CONTINENTAL

The Values and Institutions of the United States and Canada

DIVIDE

SEYMOUR MARTIN LIPSET

ROUTLEDGE
NEW YORK ▪ LONDON

To Max, Michael, and Sydnee,
for the future

First published in 1990 by

Routledge
An imprint of Routledge, Chapman and Hall, Inc.
29 West 35th Street
New York, N.Y. 10001

Published in Great Britain by

Routledge
11 New Fetter Lane
London EC4P 4EE

Paperback published in 1991

Library of Congress Cataloging in Publication Data

Lipset, Seymour Martin.
    Continental divide : the values and institutions of the United
States and Canada / Seymour Martin Lipset.
        p.   cm.
    Includes bibliographical references.
    1. United States—Civilization. 2. Canada—Civilization. I. Title.
ISBN 0-415-90309-2
ISBN 0-415-90385-8 (pb)
E169.1.L545 1990
303.48'273071—dc20   89-48660

British Library Cataloguing in Publication Data also available

Contents

Tables

Acknowledgments

Acknowledgments, as John Le Carré notes, "can be as tedious as credits at the cinema," yet they are necessary since a serious scholarly work cannot — or rather should not — be conducted without drawing on the assistance of others. In this case, I am deeply indebted to many for assistance far beyond any call of duty or friendship. Some devoted many hours to making this a better book.

S. Delbert Clark, of the University of Toronto, introduced me to the comparative study of North America more than 40 years ago, when I was a young colleague of his; fortunately he is still able to correct my errors. Robert K. Merton, my teacher and friend at Columbia University and during the past year my colleague at the Russell Sage Foundation, introduced me to the exciting world of sociological analysis close to half a century ago, and in 1988–89 he spent endless hours going over this book, much as he had done with some of my earlier ones.

Friends and erstwhile colleagues, such as Daniel Bell, Reinhard Bendix, Nathan Glazer, Earl Raab, and David Riesman, have taught me more than they realize about American society over the years. During my year at Russell Sage, Joel Silbey was quickly responsive to all my queries about American history. My emphasis on comparative analysis has benefited repeatedly from the critical commentaries of Larry Diamond, Mattei Dogan, Shmuel Eisenstadt, Alex Inkeles, and Juan Linz, and particularly from the incomparable genius of my friend and sometime collaborator, the late Stein Rokkan.

A number of Canadian scholars have suggested research leads, challenged my generalizations, or meticulously read over this manuscript. They include Robert Brym, James Curtis, David Flaherty, Richard Helmes-Hayes, Richard Lipsey, John Meisel, Mildred Schwartz, and Dennis Wrong. John Porter and Frank Underhill, both now deceased, played major roles in helping to formulate my basic conceptions of Canada and the United States.

My introduction to and awareness of Canada's creative cultures owe much to Edith Fowke and Northrop Frye.

I have drawn here on unpublished public opinion data that I received from various polling agencies and academics. Among those to whom I am greatly indebted for such materials are Allan Gregg of Decima, Graham Huber and Peter MacIntosh of the American and Canadian Gallup polls, Martin Goldfarb of Goldfarb Consultants of Toronto, Frank Lacy of the Contemporary Research Centre of Toronto, Gene Heaton of the Opinion Research Corporation of Princeton, Yves Corbeil of CROP of Montreal, Everett Ladd of the Roper Data Center of the University of Connecticut, Paul Sniderman of Stanford University, and Erik Olin Wright of the University of Wisconsin.

Three Stanford University students and assistants — Sarah Corse, Katherine Teghtsoonian, and John Torres — have worked with me over the years on my Canada-United States research; they made this book possible. Denise Darensbourg of the Russell Sage Foundation and Janet Shaw of the Hoover Institution put in more work on this book than anyone other than myself. Lenore d'Anjou did an excellent job of copy-editing, catching errors and infelicities of style. Barry Norris of the C.D. Howe Institute also helped greatly to correct the work. My morale was sustained by affection and support from Sydnee Guyer. I am deeply grateful.

Three research centers, the Hoover Institution of Stanford University, the C.D. Howe Institute, and the Russell Sage Foundation have supported my studies in this area. I am deeply grateful to their heads: W. Glenn Campbell, Maureen Farrow, and Eric Wanner. The C.D. Howe Institute commissioned the work as a short monograph. The Russell Sage Foundation provided me with a research year in which I could devote my time entirely to reworking and enlarging it as a book. The Hoover Institution has given extensively of its resources to facilitate my scholarship since 1975, without ever inquiring as to what, why, or how.

In addition to institutional backing, I have received much-appreciated and helpful grants for research on the United States and Canada from the William Donner Foundation and the Academic Office of the Canadian Department of External Affairs.

I have drawn on my previous articles in this area, and I am indebted to those who published them.[1] I learned much from the writings of various Canadian sociologists, as the endnotes should indicate.

My last acknowledgment is the most important. Elsie Braun Lipset accompanied me as a raw, scared graduate student to Regina, Saskatchewan in 1945. She made my doctoral research possible and better. She lived with me for two years in Toronto, and for more than forty in other cities in the United States and elsewhere. There is no way to describe the importance of her life for me and many others. She was an American who deeply loved her country, but some of that feeling carried over to Canada. I am glad that she once was able to tell Pierre Trudeau what his country and its hospitality meant to us. She died on February 27, 1987. Some die too young, as John F. Kennedy noted. We miss her.

Seymour Martin Lipset
Russell Sage Foundation
June 1989

A publication of the Canadian-American Committee, sponsored by the C.D. Howe Institute (Canada) and the National Planning Association (U.S.A.)

The Canadian-American Committee was established in 1957 to study the broad range of factors affecting the relationship between Canada and the United States. Its members are business, labor, agricultural, and professional leaders from the private sector in the two countries. The Committee's two sponsoring organizations are nonprofit research institutions.

Preface

Knowledge of Canada or the United States is the best way to gain insight into the other North American country. Nations can be understood only in comparative perspective. And the more similar the units being compared, the more possible it should be to isolate the factors responsible for differences between them. Looking intensively at Canada and the United States sheds light on both of them.

Societies vary in their organizing principles, in their basic beliefs about the sources of authority and values, and in their conceptions about the nature of their societies. The two nations once part of British North America were separated by the outcome of the American Revolution. One, the country of the Revolution, elaborated on the populist and meritocratic themes subsumed in stating the objectives of the good society as "life, liberty, and the pursuit of happiness." The founding fathers of the counterrevolutionary nation defined their rationale as "peace, order, and good government" when they put together the new Dominion of Canada in 1867. The source of authority for one, as stated in the preamble to its Constitution, was "the people," and the document was submitted for ratification by the state legislatures. The other saw its new government as a continuation of the ancient English monarchy and sent its constitution to London to be enacted by the British Parliament and proclaimed by the Queen. The revolutionary Republic was suspicious of state authority and adopted a power-constraining bill of rights, which produced a strong emphasis on due process, judicial power, and litigiousness. The counterrevolutionary dominion followed the Westminster model, with power centered in a cabinet based on a parliamentary majority and with no limits on the authority of the state other than those derived from a division of jurisdictions between national and provincial governments. The American Constitution rejected church establishment; the Canadian did not.

This book is an interpretive work. It seeks to throw light on the values and culture of two highly similar nations, most of whose peoples speak the same language (I am not forgetting the quarter of Canadians who are Francophones), who are among the richest in the developed world, who inhabit comparably and highly urbanized environments and live in complex, socially heterogeneous, continent-spanning federal unions. But as I shall attempt to demonstrate, they vary in *consistent ways* across a broad spectrum of behavior, institutions, and values. The differences reflect the basic organizing principles.

Most of the evidence I have located is congruent with my basic line of argument, but in no sense am I testing hypotheses. As with much macrosocietal comparative and historical analysis, I seek to sustain my interpretation by showing that there is a considerable body of confirmatory data. My main stress is on the role of national values in affecting behavior and institutions. This emphasis inevitably leads me to highlight certain factors and pay less attention to other relevant ones, particularly those that are structural — economic, geographic, demographic, and so on. Efforts that focus on the latter produce different, though not necessarily contradictory, interpretations of causal processes.

Social scientists should not feel inhibited about admitting that one of their main methods is *dialogue*. In large measure, the very meaning of scholarly verification in qualitative fields (and even to a considerable extent in some quantitative ones) is the examination of the same problem by different people operating with alternative approaches. As long as we agree about the meaning of hypotheses and the nature of evidence, the dialogue can result in replication and the growth of knowledge. [1]

Thus, the materials for this work are drawn from diverse sources: historical accounts, critical interpretations of literature and other creative arts, social scientists' quantitative analyses and qualitative studies of institutions such as religion, law, and government, as well as aggregate national statistics and survey data gathered by social scientists and commercial pollsters. In looking at discussions of crossnational differences in the creative arts, I seek to point up the images intellectuals present of the way the two peoples behave. National cultures are created and sustained by such perceptions.

Much of what Canadian intellectuals, both scholars and creative artists, write about their own country is presented in a comparative context — that is, with reference to the nation to the south. They frequently seek to describe what Canada is about by stressing what it is not: the United States. These analyses are important, as indications of how Canadians view themselves and often as serious crossnational analytical comparisons of institutions and behavior. I rely on them for descriptions of many areas in which I must acknowledge little expertise. In using secondary sources, I have looked for some consensus by the (usually Canadian) authorities. A very wise British sociologist, Tom Marshall, once justified accepting such expert testimony in logical terms:

> Sociologists must inevitably rely extensively on secondary authorities, without going back to the original sources. They do this partly because life is too short to do anything else when using the comparative method, and they need data assembled from a wide...field, and partly because original sources are very tricky things to use....It is the business of [scholars in different fields] to give to others the results of their careful professional assessment. And surely they will not rebuke the sociologists for putting faith in what...[they] write.[2]

Beyond drawing extensively on published comparative scholarly analyses, I have used a considerable amount of crossnational public opinion data. For the most part, results are compared for the two countries; when available, findings are also presented separately for English and French Canada, which are clearly distinct cultures.

Interpreting crossnational poll results presents serious methodological problems. Sampling procedures may differ. Attitudes may change over time. Pollsters frequently use different questions when dealing with similar topics. And dissimilarities in question-wording may result in variations in findings.

Even when queries are worded identically, their meaning to respondents may vary across borders or in different periods. Thus, a question about the power of the same institution, such as business, labor unions, or government, may have different implications if actual power varies across boundary lines. The Canadian labor movement is proportionately twice the size of the American. Big business is much more highly concentrated in

Canada than in the United States. The government plays a larger role in the economy and in providing welfare services in the north than in the south. Since the context of questions about these institutions clearly differs, apparently similar responses may have dissimilar connotations across the border.

The temporal context can also affect reactions to an issue by giving different meanings to an identical question — for example, as a result of changes in rates of unemployment or inflation. The popularity of the incumbent administration can affect responses to questions about the role of government. Thus, if the approval rating of Prime Minister Brian Mulroney is much lower than that of President George Bush at some given moment, as it was in March 1989, Canadians might generally voice less faith than Americans in the readiness of "government to act in the public interest." They did so — with that answer from 63 percent of Americans but only 56 percent of Canadians in the *Maclean's*-Decima poll taken at the time,[3] even though much evidence presented in that survey and in this book indicates that the northern people are basically less suspicious of the state than their southern neighbors.

Readers should also note that the national differences reported by crossborder opinion polls are frequently small — five to ten percentage points. Given the structural similarities between the two North American societies and the fact that they differ in comparable ways from Britain and much of Europe, there is no reason to anticipate large differences. In general, for samples composed of 1,000 to 2,000 people, a difference of four percentage points is statistically significant. But I do not rely on significance tests. There are too many possible sources of error to justify such use. Rather, I emphasize theoretical or logical consistency — that is, do the differences between Canadians and Americans reported here correspond to those anticipated by the assumed variations in organizing principles and national values? The relationship to the logic of the argument is more important than the statistical significance of single differences.

Unfortunately, as a crossborder opinion survey of Canadians and Americans gathered early in 1989 for *Maclean's* magazine documents, Americans know very little or nothing about their northern neighbor, though many Canadians know a great deal about the country next door.[4] The residents of the United States have little opportunity to learn since their schools and mass media rarely discuss Canada, while Canadians are exposed to considerable information about their neighbor. A content analysis of television newscasts in both countries during the final three weeks of October 1985 found the three American networks reporting almost no news about events to the north, while the two English-language Canadian ones devoted an average of one-seventh of their time to American topics, and even the two French-language networks devoted 11 and 5 percent of their time to it.[5]

An American long concerned with Canada, my interest has stemmed in large measure from a desire to understand the United States better. As noted, it is precisely because the two North American democracies have so much in common that they permit students of each to gain insights into the factors that cause variations. My first book, *Agrarian Socialism: The Cooperative Commonwealth Federation in Saskatchewan*, which dealt with North America's first socialist government above the level of a municipality, was an attempt to answer the question: Why is there no effective socialist movement in the United States?[6] My continuing work on the two countries is part of an effort to explore the unique character of much of American society, what has been called American exceptionalism.[7] I strongly support Robin Winks in his argument that

> the historian [or social science analyst] of the United States who is ignorant of Canadian history [society] is ignorant of his own history [society]....In short, the reason Americans should study Canadian history [society and politics] is to learn more about themselves, about how they differ from and how they are similar to others.[8]

The converse, of course, holds for Canadians (although they need much less urging on the subject than Americans do).

I hope that this book will prove useful even to those who disagree with its emphasis on the influence of values as sources of variation in national behavior. Just as I have drawn on the works of some whose theoretical premises I reject, I trust that the extensive documentation of what Canada and the United States are like will be helpful to all those interested in understanding what the United States and/or Canada are all about.

Finally, I would note the title, *Continental Divide*, is intended to emphasize the distinctive character of the two nations from 1783 to the present. It obviously does not refer to the geographical use of the term, the division between the flows of rivers east or west in the Rocky Mountains. As it happens, in the motion picture, "Continental Divide," John Belushi is shown picking up and reading my book, *Political Man*. This act inspired the use of the title for this analysis of the social and political continental divide.

1

Revolution and Counterrevolution: The Introduction

Americans do not know but Canadians cannot forget that two nations, not one, came out of the American Revolution. The United States is the country of the revolution, Canada of the counterrevolution. These very different formative events set indelible marks on the two nations. One celebrates the overthrow of an oppressive state, the triumph of the people, a successful effort to create a type of government never seen before. The other commemorates a defeat and a long struggle to preserve a historical source of legitimacy: government's deriving its title-to-rule from a monarchy linked to church establishment. Government power is feared in the south; uninhibited popular sovereignty has been a concern in the north.

The effort to create a form of rule derived from the people, and stressing individualism made America "exceptional," to use Tocqueville's formulation.[1] The desire to build free institutions within a strong monarchical state made Canada distinctive, different from its mother country but also from its sibling across the border.

Americans are descended from winners, Canadians, as their writers frequently reiterate, from losers. As a result, Robertson Davies observes, America "has developed myths and Canada has developed none....Canadians tend to be great deprecators — especially of themselves."[2] The United States has a pantheon of heroes in its founding fathers. Canada remembers the names of some of the people who straggled across what became the New England border into Nova Scotia and New Brunswick, and over the Niagara frontier in the area that would be called Ontario, but there were no inspired national leaders, no ideologists, no political theorists who continue to influence debate today. The magnitude of the difference is exemplified in Davies' report that he was reared as a Canadian "to know that Washington was a scoundrel, and I wanted nothing to do with him."[3]

The very organizing principles that framed these nations, the central cores around which institutions and events were to accommodate, were different. One was Whig and classically liberal or libertarian — doctrines that emphasize distrust of the state, egalitarianism, and populism — reinforced by a voluntaristic and congregational religious tradition. The other was Tory and conservative in the British and European sense — accepting of the need for a strong state, for respect for authority, for deference — and endorsed by hierarchically organized religions that supported and were supported by the state.

Two centuries after the Revolution that gave birth to these two nations and societies, I seek to compare them. Located on the same continent, with the majority of their populations speaking the same language (although important minorities do not), they are probably as alike as any other two peoples on earth. But, as we shall see, they are also somewhat dissimilar in political and religious institutions and in culture and values. They share many of the same ecological and demographic conditions, approximately the same level of economic development, and similar rates of upward and downward social mobility on a mass level. Today they are both wealthy and democratic societies, but they still march to a different drummer, as did the rebels and loyalists, the Whigs and the Tories, two centuries ago. And if the people of each want to understand why they are what they are today, they can do so best by understanding what they are not: the people of the republic or of the kingdom across the common border.

In emphasizing the continued influence of the revolution-counterrevolution distinction, I am not trying to suggest that America and Canada are still Whig and Tory societies in the late 18th-century sense of these terms. Canada obviously no longer approves of hierarchy and rule by the elite: it has increasingly accepted the individualistic values and some of the institutions derived from the Revolution. The United States, faced with the need to come to terms with problems posed generally by industrialization, urbanization, and its emergence as the leading actor in the world system and particularly with the trauma of the Great Depression and the protest wave of the 1960s, has modified its values. It has long since given up its unwillingness to use government to deal with social and economic problems or to recognize group rights and needs as distinct from those of the individual.

The most striking change in the north was the 1982 incorporation in the constitution of a due-process bill of rights. The Canadian Charter of Rights and Freedoms is not the American Bill of Rights. It preserves the principle of parliamentary supremacy and places less emphasis on individual, as distinct from group, rights than does the American document. But the Charter brings Canada much closer to the American stress on protection of the individual and acceptance of judicial supremacy with its accompanying encouragement to litigiousness than is true of other parliamentary countries. In spite of this and other changes, Canada, as we shall see, remains more respectful of authority, more willing to use the state, and more supportive of a group basis of rights than its neighbor. The statist tradition spawned by Toryism has been strengthened by the emergence of electorally viable social democratic parties in both English and French Canada. The country has an extensive welfare state and considerable government ownership; its trade union movement is much larger proportionately than the American; and the constitutional rights to ethnocultural survival given to French Canadians have been extended greatly, as have those of other ethnic groups not of Anglo-Saxon background.

Meanwhile, the United States has, like all other industrialized nations, strengthened the power of government, greatly increased its revenues, and become a welfare state. Through adopting affirmative action and other group-related policies, the nation has moved somewhat away from its historic emphasis on defining equality and due-process rights in individualistic terms and toward concern for equal treatment for collectivities. Yet when viewed in comparative international terms, it, like Canada, continues to reflect its organizing principles. The United States has one of the weakest sets of welfare provisions in the developed world; it is alone among industrialized nations in having no effective socialist or labor party; the percentage of its labor force organized in its trade union movement is the smallest in the industrial world; since World War II, its courts have extensively extended the protection of individual rights; and it still leads the world in opportunities for individual social mobility into upper-echelon positions through higher education.

In comparison to Great Britain and much of Europe, Canada and the United States share the same values, but in Canada they are held more tentatively. Canada's closer links to its European origins have helped perpetuate elements of an older set of beliefs and more conservative behavior. Thus, although equality of respect and of achievement are valued in both societies, in Canada the emphasis has been somewhat less than in the United States, and therefore the contrast remains one of degree.

Disrespect for authority and crime and deviance rates have increased on both sides of the border, as they have throughout the West, but Canada continues to exhibit more deference to elites and to have much lower crime rates than the United States. Traditional religious beliefs and practices have weakened throughout North America, but at the end of the 20th century, the United States remains the most devout of industrialized democratic nations, while Canada is much less so. The difference seems to lie in the sectarian evangelical and fundamentalist background of Americans in contrast to the more state-related and less individualistic and moralistic church traditions of Canada.

Free Trade and Cultural Distinctiveness

This book appears at the very start of an important change in the relations between Canada and the United States: the ratification of the free trade treaty. Canadians are deeply divided about the agreement, some looking forward to the economic benefits of closer ties across the border and others fearing it will lead to the demise of their distinct culture and perhaps even of their country as a separate state. The leaders of the latter group are Anglophone intellectuals,[4] and although the focus of their argument is now on the effects of free trade, their criticisms of American influence long predate the drafting of the treaty. What they fear is that their country will be flooded with American cultural products, and that the distinct character of its intellectual output will be lost in the much larger, more affluent, and more aggressive society to the south. Some also worry that Canada will become, in effect or in reality, the 51st American state.

In contrast, Americans, outside segments of the business community, are unaware that anything important may be happening to the relationship. As is all too characteristic of the ties between the giant Republic and its neighbor, the people of the United States simply take Canadians for granted, like close relatives down the road. No Americans have voiced sociocultural anxieties about the treaty. No one has indicated concern that closer involvement with Canada will have any particular effect on American society. There has, of course, been some debate about the impact of the free trade agreement on the American economy. But since few in the United States have seriously considered the possibility that the treaty could eventually lead to a common North American polity, there has been no analysis of the possible effects of Canadian participation in a single political system with the United States. Yet the argument can certainly be made that Canadians would be a force for moving the United States to the left, that the majority of Canadians would probably vote with the Democrats, that many of them would support the left wing of the Democratic Party or seek to build an electorally viable socialist party, such as exists in Canada. Various of Canada's institutions, particularly its provisions for government health care, have already been advocated as models for Americans to adopt. The consequences of a North American political union would also include having to deal with the disparity between Canada's parliamentary-cabinet form of government with its disciplined parliamentary parties and the U.S. system of divided powers with little party discipline.

North of the border, the discussion about the possible effects of the treaty has returned the subjects of national identity and values to central attention. These topics have long been debated, although Canada's internationally acclaimed literary critic, Northrop Frye, argues that his country "has passed from a pre-national to a post-national phase without ever having become a nation."[5] The free trade argument will continue in Canada, in spite of ratification. Its Anglophone intellectuals, the majority of whom strongly opposed the agreement, see it as creating conditions that will undermine the country's "soul," to use the imagery of Robertson Davies, who concludes, "Debate will not cease."[6]

The dialogue has revived the highly controversial issues of the extent to which bilingual, multicultural Canada can be considered one nation and whether the culture of its Anglophone majority is distinct from that of its neighbor to the south. Francophone Canadians, who are roughly a quarter of the population, tend to say it is not. As one analyst puts it:

> When articles on English-Canadian culture...appear in Quebec, they are likely to be headed by a title like "Does English Canada really exist?", betraying a commonly held belief that English Canada is culturally only a region of the United States.[7]

Over the years, some distinguished Anglophone Canadians, such as Goldwyn Smith in the late 19th century and Frank Underhill in the mid-20th, have believed that English-speaking Canada and the United States were destined to wind up in the same polity. Most recently, Peter Brimelow, a British journalist long resident in Canada before moving to the United States, concludes that "contemporary Canadian nationalism is a fraud." He contends that Canada "is not a nation," that "all of Anglophone Canada is essentially part of a greater English-speaking North American nation."[8]

Most Canadians reject this line of argument. It also runs against the observations, past and present, of many commentators on North American societies. Friedrich Engels in the 1880s and James Bryce a few decades later both stressed "marked differences" — surprisingly similar ones — between the two societies.[9] As will be evident in these pages, many students of politics, culture, and religion continue to note sharp contrasts.

In the context of the debate on the free trade treaty, many English-speaking Canadian intellectuals argue the existence of a distinct national value system less materialistic and culturally superior to that of the United States. They emphasize that though both North American countries differ greatly from postfeudal European nations, Canada bears more of a resemblance to Britain and France than does the United States. In attempting to explain the differences, often with a focus on the lesser economic development in the north (a difference that was much greater in the past than it is currently), many scholars have assumed that Canadians are quiet Americans, less flamboyant, less aggressive. As the sociologist Kaspar Naegele puts it:

> In Canada there seems to be a greater acceptance of limita-
> tion, of hierarchical patterns. There seems to be less op-
> timism, less faith in the future, less willingness to risk capital
> or reputation. In contrast to America, Canada is a country of
> greater caution, reserve, and restraint.[10]

The assumption that Americans are less class-aware and less deferential to social superiors and authority than are Canadians should, if valid, be reflected in socialization processes. Some striking evidence to that effect is present in a mid-1970s study of child-rearing values in ten societies including the United States, English Canada, and French Canada. In it, American parents "stand out as permissive and lenient," while, to the researchers' surprise, "the English-Canadian parents turned out to be consistently harsher disciplinarians than their American counterparts" and French-Canadian parents were somewhat less severe but "very similar to Anglo-Canadian parents." Overall, however, the three North American groups resembled each other more than they did the six others sampled.[11] Thus, the comparative analysis of orientations to child-rearing in eight countries documents the basic premise that the values and behavior of Americans and Canadians differ in systematic ways and that they have more in common with each other than they do with Europeans.

Organizing Principles

This book focuses on the sources and nature of the cultural and value differences between the two countries. It does not pretend to be an objective study. Rather, it is what the anthropologist Clifford Geertz calls an interpretative essay. In it, I try to interpret aspects of North American cultures as reflections of their key organizing principles derived from their varying histories and ecologies. By culture, I mean, in Geertz's words, "an historically transmitted pattern of meanings embodied in symbols, a system of inherited conceptions expressed in symbolic forms by means of which men communicate, perpetuate, and develop their knowledge about and attitudes toward life."[12] Culture sets boundaries and contexts within which action takes place. Values are the prescriptive parts.

My central argument is that the two countries differ in their basic organizing principles. Canada has been and is a more class-aware, elitist, law-abiding, statist, collectivity-oriented, and particularistic (group-oriented) society than the United States. These fundamental distinctions stem in large part from the American Revolution and the diverse social and environmental ecologies flowing from the division of British North America. The social effects of this separation were then reinforced by variations in literature, religious traditions, political and legal institutions, and socioeconomic structures.

In the south, the colonists' emphases on individualism and achievement orientation were important motivating forces in the launching of the American Revolution. The crystallization of such attitudes in the Declaration of Independence provided a basis for their reinforcement and encouragement throughout subsequent American history. Thus, the United States remained throughout the 19th and early 20th centuries the extreme example of a classically liberal or Lockean society, one that rejected the assumptions of the alliance of throne and altar, of ascriptive elitism, of mercantilism, of noblesse oblige, of communitarianism. Friedrich Engels, among other foreign visitors, noted that in comparison to Europe, the United States was "purely bourgeois, so entirely without a feudal past."[13]

By contrast, both English- and French-speaking Canadians sought to preserve their values and culture by reacting against liberal revolutions. English-speaking Canada exists because its people opposed the Declaration of Independence; French-speaking Canada, whose leaders were mostly Roman Catholic clerics, also sought to isolate itself from the anticlerical, democratic values of the French Revolution.[14] The elites of both linguistic groups, after 1783 and 1789, consciously attempted to create a conservative, monarchical, and ecclesiastical society in North America. They saw a need to use the state to protect minority cultures: English Canadians against Yankees, French Canadians against Anglophones. In the United States, on the other hand, the Atlantic Ocean provided an effective barrier against the major locus of perceived threat — Britain — which helped sustain the ideological commitment to a weak state that did not have to maintain extensive military forces. On both sides of the border, these initial organizing principles served to structure subsequent developments.

It is important to recognize that an examination of the cultures, values, and characters of nations must be comparative. The assertion that the United States or Canada is a materialistic nation or that it is achievement-oriented obviously does not refer to these characteristics in any absolute sense. To say, for example, that a national value system is egalitarian does not imply the absence of severe differences in power, income, wealth, and status. What it means is that, in a comparative sense, the people of that nation tend to emphasize universalistic criteria in judging others and tend to de-emphasize the institutionalization of hierarchical differences.

Perspectives on the American Revolution

What appear as significant differences when viewed through one lens may seem to be minor variations when viewed through another. For example, Louis Hartz, an American political scientist, argues that Canada, the United States, and other overseas European societies were largely settled by middle-class emigrants and were thus all "fragment cultures," lacking both the privileged aristocratic class and the deferential peasantry of the European "whole." Over time, the absence of a traditional right transmuted the original liberal or radical doctrines into conservative dogmas of the "fragment." It is impossible, Hartz claims, to build an ideological left in the fragment cultures because there is no hereditary aristocracy against whom to rebel, because there is no feudally derived emphasis on social status to define class identities, and because the philosophical bases on which an ideological left might be founded are already institutionalized as part of the received liberal and radical tradition of the society.[15]

For Hartz, then, the American Revolution cannot be a watershed marking a radical distinction between the value system developing in the postrevolutionary United States and that emerging in counterrevolutionary Canada. Although he notes that English Canada is "etched with a Tory streak coming out of the American Revolution," for him the differences between the two countries are of less significance than the traits common to both that set them off from European societies.[16]

My analysis, in contrast, emphasizes a somewhat greater degree of continuity between the communitarian and elitist aspects of monarchical Britain and the character of Canadian value orientations. I agree with S.D. Clark, the foremost Canadian analyst of North American values and institutions, who notes, "Whereas the American nation was a product of the revolutionary spirit, the Canadian nation grew mainly out of forces of a counter-revolutionary character."[17]

Is the distinction between revolution and counterrevolution an appropriate one for dealing with the two nations that stem from the American Revolution? An answer requires discussion of how revolutionary the American Revolution was — an issue that inherently remains unresolved. Some see it as an essentially moderate political change that, unlike the French Revolution, did little to transform social relationships and had a minor ideological impact domestically and internationally.

Postrevolutionary developments in Canada and the United States form the most relevant evidence for any evaluation, and in a sense examining that record is what this book is about. Canada, as many of its historians and cultural critics reiterate, was formed as a counterrevolutionary monarchical society that valued hierarchy in class relations and religion and authority and deference in politics. Its leaders looked askance at the vulgar, populist, upstart new state to the south. In contrast, the United States was founded as a nation seeking to explicate a set of political and religious ideals that emphasized liberty, saw danger in concentrated government power, and increasingly stressed populism and equality of opportunity and of social relations. Thus, although the French Revolution, the other great 18th-century upheaval, is more generally regarded as a "real" revolution, the American one was revolutionary indeed. Some statistics drawn from the work of students of comparative revolutions, R.R. Palmer and Patrice Higonnet, point up the radical effects of the latter. As much property was confiscated in the United States as in France on a per capita basis. Many more people were political emigrés from America than from France.[18]

Another indication of the truly revolutionary character of the American Revolution is its influence on subsequent events in France. Forrest McDonald finds a correlation between the communities of residence of the 8,000 French "veterans of the land phase of the war for American Independence" and the centers of agrarian radicalism in France between 1789 and 1792. McDonald emphasizes:

> On their subsequent discharge and return to their homes in France, these soldiers spread the idea they had seen in practice. When, in 1789, financial crisis, general discontent, and the weakness of the monarchy combined to make revolutionary action possible in France, these veterans formed the dynamic element in a movement which guaranteed the completion of the Revolution by the destruction of economic feudalism.[19]

Also pertinent is the fact that although the American leaders were not populists, an egalitarian image of the Revolution emerged over time and became part of what Abraham Lincoln called the American political religion and Gunnar Myrdal referred to as the American creed. It is a value system whose basic content today stems from egalitarian conceptions of the Declaration of Independence.[20] Although the United States was a slave society when its leaders declared that all men are created equal, Thomas Jefferson, who wrote that statement, felt — and was eventually proved correct — that it would undermine slavery, that the idea of equality would have a continuing effect, once it was proclaimed as a basis for American independence.[21]

Looking over the sweep of the history of the two countries, Higonnet concludes that

> the basic fact of America's political biography is that its revolutionary and liberal tradition has survived as the sustaining framework of its modern institutions....French republicanism cannot lay claim to such successes....
>
> Republican doctrine did not coalesce around a complementary blend of practical and transcendental values in France as it did in revolutionary America. In consequence, its most durable if inadvertent effect was to reinforce the strength of the centralized bureaucratic state.[22]

Revolutionary periods of turmoil and instability have a way of extending themselves far beyond what those originally participating in them want. By the end of the 1790s, the Federalists, the conservative party favored by the more elitist elements and opposed to the French Revolution, were declining and ultimately disappeared. They could not find an electoral base for their essentially pro-business position in an overwhelmingly agrarian society.[23] The Jeffersonian Democrats, who were more egalitarian and also more supportive of the French Revolution, came to power and remained dominant. Succeeding opponents of the Democratic Party, the Whigs and the Republicans, chose names that identified them with the revolutionary and Jeffersonian traditions.

Another indication of the strength of egalitarian values in the United States was the success of the struggle to extend suffrage to all males almost nationwide a decade before the Civil War. This populist move came long before parallel developments in any other country. Canada, for example, did not have full manhood suffrage until early in the 20th century.[24]

The continued weakening of conservative forces and institutions in the United States can be exemplified by changes in the religious arena as well. British America had church establishment at the time of the Revolution, and the policy continued in many states after independence. But after a 50-year struggle (New Hampshire kept church establishment until 1833), the principle of separation of church and state was accepted throughout the United States.

From the beginning, America was heir to a Calvinistic Puritanism that was stronger in many of the colonies than in the mother country, and it was congenial to modernity in a sense that the Anglican Church in English Canada and the Gallican Church in Quebec were not. The two denominations, Methodist and Baptist, that became dominant in America stressed religious doctrines that supported "anti-aristocratic tendencies."[25] During and after the Revolution, the Calvinist doctrine of innate predestination was gradually supplanted by Arminian belief, which emphasized the personal attainment of grace embodied in "doctrines of free will, free grace, and unlimited hope for the conversion of all men." Even more than Calvinism, it served as a religious counterpart to the democratic goals of equality and achievement.[26] Arminianism was not only an evangelical, revivalistic religion but also a reflection of the fact that,

> in a period when the special privileges of individuals were being called into question or destroyed, there would naturally be less favor for that form of theology which was dominated by the doctrine of the especial election of a part of mankind, a growing favor for those forms which seemed more distinctly to be based upon the idea of the natural equality of all men.[27]

Righteousness was to be rewarded both in this life and in the hereafter.

The Canadian Identity

Like all the British North American colonies before the Revolution, the settled areas that were to become Canada had a considerable degree of political autonomy, and they maintained it. In 1776, the northern British colonies were Newfoundland, Nova Scotia, the Island of Saint John (soon to be renamed Prince Edward Island), and Quebec (which then included much of present-day Ontario), the last two having been formally ceded to Britain by France in 1763 by the Treaty of Paris. What became Ontario and New Brunswick, as well as much of Nova Scotia and the Eastern Townships portion of Quebec, were primarily settled by Tories fleeing the Revolution in the more southern colonies.

The colonists who marched north after 1783, turning their backs on the Revolution, had to justify their great refusal, had to explain why they did not support independence. Such a decision presumably reflects a belief that the choice is morally superior to what others have done. And since the late 18th century, most Canadians have felt there is something not quite right with what the United States came to be. Nineteenth-century Canadian spokespersons, politicians, and intellectuals emphasized the crudity of American "mobocracy." They were not impressed by the advantages gained from democracy as distinct from liberty — the latter subsumed in the whole complex of English values that has been referred to as elitism but that can be seen as necessary to protect minority rights from populist excesses. They believed, in short, that "freedom wears a crown."[28]

The argument that monarchy can be viewed as a superior "guarantee of liberty and freedom" is restated in 1988 form by an expatriate Canadian scholar, John Conway.

> In the United States, popular sovereignty assumes many of the characteristics of Rousseau's general will. The sovereign people are always right. This means that Americans should, and generally do, conform to the "American way of life."
>
> By contrast, the Canadian nation, formed as it was by formal acts of allegiance...accepting the sovereignty of the British monarch, has allowed for more genuine diversity, for greater freedom for the individual to be himself and for the group to express its own cranky values.[29]

Thus, Canadians have argued (and still do) that the presumed greater political intolerance in the United States is a consequence of the Revolution, that repression of minority opinion must occur in a society with unlimited popular rule. Conversely, the British and American Tories fought for the protection of the rule of law and traditional values, including the rights of dissidents, eccentrics, and cranks. As the Canadian historian W.L. Morton puts it:

> The monarchy, in short, subsumed a heterogeneous and conservative society governed in freedom under law, law upheld by monarchy, where the republic would have levelled the diversities and made uniform the various groups by break-

ing them down into individuals, free indeed, but bound by social conformity and regimented by an inherent social intolerance.[30]

The greater sense of restraint in Canada and other elitist democracies is seen as inhibiting the kind of mass conformist outbursts that have occurred south of the border. Writing in the 1920s, James Bryce contended that Canada suffered much less from "demagogism" than the United States and other democracies. He explained the absence of this malady by the greater respect for authority, a "habit...formed under governments that were...monarchial in fact as well as in name...[that] has persisted."[31]

The sociologist S.D. Clark also suggests that deferential respect for elites is more widespread in Canada than in the United States. The emphasis on diffuseness and elitism in Canada, he says, is reflected in the ability of more unified and influential elites to control the system so as to inhibit the emergence of populist movements expressing political intolerance. McCarthyism, like Coughlinism and the Ku Klux Klan, reflected the greater strength of populist, anti-elitist values south of the border:

> The attack of Joseph McCarthy upon Communist influences in the government of the United States is a clear and genuine expression of the American frontier...spirit....In Canada it would be hard to conceive of a state of political freedom great enough to permit the kind of attacks upon responsible leaders of the government which have been carried out in the United States. More careful examination of the American community in general, and perhaps of the academic community in particular, would probably reveal that, in spite of the witch hunts in that country, the people of the United States enjoy in fact a much greater degree of freedom than do the people of Canada.[32]

Pointing to the same factors and outcomes, the Canadian historian Kenneth McNaught comes up with a different estimate of which country is more free. He argues that the greater strength of elitism north of the border means that Canadians have more freedom. As he puts the case, in nonpopulist societies such as Canada, "confidence in the social order minimizes resort to witch-hunting. Genuinely conservative societies feel less need to require ideological conformity than do those [such as the United States] in which the power of government is forever suspect."[33]

In Canada, state-related religion provided the country with a hierarchical and tradition-rooted control mechanism that was largely lacking in the United States. In English Canada, the Anglican church "set a standard of dignity for all the leading denominations which was absent in the United States."[34] Because of the stronger tie between church and state, religious development north of the border, in contrast to the Republic, has been less prone to both fundamentalism and evangelicalism. Both the Church of England and the Roman Catholic Church, hierarchically organized and receiving overt governmental support, gave strong support to the established political and social order. Hence, one found mutually reinforcing conservative forces at the summits of the class, church, and political structures.

Conclusion

The variations between Canadian and American value systems and institutions provide a good illustration of Max Weber's dictum that current differences among social structures can often be linked to specific historical events that set a particular process in motion in one nation or unit and a different one in a second. Weber used the analogy of a dice game in which each time the dice come up with a certain number they are loaded toward coming up with that number again. That is, a decision in one direction tends to reinforce those elements that are congruent with it. In other words, historical events establish values and predispositions, and these in turn affect later events.[35]

A concrete illustration of how this process works can be seen by examining the broad sweep of Canadian history from the time of the American Revolution through to the establishment of the Dominion of Canada in 1867. It was not just in 1776 that those to the north opted for the more conservative path. Democratic or populist elements lost their battle on many occasions. As Frank Underhill sums up his country's history:

> Our forefathers made the great refusal in 1776 when they declined to join the revolting American colonies. They made

it again in 1812 when they repelled American invasions. They made it again in 1837 when they rejected a revolution motivated by ideals of Jacksonian democracy, and opted for a staid, moderate, respectable British Whiggism which they called "Responsible Government." They made it once more in 1867 when the separate British colonies joined to set up a new nationality in order to preempt [American] expansionism.[36]

This sequence is understandable in view of the fact that many Loyalists — those most opposed to the populist egalitarianism of the Revolution — emigrated to Canada. As J.M.S. Careless, another Canadian historian, notes, it was they who formed the "backbone of...resistance" to American invasion in 1812.[37] The Revolution and the subsequent migration north by those opposed to the values it embodied loaded the dice toward more conservative postures in Canada than in the United States.

The relative significance of Canadian-American value differences has generated a great deal of debate. The argument is essentially between those like myself, who emphasize the distinctiveness of the two countries' values and the ways they affect behavior, beliefs, and institutional arrangements, and those who place primary importance on various structural factors, particularly geographic, economic, and political differences. This debate is not a matter of alternative, mutually exclusive hypotheses. Rather, one may conclude that each of several different variables is necessary but not sufficient to produce the results sometimes credited to one of them alone.

When one carefully examines the arguments of those identified as adhering to the value or structural interpretation of the sources of Canadian-American differences, it becomes apparent that most of the distinctions are really matters of emphasis. For example, my own analysis takes into account that the two nations do vary in their ecology, demography, and economy and that these differences have exerted an important influence on the development of values and attitudes on both sides of the border. Canada controls an area that is larger than its southern neighbor's but much less hospitable to human habitation in terms of climate and resources. Its geographical immensity and relatively weak population base have contributed to an emphasis on direct government involvement in the economy to provide various services for which sufficient private capital or a profitable market have not been available.[38] South of the border, the anti-statist emphasis subsumed in the revolutionary ideology was not challenged by the need to call on the state to intervene economically to protect the nation's independence against a powerful neighbor.[39]

In a similar way, the analysts who emphasize the significance of structural factors also acknowledge the role that values play in affecting the development of political and economic differences across the border. A good example can be found in the writing of Friedrich Engels, the co-founder of the most influential structural approach of all. Following a visit to both countries in 1888, he became one of the first writers to contend that Canada's economic backwardness compared to the United States was primarily a function of its value system.[40] Canada's pre-eminent economic historian, Harold Innis, who strongly emphasizes structural factors such as the "hard" character of the Canadian frontier in affecting national orientations, also notes the importance of "the essentially counter-revolutionary traditions, represented by the United Empire Loyalists and by the Church in French Canada, which escaped the influences of the French Revolution."[41]

As the saying goes, the proof of the pudding is in the eating, or in this case the reading. Whether my emphasis on the continued influence of different crossborder organizing principles helps to explain the distinctive cultures of Canada and the United States is for the reader to decide.

2

The American Ideology

The United States is unique among developed nations in defining its raison d'être ideologically. As Richard Hofstadter notes, "It has been our fate as a nation not to have ideologies but to be one."[1] In so saying, he was reiterating Ralph Waldo Emerson's and Abraham Lincoln's emphasis on the country's "political religion," alluding in effect to the former's statement that becoming an American was a religious — that is, ideological — act. Other countries' sense of themselves is derived from a common history, not an ideology. Canada, as its leading socialist historian Kenneth McNaught asserts proudly, "is an ancient monarchy, and has always been one....Like most monarchies that have survived into the modern world, the Canadian...shares with other such states an abiding respect for continuity." Unlike the United States, Canada stresses "historical continuity...[as] the basis of legitimacy."[2]

Winston Churchill once gave vivid evidence of the difference between a nation rooted in history and one defined by ideology. In objecting to a 1940 proposal to outlaw the Communist Party, which was then antiwar, he told the House of Commons that as far as he knew the party was composed of Englishmen and he did not fear an Englishman. In Europe and Canada, nationality is related to community; one cannot become un-English, or un-Swedish. Being an American, however, is an ideological commitment. It is not a matter of birth. Those who reject American values are un-American.

Antistatism

The American Revolution sharply weakened the social values of noblesse oblige and organic community, which had been linked to Tory sentiments, and strengthened the individualistic and antistatist ones. This is evident in the fact that, as H.G. Wells pointed out more than 80 years ago, the United States not only lacks a viable socialist party but has also never developed a British- or European-type conservative or Tory one. The country is and has been dominated by pure bourgeois, individualistic values.[3] As Wells put it, "Essentially America is a middle-class [which has] become a community and so its essential problems are the problems of a modern individualistic society, stark and clear." He enunciated a theory of America as a liberal society, in the classic antistatist meaning of the term:[4]

> It is not difficult to show, for example, that the two great political parties in America represent only one English party, the middle-class Liberal Party....There are no Tories...and no Labor Party....[T]he new world [was left] to the Whigs and Nonconformists and to those less constructive, less logical, more popular and liberating thinkers who became Radicals in England, and Jeffersonians and then Democrats in America. All Americans are, from the English point of view, Liberals of one sort or another....
>
> The liberalism of the eighteenth century was essentially the rebellion...against the monarchical and aristocratic state — against hereditary privilege, against restrictions on bargains. Its spirit was essentially anarchistic — the antithesis of Socialism. It was the anti-State.[5]

Fighting against a centralized monarchical state, the founding fathers distrusted a strong unified government. As Leo Strauss, the major modern political theorist of classically liberal bent, notes: "The United States of America may be said to be the only country in the world which was founded in explicit opposition to Machiavellian principles," to the power of the Prince.[6] The chronic antagonism to the state derived from the American Revolution has been institutionalized in the unique division of powers, the internally conflicted form of government that distinguishes the United States from parliamentary regimes, such as

Canada's, where the parliament (more realistically, the cabinet), has relatively unchecked power, much like that held by an absolute monarch. The first American constitution, the Articles of Confederation, did not even provide for a federal executive. Authority was put in the hands of the Congress, which had limits on its powers. The United States' second and continuing constitution is distinguished from all others in providing for an elaborate system of checks and balances on the executive and the two houses of Congress, each of which has a different term of office so as to make concurrence among them difficult. No other elected national government except the Swiss is as limited in its powers. And the American public indicates in opinion surveys that it continues to favor a divided government and a weak state. Whenever pollsters ask samples of the population whether they prefer the president and both houses of Congress to be controlled by one party or divided between two, they choose the latter response by goodly majorities. In 1988, that was the choice they made in principle, by a 20 percent majority in opinion polls, and in fact, in the elections. They also invariably indicate a preference for small governmental units over large ones.[7]

The linkage of such patterns to divergent historical experiences was brought out in the early 1980s by then Canadian Minister of Justice Mark MacGuigan. In comparing the two North American democracies, he noted:

> The United States was born in the spirit of revolution against a government perceived to be tyrannical. Its anti-tyrannical bias was written into the Constitution as the separation of powers to insure that no executive would ever again become too powerful.

In Canada, which had no comparable background, "the state was perceived as a benign presence," one whose help was needed in "the struggle for survival" against geography and climate.[8]

In a brilliant article entitled "The State as a Conceptual Variable," J.P. Nettl lays out the enormous differences between the Euro-Canadian conception of the state and the American. As he emphasizes, the latter is characterized by "relative statelessness." In the United States "only law is sovereign." The weakness of the state and the emphasis on a constitutionally mandated division of powers give lawyers a uniquely powerful role in America and make its people exceptionally litigious. Unlike the situation in Europe and Canada, "[I]n the United States, the law and its practitioners have perhaps been the most important single factor making for political and social change and have time and again proved to be the normal instrument for bringing it about."[9]

The Revolution Continued

Like all revolutions, the American one started with small, relatively unimportant demands that grew, during and after the conflict, far beyond the vision of the original participants. A good example of this extension is contained in the interesting correspondence between Abigail and John Adams concerning the rights of women. Writing to John in Philadelphia in March 1776, Abigail told him that when drafting the new code of laws,

> I desire you would remember the ladies and be more generous and favorable to them than your ancestors. Do not put such unlimited power into the hands of the husbands. Remember, all men would be tyrants if they could. If particular care and attention is not paid to the ladies, we are determined to foment a rebellion, and will not hold ourselves bound by any laws in which we have no voice or representation.[10]

Although John rejected her advice, he wrote back noting that the revolution was disrupting all forms of authority:

> We have been told that our struggle has loosened the bonds of government everywhere; that children and apprentices are disobedient; that schools and colleges were grown turbulent; that Indians slighted their guardians, and negroes grew insolent to their masters....[Y]our letter was the first intimation that another tribe, more numerous and powerful than all the rest, were grown discontented.[11]

John Adams was opposed to a broad extension of equality, as were most of the people associated with him, but they had started and legitimated a process that grew out of their control. It was difficult to restrain not only during their own period; it remained out of the control of succeeding, potentially ascriptive elites.

Efforts to enlarge the meaning of equality in institutional terms have continued from the conflicts about the common school and the suffrage to present-day ones about the position of minorities and women. The success of the struggle to extend manhood suffrage to all indicates the strength of egalitarian and populist values in early 19th-century United States.

The vigor of egalitarian sentiments in the United States can be found in the record of a movement that failed: the Workingmen's Party. The first party anywhere in the world that called itself "labor" or "workingmen's," it had strength in New York, Philadelphia, Boston, and other coastal cities in the late 1820s and early 1830s,[12] and it gave Karl Marx the idea that the workers would come to class consciousness.[13]

The most interesting fact about the Workingmen's Party, in my judgment, is not its position as the world's first labor party but its radical egalitarian stance with respect to the family, one that makes Communists appear conservative. The Workingmen were not socialists — they did not propose nationalization of property, they did not object to the private enterprise system or to great variation in achieved income and status — but they sought to institutionalize an extreme form of equality of opportunity. In the late 1820s, they argued that given the existence of rich and poor, cultured and uncultured people, it was impossible to speak of equality of opportunity for children who start life in different family environments. They contended that equality of opportunity could not be secured by sending children to what was called a common school since their home lives and cultural backgrounds varied so greatly by economic class. The New York wing of the party proposed, in effect, to nationalize the children: rich and poor alike would be required by law, from age six on, to attend state-supported boarding schools, so that regardless of family background, all would have a common environment for 24 hours a day. The Workingmen felt that this was the only way to guarantee true equality of opportunity in the race for success.

This radical proposal did not have much popular appeal, but the fact that the party received as much as 15 percent of the vote in New York indicates the extent to which sophisticated concerns for egalitarianism were current in Jacksonian America — it was not just a "get rich quick" society.

If early U.S. history can be written as a triumph for the more leftist Jeffersonian-Jacksonian and antislavery tendencies, north of the border conservative forces continued to win out for the century after the American Revolution.[14] Of course, neither society was homogeneous politically, but, as indicated earlier, in the north the more populist and egalitarian factions lost while the equivalent groups of Americans were winning. It is interesting and important to note that in Canada many liberals tended to view the United States positively, but, unlike their American compeers, they were outside their national tradition.

Meritocracy

The societal variables that have reinforced the U.S. political culture relate mainly to the unique American class structure and religious system. Tocqueville noted these elements in the 1830s when he defined American egalitarianism by two terms: equality of respect and equality of opportunity. By the first he meant the emphasis on egalitarian social relations, the absence of a demand that those lower in the social order give overt deference to their betters, and by the second, the stress on meritocracy, on equal opportunity for all to rise economically and socially. Both stemmed from the fact that America was formed as a new settler society and from the revolutionary ideology. Tocqueville was, of course, aware of enormous variations in income, power, and status, and of strong focus on the attainment of wealth.[15] But he emphasized that, regardless of steep inequalities, Americans did not require the lower strata to acknowledge their inferiority, to bow to their betters.

From early in the history of the Republic, the concern with meritocracy was present in the ideology and reality of the educational system. It would ultimately expand until the United States came to lead the world in the proportion of the population attending various levels — elementary, high school, and college. Another, equally important result was the emergence of the concept of the common school in the early 19th century. Its advocates, though less radical than the Workingmen, proposed that all children, regardless of origins, status, or wealth, should attend the same school, that there should not be a class-differentiated system. They rejected as models those that existed in Britain, France, and Germany, opposing as explicitly elitist systems that limited access to academic high schools to a small part of the population.

Meritocracy was reflected in the 19th-century American economy, which, compared to the European economies, was characterized by more market freedom, more individual ownership of the land, and a higher wage-income structure, all sustained by the classically liberal national ideology. From the Revolution on, the United States was the laissez-faire country *par excellence* — and a wildly successful one. Almost from its start, it had an expanding economic system, and it had become the wealthiest in the world by the second half of the 19th century.

Unlike the situation in many European countries, where economic materialism was viewed by the social and religious establishments — that is, the traditional aristocracy and the church — as conducive to vulgar behavior and immorality, hard work and economic ambition were perceived in the United States as the proper activity of a moral man. Writing in the 1850s, a visiting Swiss theologian, Philip Schaff, commented that the "acquisition of riches is to them [the Americans] only a help toward higher spiritual and moral ends."[16] Friedrich Engels and Max Weber, among many, emphasized that the United States was the only pure bourgeois country, the only one that was not postfeudal.[17] As Weber noted, "no medieval antecedents or complicating institutional heritage [served] to mitigate the impact of the Protestant ethic on American economic development."[18] Similar arguments were made in the 1920s by the gifted Italian Communist theoretician, Antonio Gramsci.[19] America was able to avoid the remnants of mercantilism, statist regulations, church establishment, and aristocracy and the emphasis on social class that the postfeudal countries inherited. Engels, Weber, and Gramsci stressed the United States' unique origins and resultant value system as a major source of its economic and political development. Its secular, Adam Smith, liberal orientation tied in with various aspects derived from its special religious tradition: the dominance of the Protestant sects that Weber emphasized as facilitating the rise of capitalism.[20]

The Ideology

The United States, as a country organized around an ideology, embraces a set of dogmas about the nature of a good society. As noted, the American creed can be subsumed in four words: antistatism, individualism, populism, and egalitarianism. The implications of the latter two were spelled out by Hermann Keyserling and Leon Samson, discussing, in the late 1920s and early 1930s, the weakness of socialist parties in the United States.[21] They argued that the movements had little appeal because the social content of socialism, property relations apart (which is, of course, a big apart) is identical with what Americans think they already have — namely, a democratic, socially classless society that is anti-elitist.

Leon Samson, a radical socialist, drew these conclusions from an examination of Americanism as ideology.

When we examine the meaning of Americanism, we discover that Americanism is to the American not a tradition or a territory, not what France is to a Frenchman or England to an Englishman, but a doctrine — what socialism is to a socialist. Like socialism, Americanism is looked upon...as a highly attenuated, conceptualized, platonic, impersonal attraction toward a system of ideas, a solemn assent to a handful of final notions — democracy, liberty, opportunity, to all of which the American adheres rationalistically much as a socialist adheres to his socialism — because it does him good, because it gives him work, because, so he thinks, it guarantees him happiness. Americanism has thus served as a substitute for socialism. Every concept in socialism has its substitutive counter-concept in Americanism, and that is why the socialist argument falls so fruitlessly on the American ear....The American does not want to listen to socialism, since he thinks he already has it.[22]

Samson argued that American conservatives, Republicans, and businessmen, whom he preferred to quote to illustrate his own theses, use language, concepts, and goals that in Europe are only voiced by socialists. Thus, he pointed out that President Herbert Hoover took Europe as a negative model, saying that, in the United States, "[W]e resent class distinction because there can be no rise for the individual through the frozen strata of classes."

Hoover emphasized the abolition of poverty as a goal of the American system.

In the early 1970s, Michael Harrington, the major leader of American socialism, expressed strong agreement with Samson, noting:

> [I]t was America's receptivity to utopia, not its hostility, that was a major factor inhibiting the development of a socialist movement....[T]he country's image of itself contained so many socialist elements that one did not have to go to a separate movement opposed to the status quo in order to give vent to socialist emotions.[23]

In August 1988, Harrington reiterated the argument in a television interview, saying that social relations among the classes are more egalitarian and socialist-like in America than in other societies, including Sweden and Canada.[24] A comparative analysis of Sweden and the United States by an American scholar who also happens to be a social democrat makes a similar point. Steven Kelman stresses the continued impact of deference values in Sweden and self-assertive ones in the United States. Swedes exhibit "deference to the wishes of the state," while Americans seek "to define and pursue their own goals."[25]

The ultimate source of authority in the American system is specified in the preamble to the U.S. Constitution, which starts "We, the People of the United States." Populism is limited in America, however, by constitutionalism. As noted, the revolutionary Americans feared the power of a unified central state. The antistatist, anti-authoritarian component of the American ideology is another major source of the continued weakness of socialism in the United States.

Individualism

The American radical is much more sympathetic to anarchism, libertarianism, and syndicalism than to state collectivism. Given the emphasis on antistatist individualism, "it was the attribute of collectivism or statism...that [constituted] the central negative image" of socialism for Americans.[26] If the United States ever gets a major radical movement, it will be closer to anarchism than to socialism. This notion, which is implicit in H.G. Wells' analysis, can be seen in the historical ideologies of American labor movements. The moderate one, the American Federation of Labor (AFL), was syndicalist. The radical one, the Industrial Workers of the World (IWW or "Wobblies"), was anarchosyndicalist. Both the AFL and the IWW regarded the state as an enemy and felt that government-owned industry would be much more difficult than private companies for the workers and unions to oppose. Samuel Gompers, the leader of the AFL for four decades, emphasized that what the state can give the state can take away, that the workers must rely on themselves. Gompers and the old AFL were not conservative; they were syndicalist and extremely militant. In 1920 Gompers described himself as "three quarters anarchist."[27]

Near-anarchism could also be seen in the ideology and organizational structure of the New Left of the 1960s, which stressed decentralization and community control. There are clearly strong links between the orientations of the IWW and the early New Left, both extremely American movements reflecting the continued vitality of U.S. emphasis on individualism and antistatism. The new radicals' reliance on confrontationist tactics and other forms of civil disobedience also follows the traditions of the American labor movement and the Wobblies. One of the most influential professorial influences on the early New Left was the historian William Appleman Williams, whose students started the movement's major theoretical organ, *Studies on the Left*. He reflects this association in his strong preference for Herbert Hoover over Franklin Roosevelt as embodying the best in the American capitalist tradition. Hoover is to be preferred since his solution for the crisis of capitalism lay not in strengthening the power of the central state but in proposing "that American capitalism should cope with its economic problems by voluntaristic but nevertheless organized cooperation within and between each major sector of the economy."[28]

The ideological congruence between academic spokespersons of the radical left and right can be found in an anthology of articles from *Studies on the Left*. In introducing an essay by laissez-faire economist Murray Rothbard, the New Left editors comment, "He is a free-market conservative and individualist whose anti-imperialism and proscriptions of bureaucracy and the corporatist state coincide with those of the New Left."[29]

Another early academic stimulator of the student New Left, C. Wright Mills, also exhibits a strong admiration for the competitive, free-yeoman tradition of American free enterprise and decentralized politics. There is perhaps no more favorable portrait of the operation and consequences of the pre-Civil War American economy and polity than the one presented by Mills. He describes early 19th-century America as having been an almost perfect utopia, with property widely and equitably distributed, with property ownership providing security and protection against tyranny, and with rapid and continuing social mobility so that few remained propertyless for long. Mills sees the early United States as close to a libertarian society. "Political authority, the traditional mode of social integration, became a loose framework of protection rather than a centralized engine of domination; it too was largely unseen and for long periods very slight."[30]

The individualist proclivities of the American left are also reflected in the special role played by anarchist and decentralist socialist intellectuals such as Noam Chomsky, David Dellinger, and Staughton Lynd. Such men were influential in strengthening the antistatist components of New Left ideology.

The American New Left even found common ground with some whose penchant for individualism first led them to right-wing politics. The "libertarian" faction of the Young Americans for Freedom, oriented to Barry Goldwater and William Buckley, cooperated with the decentralizers of the New Left. Both groups found a common cause in their rejection of the welfare state, of the Vietnam War, and of large bureaucratic organizations. Karl Hess, Senator Goldwater's main speechwriter in the 1964 presidential campaign, even served as an editor of the New Left organ *Ramparts* while insisting that he had not changed his political beliefs in any substantial manner.

Indicative of this congruence of ideological concerns was the composition of the board of the National Taxpayers' Union, an organization formed largely by conservatives and dedicated to "individual liberty and financial security for the American taxpayer" that actively lobbied during the 1970s against high taxes and the big bureaucratic welfare state. Its board included not only such eminent conservatives as Ludwig von Mises, Henry Hazlitt, and Felix Morley but also Noam Chomsky, Karl Hess, and Marcus Raskin — the head of the Institute for Policy Studies, the New Left think tank, and codefendant with Dr. Benjamin Spock in the Boston draft conspiracy trial. In commenting on the National Taxpayers' Union, New Left columnist David Deitch points out some of the sources of agreement between the ideological extremes in America.

> If the decentralization of government is a key place where New Left and Old Right have touched bases, taxation, the handmaiden of big government, is the arch enemy of libertarians everywhere....Its [the National Taxpayers' Union's] board of directors is a left-right alliance of strange bedfellows made comfortable by a single-minded devotion to tax cutting and the social possibilities that might accrue from a less elephantine government....There is overwhelming agreement [among them] that whether known as the "corporate state" or "big government" the growth of institutions has resulted in a significant loss of freedom.[31]

According to Deitch, the group was concerned that its tax cuts not hurt "needy recipients such as welfare people." The solution to the problem was

> a proposal for a system of tax credits for any individual or group that provides private support for welfare recipients....The law now permits charitable contributions to be deducted from gross income, but the new proposal would make it even more attractive to make private support contributions by granting an outright cut.[32]

It is difficult to realize that this proposal was made by an organization whose leaders included some of the leading left-wing radicals in America. To find anything resembling it, one must go back at least to the literature in opposition to federal welfare programs presented by the ultrarightist Liberty League in the 1930s.

Populism

Populism, the belief that the will of the people should dominate elites, that the public choice is superior to professionalism, was not part of the original revolutionary ideology. But as the creed was elaborated, populism became part of the U.S. national belief system. Institutionally, the change was reflected first in the early extension of the suffrage to all white males and subsequently in the passage of the 16th amendment providing for the popular election of senators, in the direct election of judges in state and local jurisdictions, in the emergence of the primary system of nominating candidates for public office, and in the diffusion of the initiative and referendum — that is, direct citizen involvement in legislative enactments — in most states.

That populism is stronger in America than in Canada is reflected in the very limited use of referenda north of the border[33] and in the considerable difference in the extent to which the two publics have insisted on the right to elect officials or to change appointed ones in tandem with the outcomes of elections. In Canada, legal officers tend to have life tenure, and are not directly involved in politics. Judges in Canada at every level are appointed for life. Crown attorneys are designated by provincial governments for indefinite terms and are rarely terminated before retirement. They are not fired when a new party comes to power, and since they are prohibited from political activity, they are never under pressure to handle cases in a way that might facilitate their re-election or attainment of higher electoral office.[34]

In the United States, almost all the major figures in law enforcement at the state and local government level, including judges and the heads of the prosecutor's offices and police forces, are chosen by the voters or appointed by elected officials. Most of the almost 60,000 elected county officeholders are "justices of the peace, county or probate judges, constables, clerks and coroners."[35]

The United States has an extensive pattern of local community and specific-activities governments within metropolitan areas. Compared to other democratic countries, including Canada, "the American standard metropolitan statistical areas are characterized by an astonishing number of independent municipalities and special-purpose bodies."[36] There are more than 1,000 such governments in metropolitan Chicago alone.

Albert Shanker, the president of the American Federation of Teachers, places a large part of the responsibility for the failings of public education in the United States on populism in the school system. As he argues:

> Only the U.S. has local school boards as we know them. The U.S. is the only place where a superintendent must face the school board in a public meeting every week or two and answer for any mishap that has occurred in the schools. It is the only place where the school superintendent must manage a system and try to protect his job by maintaining majority support on the school board. In European [and Canadian] systems, although elected officials are, of course, ultimately responsible to the public, school managers have much more freedom to run the schools without such direct and constant oversight.[37]

More offices are open to election in America and such contests are much more frequent there than in any other society. According to a 1987 U.S. Census Bureau study, there are 504,404 popularly elected officials in the United States, or about one for every 478 citizens. Most of those elected — 485,691 — hold local offices; another 18,171 are in state offices, about half of them are administrative officials and judges.[38] Since many are elected to one- or two-year terms, considerably more than a million contests, including primaries, must occur in every four-year cycle.

This predilection for the populist choice of officials is not merely a carryover from the past. The number of elective positions increased between 1977 and 1987 by more than 10,000, while the direct involvement of the electorate in the candidate nomination process continues to grow.

The ballot-box consequences of U.S. populism do not stop at the election of officials. State and local governments submit many proposed laws, bond issues, and constitutional amendments to popular votes, which never or rarely occurs in Canada and other parliamentary polities. In many American states, the citizenry can initiate legislation through petition and frequently do so. That right does not exist north of the border. Noting that in 1988, "a total of 230 propositions were voted on" in the United States, Austin Ranney, the foremost expert on the subject, describes the effect of populism on him as a California voter:

On November 8, I, like every Berkeley voter, was called upon to vote on twenty-nine state propositions (we had already voted on twelve propositions in June), five Alameda County propositions, and eight city propositions. But that was not all: I was also asked to make choices for president, U.S. senator, U.S. representative, state senator, state representative, and a number of county and city offices. In the manner of political scientists of my generation, I made a simple count and found that I had a grand total of sixty-one decisions to make![39]

It is well known that Americans make a poor showing at the polls; only 50 percent voted in the 1988 presidential contest,[40] and far fewer take part in primaries and lower-level elections. In contrast, 75 percent or more of citizens have voted in recent national and provincial contests in Canada. Ironically, it can be argued that part of the responsibility for the relatively poor turnout below the border is the greater institutionalization of populism there.

There are other differences between U.S. and Canadian elections. In Canada, political parties are much stronger than in the United States, since a parliamentary system requires discipline — party voting by elected members, who are denied renomination if they deviate. Conversely, of course, the American divided-powers system places little pressure on members of Congress to support their party's president or leader in the House or Senate. Renomination and re-election depend almost totally on the ability to reach out to the local electorate, not on endorsement or support by the party. Canadians vote for party in national elections; there is almost no personal vote. Americans are much more disposed to back individuals, not party, in congressional contests. And with the continuing decline of party in the United States produced by populist-inspired reforms, the same pattern increasingly occurs on the presidential level.

The frequency with which Americans are called to the polls, the prolonged campaigns, and the tactics of mud slinging and character assassination inherent in contests that focus on individuals rather than on weak parties all appear to discourage participation in U.S. elections. The decline in the power of the organized parties — of what used to be called the "machines" — to nominate candidates and to mobilize people to vote has meant that fewer people take part.[41] Populism clearly does not explain all of the phenomenon. Many properly point to the difficulty in voting that Americans face because of eligibility requirements, particularly the need to register to be on the voters' list.[42] Canadians do not have to do so. They are placed on the list by publicly employed canvassers who go door to door. American requirements have been sharply reduced since the 1960s. Some states have eliminated registration or permit citizens to register on election day and then vote, and the jurisdictions with less stringent requirements do have higher levels of participation than those with more. Nevertheless, the reforms have been accompanied by rates of decline in voting paralleling the falloff in other states. Ironically, as the American electorate gains more formal power, the voting-participation gap between the United States and Canada grows.

The same differentiating factors are seemingly reflected in administrative practices at the national level. The dividing line between political appointees and permanent civil servants is drawn much higher in parliamentary countries, including Canada, than in the United States. A newly elected president, even when one of the same party as the person succeeded, is responsible for thousands of appointments. Alexander Brady, a Canadian student of comparative political institutions, strongly emphasizes these differences:

> In Ottawa,....the dividing line between the politician craving publicity and the permanent official cherishing anonymity is drawn higher in the administrative hierarchy than in Washington. A political party replacing another in power does not, as in the United States, introduce to public office a new and large retinue of top advisors and administrators. It assumes that in the civil service it will find a reliable and competent corps of officials to supplement its thinking and implement its decisions. The deputy-minister as the permanent chief of a department is a non-political figure who normally brings to the aid of his minister the resources of seasoned experience and knowledge.[43]

Conversely, as the American political scientists Edward Banfield and James Wilson point out:

[O]ur government [in the United States] is permeated with politics. This is because our constitutional structure and our traditions afford individuals manifold opportunities not only to bring their special interests to the attention of public officials but also — and this is the important thing — to compel officials to bargain and to make compromises....[T]here is virtually no sphere of "administration" apart from politics.[44]

Such a comment underlines the populist sentiments and structures that pervade the American polity. The strong egalitarian emphasis in the United States, which presses for expression in the *vox populi*, makes Americans derisive and critical of their politicians and government bureaucrats.

Liberalism

In the United States, unlike Europe and Canada, conservatism is associated with the national tradition of suspicion of government, with classical liberalism. Ronald Reagan and Milton Friedman, the two names most identified with this ideology, define conservatism in America; the word still means laissez faire and also implies rejection of aristocracy and social class hierarchy. But, as noted, the American Left also adheres to these latter values.

As recently as April and June 1987, two leading transAtlantic right-wing intellectuals, Max Beloff (Lord Beloff) and Irving Kristol, debated the uses of titles in the British magazine *Encounter*. Kristol argued that Britain "is soured by a set of very thin, but tenacious, aristocratic pretentions...[which] foreclose opportunities and repress a spirit of equality that has yet to find its full expression." Hence the frustration of many, "which makes British life...so cheerless, so abounding in resentment." Like Tocqueville, he held up "social equality" as making "other inequalities tolerable in modern democracy." Beloff, a Tory, contended that what threatens conservatism in Britain "is not its remaining links with the aristocratic tradition, but its alleged indifference to some of the abuses of capitalism. It is not the Dukes who lose us votes, but the 'malefactors of great wealth.'" He wondered "why Mr. Kristol believes himself to be a 'conservative,'" since he is "as incapable as most Americans of being a conservative in any profound sense." Lord Beloff concluded, "Conservatism must have a 'Tory' element or it is only the old 'Manchester School,' [that is, liberalism]."[45]

Canada's most distinguished conservative intellectual, George Grant, emphasizes in his *Lament for a Nation* that

> Americans who call themselves "conservatives" have the right to that title only in a particular sense. In fact, they are old-fashioned liberals....Their concentration on freedom from governmental interference has more to do with nineteenth century liberalism than with traditional conservatism, which asserts the right of the community to restrain freedom in the name of the common good.[46]

Grant bemoans the fact that American conservatism, with its stress on the virtues of competition and links to business ideology, focuses on the rights of individuals and ignores communal rights and obligations. He notes that there has been no place in the American political philosophy "for the organic conservatism that pre-dated the age of progress. Indeed, the United States is the only society on earth that has no traditions from before the age of progress." He reiterates the words of H.G. Wells, voiced more than half a century ago: the Americans' "'right-wing' and 'left-wing' are just different species of liberalism."[47]

Conclusion

To what extent is it still possible to speak of an American ideology? It is obvious that America, Canada, and the rest of the western world have changed greatly over the past two centuries. They have all become industrialized, urbanized, better educated. The postfeudal elements that existed in many European countries have declined enormously. In terms of social structure, they are becoming Americanized. A striking example is the emergence of Margaret Thatcher and the so-called drys as dominant within the British Conservative Party. Thatcher represents the trend toward social modernization. She seeks to eliminate postfeudal values and institutions, including mercantilist-socialist policies. She detests the aristocracy and much prefers self-made entrepreneurs. In the process of trying to create a fully bourgeois nation — that is, one that is more like the United States — she is transforming the Conservative Party into a classically liberal one with an American ideology, Canadian Conservatives, while still more supportive of statist-Toryism than their British compeers, have also moved in a Thatcher-Reagan direction.

The changes that have occurred still leave many differences, however. The United States and Canada continue to vary along lines that flow from their distinctive national traditions, although Canada today resembles its southern neighbor in economic structure. In a sense, the changes in the two countries resemble movement along railway tracks on parallel lines; the gap between them remains, even though the movement in behavior and values over time has been enormous. The United States is still more religious, more patriotic, more populist and anti-elitist, more committed to higher education for the majority and hence to meritocracy, and more socially egalitarian than Canada and other developed countries. It remains the least statist western nation in terms of public effort, benefits, and employment.[48] Not surprisingly, crossnational polls (to be presented later) continue to reveal Americans as less favoring large welfare programs and an active role for government in the economy than the citizens of Canada and European countries. Conversely, Americans continue to show a marked preference for private efforts in welfare as in industry; they lead the world in philanthropic giving. As Nathan Glazer reports, "[N]on-public resources in American welfare are greater than is found in any other major nation."[49]

Two major 20th-century changes in the United States do, however, apparently contradict the original creed with its emphasis on antistatism and individual rights: first, the introduction in the 1930s of a planning-welfare-state emphasis accompanied by greater class consciousness and trade union growth, subsumed in Richard Hofstadter's phrase "social democratic tinge"; and, second, the increased focus on ethnic, racial, and gender rights in the 1960s and beyond.[50]

The earlier change has had a continuing impact in the form of a much-expanded government. Even under presidents Reagan and Bush, the country has remained committed to many welfare and regulatory objectives, but the growth has been slowed and in some cases reversed. Popular sentiment seeks to limit welfare and opposes some state involvement in the economy that once had considerable support. As of the end of the 1980s, the economic role of government is weaker in the United States than in any other industrialized economy.

The focus on nonclass forms of group rights is, however, still a dynamic force. Affirmative action quotas, first introduced in 1969 by the Nixon administration, implicitly assume the Euro-Canadian emphasis on group rights and the socialist concern for equality of results. The policy did not derive from pressure from the American left or working-class groups; rather, it reflected an effort by the white elite to meet the militant demands of blacks for economic equality. A conservative Republican, Laurence Silberman, now a Reagan judicial appointee and then assistant secretary of labor, concluded that individual redress to the courts for antidiscrimination judgments would not do much to open discriminatory parts of the labor market to blacks. He drafted an administrative order providing for a quota for blacks in the Philadelphia construction industry.

The Nixon and subsequent administrations have applied the principle of "communal rights," to use George Grant's language, to other minorities and women and to many areas of the society, including universities. This policy clearly involves an effort to guarantee equal results to groups. It has persisted through liberal and conservative administrations, even though opinion polls repeatedly report that overwhelming majorities of whites and pluralities of blacks believe that the principle of equal opportunity should apply to individuals, that special preference or quota guarantees should not be accorded to members of groups that, like blacks, are underrepresented in privileged job or educational categories. Seemingly, American elites, including many Republican and most Democratic leaders, feel the national creed has to be amended to make up for the past treatment of blacks, and this concern has been extended to other groups perceived as lacking equal rights because of ascriptive or biological traits: Hispanics, native Americans, Asians, women, the handicapped, and, to some degree, homosexuals. The Supreme Court has, however, gradually been modifying, though not eliminating, the impact of these policies by accepting the argument that they violate the equal-protection sections of the Bill of Rights, which emphasize individual, not group, rights.

These changes, moreover, have not basically modified the American emphases on individual success and equality of opportunity, rather than of results.[51] Affirmative action group rights have been defended since the 1960s as "compensatory action"; compensation for past discrimination is consistent with the egalitarian creed since it essentially makes the conditions of competition "fairer" without violating the notion of a competitive system.[52] The United States continues to be exceptional among developed nations in the low level of support it provides for the poor in welfare, housing, and medical care. As a result, though the wealthiest country in the world, the proportion of its people living in poverty is the highest among the developed nations, according to detailed statistical analyses of the Luxembourg Income Study data, the most comprehensive available.[53] The United States also ranks last among ten countries (six in Europe, plus Australia, Canada, and Israel) in comparisons of equality of income distribution.[54] In 1986, more than twice the proportion of children were living in poverty in the United States as in Canada — 19.8 percent compared to 8.6 percent. (The difference was not one of racial composition for it held for white children alone — 15.8 percent of whom are in poverty families in America.)[55]

Sacvan Bercovitch, a Canadian scholar named after two executed Italian-American anarchists, gives striking testimony to the way the continued vitality of the American creed first affected him as a Canadian, inexperienced with the power of a national ideology. He observes that Americans fight each other intensely in their efforts to defend or expand the American creed. Pre-Civil War leaders of the antislavery struggle, such as Frederick Douglas and William Lloyd Garrison, founders of American feminism, such as Elizabeth Cady Stanton, and mid-20th-century American Communists, he notes, demanded changes in order, in the words of Frederick Douglas, to live up to "the genius of American institutions, [to] fulfill its sacred mission."[56] Bercovitch first entered the United States during the conflict-ridden 1960s. Expressing his reaction to the creedal passions of the era, he writes:

My first encounter with American consensus was in the late sixties, when I crossed the border into the United States and found myself inside the myth of America. Not of North America, for the myth stopped short of the Canadian and Mexican borders, but of a country that despite its arbitrary frontiers, despite its bewildering mix of race and creed, could believe in something called the True America, and could invest that patent fiction with all the moral and emotional appeal of a religious symbol....Here was the Jewish anarchist Paul Goodman berating the Midwest for abandoning the promise; here, the descendant of American slaves, Martin Luther King, denouncing injustice as a violation of the American way; here, an endless debate about national destiny,....conservatives scavenging for un-Americans, New Left historians recalling the country to its sacred mission.[57]

And he went on to emphasize:

Nothing in my Canadian background had prepared me for that spectacle....It gave me something of an anthropologist's sense of wonder at the symbol of the tribe....To a Canadian skeptic, a gentile in God's country...[here was] a pluralistic, pragmatic people...bound together by an ideological consensus.

Let me repeat that mundane phrase: *ideological consensus*. For it wasn't the idea of exceptionalism that I discovered in '68....It was a hundred sects and factions, each apparently different from the others, yet all celebrating the same mission.[58]

As noted, Antonio Gramsci also believed that Americanism is an ideology. He wrote in the 1920s that before Italy could become socialist, it had to Americanize socially as well as economically, a development he viewed positively. Like earlier Marxists, he saw the United States as the epitome of a bourgeois democratic society, one that lacked the traditional precapitalist elements still to be found in Italy and other European cultures.[59] Of course, as indicated above, the industrialized European countries have begun to resemble the United States economically and socially, in being more affluent and less status conscious. In the process, their socialist movements (and the Italian Communist Party) have redefined their objectives in terms which resemble those of the American Democratic Party. Their conservatives, like Margaret Thatcher and Brian Mulroney, increasingly accept the classical liberal ideology, one that is also impacting on their lefts. Yet even given the structural convergences, the extent to which America is still exceptional, to use Tocqueville's phrase, is astonishing. [60]

3

The Canadian Identity

National identity is the quintessential Canadian issue. Almost alone among modern developed countries, Canada has continued to debate its self-conception to the present day. One of its leading historians notes that it

> has suffered for more than a century from a somewhat more orthodox and less titillating version of Portnoy's complaint: the inability to develop a secure and unique identity. And so...intellectuals and politicians have attempted to play psychiatrist to the Canadian Portnoy, hoping to discover a national identity.[1]

As if to illustrate his point, Margaret Atwood comments ironically, "If the national mental illness of the United States is megalomania, that of Canada is paranoid schizophrenia."[2]

The reasons for this uncertainty are clear. Canada is a residual country. It is that part of British North America that did not support the Revolution. Before 1776, Anglophone Canadians possessed the same traits that distinguished other American colonists from the British. Then, as noted in the preceding chapter, the new nation to the south developed a political identity formulated around the values set out in the Declaration of Independence. Americanism became and has remained a political ideology.[3] There is no ideology of Canadianism, although Canada has a Tory tradition derived from Britain and is, like the United States, descended from a North American settler and frontier society.

The country gradually evolved as an independent nation, but the unification of the provinces of British North America into the Dominion of Canada in 1867 was not an act in defiance of the British Crown. Rather, it reflected the fact that Britain had sought for some decades to give up much of its responsibility for the territories and wanted their people to take political responsibility for their own domestic governments while remaining part of the British Empire. The provinces united after the American Civil War, under Tory leadership, in large part because they feared they would be easy targets for takeover or absorption by the massive, war-trained army of the United States if they remained separate. Many people, especially in the Maritime provinces, wanted to remain more closely linked to Britain, but representatives of London urged them to join the new Confederation.

Opposing the democratic efforts of reformers within the autonomous provinces, the Tories favored a strong federal state that could help develop British North America economically by providing capital.[4] "Canadian confederation was expressive of Tory values"; it was designed to "counteract democracy and ensure constitutional liberty" and was resisted by the liberal and continentalist elements.[5]

The leaders of the Confederation movement were monarchists who favored a strong state. During the Confederation debates of 1865, "[w]henever one of the Fathers of Confederation called upon *authority* he called upon the Crown, what was called the 'monarchical principle.' Devotion to the Crown was the one element that all the Fathers of Confederation shared."[6] Consequently, as one of them, Thomas D'Arcy McGee, declared,

> Unlike our neighbors [the American Constitutional Fathers], we had no questions of sovereignty to raise. We have been saved from all embarrassment on the subject of sovereignty by simply recognizing it as it already exists, in the Queen of Great Britain and Ireland.[7]

As the historian William Stahl emphasizes:

> It is clear why the Fathers of Confederation spoke of "peace, order, and good government" rather than "life, liberty, and the pursuit of happiness." The virtues of monarchy subordinate the individual to the community. Instead of liberty and

happiness, loyalty and responsibility are stressed. Freedom
may be a watchword, but equality is not, and freedom is always tempered and circumscribed by obligations and the
rights of others. But if subordination is preached, subser-
vience is not....The individual curbs his or her egoism because not to do so would make life in family and community
intolerable. And over all is emphasized the personal nature
of social and political relationships. Monarchy is but the family writ large.[8]

The emphasis on order in Canada and on liberty in the
United States has had consequences for each. As one Canadian
popular writer, Pierre Berton, points out:

The other side of the coin of order and security is authority.
We've always accepted more governmental control over our
lives than...[Americans] have — and fewer civil liberties...[But] the other side of the coin of liberty is license, sometimes anarchy. It seems to us that...Americans have been
more willing to suffer violence in...[their] lives than we have
for the sake of individual freedom.[9]

Americans, from the days of the Revolution on, have resisted
authority, demanded their rights, and preferred weak government, while Canadians have complained less, been less
aggressive, and desired a strong paternalistic government. Berton believes it significant that as a soldier he "asked for 'leave,' a
word that suggests permission....[while American] G.I.s were
granted 'liberty,' a word that implies escape."[10] A summary of
Berton's conclusions notes, Canadians "are law-abiding, deferential toward authority, cautious, prudent, elitist, moralistic,
tolerant (of ethnic differences), cool, unemotional and solemn."[11]
Similar statements have been made by literally hundreds of
Canadian writers, journalists, and social scientists in differentiating their country from its neighbor. Many of their assumptions
can be validated statistically, as will be shown later. What is
equally relevant is the extent to which Canadians arc steadily exposed to this self-image, the extent to which it forms a set of
organizing principles to which they are socialized.
The process was evident in the content of a television documentary produced in 1986 by Marshall McLuhan's daughter,
Stephanie.[12] It included a variety of statements by leading

Canadians, as well as expatriates, elaborating on the characteristics of their people in terms corresponding closely to the social science generalizations. They illustrate how a society tells its people what they are supposed to be like. Novelist Margaret Atwood commented, "Americans love success, worship success," while "Canadians are suspicious of success." Journalist Peter Newman emphasized that "Canadians defer to authority," that "we are more laid back up here," there is not the "push and drive you see down in the States." Sidney Gruson of the *New York Times* told the audience, "My Canadian background made me look on crises with less heat than if I were an American." Sondra Gotlieb, wife of the then ambassador to the United States, noted, "Canadians have an image of moderateness....They are solid, reliable, decent...[but] a little bit dull." And, Pierre Berton said to the viewers, "We don't have the superpatriotism you see south of the border. We don't express ourselves emotionally. We are more phlegmatic than the Americans."

Canadians repeatedly remind themselves that they are and should be the quiet North Americans. On April 7, 1989, Ottawa experienced a dramatic hostage-taking event: a passenger-laden bus was seized on the highway and the hijacker (whose motives remain unclear) had it driven to Parliament Hill, where it remained for several hours until he was convinced to surrender. A few days later, Charles Gordon, a leading journalist, devoted a page-long column in *Maclean's*, the country's largest-circulation weekly newsmagazine, to a discussion of how the reaction to the occurrence "could only have happened in Canada." No one panicked, no guns were fired, no business or government offices in the area were shut down. A press conference for the president of Costa Rica continued in a nearby building. Evening social events were not postponed. Television news did not show "what TV audiences the world over have come to expect whenever a crisis occurs — fire trucks whizzing around with sirens blaring, helicopters whirring overhead." Gordon proudly told his fellow citizens how symbolic of the country's character it all was:

> Pictures not showing helicopters were Canadian pictures, for certain. It is difficult, in the modern world, to picture a similar scene in any other world capital — and particularly

Washington — without helicopters. But we were helicopter-less.[13]

Canadian Independence

The continuing linkage of Canada to the mother country is strikingly revealed by the most significant action a nation can take: the declaration of war. It has been understood that when the British Parliament voted for war, Canada would follow suit. Thus, Canada sent troops to fight at Britain's side during the Boer War. It entered both World War I and World War II on the heels of the mother country (although Prime Minister Mackenzie King postponed the 1939 vote in Parliament for a week, so as to emphasize Canada's independence).[14]

Until recently, the constitution of the Canadian confederation was the *British North America Act*, proclaimed by Queen Victoria in 1867. Only in 1982 did Canada request the British Parliament to give up formal control (something it had wanted to do since at least the early 1930s). Not until 1947 did Canadians even secure a separate status as citizens of their own country, as distinct from British subjects. Before 1949, their ultimate court of appeal was the Privy Council of Great Britain. Canadian lawyers had to go to London to argue constitutional cases, as well as other kinds of appeals. Prior to 1975, British citizens living in Canada could vote in national elections without filing for Canadian citizenship, and they did not lose their automatic right to enter Canada until the passage of the *Immigration Act* of 1978. The Maple Leaf became the national flag in 1965, and "O Canada" was approved as the national anthem — replacing "God Save the Queen" — only in 1967 and was not officially so designated until 1980. But, of course, as one British magazine notes, unlike Americans, "Canadians do not chant an oath of allegiance or salute the flag."[15]

The Counterrevolution Continued

Although the content and extent of the differences between Canada and the United States have changed in the course of time, many present-day variations still reflect the impact of the American Revolution. Much of the writing on comparative aspects of culture, politics, economy, religion, law, and literature in North America emphasizes the causal importance of the different origins of the two nations. As noted earlier, Canadian historians point out that in their country the democratic or populist elements lost their battle on many occasions. Some stress the significance of the failure of the 1837 rebellions, which, according to political scientist Philip Resnick, might have "fostered a liberal state, possibly a cross between American presidential and English parliamentary in form" and, more important, "would have entailed, as revolutions have elsewhere, a politicization that we rarely experience and seldom imagine in this country."[16] One of Canada's ablest historians, Frank Underhill, says of the long-term conservatism and resistance to Americanism of his country's history: "It would be hard to overestimate the amount of energy we have devoted to this cause."[17]

The legitimation of conservatism in Canada flowed from the rejection of the American and French revolutions, and from patterns of emigration and immigration that reinforced right-wing trends. The latter, which began very early, included the departure of bourgeois and rationalist elements from Quebec in 1760 after the British conquest and, from 1789 on, the arrival there of conservative priests from France, who had a "notable role in developing the classical colleges and parish schools [and]...instilled a horror of the French Revolution."[18] After 1783, most Congregational pro-Revolution clergy moved from the English-speaking areas to New England, and an estimated 50,000 Loyalists, including many Anglican priests, crossed the new border in the opposite direction.

Throughout the 19th and early 20th centuries, the United States remained the extreme example of a classically liberal or Lockean society, rejecting the assumptions of the alliance of throne and altar, of ascriptive elitism, of mercantilism, of noblesse oblige, of communitarianism. Canada was noticeably different. As we have seen, Friedrich Engels was among several 19th-century foreign visitors who noted that Canada preserved a more European society than the "purely bourgeois" United States.[19] More recently, the Canadian Marxist sociologist Arthur Davis observed:

[The] American colonies broke their ties with England, and
the philosophy of laissez-faire Manchesterism could run wild
until the rise of new internal oppositions late in the
nineteenth century....In England, on the other hand, elements of pre-industrial classes and values survived industrialization. The first reforms in the nineteenth century
were sparked, not by the "new men of Manchester," but by
Tories from the old landed classes motivated by feudal norms
like noblesse oblige. Something of these restraining values
seem to have carried over into English Canada.[20]

Another Canadian left-wing social scientist elaborates on the
way that Toryism, which emphasizes "the need for more conscious control over the processes of a...society," took root,
survived, and deeply influenced Canadian culture and politics.

[I]n the transfer of cultural and political baggage to the British
North American colonies, Toryism found an environment in
which, rather paradoxically considering the absence of a
feudal past, it was to play a more important role as a legitimiz-
ing ideology of capitalist development than it ever did in its
English homeland. In colonial Canada, both inherited Tory
images and the learned experience of development in the
peculiar circumstances of that time and place led to a domination of the Tory image of the state over the more liberal
laissez-faire concept....The emphasis on *control* of the processes of national development, the element of the collective will
of the dominant class expressed through the public institutions of the state, while seemingly anachronistic in an increasingly laissez-faire Britain, was crucially relevant to a
thinly settled frontier colony struggling on the fringes of a
growing economic and political power to the south.[21]

Ironically, other modern scholars who see Canada as a more
British- or European-type conservative society emphasize that
the values inherent in monarchically rooted Tory conservatism
give rise in the modern world to support for social democratic
redistributive and welfare policies.[22] The historian of Canadian
socialism, Gad Horowitz, notes that "socialism has more in common with Toryism than with [classic] liberalism, for liberalism is
possessive individualism, while socialism and Toryism are var-
iants of collectivism."[23] Conversely, a dominant laissez-faire
Lockean tradition is antithetical to such programs. Northrop Frye
calls attention to this alliance of opposites: "The Canadian point

of view is at once more conservative and more radical than Whiggery [the liberal ideology of the American Revolution], closer both to aristocracy and to democracy [equality]."[24]

These ideological differences in the two countries have been reinforced by institutional factors, particularly religious and political ones.[25] The American tradition and law place more emphasis on separation of church and state than do the Canadian. Since pre-Revolutionary times, a large majority of Americans have adhered to the Protestant sects that opposed the established state church in England. For most of the 19th century, the majority of Canadians belonged to either the Roman Catholic or the Anglican Church. Both are hierarchically organized and were state-established in Europe. In this century, the Anglican Church has declined greatly in relative strength in Canada; today the United Church, a unification of a considerable majority of the Anglophone sectarians, is by far the largest Protestant denomination, currently including close to one-fifth of the population. Although efforts to sustain church establishment ultimately failed in Canada, some state support of religious institutions, particularly schools, exists today in all provinces.[26] Hence religion has contributed to anti-elitist and individualistic beliefs in the United States and has countered them in Canada.

Analyzing Canadian politics in the 1980s, political scientists William Christian and Colin Campbell emphasize the continuing impact of political institutions that reflect Tory values. They call attention to the historically conditioned greater role of government in Canadian society and the economy, emphasizing that

> political institutions themselves embody and reflect political ideas, and perpetuate them as they accustom participants in the institutions to the values that are implicit in the system they represent....The successful operation in Canada of a Tory/collectivist constitution for well over a century gives us considerable grounds for the belief that such values are acceptable and legitimate to large numbers of Canadians.[27]

Structural Influences

As noted in Chapter 1, most analysts agree that Canadian values and behavior are different from American, but some also point to the causal impact of the variations in the government, ecology, demography, and economy of the two nations. It can be argued that any one of a number of factors would have produced similar results, particularly the greater emphases on the state and communitarianism in the north and on individualism and laissez faire in the south. Values derived from the different founding ethoses helped to establish these, but they have been reinforced by the contrasts in the political systems, geography, and population base.

The most obvious difference between the countries is in their governments: a parliamentary system with an executive (cabinet) that can have its way with the House of Commons, and a presidential, divided-powers system in which the executive does not control and must negotiate with both houses of Congress. In Canada, the source of authority (the Queen) and the agency of authority (the elected government) are separate: they are one in the United States, where the president, a politician, is also the head of state. The former makes for more deference and respect for government and the state than the latter.

The American Constitution with its Bill of Rights emphasizes due-process guarantees for the individual and limits on state power. Until 1982, there were few limits on the power of the Canadian Parliament and cabinet, not even on their ability to suspend the rights of free speech and assembly. The inclusion of the Canadian Charter of Rights and Freedoms in the constitution of 1982 has moved Canada a long way in the direction of American due process, but the new constitution still maintains parliamentary supremacy and does not offer many of the protections in the Bill of Rights, as will be made evident in Chapter 6.

Demographics and the environment also differ between the two countries. The harsh climate of the northern latitudes forced most Canadian settlement as far south as possible. Even today, its relatively small population (about one-tenth of the United States') is strung out in a belt reaching only about 150 miles north of the border but with an east-west span greater than the American. The results of developing and maintaining a country in this huge, sparsely populated span have been many. As S.D. Clark, the doyen of the cultural interpretation of North American comparative sociology, notes:

[G]eography, which favoured individual enterprise and limited political interference in the conduct of economic, social
and religious affairs over a large part of the continent [the
United States], favoured on this part of the continent
[Canada] large-scale bureaucratic forms of organization and
widespread intervention by the state.[28]

Moreover, the presence of a larger, more powerful neighbor to the
south has encouraged Canadians to call on the state to protect
the nation's economic independence.

Other analysts, such as Richard Gwyn, a distinguished
Canadian journalist, stress other ecological factors, including
Canada's "northernness" and its pattern of urbanization, which
is more extensive than that south of the border. He points to traits
held in common with other northern countries: "reticence, prag-
matism, wariness of public display" and social democratic
liberalism.[29]

The urban factor may not appear unique, but, as Gwyn emphasizes, there

is nothing like...[Canadian cities] in the United States. Most
Canadians live in them, while the dominant American pattern is the suburb....Canadians have figured out how to make
their cities work for them; Americans work in their cities and
live outside them.[30]

This thesis has been elaborated and documented by two ur-
banologists, Michael Goldberg and John Mercer, who stress the
many differences between cities north and south of the border —
for example, crime rates, the incidence of slums, and cleanliness
— that reflect variations in national "values and attitudes."[31]

Comparison of the frontier experiences of the two countries
encapsulates the ways in which values and structural factors in-
teract to produce different outcomes. Inasmuch as Canada had
to be on guard against the United States' expansionist tendencies, it could not leave its frontier communities unprotected or
autonomous. Moreover, "it was in the established tradition of
British North America that the power of the civil authority should
operate well in advance of the spread of settlement."[32]

Law and order, in the form of the centrally controlled North-
West Mounted Police, moved into the Canadian west before and

along with the settlers. This contributed to a deeper respect for the institutions of law and order on the Canadian frontier than on the American, thus undermining the development of individualism and disrespect for authority that has been more characteristic of the United States. (These phenomena are discussed in more detail in Chapter 6.)

National Images

Given the contrasts between the Canadian historical experience and the American one, it is not surprising that the peoples of the two countries have formed their self-conceptions in disparate ways. The United States, as we have seen, was organized around what Abraham Lincoln called a "political religion." As a result, as Sacvan Bercovitch notes, both left and right take sustenance from the American creed. Canada never developed its own universalistic ideology.[33]

Comparing political science textbooks north and south of the border, Alan Cairns emphasizes:

> There is no Canadian creed against which a Canadian text could judge the system's performance and find it lacking. Had Gunnar Myrdal written of Canada he could not have contradicted prevailing inequalities with an official creed of equality. The Anglophone political scientists of a country endowed with a counter-revolutionary tradition have felt minimal compulsion to explore the meaning and development of Canadianism.[34]

Analysts of literature draw similar conclusions. Thus, A.J.M. Smith suggests that the emphasis on a national creed has made American writing "critical and profoundly subversive," while in Canada, without an ideal to contrast with the country's reality, literature has been more conservative.[35] Margaret Atwood notes that, unlike Canada, the United States "holds out a hope, never fulfilled but always promised, of a Utopia, the perfect human society." She points out that most 20th-century American literature is about the "gap between the promise and the actuality, between the imagined ideal...and the actual squalid materialistic dotty small town, nasty city, or redneck-filled outback."[36]

In an analysis of fiction in English Canada and the United States, the literary critic Stanley Fogel emphasizes the same distinctions:

> A comparison of contemporary literature in English Canada and the United States reveals a startling disparity in the two perceptions of here. Here for American writers is a monolith, often named, which must be combatted, reviled, or exorcised. The American here comes with a clearly formed set of characteristics and an apparently universally grasped ideology. Canada's here is rarely named in the pages of contemporary Canadian writers; it cannot be named....[T]he ideological baggage, which goes with the United States, does not encumber Canada. The latter country, therefore, is not the object of writers' thrusts or assaults.[37]

As we have seen, the ideology of the American Revolution provides a raison d'être for the Republic — it explains why the United States came into being and what it means to be American. But Canada "arrived at freedom through evolution in allegiance and not by revolutionary compact." Hence, its "final governing force...is tradition and convention."[38] The country could not offer its citizens "the prospect of a fresh start...because (as the Canadian poet Douglas Le Pan put it) Canada is 'a country without a mythology.'"[39] To justify separate national existence, Canadians have deprecated American values and institutions, mainly those seen as derived from an excessive emphasis on competition, which they once identified as an outgrowth of mass democracy and equalitarianism but which in recent years are explained by their intellectuals as endemic in the hegemonic capitalist values and institutions.

Canadians have tended to define themselves not in terms of their own national history and traditions but by reference to what they are *not:* Americans. Canadians are the world's oldest and most continuing un-Americans.[40] "Without at least a touch of anti-Americanism, Canada would have no reason to exist."[41] Evidence drawn from "popular fiction, westerns, science and spy thrillers" documents "persistent...Canadian fears" about the United States.[42] Until fairly recently, the predominant form that negation took was conservative, monarchical, and ecclesiastical.

Formative national events and images — revolution and counterrevolution, rebels and Loyalists — continued to affect the way the two countries regarded themselves from the 19th century into the pre-World War II era.[43] A student of Canadian writings on America calls attention to various comments in the 1920s by Canadian observers who "discern and condemn an excessive egalitarian quality derived from notions of independence and democracy which have been set free during the Revolution."[44]

In a comparative study of modern democracies published in the early 1920s, James Bryce also noted such persistent differences flowing from divergent histories.[45] Like many Canadian and British writers, Bryce viewed most dissimilarities between the two North American democracies as reflecting credit on Canada. It did not exhibit the "spirit of license, the contempt of authority, the negligence in enforcing the laws" found in the United States and other populist countries. He stressed the enduring adherence of both Canadian language groups to prerevolutionary values.[46] Their concern with "order and harmony" reflected "the ideals of authority and natural hierarchy."[47]

A summary of Canadians' beliefs about Americans and themselves as reported in sociological surveys taken among Anglophones in the 1930s points up the way the northerners justified themselves:

> The typical American, in Canadian eyes at least, was brash and arrogant, with little respect for law and order and even less respect for the sanctity of marriage. This tells us little of what Americans were really like but it tells us a great deal of what Canadians thought of themselves....
>
> It is noteworthy that the qualities which seemed to distinguish Canadians — and to reveal their superiority — were qualities which clearly reflected conservative attitudes. The emphasis was on respect for traditional institutions....Rugged individualism was not necessarily seen as a sin but it was closely tempered by the values associated with...social conformity....
>
> The subject matter in Canadian schools...suggested a respect for inherited traditions....[T]he American myth of a new and unfettered society in the new world never appeared in the Canadian textbooks.[48]

Pre–World War II Canadians were not, of course, united in their view of themselves or their neighbor. During the 1920s, judgments varied along political lines. Conservatives stressed the Tory emphasis on the use of the state to foster noblesse-oblige objectives and were especially deprecating about egalitarianism and democracy in the United States.[49] They wished to maintain the British tie and even to strengthen the link to the Empire. In contrast, many Liberals were continentalists, adhering to traditions that were closer to those of the Americans. At the same time, radicals tended to be more nationalistic in their sentiments. Canadian leftists, then as later, worried about an American takeover of their country.

Whatever the motives of different groups, the conception Canadians had of what was good about Canada and bad about the United States influenced their values and behavior. Those who said that Canadians — by not being as materialistic, achievement-oriented and competitive as Americans — were morally superior taught their children not to be as competitive or aggressive. The stress in Canadian schooling on the value of high culture, as distinct from functionally practical subjects, both described and influenced the content of education.

Values and structures change. Canada and the United States have both followed the general tendencies of most western nations toward greater acceptance of communitarian welfare and egalitarian objectives, a decline in religious commitment, smaller nuclear families, an increase in educational attainment, a greater role for government, continued economic growth, a higher standard of living, more leisure, increased longevity, growing urbanization, and a shift in the composition of the economy from primary and secondary industries toward tertiary and high-tech and information-based ones. With these developments has come the decline of many cultural traits associated with pre-industrial society, particularly with respect to emphasis on stratification differences associated with religion and inherited social status, gender, race, or ethnicity. These changes have not, however, led to a falloff in national or group consciousness, particularly among ethnic or linguistic minorities, whose self-awareness and political organization have frequently increased; the behavior of the Québécois in Canada and the blacks and Hispanics in the United

States provides examples (which will be dealt with in subsequent chapters).

The cultural and structural differences among western countries generally and between Canada and the United States in particular have declined in some respects. The diffusion of values, the comparable economic changes, and the development of rapid transportation and almost instantaneous communication seem to be producing a common western culture. Yet, many traditional national differences persist, some in weaker form, and new ones emerge (an example is the rate of unionization, which is now much higher in Canada than in the United States). As Gwyn notes, Canadians have become

> a quite distinct kind of North American...utterly unlike [those in the United States] in their political cultures so that they are as distinct from each other as are the Germans from the French, say, even though both are European just as Canadians and Americans are both North Americans.[50]

Meanwhile, in Prime Minister Mackenzie King's words, "if some countries have too much history, [Canada] has too much geography."[51] Unlike the United States, it finds little to celebrate: no revolution, no declaration of independence, no civil war to free the slaves. Its first (1867) constitution was drawn up by conservatives who did not express themselves "in popular language. They did not speak the language of the Rights of Man or of life, liberty, and the pursuit of happiness." That constitution, argues Philip Resnick, was the legitimating "document of the Canadian counter-revolution."[52]

This discussion continues in the next chapter with an analysis of the way the content and style of creative culture, particularly literature, in Canada has helped to form and distribute the country's image of itself. Since that identity has emerged in reaction to conceptions of the United States, Canadian literary critics have also commented about American writing and identity, about the American dream.

4

Literature and Myths:
Canadian Perspectives

Canada, as we have seen, lacks an ideology, but it has a strong identity, one that is reflected in its increasingly important literature and other creative arts. And these have helped both to form and to reflect the national self-image. As Ronald Sutherland, a Canadian literary critic, emphasizes, "[t]he greatest writers of a nation...respond to the forces that condition a nation's philosophy of life, and they in turn condition that philosophy."[1] A striking example of the way novelists reinforce national self-conceptions can be found in *The Lyre of Orpheus*, the most recent novel by Robertson Davies. He gives voice to Canadians' consensus that they lack a capacity for excellence and achievement, that they value mediocrity. Non-Canadian characters in the story are described as "possessed by ambition," as seeking "real adventure." But in referring to "the Canadians," he notes:

> [T]hey closed up at any imputation of high motives, of splendid intention, of association with what might be great, and therefore dangerous. They were not wholly of the grey majority of their people; they lived in a larger world than that, but they wore the greyness as a protective outer garment. They did not murmur the national prayer: "O God, grant me mediocrity and comfort; protect me from the radiance of Thy light." Nevertheless, they knew how difficult and disquieting too bold a spirit might be. They settled to their plates, and made small talk.[2]

American novelists, though they rarely use Canada as a set-
ting, have occasionally added to these stereotypes. Thus, in John
Irving's latest book, *A Prayer for Owen Meany*, his American-born
protagonist, while living in Toronto, is rebuked for his outspoken-
ness: "It's very American — to have opinions as...strong as your
opinions. It's very Canadian to distrust strong opinions....Your
anger — that's not very Canadian either."[3]

Looking at how Canadians have analyzed their creative culture, contrasting it with that in the United States often sheds light
on the national differences. More important, it bears on the emergence of national identities. Canadian literary critics see their
country's literature as reflecting defeat, difficult physical circumstances, and an uninteresting history, while they contend
that American writers perceive their country in optimistic, trium-
phant terms, blessed by nature and events.[4] Thus, in comparing
fiction across the border, Canadian literary critics tend to accept
the emphasis of some of their U.S. peers, such as R.W.B. Lewis,
on the innocent Adam, who began traditionless, as the authentic symbol of the American.[5] The Canadian literary image is
identified with Noah, who made a new start but brought with him
the weight of a failed history.[6]

In explaining the differences, some critics focus on the contrasting effects of the American Revolution on the way North
American novelists (and populations) view the world. Others emphasize how living next door to a powerful or weak country affects
the content of a national literature in ways paralleling the traditional power positions of men and women. They suggest that as
a result of the differing histories, Canadian writers identify with
women more than Americans do and, perhaps more interesting-
ly, are therefore female in greater proportions than those in the
United States.[7]

This chapter largely focuses on the views of creative culture
in Canada and the United States. Many of the analyses presume
different contents and styles reflecting variations in the two
countries' organizing principles. Two points must be noted. First,
the sources used are almost all Canadian. Ignorant of Canada,
Americans have had almost nothing to say about the creative arts
in a comparative North American context. Hence, what is reported
in this chapter is basically a continuation of the discussion about

Canadian identity, about the ways intellectuals in the north see their nation and its neighbor.[8]

Second, such efforts invariably exaggerate differences and imply much greater coherence than exists. Canadians see their culture as pessimistic and introverted, stemming from the country's historic failures and inherent weaknesses. They view American literature and art as optimistic and outgoing, as outgrowths of political and economic successes and great power. However valid, these overall generalizations clearly ignore enormous differences within each society. The literature of the white south, a defeated region, that of American blacks, a people suffering from the effects of slavery and racism, and that stemming from the declining old New England upper class, all can match Canadian writing in pessimism. Still, as I hope will be evident, there are basic crossborder differences in predominant artistic themes that testify to the ways in which creative culture forms, sustains, and exhibits national values.

Revolution and Counterrevolution

The theme of revolution and counterrevolution has been developed in comparative analyses of North American creative arts by many writers: Claude Bissell, R. Bruce Elder, Edgar Friedenberg, Northrop Frye, Mary Jean Green, Dick Harrison, Douglas Le Pan, Norman Newton, A.J.M. Smith, Ronald Sutherland, and others. Sutherland notes that the national traits of Canadians and Americans that sprouted at the time of the Revolution "became powerful conditioning forces in American and Canadian culture and literature."[9] Frye emphasizes that a "culture founded on a revolutionary tradition, like that of the United States, is bound to show very different assumptions and imaginative patterns from those of a culture that rejects or distrusts revolution."[10] Modern Canadian intellectual radicalism "has something in common with the Toryism it opposes."[11]

Canadians describe American fiction as more outgoing, more optimistic, more populist, and more likely to contain violence than their own. "The strong romantic tradition in Canadian literature has much to do with its original conservatism," says Claude Bissell.[12] Canadian novelists have favored more aesthetic styles than Americans have. Bissell, who works in comparative English language studies, notes that Canadian novels fit in more as part "of European than American literature."[13]

Canadian writers have consciously tried "to dissent from American values....The formal conservatism of their writing is consistent with the conservative outlook their fiction has habitually expressed," notes T.D. Maclulich. Conversely, he continues, literature in the United States has been prone to reflect populist and egalitarian themes. Much of Canadian writing has been described as being in a "Tory mode" — a term referring to styles "marked by a high incidence of slightly old-fashioned syntactic habits." Until recently, it "has been the most common manner in Canadian fiction," reflecting an effort "to keep alive...a way of life that differs from the way of life pursued in the country to the south."[14]

In comparing North American writing, Margaret Atwood suggests that the symbol for the United States is "the Frontier," which implies "a place that is *new*, where the old order can be discarded." The central image for Canada, based on numerous examples of its appearance in French- and English-Canadian literature, is "Survival, *la survivance*, hanging on, staying alive." She notes the continued concern with Canada: does it exist? will it exist? what is Canadian identity? do we have an identity? As she puts it, "Canadians are forever taking the national pulse like doctors at a sickbed; the aim is not to see whether the patient will live well but simply whether he will live at all."[15]

Like others, Atwood emphasizes the difference in the way the two societies look at authority. Rebels and revolutionists are not heroes in Canadian literature.[16] She illustrates her general theme by looking at the diverse ways in which the family is treated in novels in the two countries: "In American literature the family is something the hero must repudiate and leave; it is a structure he rebels against, thereby defining his own freedom, his own frontier. The family...is something you come from and get rid of." Canadian novels treat the family quite differently, for "if in America it's a skin you shed, then in Canada it's a trap in which you're caught."[17]

Analytic Interpretations

The different ways in which Canadian and American novels treat generational, familial, and societal conflict lend themselves to analytic psychological interpretations. Both Jungian and Freudian concepts are used to account for the dissimilarities.

Robertson Davies and Robert Kroetsch see Canada, in the words of the latter, as "a much more Jungian society" than America, which can be looked at in Freudian terms.[18] Canada, having continued strong links to its past, to Britain and the monarchy, retains closer ties to its European traditions, which makes it Jungian. The United States, which broke with its archetypal myths and national family, has followed a Freudian scenario.

The literary critic Dick Harrison sees the novels of Davies and others as "private, domestic, confessional forms that dominate Canadian fiction," exhibiting a lesser Jungian emphasis on conflict, while American writing is preoccupied "with individualism, and the rejection of authority."[19] Davies himself sees American culture as reflecting "intellectual ferocity and a sort of black/white quality," while his own society appears to him as much "softer-focussed...[and] more humane."[20]

The presence of more generational conflict in American fiction than in Canadian is cited by Russell Brown as evidence that Freudian themes, albeit different ones, predominate in North American literature. According to Brown, novels south of the border emphasize rejection of the father by his sons, much as the Americans overthrew the king. Canadian fictional heroes long for the (overseas) parent who abandoned them. The variations in national literatures stem from "crucial differences between American and Canadian societies," those related to their diverse political origins.

> The fact that America, through the act of revolution, reified its break with the old sources of tradition and authority while Canada did not, marks a divergence between the two cultures that continues to make itself evident today. What is important, I wish to emphasize, is not so much the effect of the revolution (or its lack) on the day-to-day life of individuals in the two countries, it is rather the myths and the psychic con-

sequences of founding a country on revolution or on the rejection of revolution.[21]

A revolt against tradition and authority, against king and ancestral fatherland is and always must remain at some deep level an Oedipal act.[22] The writings of American authors as various as Nathaniel Hawthorne, Herman Melville, Hart Crane, Booth Tarkington, Mark Twain, Theodore Dreiser, Robert Penn Warren, Eugene O'Neill, J.D. Salinger, and Norman Mailer are identified by critics as reflecting Oedipal themes: a rejection of the father and an emotional relationship with the mother.[23]

Canadian writing, however, is said to be quite different in its treatment of the father, a variation that is

> determined by the way the nation first conceived of itself in relation to its country...of origin, its fatherland....First of all in Canadian fiction there is, inevitably, still some generational conflict, but when it is present it is more often the father that wins, victorious over the son who seems unable or unwilling to defend himself.[24]

Brown suggests that it is Telemachus whose story is reflected in a great deal of Canadian writing. Telemachus' problem is that "the king, his father, has departed, has left him to grow up fatherless in his mother's home for reasons he cannot fully grasp, or at any rate experientially comprehend." Hence he sets out at the beginning of the *Odyssey* to find his father and discover the events that took him away.[25] Among the Canadian novels Brown cites as reflecting the Telemachus syndrome are Hugh MacLennan's *Each Man's Son*,[26] Robert Kroetsch's *Badlands*, Martha Ostenso's *Wild Geese*, Margaret Laurence's *The Diviners*, and Adele Wiseman's *Crackpot*.

Brown concludes his analysis by saying,

> Oedipus and Telemachus, two different patterns of experience separated only by a border. What finally are the full implications of these two culturally-shaped attitudes, these divergent mythic patterns that lie deep within national consciousness? Many of them are already evident in the discussion which has gone before. The American desire to free oneself from the father is also a desire to escape the past with

its tradition and authority. It is no surprise that the American hero par excellence is that man without father, Adam....The American flight from history is the root of the American dream, the Horatio Alger myth, the self-made man.[27]

In Canadian writing, on the other hand, it is Noah,

the *nth* Adam, the modern man recapitulating a process handed down across untold generations stretching back to the ultimate Father, the first-namer. There are Canadian books which emphasize Noah, such as J. MacPherson's book of poems, *The Boatman*, or Robinson Crusoe, as in Leo Simpson's novel, *Arkwright* — recast in more modern terms he becomes Robinson Crusoe, the man capable through the activity of his mind of reconstructuring his civilization even in a wilderness.[28]

Gender Emphases

Mary Jean Green, an American student of Quebec literature, concurs about the importance of the revolution-counterrevolution distinction in understanding North American cultures and about the usefulness of classic psychological interpretations. She contends, however, that the family-tension pattern in Canadian novels reflects not orphanage but the stresses of the mother-daughter relationship; the daughter, like Canada, resists but does not break with her family. She agrees that the father-son conflict characterizes American fiction. According to the Freudian analysis, the son fights the father, but the daughter "though...initially overcome by hostility...can never fully abandon her very strong feelings of attachment and continuity with the mother." Hence, "the importance accorded mother-daughter interaction in the ideological context of Quebec" and Anglophone Canada as well. The theme of many recent novels in both the country's languages has been the feminine one "of rejection and reconciliation," not the more masculine sharp break.[29]

Hugh MacLennan also emphasizes his country's female characteristics in comparison to those of the more masculine United States, though from a different causal perspective. These variations are reflected in his own fiction. He suggests that Canada's feminine psychology "came into being" because of its relationship as a small country with a colossus such as the United States. MacLennan contends that Canada

> acquired a purely feminine capacity for sustaining within her nature contradictions so difficult to reconcile that most societies possessing them would be torn by periodic revolutions. Canada has acquired a good woman's hatred of quarrels, the good woman's readiness to make endless compromises for the sake of peace within the home, the good woman's knowledge that although her husband can knock her down if he chooses, she will be able to make him ashamed of himself if such an idea begins to form in his mind.[30]

Gaile McGregor also uses gender images in comparing North American fiction, agreeing that "the Canadian literary hero seems to demonstrate a distinctly [female] gender aspect," while the American is masculine. Citing novels written by men as well as women, she contends that there is an "inversion of marital sex roles" in crossborder writing. "The Canadian heroine...is strong" and dominant within the family, while the reverse is true in American fiction. The Canadian man is more "gentle and retiring." She concludes that

> though the tendency to sex inversion is not a *recognized* element in our [Canadian] national self-image, it is general enough to be seen as an important characteristic of what we might call the Canadian un-consciousness. Though the pattern of the relation implied is largely antithetical to our *overt*...value/belief system,....it is obviously a real component of *covert culture* in this country.[31]

An analysis of the story content of English-Canadian films also reports their repeated emphasis on the weak-male/strong-female syndrome. Through many different scenarios, they describe "the radical inadequacy of the male protagonist — his moral failure, especially, and most visibly, in his relationships with women." Females are characterized by "greater authenticity," having "the power to love and trust and commit themselves without adding up the cost."[32]

The assumption that the Canadian experience can be more fruitfully explored in feminine rather than in masculine terms suggests to Green an answer to the puzzle of why "women writers occupy...[more] central positions in Canadian literature in both English and French" than in American writing:

> Perhaps it is because female voices have a special resonance for the culture as a whole that, in Canada, women writers have assumed such an important role in defining a reality that is not uniquely feminine but, rather, profoundly Canadian.[33]

Elitist and Populist Styles

The varying political traditions have also been used to account for the differences in the way poetry and art developed across the border. Frye suggests these dissimilarities related to "a more distinctive attitude in Canadian poetry and in Canadian life, a more withdrawn and detached view of life which may go back to the central factor of Canadian history, the rejection of the American revolution."[34] Another critic, Norman Newton, points to a conservative emphasis in Canadian poetry that "is closely bound up with the Canadian character as it expressed itself in our formative years."[35]

Frye and Bissell emphasize that, in the former's words, in "the United States...there has been much more rugged prophecy in praise of the common man, a tradition that runs from Whitman."[36] But, as Bissell notes, "Whitman excited only feeblest discipleship in Canada." Unlike the writers in populist and egalitarian America and Australia, Canadian writers preferred English and European elitist aesthetic models.[37] "The same European tradition continues into the twentieth century."[38]

The same logic has been used to explain why Canadian art has rarely been modernist. According to critic Ross Skoggard, it is indicative of Canada's being

> one of the few Western countries that has never experienced a political revolution....Canadian artists' disaffection for revolutionary avant-garde movements reflects Canada's counter-revolutionary and loyalist past. Our distaste for confrontational politics is matched by our discomfort with confrontational culture.[39]

Movie analyst R. Bruce Elder also concludes that Canadian films eschew conflict and competition while American motion pictures emphasize them.[40]

Elder's analysis links up with that of Canadian literary critics George Bowering and Stanley Fogel, emphasizing that, in contrast to the situation in the United States, avant-garde writing, painting, and film have not flourished in Canada.[41] Bowering notes that "in Canada we hold with tenacity to realism and naturalism in our fiction," while in the United States "post-realist fiction is no longer [considered] in the avant-garde."[42] Fogel argues that "the conservative character of Canadians is responsible for the retention of traditional and the disavowal of experimental methods of fiction writing."[43] Following up the contention of Lionel Trilling and others that American writers are part of an "adversary culture," he links the social rebellion to literary innovativeness in style and form. The defensive nationalism of Canadian novelists is seen as causally related to their remaining within an old-fashioned realist tradition, to the absence of postmodern writing.

Emphasis on the crossborder variations in the importance of the postmodern — of going beyond reality — is, like all national comparisons, somewhat exaggerated. In fact, *The Canadian Postmodern* is the title of an excellent book by the comparative literature scholar Linda Hutcheon. Yet, she too repeatedly calls attention to the "continuing strength" of the "traditional realist novel" in her country and to the emphasis on "national and cultural identity" and "the relation of man to nature."[44]

The American sociologist Edgar Friedenberg, long resident in Canada, also interprets that country's culture as derived from its elitist and counterrevolutionary tradition. He contends, "With respect to the arts, Canada seems to excel particularly in those forms which have the least potential for subversion." One example, he notes, is Canada's ballet, which "has been recognized for years throughout the world; there are at least three established companies of first rank." But, he contends, ballet is "anti-mass and arty...[and] inherently counterrevolutionary." As he goes on to say, "[B]allet, though highly expressive, is also the art that provides least opportunity for spontaneity or improvisation, it is governed by an elaborate system of conventions and requires lifelong discipline of its practitioners."[45]

The Loser Syndrome

The "loser" mentality of Canadians is another theme bearing on the effects of the country's counterrevolutionary origins, one suggested by Hugh MacLennan, J.M.S. Careless, Robertson Davies, David Stouck, and others. MacLennan contends that Canadian culture reflects the fact that the three founding nationalities were defeated peoples: the English by the Americans, the French and Scots (the Scots who settled in Nova Scotia were Jacobites) by the English.[46] Careless, who stresses a Canadian "loser syndrome created by the rigors of pioneering in a northern land," also believes "Americans cannot conceive of losing unless there's a conspiracy somewhere."[47] Davies takes up the same theme in a 1989 essay, calling his country "a nation of losers, of exiles and refugees. Modern Canada is a prosperous country, but the miseries of its earliest white inhabitants are bred in the bone, and cannot, even now, be rooted out of the flesh."[48] Stouck argues that the tradition goes back well over a century:

> [T]he image of the settler as a self-pitying failure rather than a buoyant pioneer characterizes a literary tradition peopled with victims and failures. In nineteenth-century American fiction, the hero or heroine risks property, sanity and life itself, but will never surrender the dream of improvement or the sure sense of life's wonder and promise. In contrast, Canadian heroes and heroines of the same period [the mid-century] brood on inevitable failure and defeat.[49]

Such a background could be expected to produce a people uncertain about themselves and highly self-critical. In line with this deduction, one literary critic points out that major Canadian writers, such as Hubert Aquin, Marie-Claire Blais, and Leonard Cohen, have written of a society whose brave souls have been "beautiful losers" (the title of a novel by Cohen). And he contends that most good "Canadian writing...since the 1960s, is a predicate of these writers and their themes."[50] Another commentator stresses the Canadian emphasis on victims while noting that

American literature is much more focused on winners.[51] And McGregor calls attention to the "numerous Canadian critics including Dick Harrison, Margaret Atwood, and George Woodcock [who] have noted with puzzlement Canada's propensity to ignore the 'real' heroes of her history and canonize instead the 'losers.'"[52] In *Survival,* Atwood stresses that the heroes of Canadian novels "survive, but just barely. They are born losers failing to do anything but keep alive."[53]

These literary images reach out to a broader public. In its New Year's issue for 1986, the Canadian cultural monthly *Saturday Night* presented a front cover headed in large type, "Beautiful Losers — A Canadian Tradition." The story inside noted that Canada is

> not quite a country where dreams come true, not exactly a land where the good guys always win. Losses...marked our steady passage. Partaking of a [long] tradition...Canadians frequently came back from their adventures empty-handed.[54]

Comedy and Irony

Students of comedy, in both print and the movies, also point to another distinctly Canadian approach that reflects the national inferiority complex. Before World War II, the two English-Canadian writers with the greatest international reputations were the humorists Thomas Chandler Haliburton and Stephen Leacock. Suggesting that the Canadian situation is particularly propitious for comedy, the critic R.E. Walters quotes Leacock, who noted that "comparison is the very soul of humor," and in agreeing with him emphasizes that Canadians, living in a sparsely populated country and exposed to different cultures, are disposed to be comparative, to see "discrepancies and incongruities."[55] Hutcheon points to "a long tradition in Canadian letters:...Satire and laughter have been standard ways for Canadians to come to terms with where and how they live."[56]

The novelist, poet, and critic Robert Kroetsch emphasizes the willingness of his country's writers to engage in national "self-mockery and self-parody" as a response to ambiguities in the position of the Canadian: "He is the American who is contrary to the American."[57] In a discussion with Kroetsch on the subject, Geoff Hancock, the editor of *Canadian Fiction Magazine*, exemplifies the tendency by observing that "Canadians make themselves the butt of their jokes, while the Americans make somebody else the butt of theirs."[58] In an article describing Canadian writing to an American audience, Eleanor Cook notes as its most general characteristic "the tendency toward satire, self-mockery and humor."[59] Gaile McGregor links Canadians' interest in comedy to the limitations placed on their country by an inimical environment that also makes for a greater emphasis on tragedy: "The Canadian...[has] a temperamental bent toward the tragic and its complement the comic vision...[which] is carried through in our modes of literary expression."[60]

Equally relevant is the contention that Canada's lack of power makes for calculated diffidence and the use of "irony" as the forms for criticism. Walters argues, in discussing Leacock's work, that his self-deprecating "little man" is "a Canadian type, not an American."[61] Beverly Kasporich elaborates on the same theme and points to Edmund Wilson's observation that the personification by Canadian cartoonist Duncan Macpherson of a "pudgy, tramplike Canadian citizen...the 'littleman' appears to suit Canada and Canadians."[62] Wilson was convinced that Canadians tended to be more ironic than Americans. Obviously, Walter Mitty and Charlie Chaplin types are not uniquely Canadian. What these critics are emphasizing is the relative absence of serious, powerful heroes in Canadian art, the disproportionate presence of tragicomic losers.

The same point is made about English-Canadian motion pictures. Robert Fothergill, in his 1973 analysis of film content, points to a "sense of limitation and inadequacy experienced half-consciously by Canadians in their real lives," to a "defeatist fantasy."[63] More than a decade later, another film critic, Geoff Pevere, finds that this thesis helps "to account for the losers roaming around Canadian films," noting the

> persistent proliferation of outsiders as heroes in Canadian movies....And unlike the romantic American vision of the outlaw as a transcendent figure whose nowhereness permits him

an invulnerable omnipotence and godlike heroism, the Canadian outcast is defined by his being less and not greater than those communities that have rejected him.[64]

Pevere concludes that Canadian motion picture "comedies are more self-deprecating than American ones."[65]

That the disparaging self-images of Canada and Canadians found so frequently in the country's fiction correspond to feelings within its elite was brought home to me when attending a 1987 consultation for one of Canada's major foundations. The 12 distinguished Canadians present agreed that the country required examples of "excellence" to break down the aura of "mediocrity" that characterizes its major institutions and leadership. Those present included two top executives of the Canadian Broadcasting Corporation, two major business leaders, a national labor union official, an important pollster, the editors of an English-language cultural magazine and of an intellectually distinguished French-language newspaper, two prominent political figures, a top-level civil servant, and an internationally acclaimed motion picture director. Yet all were concerned with Canada's disdain for achievement and recommended that the foundation devote its resources to creating centers of excellence.

That such views were expressed by some of the most distinguished members of the Canadian establishment in a conversation with *each other* reflects the extent to which the elite of an extremely successful country has interiorized the image of mediocrity fostered by its intellectuals. Even its internationally most recognized writer and scholar, Marshall McLuhan, strongly criticized his fellow citizens and creative writers in similar terms. In the 1970s, he said there was no "serious writing going on in Canada today," that Canadians were too cautious and too lazy to create "in school or elsewhere," that it was easy to "move ahead of the rest of them" because of their general inertia.[66] These reactions may, of course, reflect the fact that Canada's principal reference group, the United States, is the highest achiever in economic, scientific, and mass culture terms. As Canadians repeatedly stress, living next to an elephant makes any other creature feel small.

Art and National Values

Russell Brown, a Canadian literary critic, stresses that "the sexual metaphor of national relationships," discussed earlier, has "real importance in the Canadian imagination and in the Canadian self-conception. The metaphor reappears constantly" in fiction and in public statements.[67] Canadian femininity has produced extreme nationalist statements, such as "the United States is like the Male — aggressive, power-mad, authoritarian, exploiting," while Canada is "passive, motherly, dependent, exploited and take for granted. Canada is the Female."[68]

In a novel published in the early 1980s, a feminist author, Susan Swan, has the married heroine describe her 19th-century situation as an acting out of unequal national relationships:

> I feel I am acting out America's relationship to the Canadas. Martin is the imperial ogre while I play the role of genteel mate who believes that if everyone is well-mannered, we can inhabit a peaceable kingdom. That is the national dream of the Canadas, isn't it? A civilized garden where lions lie down with doves. I did not see the difference until I married Martin. We possess no fantasies of conquest and domination. Indeed, to be from the Canadas is to feel as women feel — cut off from the base of power.[69]

The growth of nationalism and economic strength in Canada may, however, be reducing the usefulness of the gender metaphor in analyzing the culture and values of the two nations. Brown notes:

> Feminine Canada has broken away from the traditional sex roles at a time when they were in actuality being abandoned, has ceased trying to play the "good wife" in a harmonious, supportive relationship with her dominant "husband" nation.[70]

Canada's literary nationalisms are antinationalisms, anti-American in the case of Anglophones, and anti-Canadian in the case of Francophones. One of Canada's foremost literary critics, George Woodcock, argues, however, that many Canadian nationalists "are so in the simplest sense of the word." He notes that Canada, more than any other country, resists political centralization, that it has left itself in a position "to avoid the fevers of nationalism and to create the anti-nation," one that is independent but not intensely nationalistic.[71] And these varying political and social images, it may be noted, correspond to the stereotypical differences between men and women, as well as to those reported in behavioral research.

Conclusion

Overall, the differences between Canadian and American literature and film, whatever their sources, have contributed to the distinctive character of the two nations. American novelists, largely accepting their country's universalistic and egalitarian creed, hold up American institutions and elites to a critical light from the stance of the "adversary culture." According to Richard Hofstadter, American intellectuals have been predominantly on the left for at least the past century,[72] but they, like most of their fellow citizens, believe the United States is the best country in the world, one that should be a light unto the nations. Canadian writers focus their social criticism on the United States, in the context of seeing their own society as a better, less aggressive, gentler, more peaceable, but also more mediocre country, one that wants to live and let live, not to foster utopias. And the self-stereotype that Canadians have of themselves, that they hold out to their children, coincides not surprisingly with the image fostered by their country's nationalist intellectuals.

The dissimilarities in themes between the two North American national literatures appear to be declining. Ronald Sutherland and A.J.M. Smith call attention to the effects of the new nationalism north of the border as producing more stylistically innovative and even radical writing.[73] T.D. Maclulich, writing in 1988, emphasizes that "the state of Canadian fiction has greatly altered from what it was only twenty years ago...[and that] the Tory mode appears to be on the wane."[74] But ironically, as Sutherland points out, these changes are making Canada and its fiction more American in that they involve a greater emphasis on values such as pride in country, self-reliance, self-confidence, individualism, independence, and optimism.

It can be argued, however, that these shifts, while reducing some traditional differences, have enhanced others. The new Canadian nationalism, often linked among intellectuals to socialism and Toryism, seeks to resist increased cultural and media influence by Americans, and its weapon for so doing is the traditional Canadian remedy of state intervention. As Christian and Campbell observe in this context: "Toryism, socialism, and nationalism all share a common collectivist orientation in various forms."[75]

One area in which the relationship between values and institutions is clearly observable is religion. Two American sociologists recently contended that the greatest differences between Canada and the United States "are to be found in the religious sphere."[76] The next chapter turns to a crossnational examination of religion.

5

The Impact of Religion

The ideological streak in the American experience has been strengthened by its special religious character, one that Edmund Burke discussed in 1775 in trying to explain to the British House of Commons what the revolutionary Americans were like. He called them the Protestants of Protestantism, the dissenters of dissent, the individualists *par excellence.*[1] The United States is a country formed by Protestant dissent, by the groups known in England as the dissenters and nonconformists: Methodists, Baptists, and many other Protestant groups. The majority of the population have always belonged to, or adhered to, the sects, not to the various denominations which were or are state churches: Anglican, Catholic, Lutheran, and Orthodox.

Many modern analysts follow Burke's argument on the importance of understanding the unique character of American Protestantism. John Conway emphasizes:

[a]t the root of American political and social values...is the distinctive Puritanism of the early New England settlers....

Based as it was on the concept of the individual alone with God, unaided by a priestly or an episcopal intermediary, New England Puritanism fostered an intense individualism, which lost none of its force as Puritanism became secularized during the eighteenth and nineteenth centuries. Thoreau, in Concord in the 1840's confronting slavery and the Mexican War, declared that "the only obligation which I have a right to assume is to do at any time what I think right"....

There is no counterpart to Thoreau in Canadian history, because no settler, French or British, brought the dissidence of dissent and the protestantism of the Protestant religion to Canada's shores. Canadians cherish community, and however pragmatically, will fight vigorously to ensure that its basis is not undermined.[2]

Max Weber identified the beliefs of the sectarian Protestants as those most conducive to the kind of rational, competitive, individualistic behavior that encourages entrepreneurial success.[3] The epitome of the Protestant ethic was to be found not in the churches, but in the sects. In his classic work on the subject, *The Protestant Ethic and the Spirit of Capitalism,* Weber noted that the Puritans brought the values conducive to capitalism with them and, therefore, that "the spirit of capitalism...was present before the capitalistic order."[4] His principal examples of a secularized capitalist spirit were drawn from the writings of an American, Benjamin Franklin, which Weber quoted extensively as prototypical of the values that are most conducive to the emergence of an industrialized system.[5]

The American religious ethos was functional not only for a bourgeois economy but also, as Tocqueville noted, for a liberal polity. Since most of these sects were congregational, not hierarchical, they fostered egalitarian and populist values that were anti-elitist. Hence, both the political and religious ethoses reinforced each other.

The emphasis on voluntary associations, which so impressed Tocqueville, Weber, Gramsci, and other foreign observers as one of the distinctive American traits, was linked by them to the uniquely American system of "voluntary religion." The United States was the first country in which religious groups became voluntary — that is, not supported by the state. American ministers and laypeople consciously recognized that they had to foster a variety of voluntary associations both to maintain support for the church and to fulfill community needs.[6]

Tocqueville concluded that voluntarism was a large part of the answer to the puzzling strength of organized religion in the United States, a phenomenon that impressed most 19th-century observers and that continues to show up in this century in crossnational opinion polls taken by Gallup and others. They indicate that Americans are the most fundamentalist people in Christendom. The abundant quantitative data all indicate the enduring validity of Tocqueville's statement: "There is no country in the world where the Christian religion retains a greater influence over the souls of men than in America."[7]

National Styles

The differences between European and American political orientations can be related to variations in religious tradition and church organization. European churches have been state-financed and have called on their parishioners to support the political system. They retain hierarchical structures and corporatist values formed and institutionalized in medieval agrarian societies.

U.S. Utopian Moralism

In the United States, as noted, the emphasis on Americanism as a political ideology has led to a utopian orientation among American liberals and conservatives. Both seek to extend the good society. But the religious traditions of Protestant dissent have called on Americans to be moralistic, to follow their consciences with an unequivocal emphasis not to be found in countries whose predominant denominations have evolved from state churches. The dissenters are "the original source both of the close intermingling of religion and politics that [has] characterized subsequent American history and of the moral passion that has powered the engines of political change in America."[8] As Robert Bellah emphasizes: "The millennialism of the American Protestant tradition again and again spawned movements for social change and social reform."[9] The American Protestant religious ethos has assumed, in practice if not in theology, the perfectibility of humanity and an obligation to avoid sin, while the churches whose followers have predominated in Europe, Canada, and Australia have accepted the inherent weakness of people, their inability to escape sin and error, and the need for the church to be forgiving and protecting.[10]

Americans are utopian moralists who press hard to institutionalize virtue, to destroy evil people, and to eliminate wicked institutions and practices. They tend to view social and political dramas as morality plays, as battles between God and the devil, so that compromise is virtually unthinkable.[11] As Samuel Huntington notes, Americans give to their nation and its creed "many of the attributes and functions of a church."[12] These are reflected in the American "civic religion," which has provided "a religious dimension for the whole fabric of American life, including the political sphere." The United States is seen as the new Israel. "Europe is Egypt; America the promised land. God has led his people to establish a new sort of social order that shall be a light unto all nations."[13]

The emphasis on the religious chosenness of the United States has that meant if the country is perceived as slipping away "from the controlling obligations of the covenant," it is perceived as on the road to hell.[14] The need to assuage a sense of personal responsibility for such failings has made Americans particularly inclined to support movements for the elimination of evil — if necessary, by violent and even illegal means. A key element in the conflicts that culminated in the Civil War was the tendency of each side to view the other as essentially sinful — as an agent of Satan.

The same Protestant propensity for moralistic crusades has been expressed in various efforts to reform the rest of the world by war. It has also underlain the endeavor of numerous Americans to resist each war as immoral. For many Americans, wars must be moral or immoral; one must do God's work in supporting or opposing them. Linked to Protestant sectarianism, conscientious objection to military service was until recently largely an American phenomenon. The resisters to the Vietnam War re-enacted a two-century Protestant sense of personal responsibility that led the intensely committed to follow their consciences. In other Christian countries, state churches have called for and legitimated obedience to state authority. The American sectarians, however, have taken it as a matter of course that the individual should obey his conscience, not the state. Conscientious objection has existed in other countries, including Britain and Canada, but there it stemmed from the minority who were dissenters, and consequently it has been a less significant phenomenon.

The passion unleashed by the anti-Vietnam War movement was strongly related to basic aspects of the religiously derived American value system. To decry wars and to refuse to go to them is at least as American as apple pie. Sol Tax, comparing the extent of antiwar activity throughout American history, concluded, as of 1967, that the Vietnam War was only the country's fourth least popular military conflict with a foreign enemy since the Revolutionary War.[15] The War of 1812 was intensely unpopular in New England; some states threatened to secede on the issue.[16] Abraham Lincoln and many Whigs denounced the Mexican War. The abolitionists regarded it as an immoral conflict fought to extend the domain of slavery. Indeed, the Mexican army was able to form units composed of American deserters.[17] The antidraft riots of 1863 were the bloodiest in American history.[18] Professors and other intellectuals were vilified in the press and pulpit as traitors for their opposition to the Spanish-American War. The antiwar Socialist Party secured its largest vote in history in many cities in the 1917 municipal elections.[19] American entry into World War II was strongly opposed by an extensive mass movement. Had the United States entered in any way other than as an answer to an attack, it is clear that a large segment of the country would have continued its opposition to the conflict after Congress declared war. Opinion surveys taken within two years of the beginning of the Korean War reported significant majority opposition to it among the general population and among college students.[20]

America's initial reaction to conflicts with "evil empires" has often been one that implied no compromise. After each major Communist triumph — Russia, China, North Korea, Cuba, Vietnam — the United States went through a period of refusing to "recognize" the unforgivable, temporary victory of evil. This behavior contrasts with that of Anglican conservatives, such as Churchill, and Catholic rightists, such as de Gaulle and Franco, whose opposition to Communism did not require nonrecognition. Franco's Spain dealt with Castro soon after he took power.

Americans have been unique in their emphasis on nonrecognition of "evil" foreign regimes. The principle is related to the insistence that wars must end with the unconditional surrender of the Satanic enemy. The United States rarely sees itself merely defending national interests. Foreign conflicts invariably involve a battle of good versus evil. George Kennan, among others, writes perceptively of the consequences of this utopian approach to foreign affairs.[21]

Canadian Coexistence

In contrast, Canadian religion, dominated by church (Anglican and Catholic) and ecumenical (United Church) traditions, has not emphasized moralism. The country's leading sociologist of religion, Reginald Bibby, notes that its "religious groups are expected to co-exist for servicing. In the United States, the pursuit of truth means that religious groups are allowed to compete for truth." He explains the variations as consequences of "our countries' respective revolutions." Canada has been shaped by its gradual, nonviolent separation from Britain and its need to work out agreements among disparate cultures rather than assimilate them into one. Its history does not express any national truth.

> Americans, on the other hand, made their dramatic break with England and set out to establish a distinctive nation. Their "charter myth" included the belief that the country had been founded by God to give leadership to the world.[22]

Or as John Conway puts it, "Canada has...lacked the sense of mission of divinely inspired singularity, which has been part of American consciousness since the time of John Winthrop."[23]

These differences bear on the ways the two peoples look at politics. Americans are much more prone to see conflicts as reflecting moral concerns. Canadian activities are affected by a "sense of the permanent imperfection of man, of Original Sin" that undermines any propensity to take part in a crusade against an immoral enemy, an "evil empire." Canada has not followed U.S. policy with respect to nonrecognition of Communist states, as evident in its early recognition of and trading with Castro's Cuba, its opposition to "every attempt to require an ideological means test for United Nations membership," its refusal to apply sanctions against Poland or to support the American takeover of Grenada, and its disagreement with the United States' policy toward Nicaragua.[24]

Voluntarism and Statism

The elimination of established religion in the United States, as Tocqueville argued, greatly strengthened religion there. Voluntary institutions that rely on their members for funds and must compete with each other for support are likely to be stronger than those supported by the state. Moreover, voluntarism, together with the considerable strength of dissenting and anti-statist Methodist and Baptist denominations, meant that religion not only contributed to the economic orientation of the people but also reinforced the egalitarian and democratic ethoses. Tocqueville pointed out that all American denominations were minorities and hence had an interest in liberty and a weak state.[25]

Harold Innis underscores the source of Canada's religious orientations when he writes that a "counter-revolutionary tradition implies an emphasis on ecclesiasticism."[26] The majority of the Canadian population adhere to churches, not sects, to denominations that are hierarchical and have a long history of state support. Canada has

> never succeeded in drawing with any precision a line between areas in which the state has a legitimate interest and those that ought to be left to the voluntary activities of the churches....[F]ew Canadians find "the separation of Church and State" an acceptable description either of their situation or of their ideal for it.[27]

As William Kilbourn puts it: "There is a lingering aura of the European established church in Canada."[28] Both the Church of England and the Roman Catholic Church, in return for government support, endorsed the established political and social orders up to the post-World War II era. Hence, there were mutually reinforcing conservative forces at the summits of the class, church, and political structures.[29]

Comparing French and English Canada points up differences and similarities. The French colonists were, of course, Catholic, and they had brought with them to North America the apparatus and values of their country's established church. Ironically, that church became even more entrenched after the British Conquest. The *Quebec Act* of 1774 not only assured *les Canadiens* of the right to use French law in the civil courts, to remain Catholic, and to be appointed to the governor's executive council (Québécois were the first Roman Catholics permitted to hold such offices anywhere in British dominions); it also allowed the Catholic Church to hold property and gave it legal authority to collect tithes. Most of the bourgeoisie having fled New France soon after its fall, the leaders of the largely rural and uneducated people were the Roman Catholic clergy and the *seigneurs*, the large landholders.[30] The *Quebec Act* was a successful advance payment on their loyalty; in a longer-term result, the Roman Catholic Church became, in effect, the state church of French Canada, a position it enjoyed until the 1960s, when the forces of modernization and secularization eroded much of its authority.[31]

In English Canada, the Anglicans failed in their effort to become a "national" church. Still, they helped form the founding ethos of the country and to legitimate

> monarchy, aristocracy, and British constitutionalism...[as]
> part of a sacred scenario; and by the same token,....[their] condemnation of mass democracy, egalitarianism, republicanism and revolution as the work of the devil, left an indelible mark on English-Canadian political life. It appears reasonable that the conservative, counter-revolutionary, "law-and-order" identity which some observers...perceive as...distinctively English-Canadian is, at least in some measure, the legacy of the Anglican Church.[32]

Writing of the overall present-day situation, two American sociologists of religion, Rodney Stark and William Bainbridge, note that

> [e]ach of the three largest Canadian denominations has much the quality of an established church. The Anglican Church is an extension of the established Church of England, and the United Church lays some claim to being the Canadian national Protestant denomination. Geographically concentrated

as it is, Catholicism approaches the status of a fully established church in many areas.[33]

The Nationalization of Religion

Just as religious practices and institutions can reinforce the
general value orientations prevalent in a national community, so,
conversely, can values influence religion, as demonstrated in
crossborder analyses. In the United States, there has been an "acceptance by the...[Catholic Church] of the role of voluntary
association...as the most it could hope for."[34] Thus, as the French
Dominican R.L. Bruckberger argues, the Catholic Church in the
United States has taken over many of the characteristics of
Protestantism, including a strong emphasis on individual moralism.[35] As a result, the Vatican has frowned on the American
church and has, in fact, not treated it as well as the Canadian af-
filiate. This is reflected in a significantly lower ratio of honors —
saints and cardinals — to the Catholic population south of the
border than in Canada.

The tension between the Catholic Church and its American
branch, according to Kenneth Westhues, is a result of the difference

> between that world-view, espoused by the American state,
> which takes the individual as the basic reality of social life,
> and the church's world-view, which defines the group as
> primary. American non-recognition of the church is thus not
> merely a political matter....It is instead a genuinely sociologi-
> cal issue, resting as it does on a fundamental conflict of
> values.[36]

The "major question always before the Catholic Church in
the United States has been how far to assimilate to the American
way of life." This question "has never arisen in Canada, basically for the lack of a national ideology for defining what the
Canadian way of life is or ought to be." In any case, "corporatist
values have never been defeated in Canada to the extent they have
in the United States."[37]

A comparative study of the role of mainline Protestantism in
Canada and the United States notes that the close linkage of sec-

tarian Protestantism to the American national identity led to the emergence of what Robert Bellah describes as America's "civil religion."[38] A summary of Bellah's views notes: "This civil religion expressed the conviction that in public and cultural affairs men and women are pursuing the will of God." Canada's civil religion, the paraphrase continues, is quite different:

> It consists in the religious legitimation of sovereignty, a practice which it inherited from Britain. The American civil religion sanctifies the future to be built whereas the Canadian civil religion upholds the authority already established.[39]

The American voluntaristic and sectarian religious tradition has encouraged many new denominations, such as those of the Mormons, Seventh Day Adventists, Christian Scientists, and Jehovah's Witnesses, while the Canadian tradition has been much less theologically fecund.[40] Research documents the tight character of the religious market north of the border. As noted earlier, most Canadians remain "encased" within the three major churches: Roman Catholic, Anglican, and United.[41] Religious innovation has been more limited "because of the presence of institutional controls in which alliances between the state and established religious institutions deliberately sought to discourage religious experimentation."[42] Conversely, in the United States,

> As with other sectors of American life — the economy, education, and politics, for example — the religion market was technically "up for grabs"....[R]eligion in the U.S...is marketed with the flair and aggressiveness of a "hot" commercial commodity.[43]

Canada's most important religious creation, the United Church, which brought together the Methodists, the Congregationalists, the Evangelical Brethren, and most Presbyterians into one denomination in 1925, attests to a tolerance for diversity among Canadian sectarians. Such unity has never been approached in America, where denominational passion and belief undercut all ecumenical efforts. Union could occur in Canada, because

in a country which valued practice over theory, these churches had grown together....Canon Carmichael, writing on the
subject in 1887, found no major differences among the
Canadian churches of non-conforming origin and only a few
major differences between these...and the Anglican
Church.[44]

Opinion Poll Evidence

The generalizations drawn from historical and institutional
analyses concerning the distinctions between American and Canadian religion can be documented statistically in the findings of
crossnational opinion polls. The survey data indicate that Americans are more likely than Canadians to believe in God, to attend
church regularly, and to adhere to evangelical and moralistic
beliefs. The strength of Protestant evangelical, sectarian, and fundamentalist religion south of the border means that traditional
values related to sex, family, and morality in general are stronger
there than in Canada.

Over the years, the Gallup polls have asked comparable
questions bearing on religion that have revealed consistent, if
moderate, size differences. For some time, 95 to 96 percent of
Americans, compared to 86 to 87 percent of Canadians, have reported they are believers. In polls taken during the 1980s, about
40 percent of Americans and somewhat more than 30 percent of
Canadians indicated they had been to a "church or synagogue in
the last seven days." Catholics in both countries show a higher
rate of attendance than Protestants, about 15 percentage points
more on average. Since the proportion of Catholics is greater in
Canada, the national differences increase when religion is held
constant.

The most extensive materials on belief in North America were
gathered by the Gallup polls in two international studies, one
taken for the Kettering Foundation in 1975 and the other sponsored by CARA (Centre for Applied Research in the Apostolate) in
the early 1980s.[45] The Kettering-Gallup survey reported a gap of
20 percentage points between Americans and Canadians who
responded "very important" to the question: "How important to
you are your religious beliefs?" (56 to 36). The difference with

respect to belief in "life after death" was 15 points (69 to 54). Among those who reported a belief in God, two-thirds of the Americans and half of the Canadians said God observes their "actions and rewards or punishes...for them."

Although the published version of the Kettering Report presents only national totals, the CARA report differentiates its Canadian respondents by language (English and French), though not by religious affiliation. According to its findings, Americans are more religious and more moralistic than Canadians. In response to the question, "How important is God in your life?" answered on a ten-point scale from 1, meaning not at all, to 10, meaning very important, 59 percent of Americans placed themselves on scale point 9 or 10, as opposed to 44 percent of English Canadians and 47 percent of French Canadians. Sixty-five percent of Americans said they believe "there is a personal God," compared to 49 percent of English Canadians and 56 percent of French Canadians. Respondents were asked whether they accepted each of the Ten Commandments fully or to a limited extent and whether it should apply to others. Averaging answers about all the commandments shows that 83 percent of Americans said that they apply fully to themselves; the comparable mean response north of the border was 76 percent of English Canadians and 67 percent of French Canadians. The same pattern held for the second part of these questions: 36 percent of Americans said the commandments are meant to apply fully to other people; on the average, 28 percent of English Canadians and 23 percent of French Canadians agreed.

The CARA questions designed to measure fundamentalism showed Americans far outnumbering Canadians in expressing such beliefs, and Anglophone Canadians were more likely than Francophones to hold them. Thus, when asked whether they believed in "the devil," 66 percent of Americans said yes, as did 46 percent of English Canadians and only 25 percent of French Canadians. The differences in responses to items about belief in "hell" followed the same pattern: 67 percent for Americans, 45 percent for English Canadians, and 22 percent for French Can-adians. The overwhelming majority of Americans — 84 percent — said they believed in the existence of heaven, as did 73 percent of English Canadians and 58 percent of French

Canadians. Seventy-one percent of Americans expressed belief in life after death, compared to 61 percent of Anglophone Canadians and 63 percent of Francophones. A question on belief in a soul produced 88 percent of Americans saying yes, compared to 80 percent of each Canadian linguistic group.

Comparisons of Canadian and American Gallup polls taken during the late 1960s also demonstrate that Canadians are less moralistic or fundamentalist than Americans.

> In 1968 the CIPO and AIPO questioned national samples of Canadians and Americans about a variety of religious beliefs. Generally speaking, American responses tended to be more fundamentalistic than Canadian responses....Thirty-seven percent of the Canadian sample believed in the devil, compared to 60% of the Americans. Fifty-five percent of Canadians and 73% of Americans expressed a belief in life after death. Seventy-two percent of the former and 85% of the latter expressed a belief in heaven, while 40% of Canadians and 65% of Americans expressed a belief in hell.[46]

An unusual source of evidence of the greater emphasis on religion in the United States comes from a content analysis of the values reflected in magazines in Canada and the United States. It measured the proportion of sentences devoted to various themes, coding as religious-philosophical those that incorporated "material concerning contact with an 'ultimate reality' or referring to some form of 'ultimate meaning' in life...concerns with God, a Supreme Being, faith, Supreme Knowledge, creed, devotion, after-life (e.g. reincarnation, heaven, hell), mysticism, the occult, etc." The American magazines dealt with such themes two and a half times more frequently than Canadian ones.[47]

Congruent with the variation in religious practice and belief, the CARA-Gallup data suggest that with respect to sexual behavior, the sectarian Americans are more puritanical than the more ecumenically Protestant Anglo-Canadians, and the predominantly Catholic Francophones are the most tolerant of the three groups. In reaction to the statement, "Marriage is an outdated institution," 19 percent of French Canadians agreed, as did 11 percent of English Canadians and 7 percent of Americans. Francophone Canadians (24 percent) were also more likely than Anglophone Canadians and Americans (18 percent) to believe that "individuals should have a chance to enjoy complete sexual freedom without being restricted." Reacting to the statement, "a woman wants to have a child as a single parent but she doesn't want to have a stable relationship with a man," 58 percent of Americans voiced disapproval, compared to 53 percent of Anglo-Canadians and 34 percent of Francophones.

A similar pattern was reflected in replies to "[S]omeone says that sexual activity cannot entirely be left up to individual choice, there have to be moral rules to which everyone adheres." Fifty-one percent of Americans agreed, as did 49 percent of English Canadians but only 34 percent of French Canadians.

Earlier survey data, largely from the files of the Gallup polls in the two countries, yield similar national differences. Thus, "in 1969, 73% of a national sample of Americans and 49% of a similar sample of Canadians said they would 'find pictures of nudes in magazines' objectionable." Seventy-six percent of Americans and two-thirds of Canadians found "topless night club waitresses objectionable." Comparable variations showed up in responses to questions about sex on television.[48]

In the late 1960s and early 1970s, Americans were more likely than Canadians to believe that "it is wrong for people to have sex relations before marriage." In 1969, 68 percent of Americans agreed, whereas the percentage for Canadians for 1970 was 57 percent. By 1973, the American figure had dropped to 48 percent while the Canadian had fallen to 36 percent.[49]

Theological Changes

Much of organized Christendom has changed its orientation to the secular world in the postwar decades. The traditionally established churches have become the foremost exponents of liberation theology and of values close to those of socialism. The shift from having been supporters of conservative, often reactionary, politics is linked to the fact that the churches, particularly much of Roman Catholicism but important parts of Anglicanism as well, have always viewed capitalism and the bourgeoisie with suspicion. Like the aristocracy and gentry, the churches disliked the logic of bourgeois society and regarded the business class as materialistic, rationalist, liberal, and frequently anticlerical. Before World War II, the churches in Europe, Latin America, and Canada were allied to right-wing forces, but usually to their corporatist and antibourgeois elements.

The destruction of fascism during World War II helped to delegitimate such politics. Since then, in much of the developed and Latin American worlds, many in the churches have turned toward a left-wing, anticapitalist, and communitarian position. Both Canadian and American Catholicism have moved to the left, but the Canadian church — operating in a more statist and communitarian society in which sectarian stimulated individualism is much weaker — has gone further. In 1988, the American socialist magazine *Dissent* reprinted a statement by the Canadian bishops on social policy because the editors correctly viewed it as basically socialist.[50] The parallel document by the American bishops is much more moderate, calling for an extension of the welfare state.

In Canada, the United Church has endorsed the statement issued by the hierarchy of its Catholic co-nationals. Unlike the American evangelical sects, which have become increasingly conservative and whose white followers now vote for Republican presidential nominees, the United Church "has been a major force in the last 30 years in pressing for increased spending on social welfare programs and for the rights of prisoners, workers and Canada's native people."[51]

Conclusion

The differences between religion in Canada and in the United States are large and clear-cut. America remains under the strong influence of the Protestant sects. Its northern neighbor adheres to two churches, Catholic and Anglican, and an ecumenical Protestant denomination that has moved far from the sectarian origins of its component units toward churchlike communitarian values.

The overwhelming majority of Canadians (87 percent) belong to these three mainline denominations. Conservative evangelicals — groups of Baptists, Nazarenes, Pentecostals, Adventists, and so on — constitute only 7 percent of Canadians, with that figure including the 3 percent of the population who are Baptists.[52] Fully one-fifth of Americans adhere to a Baptist church.[53] In the United States, according to Gallup polls taken in 1984, 38 percent hold a literal, fundamentalist view of the bible, and 22 percent can be grouped as evangelicals. Among whites, these beliefs are linked to political as well as social conservatism.

In summing up the differences, a student of comparative North American religion notes:

> Canadian and American christianity differ explicitly in shape as well as context: in shape, because the dominant Canadian christian churches accept the importance of historical continuity, ritual, national organization, and a public role for their churches, while Americans give priority to belief sincerely held, strongly claimed and privately enjoyed at home or within the local congregation....
>
> Christian fundamentalism is also significantly different in the two countries. [In Canada] [i]t does not have the same media presence, numbers or influence as in the States....Nor do their preachers emphasize the same beliefs....Fundamentalism as it exists in the United States does not exist in Canada.[54]

Clearly, the different religious traditions of the two countries help to explain much of their varying secular behavior and belief.

National values find institutional expression not only in religion. Laws and the way individuals are treated under and react to them also determine and reflect the basic national ethos, as the next chapter details.

6

Law and Deviance

Efforts to distinguish Canada and the United States almost invariably point to the greater respect for law and those who uphold it north of the border. Writers and historians have reiterated the distinction in illustrating the varying organizing principles of the two societies. As Margaret Atwood notes, "Canada must be the only country in the world where a policeman [the Mountie] is used as a national symbol."[1] Gaile McGregor quotes Susan Wood:

> The archetypical scene south of the border might show the lone hero confronting his foes at high noon; but a typical scene in western Canadian fiction shows the American desperado surrendering his six-shooter at the quiet, firm command of a Canadian Mountie.[2]

As McGregor herself points out, in Canada, unlike the case in the United States, "the culture hero is not the gunslinger, triumphing over opposition by a demonstration of natural powers and anarchistic individual will, but rather the Law itself: impersonal, all embracing, pre-eminently social."[3]

Disparate Frontiers

These divergences, of course, stem from the two countries' dissimilar histories: the successful revolt in one and the reaffirmation of the monarchical base of legitimacy in the other. A related source is policies undertaken to keep their western frontiers British or Canadian, policies that resulted in contrasts between authorities on the frontiers, populist and settler-dominated in the United States but central-government- controlled in Canada.[4]

The disparate ways the frontiers of North America were settled reinforced these differences. As prairie-reared Canadian novelist Wallace Stegner notes, "In the American West men came before law, but in...[western Canada] the law was there before settlers, before even cattlemen, and not merely law but law enforcement."[5] The historian Kenneth McNaught points out, "Canadian prime minister Alexander Mackenzie...founded the... North West Mounted Police for the specific purpose of ensuring a non-American type of development in the prairie west."[6]

Those rugged individualists — the cowboy, the frontiersman, and even the vigilante — not the uniformed, disciplined Mountie, are the heroes of American western settlement.[7] The frontiersman, on the other hand, has never been a figure for special glorification in Canadian literature as he has been in American. Conversely, the Mountie has been treated in laudatory fashion by historians, journalists, and novelists.[8] (The Mountie was, of course, taken over by the American movies; in expatriate form, the original Canadian fictional views of the Mountie as an organization man defending authority, as the champion of "an anti-revolutionary, conservative, hierarchical society," disappeared. He became "the Hollywood Mountie, a democratic, individualistic hero to be distinguished from a U.S. marshall only by his red tunic.")[9]

On the American frontier, the quality of law enforcement often depended on local police authorities who reflected the values of the frontierspeople, including their prejudice against Indians and their lack of understanding for legal procedures incorporating the guarantees of due process. In Canada, Indian chiefs

> were impressed by the fact that, if Indians were punished for crimes against the whites, the whites were equally punished for outrages against the Indians. Their previous experience [with American whites] had taught them to appreciate such impartial justice.[10]

Comparing the situation during the gold rushes in California and British Columbia in the mid-19th century and in Alaska and the Klondike in the 1890s, the poet and writer Douglas Fetherling documents great dissimilarities. The Queen's peace was maintained even in the mining camps, which were characterized by violence and lack of discipline in the United States. Conditions on the American western mining frontier differed greatly from those in British Columbia, where there were no vigilantes or massacres of Indians.[11] In the Klondike, "Canadian values [upheld by the Mounties and 200 soldiers] stood firm against the 'rampant Americanism' [80 percent of the Klondike miners were Americans] spilling across from towns like Skagway, Alaska, run by thugs."[12] The Canadian experience in the west and north did not undermine the bases of authority; Canadians on the edge of settlement retained a more deeply internalized sense of obligation, of the need to conform to the rules even when there was no visible threat of coercion.[13]

Canadians' behavior still reflects such values, a conclusion attested to in 1987 by Richard Lipsey, one of the country's leading economists: "I have stood on a street corner in Toronto with a single other pedestrian, and with not a car in sight, waiting for the light to turn green — behavior unimaginable in most large U.S. cities." And he goes on to note that given "the much greater respect for...the police" north of the border, "Canadian cities...are relatively safe in ways that few large U.S. cities are."[14]

The Differing Functions of Law

The difference in the role of and respect for law that emerged in the two societies provides, in Guy Rocher's words, "some ground to assert that law can be regarded both a reflection of and an active agent in the structure and evolution of a society and its culture."[15] Rocher emphasizes the "fundamental difference between the sociological function of law in Canada and the United States."

Throughout the history of the United States, common law and the courts have been perceived and used as a check on the power of the State. "American jurisprudence reflects a concern for limiting governmental coercion over individuals." In Canada, the courts have been much more closely identified with the State, and perceived as the arm of the State.[16]

These variations are linked to the historical emphasis on the rights and obligations of the community in comparison to those of the citizen. As noted earlier, the concern of Canada's fathers of Confederation with "peace, order, and good government" implies control of and protection for the society. The parallel stress by America's founding fathers on "life, liberty, and the pursuit of happiness" suggests upholding the rights of the individual. The American commitment to personal rights, including those of political dissidents and people accused of crime, is inherent in the due-process model, which involves various legal inhibitions on the power of the police and prosecutors. The crime-control model, more evident in Canada and Europe, emphasizes the maintenance of law and order and is less protective of the rights of the accused and of individuals generally.[17] As John Hagan and Jeffrey Leon point out:

> The due process model is much concerned with exclusionary rights of evidence, the right to counsel, and other procedural safeguards thought useful in protecting accused persons from unjust applications of criminal sanctions....[T]he crime-control model places heavy emphasis on the repression of criminal conduct, arguing that only by insuring order can individuals in a society be guaranteed personal freedom. It is for this reason that advocates of crime control are less anxious to presume the innocence of accused persons and to protect such persons against sometimes dubious findings of guilt.[18]

The Canadian government has greater legal power than the American to restrict freedom of speech and to invade personal privacy. Prior to the adoption of the Canadian Charter of Rights and Freedoms in 1982, it was able, acting through an order-in-council, to limit public discussion of particular issues and, as in 1970 during the Quebec crisis, to impose a form of military control.[19] Comparing American and Canadian public reactions to violations of privacy by the government, Alan Westin writes:

> [I]t is important to note that in Canada there have been some incidents which, had they happened in the United States, would probably have led to great *causes célèbres*. Most Canadians seem to have accepted Royal Canadian Mounted Police break-ins without warrants between 1970 and 1978, and also the RCMP's secret access to income tax information, and to personal health information from the Ontario Health Insurance Plan. If I read the Canadian scene correctly, these did not shock and outrage most Canadians.[20]

Evidence that Westin's assumptions are correct can be found in the 1989 *Maclean's*-Decima poll, which reported that Americans are more likely than Canadians, by 56 to 49 percent, to oppose the national government's being given the power to "remove all civil rights" during "times of crises." The crossborder difference is much greater when the comparison is limited to Anglophone Canadians and Americans. Only 45 percent of the former reject the power to revoke civil liberty guarantees. Two-thirds (67 percent) of French Canadians, who had experienced such intervention in 1970, are against allowing the Anglophone-controlled federal government to do it again.

The lesser respect for the law — for the rules of the game — in the United States may be viewed as inherent in a system in which egalitarianism is strongly valued and diffuse elitism is lacking. Generalized deference is not accorded to the state or those at the top in the United States; therefore, there is a greater propensity to redefine or ignore the rules. While Canadians incline toward the use of "lawful" and institutionalized means for altering regulations that they believe unjust, Americans seem more disposed to employ informal, aggressive, and sometimes extralegal means to correct what they perceive as wrong.

Crime, Crime Rates, and Gun Control

The greater lawlessness and corruption in the United States can also be attributed in part to a stronger emphasis on achievement. As Robert Merton points out, such an orientation means that "[t]he moral mandate to achieve success thus exerts pressure to succeed, by fair means if possible and by foul means if necessary."[21] This suggests that, since Americans are more likely than their Canadian neighbors to be concerned with the achievement of *ends* — particularly pecuniary success — they will be less concerned with the use of the socially appropriate *means*. Hence, we should expect a higher incidence of deviations from conventional norms south of the border.

That Canadians and Americans vary in the expected direction is demonstrated strikingly in the aggregate differences between the two with respect to crime rates for violent offenses, differences that have "endured over time."[22] Americans are much more prone than Canadians to commit offenses such as homicide, robbery, assault, and rape. In 1977, the murder rate for Canada was 3.0 per 100,000 population; for the United States, it was 8.8. Ten years later, the respective rates were 2.2 and 8.3.[23] The evidence indicates that the disparity in the two countries' violent crime rates "increased rather substantially" between the 1960s and 1980s.[24] There is, however, much less difference between the two with respect to nonviolent crimes involving property, such as theft and burglary.[25]

Crossborder variations are also reported in a comprehensive analysis of differences in rates of violence in many countries. The United States not only has a much higher rate of homicide than Canada (and all other developed countries); it is also considerably higher than Canada with respect to political violence.[26] Data reported in the *World Handbook of Political and Social Indicators* demonstrate that Canadians were much less likely than Americans to engage in protest demonstrations or riots between 1948 and 1982 (see Table 1). Although the U.S. population outnumbers the Canadian by about 10:1, the ratios for political protests have been two to four times as large — that is, 20:1 to 40:1.

Given the Canadian-U.S. differences in rates of violent crime, it is not surprising that Americans are more fearful than Canadians of being unprotected after dark. The Gallup polls have inquired in both countries: "Is there any area right around here — that is, within a mile — where you would be afraid to walk alone at night?" In the mid-1970s, 31 percent of the northern population but 40 percent of those south of the border said yes. The gap between the countries was wider — 27 and 45 percent — when Gallup repeated the question in the mid-1980s.[27] The earlier surveys found that Americans were more likely than

Table 1
Political Protest and Violence
in Canada and the United States, 1948–82

	Protest demonstrations	Riots	Deaths from political violence
Canada			
1948–67	27	29	8
1968–77	33	5	4
1978–82	13	0	—
United States			
1948–67	1,179	683	320
1968–77	1,005	149	114
1978–82	1,166	93	—

Source: Incidence for 1948–77 calculated from data in Charles Lewis Taylor and David A. Jodice, *World Handbook of Political and Social Indicators*, 3d ed., vol. 2 (New Haven: Yale University Press, 1983), pp. 19–25, 33–36, 47–51. The data for 1978–82 are not in the book but were supplied to me by Professor Taylor.

Canadians to report having been crime victims in the past five years: the figures were 17 and 12 percent respectively for housebreaking and 26 and 21 percent for theft of money or property.[28] When the *Maclean's*-Decima poll asked comparable questions in 1989, it had similar results with respect to experience with crime: 26 percent in the United States and 21 percent in Canada said they had "been robbed or assaulted." Americans were more fearful than Canadians of walking "the streets of your community" alone at night; 31 percent of Americans and 24 percent of Canadians felt this way.[29]

The available information on the incidence of drug abuse and alcoholism also places the United States significantly ahead of Canada. The generalization holds up with different bases of comparison, arrests for the use of serious illegal drugs, reports by samples of high school and postsecondary students on the use of marijuana, LSD, and amphetamines, and estimates of the extent of alcoholism derived from comparative statistics on liver-cirrhosis deaths.[30]

The lower rates of crime and violence in Canada are accompanied by greater respect for the police, more public endorsement for stronger punishment of criminals, and a higher level of support for gun-control legislation. Various studies of the attitudes of American police indicate that they commonly complain of being looked down on by the public.[31] Conversely, "the Royal Canadian Mounted Police celebrated its hundredth birthday in 1973 and was honored across the country....[One] could not imagine...a similar outpouring of good wishes on the anniversary of Scotland Yard or the FBI."[32]

A review of local studies suggests "that Canadians have a much more favorable impression of the police than their American counterparts."[33] Crossnational opinion surveys yield similar findings. When asked by the Canadian Gallup poll in 1978 to rate the local and provincial police forces and the Royal Canadian Mounted Police, a large majority said "excellent or good" for each — respectively, 64 percent for the first two and 61 percent for the latter.[34] The corresponding approvals reported by the Harris survey for local, state, and federal law enforcement officials in the United States in 1981 were 62, 57, and 48 percent. In the early 1980s, the comparative value surveys conducted by Gallup for CARA found more Canadians (86 percent) than Americans (76 percent) voicing a great deal or quite a lot of confidence in the police. There was no significant difference between the two Canadian linguistic groups on this item. The crossnational variation in attitudes toward "the legal system" in the CARA study (described in Chapter 5) were similar: 63 percent of Canadians were positive, compared to 51 percent of Americans. On this question, however, Francophones revealed more confidence (72 percent) than did Anglophones (59 percent).

The magnitudes of difference here, like those reported earlier for fear of and exposure to crime, may appear small statistically, but the fact that they are consistent argues for their significance. A number of small but theoretically reinforcing variations is more convincing than a single large difference.

Attitudes toward guns and gun control present crossnational differences that are larger but just as consistent. In the United States, gun ownership has been regarded as a right linked to a constitutional guarantee established to protect citizens against the state. "Canada's policy has been a restrictive one, based on the belief [that] ownership of offensive weapons or guns is a privilege, not a right."[35] Although the majority in both countries favor gun-control legislation, Canadians have consistently been more supportive than Americans and have been much less likely to own guns.[36] When asked by the Gallup polls in 1968, "Would you favor or oppose a law which would require a person to obtain a police permit before he or she could buy a gun?" 86 percent of Canadians favored such a law, compared to 68 percent of Americans.[37] In 1975, 83 percent of Canadians voiced support compared to 67 percent of Americans.[38] In 1976–77, 72 percent of Canadians — close to three-quarters — endorsed a law to ban civilian ownership of handguns, a proposition that appealed to only 36 percent of Americans (see Table 2). Canadian gun laws were tightened considerably in 1976. Handgun permits are now issued only "after an investigation to determine crime-free status and sanity of the applicant."[39] A representative of the Justice Department noted in 1986, "[i]t is almost impossible to get a permit to carry a hand gun."[40] By March 1989, according to a *Maclean's*-Decima poll, only 3 percent of Canadians owned a handgun, in contrast to 24 percent of Americans.[41]

In line with the greater propensity of Canadians to rely on the state and their lesser concern for individual rights, they are much more willing than Americans to favor laws forbidding practices defined as objectionable. These differences show up strikingly in Table 2, which reports on crossnational attitudes in the latter 1970s to various proposed laws to ban five forms of behavior. On each item — cars in downtown areas, radios in public, smoking in public places, ownership of handguns, and door-to-door selling — Canadians were more favorable to prohibition.

The Treatment of Crime

Although Canada has lower crime rates than the United States, its citizens, in line with the crime-control model, have appeared — until recently at least — to be more disposed to favor severe treatment of criminals than their southern neighbors. As Michalos sums up in his report on North American attitudes

Table 2

Attitudes in Canada and the United States
toward Various Forms of Prohibition, 1976-77

Proposed Law Banning:	United States	Canada
Cars in downtown areas		
For	25%	42%
Against	68	46
Don't know / no answer	8	11
Transistor radios in public		
For	24	39
Against	69	49
Don't know / no answer	7	12
Smoking in all public places		
For	51	57
Against	44	38
Don't know / no answer	5	5
Handgun ownership by civilians		
For	36	72
Against	59	23
Don't know / no answer	5	5
Door-to-door salesmen		
For	39	53
Against	54	40
Don't know / no answer	7	7

Sources: United States, Roper, December 1976; Canada, CROP, February 1977.

toward crime: "Although Canadians had less crime to contend with, they tended to take a tougher line than Americans on the death penalty" and favored "stiffer prison sentences."[42] In 1969, the Canadian and American Gallup polls asked, "In your opinion, what should be the penalty or prison sentence for the following crimes: dope peddling, armed robbery, arson, passing bad checks?" For dope peddling, those who answered more than 10 years in prison constituted 85 percent in Canada and 41 percent in the United States; for armed robbery, 60 percent and 33 percent; for arson, 53 percent and 23 percent; for passing bad checks, 16 percent and 7 percent.[43]

More recent crossnational data gathered by Erik Olin Wright in 1980 in the United States and John Myles in 1983 in Canada

— using a quite different question, however — suggest the possibility that the situation has changed. Sixty-three percent of Anglophone Canadians and 60 percent of Americans strongly agreed with the statement: "In order to reduce crime, the courts should give criminals stiffer punishments." Only 43 percent of Quebec residents felt the same way.[44]

The American emphasis on due process is accompanied by a greater litigiousness and larger expenditures on law enforcement.[45] In noting the lesser propensity of Canadians to go to court, The Economist points out that, unlike Americans, they "do not stalk their country's businesses with negligence and class-action suits filed on behalf of all purported victims. Nor do they ambush their surgeons with complaints of medical malpractice."[46] The United States has many more lawyers per capita than Canada; in 1982, there were 256 lawyers per 100,000 Americans, while the corresponding figure for Canada was 118.[47] The ratio of police to population is also greater in the Republic, and the differences have been increasing steadily, as indicated in Table 3.

Criminologists John Hagan and Jeffrey Leon note that the American "antidote" for a due-process model of law enforcement, which enhances the rights of the accused,

> has been an equally significant national commitment and assignment of resources to policing and punishing deviant behavior. Thus, although an economy of scale might be expected, the United States has spent more per capita on its police than has Canada, substantially more on its courts, and more as well on corrections. A result is that the United States has produced a legal order that combines high levels of crime with a profuse and coercive police response.[48]

In contrast, says Hagan,

> Canada has been able to limit its resource commitment to crime control by reemphasizing its ideological commitment to the Burkean ideal of social order first, and individual rights second. Thus, in Canada, the police role has become preeminently symbolic, a reminder that social order ideologically precedes individual liberties....Whether the focus is restricted access to probation, discretionary right to counsel, the admissibility of illegally obtained evidence, or a range of

Table 3

Police Protection in Canada and the United States

	Number of police personnel	Number per 100,000 population
Canada (1971)	46,548	225
United States (1971)	472,066	232
Canada (1981)	53,689	220
United States (1981)	902,868	386
Canada (1985)	53,464	210
United States (1985)	1,017,679	422

Sources: For Canada: Information Canada, *Canada Year Book, 1973*, p. 82; Statistics Canada, *Canada Year Book, 1980–81*, p. 131; idem, *Canada Year Book, 1988*, pp. 2–14, 2–20. For the United States: Department of Commerce, Bureau of the Census, *Statistical Abstract of the United States, 1973*, p. 156; idem, *Statistical Abstract of the United States, 1985*, p. 176; and idem, *Statistical Abstract of the United States, 1989*, p. 176.

other issues, Canadians have demonstrated a considerable willingness to accept laws that give social order precedence over individual rights.[49]

Constitutional Protections

Constitutional Change in Canada

Although crossnational behavioral and attitudinal differences with respect to law and crime continue to the present, during the 1980s Canada has been involved in a process of changing its fundamental rules by incorporating due-process requirements along the lines of the American model. The comprehensive Canadian Charter of Rights and Freedoms, adopted in the new constitution of 1982, was designed to create a basis, absent from the old *British North America Act* (the original Canadian constitution, adopted in 1867), for judicial intervention to protect individual rights and civil liberties, one that Canadian courts have begun to practice actively.

These changes are very important, even revolutionary. They have drastically changed, although not completely eliminated, the differences between Canadian and American legal cultures. Canadian courts have been more respectful than American ones of the rest of the political system. In discussing "the judicial deference to legislative judgement" in the first years of interpreting the Charter, F.L. Morton and Leslie Pal suggest that this behavior "reflects the continued influence of the tradition of judicial self-restraint engendered by over a century of Canada's unique form of parliamentary supremacy."[50] As the historian Kenneth McNaught describes the underlying pattern:

> [O]ur judges and lawyers, supported by the press and public opinion, reject any concept of the courts as positive instruments in the political process....[P]olitical action outside the party-parliamentary structure tends automatically to be suspect — and not least because it smacks of Americanism. This deep-grained Canadian attitude of distinguishing amongst proper and improper methods of dealing with societal organization and problems reveal us as being, to some extent, what Walter Bagehot called a "deferential society."[51]

The Charter is not the American Bill of Rights. Although it places many comparable restrictions on government action, it is still not as protective of individuals accused of crime. As Edgar Friedenberg notes:

> The Crown in Canada can appeal against an acquittal in a criminal procedure and demand that the accused be tried again....The American Bill of Rights provides no person shall "for the same offense be twice put in jeopardy of his life or limb." A similar provision under Section 10 (h) of the Canadian Charter of Rights and Freedoms is made ineffective in preventing what an American court would call "double jeopardy" by the inclusion of the word "finally" — "finally acquitted," or "finally found guilty" — since the process is not considered final till the Crown has exhausted its rights to appeal [an acquittal] which under American law, it wouldn't have in the first place.[52]

The new constitution gives accused persons

> the right to obtain counsel; [but] there is no constitutional obligation on the government...to provide counsel for in-

digents....[T]he Charter does not protect generally the right to refuse to answer a question in any proceeding on the basis of possible self-incrimination....[It] provides that the right to trial by jury exists only when the maximum punishment prescribed for the offense is at least five years.[53]

Property rights are also under less constitutional protection in Canada than in the United States. As a result, the law and judicial decisions differ in the two countries. The U.S. Constitution's famous fifth amendment not only protects accused persons against self-incrimination; it and the fourteenth amendment provide that persons may not be deprived of "property without due process of law." Hence, property holders have a right to be recompensed for government action, on the federal or state level, that expropriates property or reduces property values. No corresponding rights exist in Canada in either the 1867 or 1982 constitutions. The latter proclaims the right of everyone to "life, liberty and security of the person," but it lacks any clause bearing on the "right to own and to enjoy property and not be deprived thereof except by due process of law."[54] The government can "expropriate or take property, as long as there is statutory authority." As one legal authority notes: "The Charter of Rights and Freedoms...does not enshrine property rights....Two recent court tests...have sustained the interpretation that private property rights have not been entrenched in the new constitution."[55]

In contrast to the insistence in the Bill of Rights on "due process of law," the Charter refers to "principles of fundamental justice" as the basis for assuring basic individual rights. McNaught argues that "the Charter is distinctly un-American": its basic stress is still on the "dependence of liberty on order."[56] It provides that the "guaranteed rights and freedoms set out in it," must be "prescribed by law," and are subject to such "reasonable limits...as can be demonstrably justified in a free and democratic society." Its authors assumed that Parliament would be able to define "reasonable limits."[57]

Moreover, given the continuation of parliamentary supremacy, the Canadian constitution provides that Parliament or a provincial legislature can "opt out" of many of the constitutional restrictions by inserting into a law a provision that it shall operate "notwithstanding" a particular section of the Charter.

> This section gives both Parliament and the provincial legisla-
> tures the power to override most of the *Charter*'s rights and
> freedoms, specifically, "fundamental rights," "legal rights"
> and "equality rights."....The only rights which cannot be over-
> ridden are the "democratic rights," "mobility rights,"
> "minority language educational rights," rights associated
> with the equal status of French and English in some parts of
> Canada, and an interpretation clause providing that rights
> in the *Charter* are guaranteed equally to male and female per-
> sons.[58]

Thus, Canada now has a constitution that both empowers the judiciary to overrule Parliament by ruling that legislation is inconsistent with the Charter and allows the legislative bodies to limit the authority of the courts to do so.

In the years since the Charter was enacted, Canadian legislative bodies have used their override power sparingly (although Quebec's use of it on language rights has been a major, emotion-laden issue). However, the courts, in ruling on government activity, must be aware that parliamentary bodies can overrule them if, as in the United States, they engage in extensive judicial activism and creative interpretation that go beyond sentiments widespread in the population. Perhaps the most important decisions of the Canadian Supreme Court occurred in 1988, when it declared unconstitutional limitations on abortion in federal law and restrictions on the use of languages other than French on public signs in Quebec law. As yet (1989), efforts to write new federal abortion statutes have proved unsuccessful, but Quebec used the notwithstanding clause to renew its limitations on the rights of English-speakers.

One of the leading authorities on the impact of the Charter, F.L. Morton, argues that the override section is Canada's way of dealing with the American problem of "nine non-elected permanently tenured judges...setting permanent constitutional policy." It helps to avoid "the American dilemma of allowing constitutional supremacy to degenerate into judicial supremacy."[59]

While Canadian law under the Charter is somewhat more limited in protection of individual rights than American law, it retains the traditional Canadian emphasis in favor of collective or group rights. The 1867 constitution had provisions "protecting the linguistic and religious minorities of that period. The traditional fundamental and individual rights, on the other hand, were given no protection." The situation has changed greatly with the addition of the Charter, which now protects many individual rights, but pre-eminence continues to go to "the collective rights of minorities, in particular language rights,"[60] as well as aboriginal rights and rights to sexual equality. Individual rights may be overridden by Parliament or provincial legislatures; group rights may not. The Charter also authorizes affirmative action programs. Thus, Canada's constitution still reflects "a value system in which certain collective rights are of central importance."[61]

As noted earlier, Canada also continues to place more restrictions on freedom of speech than America. Its group defamation law, passed in 1969, permits prosecution for ethnic, racial, or religious attacks.[62] Sections 281 and 282 of the criminal code, which applies nationwide, make it a criminal offense to "willfully promote hatred against any identifiable group." Although this provision is rarely used, there have been a few well-publicized cases. In 1985, an Alberta school teacher was convicted for teaching a Jewish conspiracy theory of history, including denial of the Holocaust.[63] Even more distinctive is Section 177, still on the Canadian statute books after 100 years, which forbids the spreading of "false news." It provides: "Everyone who willfully publishes a statement, tale or news that he knows is false and that causes or is likely to cause injury or mischief to a public interest is guilty of an indictable offense and is liable to imprisonment for two years."[64] The section was used in 1985 to prosecute a publisher of materials denying the Holocaust.

No comparable statutes exist south of the border, nor would they be constitutional under freedom-of-speech rulings. In Canada, indictments for the promotion of racial hatred are justified by reference to the Charter's opening section, "which allows such reasonable limits as are 'demonstrably justified in a free and democratic society.'"[65]

More controversial is the continued legitimation by Canadian courts of the offense of "scandalizing," illustrating their continued commitment to giving priority to the maintenance of order — particularly confidence in the justice system. The misdeed is an action that "scandalizes a court by deliberate acts or words that 'lower its authority' among the public." The concept arose in Britain, but it is now almost forgotten there, and "[t]he Supreme Court of the United States has rejected the whole idea as 'English foolishness'."[66] Canada, however, had a number of prosecutions for the offense before the passage of the Charter and has had at least one since. In that recent case, initiated in 1985, the accused was a lawyer who, in a press interview, vehemently attacked a court decision against a political radical suing the Mounties for defamation. The lawyer was convicted in Ontario, with the judge ruling that his statements were "a blatant attack on all judges of all courts...likely to lower the authority of the court and its respect in the public eye." The conviction was reversed by the Ontario Court of Appeals on constitutional grounds, but the justices also ruled that the Charter permitted conviction for scandalizing if the provocation were greater than in this particular case, if it "threatened to provoke public rebellion against law and order." One justice, in maintaining that conviction for scandalizing was permissible under the Charter, criticized those who would eliminate the offense for following "American precedent." He preferred to "follow...[the] more civilized standards" to be found "in the United Kingdom and other Commonwealth countries."[67] In 1988, the same court drew attention to the differences between the Charter and the Bill of Rights in affirming a conviction of two members of the Nationalist Party of Canada for having willfully promoted hatred of blacks and Jews in publications.[68]

In comparing the situation of the judiciary on both sides of the border, the Canadian legal correspondent Jeffrey Miller points up the implications of the diverse populist and elitist traditions:

> [I]n the United States, the judges who aren't politically appointed are elected and answerable to the voters. In either case, they're subject to the same disrespect as any other public official. In America, if it takes your fancy, it is almost a public duty to bad-mouth the local magistrate. In Canada as in England, symbolically at least, judges have retained the majesty that accrued to them when adjudicating had strictly divine roots, all law supposedly being God-given. They don't wear horsehair wigs any more, but they remain "Their Lordships," and many of them still regard themselves as the priestly — if underappreciated — guardians of the social order.[69]

Change in the United States

The same period that witnessed Canada's partial move away from an emphasis on the collectivity toward constitutionally protected individual rights found the United States wrestling uneasily with both its increased acceptance of community responsibility for assorted welfare objectives and its continued commitment to individualism. It has sought to resolve the dilemma through legislation and especially through judicial decisions elaborating constitutional guarantees.

Perhaps the most vivid example of both the need for enhanced government responsibility and the strength of individualism can be found in military policy. Although the United States has taken the major lead in and responsibility for the defense of the non-Communist world, it does not have a conscript army. Many of its European allies, such as France and West Germany, do. The effective political argument against the draft has not been a strategic one. A committed libertarian, Martin Anderson, used ideological grounds to lead the successful battle to persuade Richard Nixon's administration to give up conscription. Also, the legal rights of individuals in service have been extended greatly by administrative and judicial orders.

Although the reforms introduced by the Charter of Rights and Freedoms have probably brought about more change in Canada than anything that has occurred in recent times in the United States, the Republic under the Warren Supreme Court (1953–69) extended its constitutional guarantees of personal rights in dramatic fashion. The most significant such development was, of course, *Brown v. Kansas*, the 1954 school integration case, as well as later antisegregation decisions. The court ruled that public agencies could not differentiate by race — that is, collectively — that everyone must be treated equally as an individual. The subsequent introduction of affirmative action policies, which require group preferences or quotas in hiring, awarding of government contracts, and university admissions in order to assure equal representation does, of course, constitute a move to give the rights of collectivities preference over individuals. Much of the debate over these policies has been put in these terms. Opinion polls indicate that the overwhelming majority of Americans (usually about 75 percent) oppose quotas linked to group identity. And ever since the *Bakke* case in 1978, involving a suit by a white denied admission to a medical school because it gave preference to blacks, the Supreme Court has gradually been undercutting, though far from eliminating, these policies. In principle, it stresses that the Constitution guarantees equal rights to individuals, not to collective categories such as those of race or gender.

The court has been even more emphatic in emphasizing protection for the individual in a variety of criminal cases, the most famous being *Miranda*, in which the decision assured accused persons of their right to be told that they do not have to speak to a police officer except in the presence of an attorney. Those arrested are now guaranteed legal representation if they cannot afford counsel. The courts have extended the meaning of entrapment. The rights of those subject to capital punishment have been particularly strengthened by judicially set regulations (although the court has accepted the constitutionality of imposing the death penalty). The incarcerated are now given many of the same legal protections as people outside prisons.

Perhaps the most important decision relative to politics was the Supreme Court's insistence on equal representation in local and state legislatures — that constituencies must be roughly equal in population, thus outlawing advantages to rural areas, less populous counties, and, in some cases, ethnic and racial groups. The ruling states that every person's vote should have the same impact. Equal protection has also been extended to foreign-born residents. Naturalized citizens can no longer lose their citizenship if they move abroad. More surprising have been decisions assuring illegal immigrants and their children rights to government services, including education, health, and welfare.

The original Supreme Court decision to legalize abortion, *Roe v. Wade*, involved the extension of the woman's right to privacy to noninterference by the government over her body. A constitutionally guaranteed right to personal autonomy had been enunciated in 1923 and was greatly elaborated in 1965 and 1973 in cases declaring unconstitutional laws outlawing contraception and abortion. The intense opposition to legal abortion also emphasizes individual rights — in this case, those of the fetus. The movement's lawyers stress that they do not want to challenge the privacy guarantees, which, as of 1965, set up broad new protections for individuals against invasive efforts by government. The 1965 decision, *Griswold v. Connecticut*, written by Justice Douglas, enshrined the right to privacy in constitutional law by finding it in various guarantees of the Bill of Rights. In recent years, the Supreme Court, increasingly dominated by the conservative appointees of Ronald Reagan, has been modifying but not overruling past decisions on abortion, just as it has been treating rulings on affirmative action quotas and the death penalty.

Wartime and Constitutional Rights

The emphasis on due process, free speech, and other rights of individuals as superseding the needs of the state for the maintenance of order is severely challenged during wartime. Threats to the very existence of the nation lead governments everywhere to suspend or ignore legal rights. America and Canada have not been exceptions.

In the United States, habeas corpus was suspended during the Civil War; free speech was denied opponents of the conflict in World War I, and many, particularly socialists and other radicals, were imprisoned; citizens of Japanese ancestry were placed in concentration camps on both sides of the 49th parallel during World War II for no offense other than their national origin; and a wave of intolerance against Communists and other leftists accused of complicity with them, which has entered history under the generic name of McCarthyism, swept the United States during the Korean War, a conflict with two Communist states. The courts did little to restrain the authorities, thus revealing the fragility of legal guarantees in the face of wartime hysteria.

On the positive side is the fact that these actions were generally repudiated and often legally reversed by the courts once the wars ended. After the Korean War, not only did Congress and the courts upset legislation designed to frustrate Communists and revolutionaries and limit the rights of aliens, but radicals were given more legally protected freedoms than ever before. Although the Vietnam War led to some prosecutions for antiwar activity, on the whole such behavior was less constrained than in any previous military conflict. Individual rights in the United States have been better protected since American troops left Saigon than ever before.

Conclusion

As noted earlier, a paradox of postwar change in North America has been the growth of both collective and individual values and policies. The new Canadian Charter of Rights and Freedoms has vastly increased the legal protection of individual Canadians, while the role of the state has been considerably enhanced south of the border. Yet, in spite of the changes in both countries, Canada remains much more group- and collectivity-oriented than its neighbor.

Public Opinion

Evidence that the dissimilarities in the guarantees afforded citizens in the two North American democracies correspond to differences in the values and opinions of their populations can be found in the results of a 1987 survey evaluating popular support for communal and individual rights. Four questions asked in both countries sought to measure concern for liberty in contrast to interest in an orderly society (see Table 4).[70]

The answers to the four statements indicate that Americans were disposed significantly more than Canadians to voice a preference for liberty in contrast to the perceived danger to society of disruption. The differences between Canada's two linguistic groups were inconsistent, and, on average, small. Basically, the study found that Canadians divided almost evenly in their willingness to take risks to maintain freedom of speech and assembly, while two-thirds of Americans would do so.

The national differences invert, however, when the questions posed deal with feelings about having deviants and extremists as neighbors, rather than with their possible impact on society. The CARA-Gallup values studies, made during the early 1980s, found that Canadians — Francophones particularly — were more ac-

Table 4

Support for Liberty and Order in North America
(percentage who "basically agree")

	Canadians		
Francophones	Anglophones	All	**Americans**

"It is better to live in an orderly society than to allow people so much freedom they can become disruptive."

77	61	65	51

"The idea that everyone has a right to their own opinion is being carried too far these days."

45	33	37	19

"Free speech is just not worth it if it means we have to put up with the danger to society of radical and extremist views."

38	35	36	28

"Free speech ought to be allowed for all political groups even if some of the things that these groups believe in are highly insulting and threatening to particular segments of society."

63	47	51	60

Average choosing value of social order rather than free speech for all the questions:

49	45	47	35

Note: In the first three questions, "agree" implies support for order over liberty, but it means liberty in the fourth item. Hence the percentages for the latter were inverted to calculate the averages.

Source: Paul M. Sniderman et al., "Liberty, Authority, and Community: Civil Liberties and the Canadian Political Culture" (Centre of Criminology, University of Toronto, and Survey Research Center, University of California, Berkeley, 1988), figures 9A-9D. The column for all Canadians is not in the original report. I calculated it from the data in the table, assuming three English-speakers to one French-speaker. The bottom row, giving the averages, is also my calculation.

cepting of deviants than were Americans. The latter were more likely (48 percent) than English Canadians (40 percent) or French Canadians (30 percent) to say that they were opposed to having "people with a criminal record as neighbors." Americans were also more disposed to find "emotionally unstable people" offensive as neighbors (47 percent) than were Anglophones (33 percent) or

Francophones (13 percent). And Americans exhibited less tolerance for living next to people described as "extremists." Thus, "left-wing extremists" were rejected as potential neighbors by 34 percent of Americans, 31 percent of English Canadians, and only 20 percent of French Canadians, while "right-wing extremists" were turned down by 26 percent of Americans, 24 percent of Anglophones, and 14 percent of Francophones.

It is difficult to interpret these results other than to infer that Canadians are more concerned than Americans with maintaining social order, even at the price of restricting the liberties of minorities, but are more lenient at the level of interpersonal behavior.

The hypothesis of greater tolerance in Canada is sustained by the results of Gallup polls, taken between 1963 and 1975, that inquired: "If colored people came to live next door, would you move your home?" Nine-tenths of Canadians consistently replied no, but only two-thirds of Americans gave that answer.[71] The *Maclean's*-Decima 1989 crossborder survey reported similar results to a question on respondents' feelings "if one of your children married someone from a different racial background." Almost one-third (32 percent) of Americans said they would be "unhappy"; in contrast, only 13 percent of Canadians gave that answer.[72] Too much weight should not be placed on these differences since, as Goldberg and Mercer note, it is necessary "to admit the possibility that if non-whites were as significant an urban minority as they are in many U.S. urban contexts, one might then find less willingness among Canadians to admit them as near-neighbors." Still, these analysts conclude their detailed comparative study of urban life in North America by emphasizing that "values tolerating ethnic and racial diversity and values which contribute to a less violent milieu play a role in maintaining the superior livability of the Canadian central city."[73]

The urbanologist Alan Artibise gives a similar interpretation in discussing the extensive changes in Toronto, which has gone from being an overwhelmingly Anglo-Saxon Protestant metropolis to one with a very large portion of immigrants from southern and eastern European and from Asia and the Caribbean. Noting that probably "no other North American city has undergone so much change in only thirty years," he emphasizes, "What is even more remarkable about this transformation is that it has taken place with no major violence or disorder....Toronto has managed to maintain general social tolerance among its people."[74]

The interplay between law and values in the two North American democracies can be seen as reflecting the variations in their key organizing principles established in their formative periods. The American emphasis, as stated in the Constitution and the Bill of Rights, has been on due process and the protection of the individual from state encroachments. Canadians, following organic principles, have been more focused on protection for the state and community. Variation in crime rates and attitudes toward the law and law enforcement seem to reflect these differences. Both polities have changed as Canada has moved in the due-process direction with its Charter of Rights and Freedoms while the United States has shifted somewhat in the collective-rights direction with its acceptance of group-oriented affirmative action policies.

Deviance

Many of the themes discussed thus far dealing with respect for authority, religion, and rule of law are affirmed in an extremely thorough comparative study of teenage pregnancy.[75] The research, which deals with quantitative analyses of data from 37 industrialized countries, includes case studies of six countries, two of which are Canada and the United States.

America stands out among industrialized countries and in comparison with its northern neighbor as having higher teenage fertility rates, including more abortions. These differences have "existed at least since 1971." The phenomenon is *not* to be explained by racial variations, a hypothesis that holds up when the data for whites only are examined. Given this fact, the authors conclude their broad analysis by saying, "[I]t appears that the principal explanation for the relatively high incidence of adolescent pregnancy in the United States must be sought in factors that influence the entire country." And looking at the results of opinion surveys taken in the six nations, they report "rather high negative correlations" between permissive attitudes toward sex and restrictive rules and beliefs about contraception and adolescent sexuality.[76]

As noted in Chapter 4 and reiterated in the pregnancy study, Canadians have held more liberal or permissive attitudes toward premarital and extramarital sexual relationships than Americans since the 1960s. In line with these results is the finding that cohabitation is twice as common among Canadian teenagers than American. More significantly, "60 percent of [Canadian] teenage mothers are unmarried at the time of birth. For U.S. teenagers, the proportion is 50 percent, and it is only 35 percent among U.S. whites."[77]

The fact that Canadian teenagers are much more likely than their American compeers to be unwed at the time of their child's birth must, however, be considered in tandem with the variations in fertility rates. They are greatest among females, age 15 and younger, for whom the American birth rate is four times that of the Canadian. And, the research indicates,

> [A] major part of the difference [in pregnancy rates] may be attributed to better contraceptive practice by Canadian teenagers. Studies suggest that Canadian teenagers are more likely than U.S. teenagers to be using a method currently, to use a contraceptive at first intercourse, and to be using oral contraceptives....Among teenagers practicing contraception, a higher proportion of Canadians than Americans use the pill, the most effective reversible method.[78]

Canadian women generally have shown a greater openness than have American women toward using a birth-control method that implies more conscious preparation for intercourse. They

> adopted the pill more rapidly than did U.S. women...[in] the late 1960's and early 1970's. Canadians have overwhelmingly favorable attitudes toward pill use....The pill is almost universally considered the method of choice...by teenagers.[79]

Given this background, it is not surprising that "unmarried Canadians...have fewer abortions and their overall pregnancy rate is lower." Yet, white American teenagers are much less likely than Canadians to bear illegitimate children, an outcome that the researchers believe reflects the fact that in the United States, "unwed pregnant teenagers, especially white teenagers, are under greater pressure than Canadians to legitimize the birth."[80]

How can these seemingly contradictory patterns be reconciled? The authors refer to the evidence that Americans are more intensely religious than the populations of the other countries they consider, and they suggest that "the intensity and nature of religious feeling in the United States" serve to inhibit Americans', particularly young Americans', ability to react matter-of-factly to sex and marriage. It "is romantic, but also sinful and dirty; it is flaunted but also something to be hidden"; hence, the ambivalent reaction to contraception, especially to the pill.[81]

The analysts argue that Canadians' greater reliance on effective birth control and much lower teenage fertility rates derive from these patterns, having now become the conventional way of behaving north of the border. These patterns, they say, may be linked to Canadians' greater "conservatism (which may include an aversion to risk taking)." As they point out:

> Canadians appear to be more law abiding and to have more respect for authority than Americans. The difference is immediately apparent to the U.S. visitor who is struck by the lack of graffiti and litter in the streets, even in a large metropolitan area such as Toronto,....in spite of...[a] large immigrant population of many nationalities....The difference is reflected in the youth culture: Canadian teenagers are reported to have better relations with their teachers and there is less vandalism and violence in the schools. One might hypothesize that teenagers with a positive identification with authority would follow adult norms of responsibility in sexual behavior and use of contraceptives.[82]

Conversely, the greater religiosity, anti-elitism, and propensity for law and rule violation in the United States make for confused sexual behavior. Young Americans, particularly whites, violate the religious norms by engaging in premarital intercourse but, given their moral ambivalence, do not handle contraception well; they are then likely to marry if pregnancy results.

Conclusion

The gaps between the Canadian and American societies on constitutional, juridical, behavioral (crime and deviance rates), and attitudinal scales remain large. The difference between the Tory and Whig modes continues to inform their legal systems and citizen behavior.

In emphasizing the continuing differences between Canada and the United States after the enactment of the Charter of Rights and Freedoms, it may be that I am underestimating the potential for change in Canadian values and behavior that will develop as the Charter is implemented by the courts. Although favored more by the left than the right, it probably goes further toward taking the country in an American direction than any other enacted structural change, including the Canada-U.S. Free Trade Agreement. The Charter's stress on due process and individual rights, although less stringent than that of the U.S. Bill of Rights, should increase individualism and litigiousness north of the border.

The next area to be explored is economic behavior, which, some would argue, determines values.

7

Economic Behavior and Culture

The two North American nations are the wealthiest and most productive industrialized countries in the world. As of 1986, the gross domestic product (GDP) per head for the United States in comparable purchasing power units was US$17,360, while Canada was second among the countries of the Organisation for Economic Co-operation and Development (OECD) at US$15,910. West Germany and Japan were well behind with per capita incomes of US$12,793 and US$12,210, respectively.[1]

The decline of North American production as a proportion of the worldwide product and the growth in the foreign trade deficit of the United States have led some people to worry or gloat about the weakening of the latter's international impact. There can, of course, be no argument about the fact that the American *share* of the world economy shrank in half, from 40 to 45 percent in the late 1940s to 20 to 25 percent in the late 1960s. But this change reflected the growth of other countries — an advance obviously to be welcomed — not the inability of the United States to continue to work and produce at a high level. And the increase in the importance of other economies, including Canada's, is in part a consequence of the North American and Canadian commitment to freer trade, the willingness of the two nations to import foreign-made products, which have competed successfully with domestic goods. Many European countries have more limitations on imports of Japanese and South Korean automobiles, the main foreign market for which is in North America.

In any case, the American and Canadian economies have not been doing badly even compared to the Japanese. In the 1980s,

> [T]he most notable decline in gross domestic product growth was that of Japan: its average annual growth rate between 1980 and 1986 was 58.7 percent of what it had been between 1965 and 1980. In contrast, the U.S. average annual growth rate in 1980–86 was 110.7 percent of what it had been in 1965–80.[2]

Between 1970 and 1987, the American share of the gross world product held steady at 22 to 25 percent, as did its portion of world exports generally (about 19 percent), and of technology-intensive products (about 25 percent).[3] "The percentage of the population employed (ages 15 through 64) in the United States rose from 64 percent in 1970 to 69 percent in 1987; in Western Europe, it fell from 65 percent in 1970 to 58 percent in 1987."[4]

The Canadian-U.S. differences in levels of income and occupational structures are narrower than any time in history. The Canadian economy has grown dramatically in the past quarter of a century. Between 1985 and 1989, its rate of increase was second only to Japan's. Whatever factors were responsible for the northern country's being significantly poorer than its southern neighbor before World War II have seemingly been declining or disappearing.[5] The changes apply to both English and French Canada. Nevertheless, the United States is still roughly 10 percent more productive than Canada, and the more populous country has been considerably ahead for most of the past two centuries. The large literature seeking to account for the earlier dissimilarities notes important differences in economically relevant behavior. As I will document below, the contrasts in business and work values continue to exist, although the phenomena they are supposed to explain — Canada's economic backwardness and America's advantage — have almost disappeared.

The efforts to deal with the variations in economic development between Canada and the United States and between French and English Canada in the past and to account for the greater role of government in the Canadian economy divide between emphasis on cultural and on structural factors.

The structural explanation of early American affluence notes the advantages of occupying a considerably larger habitable land mass, with enormous agricultural, animal, and mineral resources and a more clement climate. And the much greater size of the American market has given business in the United States a considerable advantage over that in its neighbor. These basic structural factors are obviously strongly related to the differing economic outcomes. Business in the United States has been ecologically and demographically advantaged compared to that in Canada. Quebec has been in a weaker position vis-à-vis English Canada. Consequently, Canada has required government capital and other assistance to establish and maintain services and industries necessary for survival in a large country with a relatively small population.

The cultural interpretation points to the congruence, noted by Max Weber, between the ethoses of Protestant sectarianism and of capitalism as related to the presence of a harder-working, more capital-maximizing population south of the border.[6] Canada, as indicated earlier, has been less Protestant sectarian than the United States and, in harmony with the Weber thesis, developed more slowly. The Weberian logic also suggests cultural reasons for the relatively tardy economic advancement of Quebec and the American south: respectively, Catholicism and slavery and their residues in values and structures.[7]

Culture and Economic Behavior

Strikingly, one of the earliest exponents of a cultural explanation for Canadian-U.S. differences was, as we have seen, the cofounder of the world's most influential structuralist theory. In writing his impressions of a brief visit to North America in 1888, Friedrich Engels emphasized the sharp variation between the values of Americans and those of Canadians, who resembled Europeans in his judgment. He noted that, north of the border, "one imagines that one is in Europe again, and then one thinks that one is in a positively retrogressing and decaying country. Here one sees how necessary the *feverish speculative spirit* of the Americans is for the rapid development of a new country." He pointed to the "economic necessity for *an infusion of Yankee blood*," not capital, if Canada was to grow, and he looked forward to its incorporation into the United States.[8]

Engels' observations are not as un-Marxian as they may appear to those who think of Marx and Engels as narrow economic determinists. In discussing the conditions for economic development in various less-industrialized areas — for example, Algeria, India, Mexico, and eastern Europe — both men emphasized the inhibiting influence of cultural factors and advocated the takeover of these societies by advanced countries, such as France, Britain, the United States, and Germany; such conquests were needed, they thought, to break up the self-reinforcing pattern of traditional values antithetical to industrialization and capital accumulation.[9]

Over the decades, various Canadians have pointed to ways through which the distinctive nature of their society has affected how its citizens do business. Herschel Hardin, an analyst of business behavior, writes:

> It was...rough egalitarianism, practical education...and the relentless psychic push to keep up in the "Lockean race" that made the exceptional United States go. To expect that [same behavior] on this side of the border, out of a French Canada tied to its clerical, feudal past, and out of an English-speaking Canada, which, although it inherited much of the spirit of liberal capitalism, was nevertheless an elitist, conservative, defensive colony — to expect it without an intense, ideological revolution — was to dream a derivative impossibility.[10]

Canadian entrepreneurs have been frequently described in fiction and popular magazines as less aggressive, less innovative, less risk-taking than their American counterparts.[11] These stereotypes remain in spite of the steady growth in the wealth of the country and the increased presence of major Canadian businesses abroad. Such comments particularly characterized the observations made by people acquainted with both nations in the 1986 TV documentary, "O Canada Eh!," described in Chapter 3.[12] An executive of the large insurance company Sun Life, Mike Wadsworth, told the TV audience:

Americans generally are harder working. They are more aware of the value of the dollar. Americans are greater risk takers, they put more emphasis on making money. Canadians are more concerned with the quality of life, they are not as anxious to make big money.

Peter Widdrington, then president of the giant beer company Labatt, spoke in a similar vein in comparing executive behavior: "In the United States, senior managers have a more aggressive style than in Canada. There is less pressure among senior people." Popular author Pierre Berton reinforced these images, stating categorically: "We are not an entrepreneurial country and never have been....There is a feeling in the Canadian establishment that it is a little bit vulgar to go after things too hard."

Writing more generally, Margaret Atwood contends:

Americans worship success, Canadians find it in slightly bad taste....One could sum up the respective stances by saying that the typical American is...unthinkingly and breezily aggressive and the Canadian...peevishly and hesitantly defensive. [13]

Public opinion surveys indicate that these stereotypes do correspond to actual national traits. Gallup polls taken in 1973 inquired: "Some people are attracted to new things and new ideas, while others are more cautious about such things. What's your own attitude to what's new?" Almost half the Americans (49 percent) said they were "attracted" to newness; only 13 percent replied "more cautious." Among the Canadians, however, more than one-third (35 percent) were cautious, while 30 percent were attracted to new things or ideas. In line with these results, crossnational surveys taken by Goldfarb Consultants, a leading Canadian market research firm, in 1982 in the United States and in 1983 in Canada, found that more Americans (69 percent) than Canadians (60 percent) agreed with the statement: "I am always willing to try new things or products." The same surveys also reported that Americans were much more likely than Canadians to say "I work well under pressure," by 70 to 53 percent.

Drawing in large part on works by students of invention, Hardin concludes that private enterprise in Canada "has been a monumental failure" in developing new technology and industry. Canadian business has rarely been involved in creating industries to process inventions by Canadians, who have had to go abroad to get their discoveries marketed.[14] The Science Council of Canada, dealing with impediments to innovation, emphasizes the "prudence" of Canadian entrepreneurs as a major obstacle.[15] Charles McMillan, recently an adviser to Prime Minister Brian Mulroney, noted, while still a professor of business:

> [T]he Canadian record of diffusion of existing technology in various areas of secondary manufacture remains relatively poor, and the traditional management values and organizational processes act as deterrents to making product innovation a major corporate strategy.[16]

Involvement in research and development (R&D) is low in Canada compared with other OECD countries. Some analysts suggest the principal reason is the Canadian economy's large component of foreign-owned, especially American-owned, companies. Yet, as Canadians Geraldine Kenney-Wallace and Fraser Mustard point out, if "one compares the expenditure of Canadian-owned firms in a variety of industrial sectors with that of U.S. companies in equivalent industrial sectors,...[the former] spend substantially less...as a percentage of their sales." The difference is not a function of size since "Sweden and Switzerland compare favorably with the United States and Japan in their levels of innovative activity." The analysts, who have documented the relative weakness of Canada in developmental and basic research, conclude that to remedy the problem would require a conscious effort to "change culture."[17]

Another interesting fact may also reflect crossborder cultural variations. Total Canadian spending on R&D is only about 1.40 percent of GDP, about half the American proportion of 2.74 percent. But comparison of the percentage of GDP spent on *government-performed* R&D in both countries shows Canada in the lead by 0.39 to 0.33 percent.[18]

It is taken for granted that the ability of nations to compete in the world market is linked to their R&D capacity. Not surprisingly, Canada does much worse than the United States in exports of high-technology products. As of 1986, such goods represented

14 percent of manufactured exports from the northern country compared to 38 percent from the southern one.[19]

Prudence and Risk

The consensus that Canadians are more cautious and conservative than Americans in their economic behavior is attested to by a variety of crossnational aggregate and opinion data. Americans are more prone to take risks. The differences show up with respect to investment strategies, savings, insurance purchases, use of credit, and consumer behavior.

The Canadian economist Jenny Podoluk reports: "[I]nvestment is a much more significant source of personal income in the United States than in Canada. Capital investment is necessary for economic development, but the risk involved has generally not appealed to Canadians."[20] Americans have been more disposed to put their money in stocks. In 1981, such investment amounted to 0.9 percent of GDP in the United States and 0.2 percent in Canada.[21] As of 1986, 13 percent of adult Canadians were stockholders; the corresponding figure for Americans in 1985 was 20 percent.[22] Needham-Harper market research, finding small but consistent differences, reported in 1986 that Canadians are somewhat more likely than Americans to say that "when making an investment, maximum safety is more important than high interest rates" (83 to 78 percent) and that "on a job, security is more important than money" (82 to 75 percent). Compared to their southern counterparts, Canadian investors and financial institutions are alleged to be less disposed to provide venture capital. According to the Science Council of Canada, they "tend consistently to avoid offering encouragement to the entrepreneur with a new technology-based product...[or to] innovative industries."[23]

Canadians have long sought opportunities for safer investment south of their border. Supposedly, "[w]hen Canadians have invested, the risky new Canadian enterprise has not been as attractive as the established American corporation."[24] Kenneth Glazier seeks to explain the phenomenon:

One reason is that Canadians traditionally have been conservative, exhibiting an inferiority complex about their own destiny as a nation and about the potential of their country....President A.H. Ross of Western Decalta Petroleum, Ltd., Calgary, in a recent annual report, said that most of Western Decalta's exploration funds are "from foreign sources because the company has not been able to find enough risk capital in Canada."

Thus, with Canadians investing in the "sure" companies of the United States, Canada has for generations suffered not only from a labor drain and a brain drain to the United States, but also from a considerably larger capital drain.[25]

This pattern is not new. The economic historian R.T. Naylor notes of the pre-World War I period:

Financial capital moved from Canada to the U.S., industrial capital back to Canada. Canadian funds went to support American stock exchanges or into corporate bonds....Canada in effect ended up "borrowing" back its money in the form of direct investments by American firms.[26]

The large Canadian insurance company Sun Life "generally preferred American investments to Canadian ones," and "Canadian brokers dealt more heavily in American than in Canadian stocks."[27]

If one controls for the sizes of the two populations and per capita gross national products, it is clear that Canadians invest much more money south of the border than Americans send north, a tendency that has grown greatly since the 1960s.[28] One-fourth of the 100 largest foreign investments in the United States, as of 1986, were held by Canadian companies.[29] Even more striking is the finding in a U.S. Commerce Department survey of the total value of direct investments in the United States that "traced assets to their ultimate owners. Britain ranked first in 1986 with $133.8 billion, *followed by Canada* with $129.5 billion, Japan, $96.7 billion, Switzerland, $79.5 billion and then the Netherlands, with $68.4 billion."[30] The *Wall Street Journal*, reporting these data in a manner typical of the way Americans tend to slight Canada, discusses the implications of the heavy British and Japanese investment, and notes some doubt that the Dutch involvement is as great as indicated, since the figures include many "foreign companies that aren't Dutch, *particularly Canadian com-*

panies, [which] channel their direct investment in the U.S. through Dutch subsidiaries...to save on U.S. withholding taxes."[31] The article totally ignores the growth and magnitude of Canadian involvement, including the possibility that Canada may be the largest foreign investor in the United States.

The overall situation has changed drastically in the past two decades. Although Canada is one-tenth the size of the United States in population, the ratio, in absolute terms, of American investment in the north to Canadian investment in the south decreased from five to one in the early 1970s to three to two as of the early 1980s to par or above by the latter years of the decade.[32] More Canadian capital is moving to the United States than is being invested by Americans in Canada.[33] Overall, too, Canadian direct investment abroad is greater than the amounts foreigners put into the country.[34] And the growth rate in ownership of capital abroad is greater for Canadians than for Americans. In an effort to reduce the outflow, the Trudeau government instituted regulations to permit Canadians to deduct 20 percent of the dividends of Canadian-owned companies for income tax purposes and to require pension funds and after-tax retirement savings to be put primarily into Canadian investments.[35] (These rules have been left in force by the Conservative government of Brian Mulroney.)

The employment of money in the United States does not mean that Canadian capitalists have been abandoning business in their country to foreigners. A summary of the research evidence on the ownership and control of the largest Canadian firms reports:

> [I]n 1946 and 1976 about 86 percent of such assets were Canadian controlled...[while] among all non-financial companies in Canada, the value of assets under foreign control...has steadily decreased from 36 percent in 1970 to 26 percent in 1981. In manufacturing alone the decline was from 58 percent in 1970 to 41 percent in 1983.[36]

Given such improvements in the patterns of economic growth and in the ratio of foreign to domestic direct ownership, and given Canada's increasingly assumption of an international role as an exporter of capital, it is puzzling that the public opinion and aggregate data still indicate that Canadians are more prudent than Americans, The record, however, is clear and consistent. Reviewing the evidence from opinion polls and aggregate data in 1988, Goldfarb Consultants comments: "Canadians are more security conscious, have a 'rainy-day' mentality, are more heavily insured and bigger savers than U.S. residents." The former show up as significantly higher than Americans on an "uncertainty avoidance index" in a study of the employees of the same multinational corporation.[37] The Science Council of Canada reports that Canadians save more than their neighbors to the south, that a greater "part of these savings go into bank deposits, pensions, and life insurance," and that Canadians proportionately have "much more life insurance in force" than Americans.[38] At the end of 1982, the average Canadian had $22,060 in life insurance coverage, compared to $19,291 for the average American.[39] In 1984, Canadians purchased $4,704 worth of insurance per capita; Americans bought $4,439 per person.[40] According to the American Council of Life Insurance, the ratio of life insurance in force to national income in the latter year was 7 percent higher in Canada than in the United States.[41] From 1980 to 1988, the household savings rate in Canada was more than twice that in the United States for all years but two, when it was almost at that ratio (for example, in 1988, it was 8.9 to 4.9 percent).[42] *New York Times* chronicler of Canadian society Andrew Malcolm, noting the fact "that there are today [1988] six million more savings accounts in Canada than there are people," explains the phenomenon by the assumption that "adversity is instinctively anticipated" north of the border, an attitude that "has produced a kind of self-fulfilling pessimism."[43]

Cumulative evidence drawn from opinion polls reinforces the aggregate findings indicating the greater economic prudence of Canadians. In 1986, Needham-Harper market research found 10 percent more Americans than Canadians making use of bank or credit cards. A year later, Decima and Cambridge Research Incorporated (CRI) reported comparable results to the question, "If you needed to make a major purchase in the next month, how willing would you be to make that purchase using credit?" Forty-five percent of Americans replied that they would be "very willing" to use credit compared to 34 percent of Canadians. The findings of surveys taken in 1968, 1970, and 1979 make it evident that these differences go back at least to the late 1960s.[44] So, too, as of 1970, Americans were more likely than English-speaking Canadians (46 to 39 percent) to report having borrowed "money from a bank or finance company" during the past year. Canadians were more inclined to "like to pay cash for everything I buy" (80 to 72 percent) and to say that "to buy anything, other than a house, on credit is unwise" (61 to 50 percent).[45] A marketing executive in the automobile industry reported in the early 1970s that the advertising used in his field varied across the border, since the "Canadian buyer is much more cost conscious...than the American."[46] Goldfarb Consultants reported the same difference at the end of the 1980s.

Values

Survey findings on values back up the hypothesis that Canadians are economically more cautious and conservative than Americans, although the differences are not enormous. In the CARA-Gallup values surveys described in Chapter 5, the answers to questions concerning values to be inculcated in the young consistently implied that Canadians are somewhat more parsimonious and less achievement-oriented than Americans. As on other measures, Anglophone Canadians fell between Americans and Francophone Canadians. From a list of 17 "qualities which children can be encouraged to learn at home," respondents were asked to choose five items that they considered "especially important." Twenty-one percent of French-speaking Canadians included "thrift, sparing money and things" in their list; so did 12 percent of Anglophones and 9 percent of Americans.

Americans are more likely than Canadians to express attitudes that suggest a greater absorption of values characteristic of the business-industrial system. The values study also posed several items dealing with feelings about work. The magnitude of the differences found varied, but the directions were again consistent. Basically, Anglophone Canadians differ from Americans in the same way their Francophone conationals do, only less so. Thus, the respondents expressing "a great deal" of "pride in the

work you do" ran 84 percent for Americans, 77 percent for
Anglophone Canadians, and 38 percent for Francophone Canadians; those saying they never felt "taken advantage of or
exploited on the job" were 37, 44, and 56 percent, respectively;
and those reporting they followed their "superior's instructions
on a job" were 68, 57, and 45 percent. Americans were, however,
least likely to choose one of the top three categories on a ten-point
scale with regard to job satisfaction: in that group were 63 percent of Americans, 69 percent of English Canadians, and 74
percent of French Canadians. This pattern of responses — the in-
verse of those reported for pride in the job and feelings of
exploitation — may reflect a greater achievement drive among
Americans, leading to more willingness to seek a better job.

The question, mentioned earlier, in which respondents chose
from among a list of "qualities which children can be encouraged
to learn at home," produced results that, on the whole, reflect the
same pattern of underlying values. Americans led English Canadians who, in turn, were ahead of French Canadians in the
percentages choosing "independence" (32, 27, and 15 percent)
and "hard work" (26, 21, and 17 percent).[47]

These results from the CARA-Gallup studies are congruent
with the findings of Quality of Life (QOL) surveys conducted in
the United States in 1971 and in Canada in 1977 and with those
of the Goldfarb Consultants polls taken in 1982–83. Comparisons
must be limited because of differences in timing and question
wording. But the QOL report concludes that the data demonstrate
"the greater importance of work in the United States than in
Canada....The work domain appears to have twice the impact...
among Americans." It emphasizes the "greater value of social
relationships in Canada and of achievement in the United
States."[48] The Goldfarb study finds that Americans exhibit a
higher "commitment to the work ethic" by an average scale score
of 8.1 to 7.5 and are more likely to value "being a leader, taking
a leadership role in things you participate in" by 7.3 to 6.4. Three
other surveys, more limited in their sample scope, "support the
proposition that Americans on the whole have a higher need for
achievement than Canadians."[49]

Corporate Networks

Whatever the variation in crossborder investment, savings rates, and beliefs related to economic matters, the available evidence on investments clearly does not confirm the frequently asserted argument that heavy foreign investment has given the Canadian business class a "peculiar dependent character" — closer ties to American business than to its own members — that has contributed "to the underdevelopment of indigenous industry."[50] In recent years, a number of Canadian sociologists have documented the opposite through network analysis, looking at the links among large firms in their country. They find dense and close intranational ties among the directors of financial and industrial concerns.[51]

> Moreover, the directorship ties among indigenous Canadian financial and non-financial firms have become more dense over time while the ties between Canadian financials and American-controlled industrials have become less dense.[52]

Firms north of the border have proportionately many more links — directors in common — than those in the south. Business networks are much more closely tied together in Canada, while they are "very weakly integrated" in America. One-fifth of U.S. corporations are "isolated," but only one-tenth of Canadian companies are.

These studies of relations among corporations bear out the finding drawn from analyses of stock ownership: a much greater concentration of ownership and control among Canadian corporations than American firms.[53] A 1984 study by the Ontario Securities Commission reports that four-fifths of the companies on the Toronto Stock Exchange's 300 Index are controlled by seven families.[54] Crossnational data reveal that Canada's 32 wealthiest families plus five conglomerates "control about one-third of the country's non-financial assets....By comparison, in the U.S. the 100 largest firms, few of which are controlled by individuals, own one-third of the non-financial assets."[55] Only 15 percent of the 500 companies on the American Standard and Poor's stock index have a large stockholder; in Canada, at least one-quarter of the stock in 93 percent of the country's largest publicly held corporations "is held by a family or conglomerate."[56] While the United States has literally thousands of small banks, Canada's five largest chartered banks almost totally dominate the industry in their country, holding 80 percent of all deposits; another five have an additional 10 percent.[57] Proportionately, Canada has five times as many billionaires as America.[58]

The concentration of wealth is encouraged north of the border by the absence of the estate and gift taxes to be found in the south, as well as by lower levies on capital gains. After an exemption on the first $600,000, American estate taxes start at a 35 percent rate, move up to 55 percent, and are applied to the appreciated value of property at the time of death, not to its original cost. Revisions in the U.S. tax law in 1987 and 1988 make it extremely difficult to evade these levies by transferring property to family members.[59] Since 1972, Canadians have been generally deemed to realize accrued capital gains at death for income tax purposes. To date, however, estate planning arrangements have substantially reduced the potential impact of this rule. Canadians also get a lifetime exemption from capital gains tax of C$500,000 for gains derived from shares of Canadian-controlled private corporations carrying on active business largely within the country. There is no comparable deduction in the United States.

The Canadian economy turns out to be organized more like the economies of much of Europe than that of the United States.[60] There is no obvious economic interpretation of these disparate North American patterns. Some may stem from variations in market size. A large part of the explanation, however, seems rooted in values and politics. Business relationships in the United States are affected by the strong anti-elitist, anti–big-business sentiments that have been institutionalized in antitrust legislation and inheritance taxes. The lower level of such feelings in Canada seemingly is reflected in the lesser emphasis on such policies in Canada.[61] Most surveys on the subject find that fewer Canadians than Americans think economic concentration threatening (see, for example, Table 5).

Canada has anticombines legislation, but it has been weakly enforced compared to that in the United States. "In Canada, government agencies have seldom directly instigated prosecution

Table 5

Feelings in Canada and the United States about Concentrated Business Power

"There's too much power concentrated in the hands of a few large companies for the good of the nation."

	Canada	United States
	percentage agreeing	
1977	66	76
1979	69	80
1981	73	79
1983	69	75
1985	64	73
1987	67	72
Average	*68*	76

Sources: For Canada, the Contemporary Research Centre (CRC); for the United States, the Opinion Research Corporation (ORC).

for reasons of anti-trust violations."[62] The American government also has been more committed than the Canadian to regulatory policies designed "to reduce pollution, to help preserve scarce environmental resources, and to deal with a range of related concerns," says Sylvia Ostry, a former high-level Canadian civil servant.[63] Ostry believes that the lesser emphasis on regulation of business in her country may reflect Canada's being "more sensitive to development and growth objectives and reluctant to enforce policies which would impede efforts in this direction." She also points to the relevance of the varying strengths of populism across the border, specifying

> the considerably stronger and more active role of U.S. interest groups, politicians, the press and other institutions in mobilizing and articulating public opinion. Consumers and environmental groups are, of course, active in Canada; but...they are often a pale reflection of their U.S. counterparts.[64]

Hence, even if Canadians are more inclined to prudence than Americans are, they should feel freer to take risks.

Ironically, in spite of the Canadian emphasis on direct state involvement in the economy through public ownership, extensive welfare programs, and a relatively high rate of taxation, business in Canada has in recent decades operated less subject to government interference than in the United States.[65] Executives of firms operating on both sides of the border attest in interviews to their awareness of this situation. Could the surprising growth of the Canadian economy and its improved position internationally reflect to some degree the fact that it is freer and less government-regulated than the American?

The ways in which regulatory efforts operate also vary considerably across the border. One analysis notes that American legislation gives regulating agencies much less discretion than the Canadian ones have and provides "private groups and individuals with substantial opportunities to use the courts to hold the regulators to the letter of the law." Canadian provisions, on the other hand, usually confer "substantial discretionary authority on the regulators," authority that is subject to "minimal judicial scrutiny." Canadian regulation "tends to trust the public service to use its expert judgment to protect legitimate interests," while American regulation is "usually public, contentious and combative" and hence more strictly and narrowly enforced.[66] The analysts suggest that the most important reason for the crossnational difference is "a pervasive [Canadian] social phenomenon born of historical tradition, which entails a greater acceptance of the legitimacy and authority of the government to attend to social concerns." The greater flexibility in Canada results in regulators' frequently delegating "monitoring of compliance to the regulated firms."[67] Regulation is simply less strict north of the border.

The combination of a strong commitment to an extensive welfare state and less emphasis on regulation of business is not as unusual as it may first appear. Many social democrats, but few American liberals, hold the belief that government should intervene where private institutions or individual resources fail but that it should be wary of trying to affect market outcomes by controls. More than three decades ago, the English economist Anthony Crosland, who held various cabinet posts — including that of Chancellor of the Exchequer — in Labour governments, told me he could not understand the logic of many American regulations, including some affecting the stock market. He felt, as apparently many Canadians do, that a market economy works best with a minimum of government interference, but that the state should take responsibility for providing services in areas where it can do so more efficiently or humanely than the private sector. This viewpoint implies that government ownership occasionally may be a preferred solution, but regulation is less likely to be so.

Evidence of the varying orientations of Canadians and Americans toward competitiveness and government ownership can be found in crossborder polls taken in 1976 by two opinion research groups, the Roper Organization in the United States and CROP in Canada. They inquired as to which policy, public ownership or antimonopoly, might be the "best way to get good quality at reasonable prices" in four industries: autos, oil, steel/metals, and chemicals. Averaging the separate responses for each industry, one finds that Americans were more disposed than Canadians to favor the anti–big-business, pro–competitive-free-market position of "break large companies into smaller companies" by 26 to 10 percent. Conversely, advocates of reform in Canada were more favorable toward partial or total governmental ownership by 21 to 13 percent. Six surveys conducted between 1977 and 1987 by the Contemporary Research Centre in Canada and the Opinion Research Corporation in the United States also indicate that Americans are consistently more likely than Canadians to believe: "Many of our largest companies ought to be broken up into smaller concerns." Averaging the responses over the ten-year period reveals 52 percent of respondents south of the border supported the policy but only 43 percent in the north.

That Canadians are less hostile than Americans to *big* business may seem surprising given the greater strength of trade unions and socialist movements north of the border. But these left-wing groups have not focused on the greater concentration of capital in Canada as an evil to be constrained. For the Tory-socialist tradition, *bigness* is simply not the problem it is for the libertarian-Whig one.

Tory-socialist sentiments may, however, be reflected in crossnational poll results revealing that Canadians are somewhat less friendly than Americans to private enterprise. From surveys conducted in the early 1980s, Goldfarb Consultants reports that, on a ten-point scale, Americans ranked the importance of a "commitment to the free enterprise system" one point higher (8.0) than Canadians (7.0). In the same period, Wright and Myles asked a battery of four questions evaluating the role of corporations, private ownership, and the profit motive. On average, Canadians were more likely than Americans (62 to 52 percent) to endorse antibusiness statements.

Conclusion

The reduction of the productivity gap between Canada and the United States and the considerable growth in many southern European and east Asian economies, once less developed, suggest either that the cultural explanations of differences in national economies are wrong or that new factors should be entered into the explanations. Essentially, the Weberian approach (to identify a body of analysis by many with one name) seems to help to account for variations in the timing of takeoffs — earliest and fastest in the Protestant, especially the sectarian, areas. But as Weber himself suggested, once economically functional behavior is institutionalized in capitalism and industrialism, it does not require the Protestant ethic or its equivalents to keep going on or to improve. Similarly, as the cultures of capitalism and industrialization diffused, they were absorbed in the non-Protestant countries of Europe as well as in east Asia, where some scholars argue that aspects of the Confucian ethic, comparable to the Protestant one with respect to a this-worldly orientation to work and rationality, helped to give them hospitality.[68]

Developments in Canada are especially intriguing since, as we have seen, it has approached the American level of productivity and wealth more closely than any other society, particularly since the 1970s. Yet, as an abundance of opinion and aggregate savings and insurance data document, the economic cultures continue to differ. Canadians are more prudent than their southern neighbors. This conundrum is difficult to explain. Perhaps caution and savings pay off, much as they have done for the Scottish diaspora in England and overseas. Or perhaps the relevant factor is not differences between national populations but the presence within a less aggressive society of a venturesome minority, large enough to take advantage of economic opportunities.

The role of Jews may be particularly important in Canada. Nine wealthy family groups control a major segment of the shares on the Toronto Stock Exchange; three of them are Jewish, and another is of Jewish background. Two of these four families emigrated to Canada after World War II. Nine of the wealthiest 32 families in Canada have similar religious origins.[69] Given that the American Jewish community is proportionately much larger than the Canadian (approximately 2.5 to 1.0) and that the latter has a more recent immigrant background, Jews have done much better in the north, though roughly one-quarter of the 400 richest families in the United States are Jewish.[70]

Despite the success of Jews (and other immigrant groups) in Canada, there is considerable Canadian literature contending that the country's economic backwardness in the past can be explained by its "dependent" relationship, first to Britain and then to the United States. Foreign investors, the argument goes, sending profits abroad inhibited growth. Most economists, however, would agree with Joseph Schumpeter that economies benefit from investment capital, regardless of its origins. The United States was in Canada's position prior to World War I, when the Republic was the world's largest recipient of foreign capital; a comprehensive historical analysis of such investment by Mira Wilkins concludes that the largely British and German funds and companies played a major role in enabling the country to develop its mines, transportation systems, and manufacturing industries.[71] That story has been repeated in Canada, and may be occurring once more in the United States today.

Meanwhile, Canadians, although much less concerned than Americans with limiting the scope of big business or family wealth through government action, have been much more disposed to call on the state to handle various matters, as the next chapter indicates.

8

Government, Welfare,
and Philanthropy

The crossborder differences in North American values, reflecting the varying organizing principles of the two polities, show up in the disparate roles assigned to government and voluntary initiative in dealing with social issues. North of the border, the Tory orientation and the smaller population relative to land mass have meant a larger number of functions for the state. The United States, set in a classically liberal-Whig mold, stands out among developed countries in the relative lack of involvement of its governments in fields such as ownership of industry, welfare, health care, and urban amenities. If Tory Canada has become, in Robertson Davies' words, a "socialist monarchy," the United States tries to follow Thomas Jefferson's dictum: "That government governs best, which governs least." If one society leans toward communitarianism — the public mobilization of resources to fulfill group objectives — the other sees individualism — private endeavor — as the way an "unseen hand" produces optimum, socially beneficial results. The evidence on this score is abundant and clear.

Government and the Economy

As of the mid-1970s, the proportion of the Canadian gross domestic product (GDP) in government hands was 41 percent, compared to 34 percent in the United States. In 1987, the ratio was 47 to 37 percent. As of 1982, "government spending in Canada [was], in proportionate terms, 24.4 percent greater than in the U.S."[1] Subtracting defense spending — roughly 2 percent of GDP for Canada and 5 to 6 percent for the United States — considerably widens the gap between the two countries.[2] In commenting on the 1989 Canadian budget proposed by the Conservative government, the *Wall Street Journal* editorialized that it "is replete with new taxes of the sort that Ronald Reagan and now George Bush have refused to support." The United States is seeking to cut the welfare state; "in Canada the welfare state by and large still rules."[3] Prime Minister Brian Mulroney has spoken of the welfare provisions as a "sacred trust."

Although both countries have some government-owned industry, the phenomenon is much more common in Canada (it is now declining there somewhat, however, reflecting efforts at privatization by both the federal and provincial governments). J.T. McLeod calls attention to "the frequent appearance of public ownership in Canada," where "the State has always dominated and shaped the economy." Unlike "the United States, [Canada] has never experienced a period of pure unadulterated laissez-faire market capitalism."[4]

Mercer and Goldberg sum up the magnitude of government involvement in the Canadian economy as of 1982:

> Of 400 top industrial firms, 25 were controlled by the federal or provincial governments. Of the top 50 industrialists, all ranked by sales, 7 were either wholly owned or controlled by the federal or provincial governments. For financial institutions, 9 of the top 25 were federally or provincially owned or controlled....Canadian governments at all levels exhibit little reticence about involvement in such diverse enterprises as railroads, airlines, aircraft manufacture, financial institutions, steel companies, oil companies, and selling and producing atomic reactors for energy generation.[5]

Although most European states are more involved in economic activities than Canada is, the latter "does appear to represent a mid-point between the European and American patterns..., both in the provisions of subsidies to the private sector and in the scope of public enterprise." Although below the norm for members of the Organisation for Economic Co-operation and Development (OECD), Canadian subsidies to business and employment in public enterprise were each five times the level of American ones during the 1970s.[6] "In Canada...the natural focus for collective activity has always been government." North of the border, private organization is not "accorded the intrinsic value in and for itself that it receives in the United States...[where] even a badly functioning private marketplace often appears to be definitionally superior to a well-functioning public agency."[7]

Medical Care, Welfare, and Education

The differences between the two countries are particularly striking with respect to the role of government in medical care. They have been well summed up in questions prepared for a Louis Harris crossnational opinion survey. The American system is one in which

> [t]he government pays most of the cost of health care for the elderly, the poor and the disabled. Most others either have health insurance paid for by their employers or have to buy it from an insurance company. Some have no insurance.

Conversely, the Canadian system is one in which

> the government pays most of the cost of health care for everyone out of taxes, and the government sets all fees charged by doctors and hospitals.

Both systems allow people to "choose their own doctors and hospitals."[8]

Canada's approach is widely supported throughout that country. Poll data for 1988 show that an overwhelming 95 percent of Canadians preferred their system to the one in the United States. Most Americans (61 percent) also voiced a preference for the Canadian system over their own when the two were presented to them by interviewers in the terms quoted above. There was much less satisfaction with "the health care services that you and your family have used in the last year" in the United States than in Canada; 35 percent of respondents were "very satisfied" in the south, compared to 67 percent in the north. Still, more than one-third of Americans (37 percent) preferred the more pluralistic system in the United States; only 3 percent of Canadians did so.[9]

In Canada, health care falls constitutionally under the purview of the provinces; thus, the system, though Ottawa funds about half of it through grants, is both legislated and administered provincially.[10] Although there are important variations from province to province in amounts paid to physicians, cost controls, and care priorities, basically the Canadian programs are highly comparable.[11] This holds true for those sponsored by governments that are strongly oriented to free enterprise, such as the Social Credit administration of British Columbia, as well as for those introduced or operated by social democratic (New Democratic Party and Parti Québécois), and Liberal, and Conservative governments. Seemingly, all Canadian politicians from left to right recognize that they cannot upset the commitment to public payment for all medical costs and to state control over the prices paid to physicians and hospitals. Obviously, there is no such consensus in the United States, where the medical profession retains much more bargaining power, even in the publicly financed sectors.

A detailed comparative analysis of the development of the welfare state in both countries by Robert Kudrle and Theodore Marmor concludes that specific welfare policies have generally been adopted earlier in Canada, are "usually...more advanced in terms of program development, coverage and benefits," and "have exhibited a steadier development." In seeking to account for these variations, they stress

> ideological differences....In every policy area it appears that general public as well as elite opinion...[has been] more supportive of state action in Canada than in the United States. This support appears to underlie not just the typically earlier enactment of policy in Canada but also subsequent changes...[in a more elaborate direction].[12]

As detailed by a former Canadian official:

> A remarkable collection of federally-inspired programs was put in place that has had the effect of providing virtually

cradle-to-grave basic protection and opportunity for every Canadian. Canadian federal and provincial governments put in place a *de facto* if not *de jure* guaranteed minimum income which embraced family allowances, a comprehensive social welfare program including widows and persons with disabilities, enriched unemployment insurance benefits, manpower training allowance, a greatly expanded post-secondary education program that covers about three-quarters of the real per student cost, old age pensions as a matter of right and an additional universal contributory pension program, subsidized housing, and a complete hospital-medical protection program.[13]

Similar Canadian-U.S. differences occur in education as well. Unlike the United States, Canada does not have a single large private university. Technically, most Canadian universities — including many of the oldest and best known — have quasi-private ownership. But public revenues supply the major portion of their funding (a large fraction is federal money, passed through the provinces, which have the constitutional responsibility for education at all levels). Operations are also regulated by the provinces. In effect, the closest American parallels are the state universities.

Elite and Public Opinion

Most of the research based on opinion polls, as well as political party programs, documents that Canadians at both the elite and the mass levels — particularly the former — are more supportive of state intervention than Americans. Summarizing surveys of high-level civil servants and federal, state, and provincial legislators taken from 1967 to 1971, Robert Presthus reports:

[T]he sharp difference between the two [national] elites on "economic liberalism," defined as a preference for "big government"....Only 17 percent of the American legislative elite rank high on this disposition, compared with fully 44 percent of their Canadian peers....[T]he direction is the same among bureaucrats, only 17 percent of whom rank high among the American sample, compared with almost 30 percent among Canadians.[14]

Differences related to party affiliation emphasize the cross-national variations. Canadian Liberal legislators scored much higher than American Democrats on economic liberalism; Canadian Conservatives were much higher than American Republicans and even higher than American Democrats.[15] A subsequent comparison of members of Parliament and of Congress, conducted in 1974–75, also found the former "better disposed to the welfare state" by a considerable margin.[16]

A more recent study (1983–84), also based on questionnaire data, compared the attitudes of American (Minnesota and North Dakota) and Canadian (Manitoba, Saskatchewan, and Ontario) legislators; it again reported that Americans were significantly less positive toward government intervention as measured by responses to items related to welfare, economic liberalism, and economic conservatism. The survey also included a number of questions dealing with specific policies and found that "the Canadians are generally more willing than the Americans to support [education] programs by authorizing heavier tax burdens." The former are also more disposed to increase "welfare and unemployment benefits" and to "relax eligibility requirements." As the researcher, Vicki Templin, notes, her policy-related study "substantiates the conclusions reached by the Presthus study" a decade earlier.[17] The Tory-Whig difference still holds up.

In discussing the 1988 elections in Canada and the United States, *The Economist* commented on the same pattern, stressing that the leaders of Canada's three largest parties, the re-elected Conservatives, the Liberals, and the social democratic New Democrats were "all to the left of the American Democratic team, Mr. Michael Dukakis and Mr. Lloyd Bentsen....Most Canadian voters, too, are committed to a quasi-welfare state."[18] Given the consensus on values among the three major parties, election campaigns now help define Canadian identity as social democratic. As the editor of the country's leading political monthly, the social democratic *Canadian Forum* observed, the 1988 election debates "on what Canada was all about" emphasized "social programs,...national standards to offset regional disparities and...[a] willingness to use government power to redress the inequalities of the market place."[19] An observation made by a Canadian commentator in the early 1950s holds even more true for the late 1980s, "at a time when the *laissez-faire* philosophy was prevailing in the rest of the Western World, there was no protest in Canada against government intervention and interference, not even from business circles."[20]

Canadian-U.S. dissimilarities in popular attitudes toward the economic role of government show up strikingly in various crossborder opinion surveys. In their 1968–70 studies of American and English-Canadian attitudes, Arnold and Tigert found that Americans were more opposed than Canadians to big government and less likely to believe that government should guarantee everyone an income.[21] Arnold, writing with James Barnes, interprets these results to mean that "Americans were...individualistic, whereas Canadians were more collectivity oriented."[22]

Other surveys provide further evidence of Canadians' greater propensity to favor a strong role for government. In 1978–79, Roper and CROP asked samples in each country to locate themselves on a seven-point scale running from "government should see to a job and a good standard of living" to the state should "let each person get ahead on his own." As expected, Americans were more likely to choose the individualistic response. Fifty-one percent opted for the three "let each person get ahead" positions, in contrast to 38 percent of their northern neighbors. In 1986, Decima in Canada and Cambridge Research Incorporated (CRI) in the United States asked cross-sections of North Americans to place themselves on an 11-point scale in reaction to the statement, "The best government is the one which governs the least." Canadian respondents were more prone to "totally disagree" (23 percent) and to exhibit any level of disagreement (42 percent) than were Americans (13 and 32 percent, respectively).

Private Efforts

Research by two sociologists, James Curtis and Ronald Lambert, indicates that Canadians also evidence a greater disposition than Americans to believe that government should take responsibility for the needy. They conclude that Canadians should be less "inclined to contribute...to fund appeals."[23] The inference is borne out by comparative materials on charitable gifts in both nations. A study by a Canadian Task Force on Funding Higher Education reports:

> Corporate giving in the United States as a percentage of pre-tax income has been roughly double the level in Canada over the past decade, and is now close to three times the current level in Canada....The different levels of corporate giving...are dramatic enough to suggest that fundamental cultural and attitudinal forces may be at work which by their very nature will permit change in Canadian giving habits to come very slowly. It may well be that the tradition of private support for worthy endeavors is far more deeply imbedded in the American psyche than in the Canadian. We Canadians appear to rely more on government than on voluntary efforts to finance such causes.[24]

The differences are significant on the individual level as well. "In Canada in 1980, individual giving was 7 times total corporate giving. In the United States in the same year, individuals gave approximately 15 times as much to charitable causes as corporations."[25] Surveys of Americans in 1985 by Yankelovich, Skelly, and White and of Canadians in 1987 by Decima also found that Canadians give less per capita than Americans. The Canadian figure for nonreligious causes is C$122, compared to US$180 south of the border. (One Canadian dollar then roughly equaled 80 American cents.)[26]

The willingness of Americans to contribute considerable sums to philanthropic works, reaching heights undreamed of elsewhere, is not only the obverse of the lack of state commitment to supporting community institutions; it is also linked to the interrelationship between voluntary religion and secular behavior discussed in Chapter 5. The emphasis on voluntarism in both religious and secular areas has clearly been mutually reinforcing. Americans are expected to be righteous, hard-working, and ambitious. Righteousness is to be rewarded both in the present and the hereafter, and the successful have an obligation to engage in good works and to share the bounty that they have attained. In a detailed history of American giving for overseas purposes, Merle Curti stresses the role played by "the doctrine of stewardship," the belief that whatever of worldly means one has belongs to God, that the holder is only God's steward and obligated to give to the poor, the distressed, and the needy. From many diaries, letters and other evidence it is clear that this factor was a dominant one in a great deal of giving.[27]

Scholarly students of philanthropy in the United States emphasize that the underlying support for private charity is sustained by American "individualistic philosophy and suspicion of government control."[28] Some indication of the past strength of these values can be seen in the American Red Cross's rejection, in January 1931, of a proposed federal appropriation of US$25 million for the relief of drought victims. The chairman of the central committee told Congress, "All we pray for is that you let us alone and let us do the job."[29] As recently as 1962, at a time when support for federal support for the arts was growing, only 5 percent of the major symphony organizations that were members of the American Symphony Orchestra League responded favorably to a League survey about federal government support of the arts; almost half took a middle-ground position, and 21 percent were opposed. As a student of the symphony notes, "Imbued with a deep suspicion of government in all its activities, and taking a certain pride in his own independence and enterprise, the American patron of the arts bitterly opposed government subsidy" until recently.[30]

In spite of the growth of the welfare and planning state, these values are not dead, not even on the left of American politics. As noted in Chapter 2, in 1971 the National Taxpayers Union, a group whose board included three then-major New Left figures and a number of conservative free-enterprise thinkers, advocated sharp cuts in the welfare responsibilities of government and changes in tax policy to encourage contributions by the wealthy.[31] The fact that some of America's leading left-wing radicals could have made such a proposal in the early 1970s attests to the continued vitality of antistatist individualism.

The tradition of private philanthropy has a long history in the United States. The Protestant ethic and the liberal emphasis on individualism and achievement combined to foster the emergence of an upper class that took its communal responsibilities seriously. As early as 1807, members of the Boston elite stated in the founding documents of the Boston Athenaeum that, in their city,

> [T]he class of persons enjoying easy circumstances, and possessing surplus wealth, is comparatively numerous. As we are not called upon for large contributions to national purposes, we shall do well to take advantage of the exemption, by taxing ourselves for those institutions, which will be attended with lasting and extensive benefit, amidst all changes of our public fortunes and political affairs.[32]

Martin Green, who called attention to this remarkable statement, notes that

> Boston merchants, and to some extent the bankers and industrialists who succeeded them, had the idea that commerce should go hand in hand with philanthropy, and even culture, and should give way to them as soon as the individual had secured himself an adequate sum.[33]

In the 19th century, they demonstrated the vitality of this sense of responsibility by their support for libraries, the symphony, the Perkins Institute for the Blind, the Lowell Institute, Harvard, and the beginnings of a complex of hospitals that remains at the summit of medical care in America today. The altruistic sentiments voiced by the founders of the Athenaeum were, of course, not the only reasons motivating major contributions by the wealthy. In a fundraising letter for Harvard in 1886, Henry Lee Higginson, a leading Boston Brahmin, stated some other goals: to "educate, and save ourselves and our families and our money from mobs."[34] James Buchanan Duke, the founder of the Duke Endowment, explained his concern for the expansion of health facilities in the 1920s by saying in a newspaper interview, "People ought to be healthy. If they ain't healthy they can't work, and if they don't work they ain't healthy. And if they can't work there ain't no profit in them."[35]

Despite the clear elements of self-interest in the philanthropy of the American Protestant wealthy, they did exhibit levels of generosity unmatched by the rich in other nations. John D. Rockefeller, who gave away more in his lifetime than any other individual, was frequently attacked, with good reason, for making his contributions for public relations and political purposes, for seeking to clean the image of "tainted money." Yet it must also be noted that, from the time he was a teenager on, he regularly gave a tenth of his earnings to charity. He was a devout Baptist who "apparently felt there was some divine cooperation in the construction of Standard Oil Company." In the words of one student of philanthropy,

> "God gave me my money," he told an interviewer in 1915. After financing establishment of the University of Chicago, Rockefeller told a campus meeting: "The good Lord gave me the money, and how could I withhold it from Chicago?" In his later years, Rockefeller mused, his wealth was an "accident of history," possible only because of the peculiar circumstances of oil and the nineteenth century, and that he was only its trustee.[36]

At the mass level, the continued linkage of voluntary religion to voluntary charity in the United States may be seen in the fact that "72 percent of all individual giving went to religious institutions" in 1985.[37] Education and health (including hospitals) were next, but far behind on the list. One study found that "the ratio of gifts to religious organizations to discretionary receipts was remarkably constant over all the income levels."[38]

The Great Depression of the 1930s, of course, brought about a fundamental change in the role of philanthropy. The state increasingly took over responsibility for welfare functions, for hospitals, for higher education, and for many other activities. Private contributions have continued to increase in absolute size, particularly since World War II, but they have become a smaller proportion of the whole, especially in nonreligious spheres.

The sources of private donations have also changed. Corporations have replaced wealthy individuals as the large contributors. Corporate gifts have come to be recognized as excellent forms of public relations. One student of philanthropy, Aileen Ross, contends:

> [T]he rise in the contributions of corporations has enabled them to take over the control of raising and allotting money to many philanthropic agencies. Management can determine the amount that will be given, and since the same men are often found on the board of a number of the larger corpora-

tions, they have come to form an "inner circle" which can control both the gifts that are given and the selection of the top executives in the philanthropic agencies and in the more important and prestigious fund-raising campaigns, such as those for hospitals and universities.[39]

It is still true, of course, that more than four-fifths of contributions continue to come from individuals. As noted, most gifts from small donors go to religious-related causes. "Education, mainly colleges and universities, is getting the largest share of corporation giving, followed closely by health and welfare agencies."[40]

In brief, the historic sources of support for voluntary activity in America still have vitality. "Each year for more than a quarter century after 1960 recorders of American philanthropy reported that total giving...had reached new highs."[41] The amount for 1987 — approximately $94 billion — was more than two and a half times as large as that a decade earlier and more than 11 times the funds raised in 1955. The sum amounted to 2.09 percent of the gross national product.[42] Canadians, conversely, are "giving thirty percent *less* to charity than they did twenty years ago."[43]

Even more impressive on the U.S. side are survey findings for 1985 and 1987 that "about 48 percent of the U.S. population volunteered some part of their time to gift-supported organizations....The estimated number of full and part-time volunteers amounted to more than 117 million,"[44] most of them presumably church-related. The numbers come close to equalling those for participation in the 1988 presidential election and are far greater than for voters in congressional, state, or municipal contests — facts that give food for thought. Even though U.S. governments now provide more fully for many activities, including the arts, once almost totally dependent on private support, the country's people, the most antistatist in the developed world, continue to be the most generous on a personal basis.[45]

Voluntary Activities: Some Controversy

In earlier publications, I generalized beyond philanthropy to argue that the more individualistic emphasis of Americans makes them "more likely to take part in voluntary activity to achieve particular goals," while Canadians are less prone to do because of their greater disposition "to rely on the state."[46] A group of four Canadian sociologists, though generally accepting of my comparative distinctions, conclude that I am empirically wrong in this case and refer to some crossborder surveys.[47] In going over the available data, I located seven sets of binational polls, taken between 1960 and 1985, that permit ten comparisons of voluntary activity. In most of the contrasts, Americans show up more active by eight to two. Considering only differences of 3 percent or more puts the United States ahead in six of the comparisons and Canadians in one; in four, the results are basically the same on either side of the border. Francophones are the least participatory in each case.

Considering these studies raises various methodological issues of response reliability, different question wordings, and differences in the timing of different surveys. As a result, I conclude that "the tentative verdict in this case must be the Scottish one, not proven." I also note, however, that, as Paul Lazarsfeld has emphasized, consistent quantitative — though very small — differences that coincide with theoretical expectations are more significant than an unanticipated large one.[48]

Contextual Effects

The results of one recent crossborder opinion survey, that of Wright and Myles taken in the early 1980s, seems to contradict the generalizations about the relative crossborder preferences for public welfare programs. The data indicate that Americans are more disposed than Canadians to favor increased spending for government social services, by 70 to 65 percent. Given that the level of such services is higher north of the border, it may be that these national differences reflect the fact Americans, having less, want more — for example, state-financed medical care, as the polls indicate — while Canadians, who have a more extensive welfare state, feel less impelled than their neighbors to ask their governments to do more.

Dissimilarities in national contexts can undermine reliance on responses to the same policy questions.[49] In any case, it must be reiterated that the responses to a single question can not be considered definitive, and that a large number of comparative findings indicate that Americans are less approving than others of welfare services. A comprehensive analysis of attitudes toward the welfare state over the past 20 years — mainly in the OECD countries, including Canada — reports that "the United States is consistently at the bottom in its support for different kinds of social welfare benefits." The one issue "on which Americans fare much better — and often the best — compared with other nations...[is] educational opportunity, assistance and spending." And as the authors, Robert Shapiro and John Young, note, these attitudes stem "from Americans' views and values concerning individualism and the equality of opportunity, as opposed to equality of outcomes for individuals."[50]

Tories and Socialists

To reiterate a key point, there is good reason to believe that social democratic movements are the other side of statist conservatism; Tories and socialists are likely to be found in the same polity, while a dominant Lockean liberal tradition inhibits the emergence of socialism.[51] Given this view, the existence of an electorally viable social democratic party, the New Democratic Party, in Canada can be seen as an outgrowth of the Tory-statist tradition and the relatively strong collectivity orientation north of the 49th parallel. And the absence of a significant socialist movement in the United States is evidence of the vitality of the antistatist and individualist values there.

The thesis that a Tory-statist tradition is conducive to the emergence of socialist movements has, however, been criticized on the grounds that such parties have been weakest in the most traditional parts of Canada: Quebec and the Atlantic provinces.[52] Answering this line of argument, William Christian and Colin Campbell suggest that the emergence in the 1960s and 1970s of a social democratic movement in Quebec — the nationalist Parti Québécois, which applied for membership in the Socialist International — reflects the propensity for the collectivism inherent in Canadian elitist values to appear in leftist form after the bulwarks of the traditional system break down. They conclude — correctly, I believe — that the development of socialist strength

> in Quebec in reaction to the incursions of liberalism and capitalism is hardly surprising...for...Quebec's stock of political ideas includes a strong collectivist element. This collectivism is deeply imbedded in Quebec's institutions: from the earliest days of New France, the government actively intervened on a broad scale in economic affairs....Quebec's collectivist past provided receptive and fruitful soil for socialist ideas once the invasion of liberal capitalism had broken the monopoly of the old conservative ideology.[53]

The continued weakness of socialist movements in the Atlantic region, the poorest and most traditional section of Canada, appears to contradict the Tory-influence hypothesis, even if these four provinces contain only 9 percent of the country's population. Their greater adherence to custom, including strong deferential and patrimonial elements, may account for their holding back. The two old parties appear to have maintained strong ties to the more impoverished electorates, ties based on personalistic relations and patronage. Moreover, these provinces' heavy dependence on government expenditures and regional transfer payments seemingly limits their freedom to move beyond the major parties, which have thus far been the only viable contenders for national office.

Evidence that the forces making for class consciousness and organization are more powerful in Canada than in the United States does appear in statistics on trade union membership. Workers in the northern country are much more heavily involved in unions than those in the south. Since the mid-1950s, union membership in the United States has been steadily declining, down to less than one-sixth of the nonagricultural labor force, while it has grown from one-quarter to close to two-fifths in Canada.

Some of the sources of these variations will be discussed in the next chapter. It can be suggested here, however, that the long postwar prosperity refurbished the antistatist and individualistic values of the United States, while in Canada economic growth in the context of the silent and postindustrial revolutions in the two linguistic areas did not challenge traditional class and collectivity orientations. From a consideration of the role of the state with respect to economic and welfare policies, it seems appropriate to turn to aspects of stratification.

9

Social Stratification, Trade Unions, and Politics

Much of the comparative discussion of North America refers implicitly, if not explicitly, to variations in stratification: hierarchy, inequality, and patterns of class sentiments. Canada began as a nation whose political and religious elites believed in an organic hierarchical society in which inferiors showed deference to their superiors. The new United States, though also a hierarchical society with slavery and indentured service, had waged its revolution partially under the banner of equality. It explicitly rejected monarchical rule and ascriptive aristocratic titles.

Respect for Status

Critical analyses of egalitarian populist democracy have continued to be voiced by Canadians, usually in the context of pointing to positive features of their society. But in recent times, similar arguments have been made by Canadian leftists, who see political repression as endemic in populism. The historian Kenneth McNaught, one of Canada's leading socialist intellectuals and the biographer of its socialist hero, J.S. Woodsworth, has emphasized over the years the positive consequences of monarchy and aristocratic elitism for liberty and radicalism. As he puts it: "Canadians are suspicious of American disrespect for authority...and insistence upon conformity to the prevailing conception of 'Americanism.'" Events in North America have "periodically re-confirmed the Canadian belief that 'freedom wears a crown.'"[1]

In discussing why the United States lacks a socialist movement and strong radical dissent, McNaught points to the absence of an upper-class "tradition of eccentricity," of a history of elitist nonconformity, such as is found in monarchical and other deferential cultures. Basically, he reiterates, as have other Canadian intellectuals, Tocqueville's analysis of the "tyranny of the multitude," emphasizing the extent to which an egalitarian society produces "other-directed" individuals concerned with what is thought of them, in contrast to the greater willingness to stand up against the multitude that is produced in a society that gives more respect and deference to high status.[2]

The underlying generalization that Canadian society remains more elitist, more respectful of status and authority, than the American is reiterated by many social scientists. Reviewing the research evidence on the subject, two of them report:

> Canadians are much more tolerant of ruling elites and oligarchy than Americans. This...social system is a logical concomitant of the other facets of the Canadian character, for which deferential and collective behaviors were seen to be more widespread than in the United States.[3]

Data bearing on the hypothesis that Canada is more elitist than the United States are reported on in four academic studies based on interview materials: one concerning national variations in value orientations, two dealing with occupational prestige, and a fourth looking at views about child-rearing practices.[4] Surveys taken in two communities situated on different sides of the border found that Americans scored lower than Canadians on an elite-orientation scale and higher on achievement values. The variations held up among age groups.[5]

Canadian evaluations of the prestige of upper-middle-class occupations turn out to be higher on the average than those in the United States, according to the results of two parallel cross-national surveys. "The tendency in Canada to rank jobs higher is greatest for the professional and semi-professional categories...where on the average the jobs are ranked about four points higher than in the U.S." Two sociologists, Peter Pineo and

John Porter, interpret this result as reflecting "a deferential element in the Canadian rankings derived from the elitist
pattern...[which is important] in Canadian society."[6]

A more recent analysis of occupational-prestige rankings in
both countries yields similar results. The comparison provides
"support, albeit of a serendipitous nature, for [the]...argument
that in the United States less emphasis is placed on hierarchical
patterns of deference." The findings indicate "stronger class
hegemony in Canada"; its privileged classes appear to have more
influence than their American compeers on judgments of the
worth of occupations.[7]

Research on child-rearing values in comparative perspective
produces further evidence "that Canadians may be more 'elitist'
than Americans." Dissimilarities across class lines are more
pronounced among Canadians, Francophone and Anglophone,
than among Americans.[8]

The assumption that Canadians are more deferential to
those on top than their neighbors implies a greater degree of class
consciousness. The most recent crossnational study (by Wright
and Myles) of the ways the citizens of the two countries perceive
classes indicates that Canadians are somewhat more class-aware
and more disposed than Americans to identify themselves as
working class. My own analysis of these early 1980s national surveys provides the limited evidence. Forty-eight percent of
Canadians, but 42 percent of Americans, said that they think of
themselves as "belonging to a particular social class." Respondents who replied they were in a class were then asked to choose
among a number of categories. More than three times as many
Canadians (28 percent) as Americans (9 percent) chose "working
class," or "poor." Those who denied class membership were asked
to place themselves among a slightly different set of alternatives.
Combining both groups of respondents reveals 35 percent of
Canadians as working-class identifiers, in contrast to 27 percent
of Americans.

Canadians living in the predominantly Anglophone provinces were much more likely to place themselves in the working
class than those living in Quebec. Among the class-aware, the
differences were 30 to 24 percent; among those forced to choose,
they were 41 to 23.[9] I know of no hypothesis that suggests a

reason for a variation of this magnitude, other than (possibly, but dubiously) the fact that industrialization occurred earlier and more extensively in Ontario than in Quebec and that socialism emerged later in French Canada than in English Canada.

Earlier studies of class identification reveal mixed results, pointing up a repeated difficulty in poll data reported in this work. As noted earlier, crossnational surveys gather data in varying contexts and often use different question-wordings in dealing with the same subject. Given the structural similarities between Canada and the United States — occupations, urbanization, dominant language, and so on — one should not expect large differences between the two countries. But varying methods help produce inconsistent results. In four Canadian surveys taken between 1965 and 1974, respondents identifying themselves as working class ranged from 30 to 45 percent.[10] The range in American surveys conducted from 1956 to 1974 was 36 to 60 percent.[11] A comprehensive methodological analysis of the different questions and results in both countries suggests that the American survey with the highest findings includes the term "working-class" in the preamble to the question "in such strong form as to constitute almost a loaded question," producing a sizable bias in favor of choosing that option, one on the order of 15 percent.[12] Given the varying question-wordings among cross-border surveys, except for the Wright-Myles one, it is impossible to come up with a reliable judgment as to which country has more class-awareness and working-class consciousness. I can only note again that the Wright-Myles sampling, the most systematically comparative study which is also the most current, gives the edge to Canada. The 1979 *Survey of Social Change in Canada* found an even higher proportion of working-class identifiers — 50 percent.[13] Thus, two bases for comparison taken during the 1979–83 period indicate more class-awareness and working-class consciousness in Canada than in the United States.

Elitism and Equalitarianism

The two key terms used here to differentiate stratification values are "elitism" and "equalitarianism." As I defined these words in earlier work, they referred to the distinction between values emphasizing that

> all persons must be given respect simply because they are human beings, [and]...the general superiority of those who hold positions of power and privilege. In an equalitarian society, the differences between low status and high status people are not stressed in social relationships and do not convey to the high status person a general claim to social deference. In contrast, in an elitist society, those who hold high positions in any structure, whether it be in business, in intellectual activities or in government, are thought to deserve, and are actually given, general respect and deference.[14]

"Equalitarianism," however, has many meanings, not all of which are incompatible with elitism. Conceptualized as "equality of result," it enters into the political arena in efforts to reduce inequality on a group level. And it can be argued that Tory stimuli, elitist in origin, produce social democratic responses — in particular, efforts to protect and upgrade the position of less privileged strata, initially legitimated by communitarian or noblesse-oblige values.

That Canadians are committed to redistributive egalitarianism, while Americans place more emphasis on meritocratic competition and equality of opportunity, can be seen in a variety of survey results. The findings of recent crossnational polls point to consistent differences between the two countries. Reporting on a survey of attitudes of college and university students in both countries, Milton Rokeach says "more American undergraduates were achievement and competence-oriented" while Canadians "were more for equality...than their American counterparts."[15] In the fall of 1979, a Japanese research group asked national samples in the two countries to choose between the two values in an indirect fashion:

> Here are two options about conditions existing in our country. Which do you happen to agree with?
>
> A. There is too much emphasis upon the principle of equality. People should be given the opportunity to choose their own economic and social life according to their individual abilities.

B. Too much liberalism has been producing increasingly wide differences in peoples' economic and social life. People
should live more equally.[16]

Forty-one percent of the Canadians and 32 percent of the
Americans chose the more egalitarian and collectivity-oriented
option B. These findings indicate that Canadians have a higher
regard for equality of result, while Americans are more achievement-oriented.[17]

The CARA-Gallup value studies put the same issue in a different way:

There are two secretaries, of the same age, doing practically
the same job. One of the secretaries finds out that the other
one earns $20 per week more than she does. She complains
to her boss. He says, quite rightly, that the other secretary is
quicker, more efficient, and more reliable at her job. In your
opinion, is it fair or not fair that one secretary is paid more
than the other?

This question is clearly — and intentionally — biased in favor
of obtaining the reply that the more productive secretary should
be paid more, and large majorities on both sides of the border
responded this way. It is interesting to note, however, that almost
twice the proportion of Francophone Canadians (32 percent) as
Americans (17 percent) said it was unfair to pay the more efficient
worker a higher rate; as was usually the case in this study,
Anglophone Canadians fell in the middle (23 percent).

The same studies found that the three North American
groups chose as expected between classic statements of the conflict between liberty and equality. Respondents were asked:

Which of these two statements comes closest to your own
opinion?

A. I find that both freedom and equality are important
but if I were to make up my mind for one or the other, I would
consider personal freedom more important, that is, everyone
can live in freedom and develop without hindrance.

B. Certainly both freedom and equality are important,
but if I were to make up my mind for one of the two, I would
consider equality more important, that is, that nobody is un-

derprivileged and that social class differences are not so
strong.

Most respondents in both countries opted for freedom over
equality, but Americans led in this preference. Seventy-two percent agreed with the first statement, compared to 64 percent of
English Canadians and 57 percent of French Canadians. Conversely, 38 percent of Francophone Canadians, 29 percent of
Anglophone Canadians, and only 20 percent of Americans said
that emphasis on the reduction of class differences is more important than freedom.

Education and Mobility

In interpreting the role of education in the class structures
of Canada and the United States, analysts often use a distinction
introduced by American sociologist Ralph Turner to explain
British and American differences. Turner says that Britain has
followed a "sponsored mobility model" — that students have been
sponsored or supported in higher educational aspirations by the
class system; higher education has been geared for a relatively
small minority, inherently from privileged backgrounds. In the
United States, a much greater emphasis has been placed on a
"contest model" — on making it possible for all, or at least a much
larger proportion than in Britain, to move up first through
elementary school, then through an expanded high school system, and finally into mass higher education.[18] As noted earlier,
the United States has led the western world in the proportions at
each level as educational opportunities have grown.

Canada, both English and French, began with a version of
the sponsored system, one oriented to classical education and
preparation for a handful of universities. Educational attainments were much more class-stratified than in the United States.
Two Canadian sociologists of education describe the crossborder
differences in the pre-World War II era:

> The Canadian system fell midway between the British spon-
> sored model and the American contest model. Class bias was
> less open than in England, more covert than in the United

States. It was nevertheless very real. The religious and ethnic basis of so much strife over such a long period effectively hid much of the class discrimination. The ideology of equality of opportunity never attained the credibility in Canada which it enjoyed in the United States, but Canadians tended to be more aware of ethnic rather than social class differences.[19]

Conceptualizing equalitarianism as meritocracy leads to the expectation that nations that rank high in valuing achievement or equality of opportunity will be less concerned with reducing inequality of condition. If the United States is more achievement-oriented and less elitist than Canada, then it should place more emphasis on educational equality as the primary mechanism for moving into the higher socioeconomic positions, and so it does. Canada should be more engaged in redistributive policies, thus upgrading the lower strata, as in fact it is. Both survey and aggregate national data indicate that

> Canada has retained a greater degree of educational inequality in the twentieth century than the U.S....The 35.5 percent of Canadians born 1947–1951 who completed nine through eleven years [of schooling] is more than two and one-half times the proportion of U.S. white males who failed to complete twelve years of schooling.[20]

The comparative literature of the 1950s called attention to the more elitist character of the Canadian system and to the fact that in Canada, as in Britain, education was more humanistic and less vocational and professional.[21] Subsequent survey data showed that these differences corresponded to public attitudes to education.[22]

Scholars of speech and literature also note that, until recently, Canada's educational system, like its other prestige institutions, rejected the American pattern of modifying approved language styles in the direction of popular speech. One linguist argues that the "part of Canadian education...which concerns itself with syntax, grammar and spelling has...been based almost exclusively on British models."[23] Another seconds that conclusion, noting that through "the deliberate policies of its

educational institutions and through the example of the CBC
[Canadian Broadcasting Corporation], Canada has long resisted
standardizing 'prestige' forms of speech in the direction of the language of the masses."[24]

During the past two decades, the number of people participating in higher education has increased greatly in both North
American societies, but there is still a considerable gap between
them. As of 1984, the proportion of the relevant Canadian age
cohort in all postsecondary education had risen to 44 percent,
but the comparable American figure had increased to 57 percent.[25] The American lead is greater when the comparison is
made in terms of full-time students in colleges and universities:
14.5 percent of 18–24 year-olds were enrolled in Canada and 22
percent in the United States as of 1985.[26] That the differences
are at least partially rooted in values is suggested by the findings
of the 1982–83 crossnational poll conducted by Goldfarb Consultants. Respondents were asked to rank the "importance of
obtaining a college education" on a scale of one to ten. The average
American placed a higher emphasis on it than did the average
Canadians, by almost one scale rank (7.9 to 7.1).

Variations in the proportion of people attending university
do not appear to affect rates of mass social mobility, movement
between the working and middle classes, or proportions of man-
ual and nonmanual occupations. A large number of studies of
such patterns emphasize similarity more than difference among
industrialized countries.[27] Comparisons between Canada and
the United States reiterate the point of little variation.[28]

The same conclusion does not hold for the origins of the more
privileged strata. Since higher education in the United States
remains more extensive than in Canada, students in the north
are still more likely to come from advantaged backgrounds than
those in the south. This in part explains the findings that the
American elites are more open than the Canadian to those of less
privileged position. It should also be recalled that there is a
greater concentration of wealth in Canada than in America, a
phenomenon that should reinforce the impact of the varying dis-
tributions in university education.

Two methodologically comprehensive efforts to compare the
sources of educational and occupational aspirations in the two

countries suggest a further dimension to the analysis: the effects of national value differences on class-relevant behavior. After noting that the research literature, as of the 1970s, indicated that "Canada is more elitist, ascriptively oriented and particularistic than the United States," the Canadian educational sociologist Sid Gilbert systematically compared the paths leading to the achievement aspirations of high school seniors in Wisconsin and Ontario. He found that socioeconomic status — family class background — plays "a greater role in determining the formation of educational and occupational aspirations of high school students in Canada than in the U.S.A." He concludes that in "the more stratified society, Canada, the family to a greater extent serves as a mechanism of status transmission."[29]

The second study reached similar conclusions in analyzing the large-scale national mobility research conducted in 1973 with samples of 33,600 in the United States and 45,000 in Canada. Richard Wanner found that parental socioeconomic status "is a more potent determinant of the likelihood of extending schooling beyond high school, particularly to university" in Canada than in America.[30]

Some analysts of change in Canadian universities refer to it as "Americanization."[31] Canada has not only sharply increased the number of universities and places for students; its institutions of higher education have also incorporated practical and vocationally relevant subjects, expanded their social sciences and graduate programs, and placed greater emphasis on faculty scholarship. As Claude Bissell, former president of the University of Toronto, emphasizes, his country has been moving away from an elitist conception of higher education.

> By endorsing a policy of open accessibility and the concept of the social value of new knowledge, Canada was, one might say, at long last accepting in its educational practices some of the concepts implicit in the American Revolution....
>
> [It was giving up] the conservative, antirevolutionary concepts that had dominated higher education in Canada — the bias to languages and philosophy, the emphasis on thoroughness in the undergraduate degree, and the untroubled merger of the religious and the secular.[32]

Yet, it must be reported that "Canada's support for university research is on a per capita basis among the lowest in the major OECD [Organisation for Economic Co-operation and Development] countries"; it was less in 1988 than in 1970, while America was at the top of the OECD list. Canada generally lacks the research-intensive universities and major research institutes that are scattered around the United States. The country's history and culture make it highly unlikely that private institutions will ever play a major role, while its governmental funding agencies find it politically difficult to make "the institutional arrangements that could create critical masses of talented scientists" or other scholars.[33]

Canadian cultural elitism still exists, of course, and shows up in the findings that it resembles Britain in recruiting its business and political administrative elites disproportionately from those without a professional or technical education. As Charles McMillan reports, "Canadian managers tend to be less well educated than their counterparts in any other industrialized country with the possible exception of Britain."[34] High-level Canadian bureaucrats also differ from those in the United States in being more likely to have a generalist, rather than a bureaucratic specialist, background. They "rarely view their career choice as a vocation," receiving promotion as they "move from ministry to ministry."[35] Not surprisingly, the proportion of university graduates receiving degrees in business and management is much greater south of the border than to the north, although the ratio, but not the absolute difference, is slowly declining: it was 14 to 5 percent in 1970–71 and reduced to 24 to 13 percent by 1983.[36] As of the latter year, Canada had fewer people per 10,000 participants in the labor force who had received bachelor's and advanced degrees in the natural sciences and engineering (12.7 and 2.3, respectively) than did Britain (13.8 and 3.5) or the United States (17.0 and 4.6).[37]

These results are reiterated in studies of business leaders, which find that Canadians not only have less specialized education than Americans but are also much more likely to have a privileged social background. As Wallace Clement reports: "[E]ntrance to the economic elite is easier for persons from outside the upper class in the United States than in Canada....[T]he

U.S. elite is more open, recruiting from a much broader class base than is the case in Canada." As of the mid-1970s, 61 percent of top Canadian executives were of upper-class origin, in comparison to 36 percent of American executives.[38]

Variations among top civil servants are reported in studies undertaken during the late 1960s and 1970s.[39] Both analyses find a much higher proportion of Canadian than of American bureaucrats with privileged class origins. Presthus explains the phenomenon "both in industry and government" as reflecting

> strong traces of the "generalist," amateur approach to administration. The Canadian higher civil service is patterned...after the British administrative class, which even today tends to symbolize traditional and charismatic bases of authority. Technical aspects of government programmes tend to be de-emphasized, while policy-making and the amateur-classicist syndrome are magnified.[40]

Campbell reports more American than Canadian civil service executives with some "type of expertise," such as "legal and analytical skills." Fewer than half (46 percent) of the Canadians "attribute importance to experience in government" as a background for jobs such as theirs, while a huge majority (85 percent) of the Americans do so. Only 29 percent of the former, in comparison to 68 percent of the latter, "cite academic training" as important.[41] The size of these crossnational differences reflects the fact that these attitudes appear rooted in the diverse practices of institutions. They are not like the opinion poll results reported earlier, which are from comparable mass publics in each country and hence generally do not differ as much.

Like many other Canadian institutions, the civil service is changing. A late 1970s survey of bureaucrats in central government agencies found that in "the past decade Canada has seen a remarkable influx of bureaucrats representing segments of the population traditionally excluded from senior positions in the public service"; many of those interviewed had "experienced rapid upward mobility."[42] These developments may reflect a decrease in educational inheritance in Canada as the system of higher education has expanded.[43]

Trade Unions and Socialist Parties

These findings about varying attitudes toward stratification and elite behavior are relevant to the crossnational differences in the strength of trade unions and the presence or absence of electorally viable socialist or social democratic parties noted earlier. Although Canada falls behind much of Europe on both items, its union movement has encompassed a significantly larger proportion of the nonagricultural labor force than has the American movement for most of the years from 1918 to the present.[44] And since 1921, class-oriented or social democratic third parties have had significant electoral strength in federal and a number of provincial elections.

The United States

Of particular interest is the growth of union density in the United States from the mid-1930s to the mid-1950s, which temporarily placed the American labor movement ahead of the Canadian in proportion of the labor force involved. The same period also witnessed a change in the political and ideological behavior of much of organized labor. The American movement became deeply involved in political action, largely in support of the Democratic Party, while the CIO (Congress of Industrial Organizations) and sections of the AFL (American Federation of Labor) adopted political programs calling for a high level of state involvement in planning the economy and sharp increases in welfare and health programs, in contradiction to the AFL's historic antistatist-syndicalist position. Social democratic factions were able to win control of the Democratic Party in a number of states, and two statewide leftist third parties, the Progressives in Wisconsin and the Farmer-Laborites in Minnesota, captured their state governments.[45]

These changes reflected, of course, the impact of the Great Depression. That unprecedented event undermined traditional American beliefs among large sectors of the population and led to a majority acceptance of the need for state action to reduce unemployment and assist those hurt by the economic collapse. As

Richard Hofstadter notes, the Depression introduced "a social democratic tinge" to American party politics that had never been present before.[46]

Analyses of contemporary public opinion polls and election results found that class factors had become highly differentiating variables. Samuel Lubell, who conducted in-depth interviews of many voters, concluded that the electoral support for President Franklin D. Roosevelt and his New Deal programs constituted

> a class-conscious vote for the first time in American history....The New Deal appears to have accomplished what the Socialists, the I.W.W. [Industrial Workers of the World] and the Communists never could approach. It has drawn a class line across the face of American politics.[47]

Moreover, a clearly identifiable class-based division in attitudes emerged in the opinion polls. The less-affluent strata, measured by both socioeconomic status and occupation, perceived redistributionist policies, government ownership, and welfare programs much more favorably than did the well-to-do.

The "social democratic tinge" declined under the impetus of the postwar economic miracle, which, despite the business cycle and occasional recessions, produced a steadily growing economy greater in terms of job creation than that in other societies given more recognition for their achievements. From 1973 to 1987, 30 million jobs were added in the United States, while the western European countries actually experienced a small decline.[48] Most of the latter also had much higher rates of unemployment than the United States, where the first seven years of the 1980s saw "the creation of hundreds of thousands of new businesses and 14 million new jobs, far and away the best performance among the advanced countries."[49] Although some people contend that the great majority of the new positions in this decade are low paying, this argument has been challenged by U.S. Bureau of Labor Statistics economists, who report, "More than half...were in occupations — such as managerial/professional, and craft and repair — where the average pay is $22,000 or more."[50]

That the postwar resurgence gave Americans renewed faith in the promise of their country as an open, meritocratic society is evidenced by federal election results (seven Republican victories in the ten presidential elections held from 1952 on) and the findings of opinion polls. Support for nationalization of various industries and socialism declined steeply. A 1975 Cambridge Research Incorporated (CRI) poll asked:

> Some people have proposed nationalization — or government takeover — of particular industries which they feel have too much influence over U.S. life and should be controlled. Would you favor or oppose government takeover of any of the following eight major industries?

In every case, decisive majorities were opposed. Similar results to related questions have been reported by a number of pollsters. Harris repeatedly found in the 1970s and 1980s that only one-tenth of respondents favored "the federal government taking over the running of most *big* businesses in this country."[51]

The electoral strength of socialist parties in the United States has been less than 1 percent in every presidential election held since World War II. This pattern is reflected in opinion polls inquiring about attitudes toward socialism. A 1942 Roper poll had found that 25 percent of the U.S. population felt that "some form of socialism would be a good thing"; in 1976 and 1981, less than half this proportion (10 and 12 percent respectively) told pollsters they would "favor...introducing socialism in the U.S." Almost everyone (90 percent of respondents) reacted positively to "free enterprise."[52] Given the evidence of the restoration of faith in traditional American values, it is understandable that support for and membership in trade unions have also fallen considerably.

Canada

In Canada, the effects of the Great Depression and the subsequent postwar economic growth have been quite different. In the first half of the 1930s, Canadians formed a vigorous social democratic party, the Co-operative Commonwealth Federation (CCF). In its reorganized format as the New Democratic Party (NDP), it has, on occasion, won first or second place in all provincial elections west of Quebec, it has taken enough seats in the federal Parliament to be an effective third party, and it began to rival the two old major parties in national opinion polls taken in the mid-1980s (although it only secured a fifth of the vote in the 1988 federal election).

As noted, many analysts explain the upswing of both union and social democratic strength in Canada as an outgrowth of the Tory-statist tradition and the continued strength of the collectivity orientation.[53] Thus, the British labor economist Henry Phelps Brown points out:

> [T]he strong tradition of Toryism in Canada laid its stress on solidarity and against individualism and the fissiparous impact of market forces. Here it found common ground with socialism and, implicitly, with the propensity of the worker to organize for the protection of the conditions of his working life.[54]

Or, as the Canadian historian Gad Horowitz puts it:

> [S]ince Toryism is strongly present in the [Canadian] political culture, at least part of the leftist reaction *against* it will be expressed in its own terms: that is, in terms of class interests and the good of the community as an organic entity (socialism) rather than in terms of the individual and his vicissitudes in the competitive struggle (liberalism), as in the United States.[55]

Many Canadian trade unions, especially those founded in the late 19th and early 20th centuries, began as affiliates of unions headquartered in the United States, and about 40 percent of Canadian union members still belong to these international unions. Affiliates in the two countries, not to mention Canada's own national unions, have, however, varied in ways that reflect the diverse national traditions.[56] Before the 1930s, the leaders of American workers, both moderate (the AFL) and radical (the IWW), opposed forming a separate labor or socialist party. As noted in Chapter 2, the first was syndicalist, the latter anarcho-syndicalist: in good American tradition, both viewed the state as enemy. In contrast, the officials of Canadian labor, though not formally socialists, repeatedly endorsed the principle of independent labor political action from the turn of the century on and were much more favorable to state intervention than their counterparts to the south. As Horowitz notes:

> The TLC [Trades and Labour Congress], though it consisted almost entirely of Canadian locals of AFL unions and was greatly influenced by Gompers, never adopted the Gompers approach *in toto*....[Unlike the AFL] the TLC...never took a stand *against* socialism. Unlike the AFL, it never adopted the phraseology of *laissez-faire* and Lockean individualism.[57]

During the 1930s, many union activists took part in the formation of the CCF. The relationship became stronger over the years. A poll of labor leaders in 1958 revealed that 45 percent of the TLC (AFL) officials surveyed supported the CCF, as did an overwhelming 93 percent of the executives of the Canadian Congress of Labour (CCL, then tied to the CIO).[58] After the two labor federations, the TLC and the CCL, merged into the Canadian Labour Congress in the mid-1950s, they joined with the CCF to form the NDP in the early 1960s. The united Canadian union movement continues officially to support the NDP.

The minority of Canadian unionists who are still in AFL-CIO affiliates remain to the left of their American counterparts. "With the exception of apolitical craft unions, Canadians invariably are in the left wing of the internationals. Canadians favor broader public health insurance plans, government ownership of basic industries."[59]

Prosperity has not undermined social democratic electoral strength or union membership in Canada. There has been no return to the values of classical liberalism, like that of the postwar United States, because these have never been the national tradition. As noted earlier, all mainstream Canadian political parties, including the now-governing Tories, remain committed to an activist welfare state, to communitarianism.[60]

Although the Canadian economy entered the postwar years weaker than the American, the long-term boom, extensive growth, upgrading of the occupational structure, higher income, and rise in standards of living also occurred in Canada. In spite of such improvements, Canadian socialism has held its own nationally, generally obtaining between a fifth and a quarter of the federal vote in English Canada. Social democracy gained a new bastion in Quebec with the rise of the Parti Québécois to major party status in the 1970s, while the NDP attained a similar position there in the opinion polls in the mid-1980s. The Canadian labor movement reached new heights of membership at the start of the 1980s — close to 40 percent of the employed labor force — with a very small dropoff in the latter part of the decade, especially in the private sector, where Canadian employers had exhibited greater vigor in resisting unionization during the 1980s than in previous postwar years.[61] Still, as of 1989, Canadian union density was more than twice that of the American.

These crossnational differences in union strength are not a function of structural variations in the two economies.[62] In fact, as the Canadian labor economist Noah Meltz documents,

> If the distribution of employment in Canada in 1980 had been the same as that in the United States, and if the rates of union organization [by industry] were the ones that actually existed, the overall union rate would have been even higher [in Canada] than it was in 1980 by approximately 10%.[63]

Curiously, given the large difference in union strength across the border, questions inquiring about attitudes toward unions, their power, and the outcomes of strikes that have been posed by the Gallup polls, Decima and CRI, Harris, NORC, and the Wright-Myles studies do not show Canadians as more pro-union than Americans. Some even find the population in the north less approving of unions and more concerned about union power, which in fact is much greater there than in the southern nation.

Some analysts of the crossborder variation in union strength contend that it results primarily from the fact that labor legislation and labor relations boards have been less union-friendly in the United States than in Canada since the late 1940s, encouraging employers in the south to campaign actively against union organizing efforts.[64] Yet, it should be noted that three national polls taken in the United States between 1977 and 1986 have shown large and increasing majorities of all nonunion American workers saying that they would vote against a union in their company in a representation election. Such responses are clearly not affected by the composition of labor boards or by employers' anti-union activities. I know of no equivalent Canadian data, but a comparison of two community surveys conducted in Canada and the United States indicates more unorganized workers willing to support unions in the north than in the south.[65]

Conclusion

The American social structure and values foster an emphasis on competitive individualism, an orientation that is not congruent with class consciousness, support for socialist or social democratic parties, or a strong union movement. Survey results provide support for these interpretations. In the CARA-Gallup values study, respondents in both Canada and the United States were asked to place themselves on a ten-point scale with respect to the following question:

> Some people feel they have completely free choice and control over the way their lives turn out, and other people feel that what they themselves do has no real effect on what happens to them. Please use the scale to indicate how much freedom of choice and control you have over the way your life turns out.

Fifty-nine percent of the Americans chose the three highest points, meaning that they felt that they had a great deal of control over the course of their lives; compared to 52 percent of the Canadians (54 percent of the Anglophones and 46 percent of the Francophones) who did so. Thus, it is evident that more Americans than Canadians believe they can control their destiny.

This greater emphasis among Americans both reflects and reinforces the attitude that individuals are responsible for the life situation in which they find themselves. In other words, they are more likely than Canadians to feel that people should be given a chance to make something of themselves but that if they fail, it is their own responsibility, not that of society or of the government. By contrast, the somewhat greater strength in Canada of the belief that a person's life is not necessarily subject to his or her control can plausibly be said to contribute to a more positive view of class (trade union) action and state intervention intended to further equality of condition. Opinion polls and politics reinforce the conclusion of Canadian novelist Robertson Davies, who is a Tory, that "beneath all of this we are a people firmly set in the socialist pattern."[66]

In the next chapter, this analysis turns to national unity, to the ways that subgroups, ethnic and regional, behave in the two societies.

10

Mosaic and Melting Pot

One of Canadians' important self-images is that their society is a "mosaic," one that gives diverse ethnic groups the right to cultural survival. It contrasts with the once-traditional American emphasis on assimilation into the "melting pot." The origin of these differing ideals, like other values discussed here, can be traced to the impact of 18th-century history. American universalism — the desire to incorporate diverse groups into a culturally unified whole — is inherent in the country's founding ideology. Canadian particularism — the preservation of subnational group loyalties, as well as the strength of the provinces vis-à-vis the federal government — is rooted in the decision of the Francophone clerical elite to remain loyal to the British monarchy as a protection against Puritanism and democratic populism across the border. Because of the importance of the French-speaking areas to British North America, the subsequent Canadian federal state incorporated protections for the linguistic minority, and the provinces assumed considerable power. The Canadian sociologist Morton Weinfeld notes that there is

> ample evidence to support the idea that Canada has generally been encouraging of ethnic diversity. The British North America Act of 1867 did not declare the absolute equality of all citizens. Rather, by recognizing certain rights for religious groups (Catholics and Protestants) and linguistic groups (English and French speakers), it legitimated a collectivist approach to the notion of rights, in contrast to the American emphasis on individual liberties. The binational origin of the

Canadian state paved the way for full acceptance of the plural nature of Canadian society and acknowledgement of the contributions, value, and rights of all Canadian minority groups.[1]

One might have thought that these differences would have declined with modernization. Most analysts used to assume that industrialization, urbanization, and the spread of education reduce ethnic and regional consciousness, that universalism supplants particularism. As Nathan Glazer and Daniel P. Moynihan point out, it was generally believed that "divisions of culture, religion, language [and race]...would inevitably lose their weight and sharpness in modern and modernizing societies, ...that common systems of education and communication would level differences."[2]

During the past three decades, however, the world has witnessed an ethnic revival in many countries.[3] The validity of the assumption that structural modernization would sharply reduce ethnic and regional diversity and the power of federal subunits has been particularly challenged by North American experience. Blacks, Québécois, Chicanos, native North Americans, and a host of other ethnic and racial groups have expressed more self-consciousness since the 1960s than at any time in the history of the continent.

It has not always been thus. Canada once stood out as a "deviant case" among developed nations, according to a study by the sociologist Marie Haug of the degree of cultural and structural pluralism in 114 countries. Using data from the 1950s and early 1960s, she devised a pluralism index based on five variables: degree of linguistic heterogeneity, racial diversity, religious variation, sectionalism, and "interest articulation by non-associational groups." Her statistical analysis revealed a negative correlation between levels of national economic development and cultural and political pluralism. Higher pluralism was "related to progressively lower per capita GNP, with 75 percent of the extremely plural societies recording less than $150 per person annually,...[with the] linear regression...accounting for 83 percent of the variation." But, in spite of the strength of this relationship, wealthy Canada scored close to the bottom on the index. Only ten countries, all in the Third World, had lower pluralism scores than Canada. Conversely, the United States placed well above the median.[4]

The differences between Canada and the United States have undoubtedly reflected in part the conflicting orientations toward minority cultures subsumed in the mosaic and melting-pot concepts. As the sociologist Arthur Davis points out:

> [E]thnic and regional differences...have been more generally accepted, more legitimized [in Canada] than they have been in our southern neighbor. There has not been as much pressure in Canada for "assimilation" as there has been in the United States....Hutterite communities unquestionably are granted more autonomy in Canada than in the United States. Likewise, the Indians of Canada, however rudely they were shunted into reservations, were seldom treated with such overt coercion as were the American Indians.[5]

Native North Americans

The crossborder dissimilarity in the situations of native North Americans can serve to illustrate the greater consideration for — perhaps more accurately, the lesser pressure put on — minority populations north of the 49th parallel. Although native people have been treated badly on both sides of the border, Canadians have shown them more respect than have Americans.[6] Writing of the situation in the latter part of the 19th century, the Canadian-reared novelist Wallace Stegner notes: "One of the most visible aspects of the international boundary was that it was a color line: blue below, red above, blue for treachery and unkept promises, red for protection and the straight tongue."[7] Although the difference was probably never that clear cut, it must be acknowledged that "Canada, despite the failures of its Indian policy, was for a time a refuge to the Sioux of Sitting Bull after they wiped out Custer's command."[8] Indian wars and settler vigilantism were all too common south of the border; the keeping of the peace and of treaties by the representatives of the Crown and central authority characterized the situation in the North.

> Canada did not suffer the long and bloody wars that marked American occupation of the far west. The Mounted Police

maintained much tighter control of western settlements and the six-shooter never became the symbol of Canadian freedom. Ottawa negotiated treaties with the plains Indians which secured relatively peaceful opening of most fertile land and the re-location of tribes on substantial "reserves." By no means an ideal permanent solution to the question of Indian-White relations, this policy at least prevented large-scale illegal dispossession of the Indians.[9]

The criminologist John Hagan relates the fact that "Canada's Native people were treated in a significantly different way than were Native people in the United States" to the lower rates of "violent crime" north of the border. As he notes: "America's treatment of both its black and Native minorities was extraordinarily violent. Canada's...has not been nearly so violent. It seems unlikely that this difference...would not have had behavioral consequences."[10]

In evaluating the record of four overseas, predominantly English-speaking countries in dealing with their aboriginal populations, the American historian Robin Winks concludes

> that the harshest race relations developed in Australia, the least harsh in New Zealand, and that the experience with white-Indian contact in the United States fell more towards the Australian side, and...in Canada more towards the New Zealand side, of the scale.[11]

Although I have not been able to locate crossnational public opinion data bearing on attitudes toward native rights, Gaile McGregor's comparison of North American fiction, described in Chapter 4, notes that Canadian literature deals with Indians much more sympathetically than does American. She points out that in

> comparison with his relatively infrequent appearances in "serious" modern American writing, the Indian has...become one of the more important personae in the Canadian....In Canada, in Atwood's words, Indians are not valued because "they are good or superior, but [because] they are persecuted." The Indian...is the "archetypical" victim.[12]

Another literary critic, Linda Hutcheon, also emphasizes the importance of the Indians for white Canadian writers "in their own search for their roots," one not found among Americans, who lack these concerns. "Canadian novels...have related the Indian and the Inuit [Eskimo] to the wilderness....[B]oth Native and nature...embody some eternal spiritual essence."[13]

This is not to say that Canada's record of behavior toward its native peoples has been perfect or even good. For much of the past century, the aboriginals north and south of the border have suffered from what was at best benign neglect and usually included outright discrimination. They show up at or near the bottom on most measures of mortality and social morbidity.[14] Nevertheless, the record is clear that the native peoples have been better able to survive in Canada than in the United States.

One great advantage of those in Canada has been geographical: many are positioned on the fringes of northern settlement, where they have had limited contact with whites. Another advantage has been demographic. As Margaret Atwood points out, in Canada, "[T]here's a lot more of them per capita."[15] The actual official proportions in the most recent decennial censuses were 2.02 percent in Canada in 1981 and 0.6 percent in the United States in 1980. Even here, however, there is evidence of ignorance and prejudice. Students of the subject suggest that the census data underestimate the number of Canadian natives. Three different estimates put them at 3 to 4 percent of the population.[16] There are "proportionately eight times as many native people[s] in Canada as in the United States,"[17] including 300,000 status Indians, more than 800,000 métis (persons of mixed ancestry) and nonstatus Indians, and 23,000 Inuit.[18]

Recent concerns for civil rights have activated the native populations in both Canada and the United States, and their legal situation has improved in both.

In the United States, Indian legal rights, particularly to self-government, have been under more formal guarantees than in Canada through judicial actions. Until recently, the American courts generally accepted the legitimacy of Indian property rights, as defined in treaties, more easily than the courts across the border. Such outcomes presumably reflected the greater commitment to due process and constitutionally protected property rights in the United States.[19] The position taken by American courts before the Civil War, that Indian tribes are "dependent sovereign nations," resulted before World War II in explicit congressional acknowledgement that the tribes should be allowed self-determination, though they remained highly dependent financially on Washington.

The legal position of Canadian natives who remained under the protection of the Crown was more ambiguous until the 1970s. Changes in the American direction occurred in tandem with the increased Canadian concern for due process, first in a bill of rights and then in the Charter of Rights and Freedoms.[20] Although these adjustments introduced a more American emphasis on individual citizens' rights, contradicting historic organic communal and particularistic values, the Charter has also encouraged Indian claims for tribal self-rule, explicitly affirming "the existing aboriginal and treaty rights of the aboriginal peoples of Canada" (section 35).[21] The native populations have been gaining effective rights to self-government since the 1970s.[22]

Historically, C.E.S. Franks notes, Canada's policy has been more consistently supportive than American of "communal land and tribal identity." The United States "has oscillated between extreme liberal individualism, and recognition of community and cultural distinctiveness." Most recently, it has been committed to "self-determination," while Canada favors "self-government." Franks' comparative study concludes: "[S]elf-government in Canada does...seem to have more content than self-government in the United States." This difference is reflected particularly in variations in policies toward northern communities in Alaska and in the Yukon and Quebec. In 1989, Canada agreed to split its vast Northwest Territories in half, giving its Inuit population political control over the eastern Arctic with a grant of C$700 million over a 15-year period.[23]

Ethnoreligious Communities

A sociologist's comparison of Mennonites in the United States and Canada also points up the ways in which the varying national values and structures have affected group behavior.

In America, the Mennonites with their ethnic and non-conformist heritage experience many difficulties with their dual

American and Mennonite loyalties. [North of the border they] tend to feel more at home in their adopted homeland ....Canadian Mennonites have not needed to deny their past or reorient their religion to embrace denominationalism to verify their acceptability as Canadians....Canadian Mennonites appear to have shared less of the strain of identity experienced by their American brethren.[24]

The differing organization of Jews in Canada and the United States also shows how the structure and behavior of an ethno-religious group may vary with national environments. Living within an accepted multinational environment, "[t]he Canadian Jewish community is much more like a European community than it is like either the British community or the American community."[25] A single national association, the Canadian Jewish Congress, makes policy for and represents all organized Jewry in Canada; there is no comparable group in the United States.[26] Canadian Jews have shown much less propensity than American Jews to assimilate to a dominant middle-class liberal Protestant pattern. American Jewish historian Jonathan Sarna notes, "In Canada, reform Judaism has been weaker and Zionism [historically] stronger than in the United States," and "Canadian Jews have remained somewhat more attached to Yiddish and Yiddish culture than have American Jews."[27] A much higher proportion of Jewish youth is enrolled in religious day schools in the north than in the south, while the intermarriage rate is lower in Canada even though the Jewish community there is much smaller than the American. Small size normally leads to greater assimilation, but the emphasis on particularistic group organization, subsumed in the mosaic concept, seemingly helps to perpetuate more solidarity in the Canadian Jewish community.[28]

A comparison of Jewish novels in the United States and Canada notes that in the former the ghetto is "American-style, which frequently means that enclosed space eventually expands toward new horizons." Canadian writers focus more on the constraints of the ghetto and even deal with the "reghetto-ization" of Jews who have escaped.[29]

The stronger community among Canadian, as compared to American, Jews is, of course, also a function of the fact that the former are a "younger group" — that is, closer in time to their immigrant origins. A considerable number of Jews came to Canada in the 1920s, after the United States' borders were largely closed to them. Yet, as Canada's foremost student of Jewish literary culture, Ruth Wisse, notes, the crossborder differences also reflect the fact that

> Canadian Jews came into a country where ethnicity is recognized. It has ethnic groups such as there were in Eastern Europe; it has already existing differences between Poles and Ukrainians and all the subgroups with their different languages. It seems to me the [Canadian] Jewish immigrants didn't come into an Anglo-Saxon culture but a land of ethnic distinction.[30]

Sarna suggests that the crossborder differences in Jewish behavior may reflect "the different religious traditions" of the two countries. He also calls attention to the fact that "the United States [has] demanded a greater degree of accommodation and outward patriotism from Jews than has Canada."[31]

Multiculturalism

Canadian ethnocultural groups have a more protective environment than American ones because of the official acceptance of multiculturalism stemming from the need to conciliate French Canadians. Ironically, Anglophone Canadians have become more committed to this concept than Francophones, many of whom prefer a two-cultures model, believing that Anglophones see in multiculturalism a way of denying the French equal status.[32] On a more positive note, the push to multiculturalism may reflect a desire to formulate "a uniquely Canadian culture or set of national characteristics...[by] defining Canadian culture in terms of the legitimate ancestral cultures which are the legacy of every Canadian defining the whole through the sum of its parts."[33] The 1969 publication of the fourth volume of the *Report* of the Royal Commission on Bilingualism and Biculturalism led the country to a commitment to helping all ethnic groups maintain their identity and culture.[34] The *Multicultural Act* of 1971 officially designates Canada as a country that is "multicultural in a bilingual framework." In a policy announcement to Parliament, the government declared:

> We believe that cultural pluralism is the very essence of Canadian identity. Every ethnic group has the right to reserve and develop its own culture and values within the Canadian context. To say that we have two official languages is not to say we have two official cultures, and no particular culture is more official than another. A policy of multiculturalism must be a policy for all Canadians.[35]

Multiculturalism is entrenched in the 1982 Canadian constitution. Section 27 of the Charter of Rights and Freedoms says: "This Charter shall be interpreted in a manner consistent with the preservation and enhancement of the multicultural heritage of Canadians." A cabinet post whose exclusive responsibility is multiculturalism was established in 1973. The government now gives grants to assorted ethnic minorities for projects designed to celebrate and extend their cultures.[36] Some school boards, including that of the City of Toronto, now provide for the teaching of "heritage languages" — that is, one or more languages that are neither French nor English and are usually those spoken by the ethnic groups living near particular schools.

Canadian political leaders often emphasize multiculturalism as a defining characteristic of the society.[37] They have "indefatigably praised the situation in which ethnic groups could retain their distinctiveness and yet be Canadian, in contrast to the American melting pot as they conceived it." In the words of Joe Clark, former prime minister and current minister of external affairs, Canada is "a community of communities."[38]

Within the American polity during the past two decades, blacks have assumed a role comparable to that of Francophones in Canada. The call for "Black Power," the judicial requirement of affirmative action quotas, and the demand for other government support policies did much to lead the United States to accept particularistic standards in dealing with other racial and ethnic groups and women. Blacks, like French Canadians, are "unmeltable ethnics," and much as Francophones have legitimated cultural autonomy for other non-Anglo-Saxon Canadians, the changing position of the blacks has helped other American groups to claim rights. In effect, the United States is replacing the ideal of the melting pot with that of the mosaic.

Both countries have moved toward one form of equality of result: affirmative action preferences or quotas for minority ethnic and racial groups and for women. (Although women do not constitute the same type of aggregate as the ethnic minorities, they have been defined legally and ideologically in comparable terms.)[39] As noted earlier, the American policy came about through administrative order in 1969 and has been the subject of continued political and judicial controversy. Enforcement declined under Ronald Reagan's administration, which took the position — held by a substantial majority of Americans, according to the opinion polls — that rights to equal treatment should be guaranteed to *individuals*, that remedial preferences should not be given to *groups*. In Canada, subsection 15.1 of the Charter of Rights and Freedoms has enshrined an American doctrine: "Every individual is equal before and under the law and has the right to the equal protection and equal benefit of the law without discrimination."[40] But to avoid the American legal debate over whether individual rights preclude special advantages to underprivileged groups, subsection 15.2 goes on to specifically authorize programs and activities directed to "the amelioration of conditions of disadvantaged individuals or groups including those that are disadvantaged because of race, national or ethnic origin, colour, religion, sex, age or mental or physical disability." As one political scientist emphasizes:

> This clause is an invitation to...government to engage in micro social engineering to readjust the status order produced by history....[It] illustrates a recurring tendency of the Canadian state...[to single] out particular groups or categories for individualized treatment.[41]

Canada and its provinces have defined more than 30 such groups as worthy of special treatment, far more than has the United States — behavior that conforms to the greater emphasis on the mosaic in the former.

The success of blacks in modifying the emphasis on individual rights in American values stems, of course, from the fact that slavery and racism have been the foremost deviation from the American creed throughout the history of the Republic. Thomas Jefferson voiced his concern over its impact on the future, noting in 1781, "I tremble for my country when I reflect that God is just."[42] In his classic analysis of American racism, *An American Dilemma*, Gunnar Myrdal emphasized in 1944 that, in spite of racist practices, white Americans, including southerners, believe in the creed, in egalitarianism. They believe they believe in equality for all. From this assumption, he anticipated that if blacks organized to demand their rights, the whites would give in.[43] This is what has happened. And in yielding politically, the white male political elite has acquiesced to the demand for group rights, for a form of equality of results. But this change does not affect economic class rights or the strength of the meritocratic belief that those who work hard will succeed.

Immigration

Both Canada and the United States are marked by having developed through massive, somewhat different influxes of heterogeneous immigrants. Canada, for much of its history, was settled by people from its founding national groups, British and French.[44] (In fact, after the British took Quebec, Canada secured relatively few settlers from France, which is not an emigrant country.) But given the country's need to fill its vast underpopulated spaces, Canada began to look with increasing success, before and after World War I, for people from non-British, non-Nordic Europe. Its Protestant, Anglo-Saxon bias continued, however, to be reflected in legislation and administrative policies, which favored newcomers from Britain. The United States, on the other hand, drew its immigrants from more diverse sources, first more Germans and Irish Catholics, and, from the 1880s on, increasingly from other parts of Europe.

The difference in the national backgrounds of settlers in the two countries reflected their dissimilar origins and links to Britain. Not only was the British tie reinforced in Canada by heavy immigration from the mother country, but it can be argued that the values of those who chose the north were somewhat different from those who went to the United States. As reports on notable newcomers attest, America was a refuge for democratic and radical emigrés. There was a flood of such immigrants after the failure of the revolutions of 1848. A few decades later, many fled eastern Europe to escape political and religious persecution. Although Canada undoubtedly received some political emigrés, there was little reason for most of them to go to a country whose image in Europe was largely as part of the British Empire.

Until after the turn of the century, both North American societies continued to absorb large inflows from the British Isles, most of them relatively poor people. Although most of the immigrants to the United States were Protestants, it attracted many more Irish Catholics than did Canada. Canada, conversely, was relatively more attractive to British Protestants, including large numbers of Northern Irish Orangemen. The two groups differed greatly, of course, in their attitudes toward England and the monarchy. It may be hypothesized that the Protestant Britons who moved to North America also made an ideological decision in choosing between Canada and the United States. To go to Canada meant remaining within the Queen's domains, inside the British Empire. To settle in the United States involved a move to a country that had rejected the monarchy and possessed an aura of populist democracy. Hence, without any evidence to test the assumption other than the ethnoreligious variations in the destinations of those who left Ireland, I suggest that the monarchical and republican parts of North America attracted different types of people. And the differences continued to produce a population more receptive to Tory-deferential values in the north than in the south, where immigrants were encouraged to follow egalitarian norms.

Before World War II, both countries had responded to tightening labor markets and internal ethnic tensions by restricting immigration, first, at the turn of the century, for Asians, and subsequently for all others. The crackdown came in the United States in the 1920s but not until the 1930s in Canada, which was more disposed to view itself as underpopulated. The immigration restriction laws reflected ethnic biases in each country. The base chosen for the American quota system was the distribution of national origins in the country as of 1890 — that is, before the heavy influx from southern and eastern Europe — when the population was mostly of northwestern European and British heritage. Canada largely sought immigrants from English- and French-speaking areas, which, in effect, meant most were from Britain with a sizable minority from the United States; Asian immigration had been restricted from the late 19th century onward.

The United States' designation of quotas favorable to Nordic Protestants is an example of the way in which the American value system can be negated. The enactment of this law in 1924 eliminated the universalistic and egalitarian principle that everyone had a right to become an American, that to become one required only that a person wished to be an American, not that the person had been lucky in choosing his or her parents. And though it is possible to argue that the imposition of numerical restrictions on immigration was necessary with the end of the open-land frontier, the fact remains that particularistic quotas constituted a fundamental violation of traditional American values.

The crusade to keep America Protestant by barring massive non-Protestant immigration is actually almost as old as the United States itself. From Thomas Jefferson's presidency to Woodrow Wilson's, there was an association among conservative politics, efforts to impose ascetic Protestant morality on the lower classes — often viewed as largely immigrant in composition — and attempts to limit immigration or to withhold equal rights from the foreign-born. In almost every generation, "old American" groups that saw themselves "displaced" — relatively demoted in status or power by processes rooted in social change and economic competition — sought to reverse these processes thorough political action. Conflict between the advocates of ascetic and nativist doctrines, usually associated with the Federalist-Whig-Republican parties, and their more culturally cosmopolitan and egalitarian opponents, most often located in the nonsouthern Democratic Party, has characterized much of American history.

An examination of the forces that precipitated the passage of immigration restriction in 1924 suggests that it did not reflect a clear-cut rejection of the American creed. Rather, in the 1920s, its enactment — together with the passage of the Prohibition amendment to the Constitution, the passage in many states of laws barring the teaching of evolution, and the rise of the Ku Klux Klan — represented the power of the backlash of provincial resentment against structural changes within the society that were weakening the social and political influence of the more fundamentalist small-town and rural Protestants. The 1920 census reported that, for the first time in American history, a majority lived in "urban areas." And the urban districts, particularly the culturally and economically dominant cities, were centers of resistance to evangelical Protestant influence, metropolises peopled by an opposition consisting of Catholics, Jews, and adherents of the liberal high-status Protestant denominations. To moralistic, small-town Protestants, these urban centers were also concentrations of drunkenness, immorality, political corruption, and cosmopolitanism. Many evangelical Protestants backed nativism because they saw evidence that the increase in the size of the non-Protestant population and the growth of the metropolises were undermining their way of life, relegating them and their communities to a minority position.[45]

Postwar Changes

The postwar era brought about a reversal in restrictive policies, initially more in Canada than in the United States. Both countries accepted refugees, first from the after-effects of Nazism and subsequently from east European Communism. By the 1960s, both had changed their legislation, first dropping the barriers against Asians and then cancelling all quotas.

In Canada, these changes were to result in a massive demographic shift as hundreds of thousands of non-British, non-French — including many Asians — came in. By the 1980s, while people of British and French descent still made up the majority of Canada's population, each of these ethnic groups was outnumbered by persons whose origins were in other countries. Of the almost 200,000 immigrants to Canada in 1961, only 15.8 percent were from Britain and Ireland, with another 3.4 percent from the United States. To state what happened in another way: in 1951, some 76.5 percent of immigrants arrived from continental Europe, with Italians in the lead; by 1981, the proportion of

Europeans had fallen to 19.5 percent, and 6.8 percent came from the United States.

Meanwhile, the composition of immigrant groups south of the border also changed. People entering the United States from the British Isles fell from 10.9 percent of all immigrants in the 1950s to 2.7 in the 1980s. "Other Europeans" also declined greatly, from 48.4 to 8.9 percent.[46]

In some ways, the contrast between the two North American countries is striking. About one-quarter of entrants to Canada in 1987 were from Europe and the United States, while about one-seventh of newcomers to America arrived from Europe and Canada. No European country now places among the top ten sources of immigration to the United States; only Britain ranks in this group in Canada. More than 40 percent of those entering both North American countries in the 1980s have been Asian.[47]

In line with their record of leading the developed world in job growth since World War II, Canada and the United States have been in the forefront of immigration-receiving countries: in 1988, America took 700,000 legal entrants and Canada more than 150,000, greater than the total to the rest of the world. There are, of course, many more undocumented immigrants in the United States. Canada takes in more legal ones per capita, though it too is home to many illegals.

At the end of the 1980s, Canada and the United States remain more universalistic and socially heterogeneous in their immigration admission patterns than other "white" First World countries. Almost three-quarters of immigrants to the United States (73 percent) come from the Third World: more than one-third from Latin America, another 8 percent from Africa, and two-fifths from Asia.[48] The Third World figure for Canada, as of 1987, is similar.[49]

These changes point to a renewed commitment by the United States to its liberal universalistic values, which were violated for four decades by discrimination based on national origins. Canada has become almost as universalistic, much less committed to a British preference, thus reversing its particularistic emphasis and pointing up its increasingly more liberal character.

Backlash in Canada?

Given Canada's increased emphasis on multiculturalism, a finding in the March 1989 *Maclean's*-Decima crossborder survey runs counter to expectations. The poll enquired: "What do you think is better for Canada / the United States: that new immigrants be encouraged to maintain their distinct culture and ways, or to change their distinct culture and ways to blend with the larger society?" Surprisingly, a larger proportion of Americans than Canadians (47 to 34 percent) thought it would be better for newcomers to preserve their culture than to assimilate.[50] Fully three-fifths of Canadians (61 percent) thought newcomers should change their culture "to blend with the larger society," compared to "only 51 percent of American respondents [who] endorsed the melting-pot model of ethnic assimilation."[51]

These findings suggest, as Allan Gregg of Decima and various other Canadian social scientists I have consulted believe, that the massive waves of immigration that Canada has absorbed in recent decades, which have made it a much more heterogeneous country in ethnic and racial terms than ever before, have led to a major shift in attitudes among people of old Canadian stock, both British and French — that a backlash against the mosaic concept is occurring. The population changes are not minor. At the end of World War II, 88 percent of Toronto's residents had origins in the British Isles; in 1989, a majority, 51 percent, were foreign born. In the country overall, 13 percent of the population belong to non-white minorities.

The more liberal American reaction may reflect that country's greater experience with absorbing immigrants, and the fact that dealing with non-whites is not a new phenomenon for its large cities. There are examples of anti-immigrant and racial backlash on both sides of the border. But the tensions of immigration absorption and ethnic-racial strife may be affecting Canadians more than their neighbors today precisely because these difficulties have been less common there in the past. In any case, the response to a single question in a recent poll does not demonstrate that Canadians have given up on cultural pluralism. When asked in April 1989 by another polling organization, Environics Research Group, whether they favor multiculturalism as a national policy, 63 percent responded affirmatively.[52]

A Note on Gender Differences

In Chapter 4, I described some telling differences between Canadian and U.S. literature, noting the proportionately greater role of women in the northern country and its greater use of themes of a strong-female / weak-male syndrome or mother-daughter relationships. These emphases do not mean that Canadian novels have not described a world in which the male is dominant or that the position of women in Canada has been superior to that of their peers below the border.[53] All the evidence, in fact, suggests that the opposite was true until recently. Canada, being a more traditional, hierarchical, religious, and Tory society, gave its women fewer rights than its more egalitarian neighbor. Canadian women were less likely than American to question their inferior position, at least in as public or militant ways.[54]

The differences in the political cultures of the two countries contributed to varying approaches by feminist advocates. Americans were influenced by the emphases on constitutional rights. And "American feminism has absorbed this culture of rights, indeed the entire history of feminism there is deeply entwined with the abolition movement in the nineteenth century and the black civil-rights movement in the 1960s." Canadian feminism, not exposed to "a political atmosphere highly charged with the rhetoric of political rights," has been more disposed than the American to pursue a wide variety of specific objectives.[55]

Canadians clearly lagged until recently. The U.S. women's suffrage movement organized earlier and remained more militant tactically.[56] A number of American states gave them the vote in the late 19th century. No Canadian province did so until World War I, and Quebec did not allow women to vote until 1940.[57] Some women (those with close relatives in the military) got the federal vote in 1918; others received it soon afterwards. Nevertheless, Canadian women were denied equal legal rights until 1929, long after women in the United States had obtained them. The key event was the "persons" case; Henrietta Muir Edwards, a leading suffragette from Alberta, was chosen for the federal Senate, but she was denied the seat on the grounds that the body's membership was constitutionally restricted to "persons" and the old British Common Law provided that "women are persons in matters of pains and penalties, but are not persons in matters of rights and privileges." The decision was finally reversed by the Privy Council of Great Britain, then Canada's highest appeals court.[58]

The militant struggle for the suffrage in the United States raised the consciousness of many American women and stimulated a sharp increase in female participation in the labor force and attendance in colleges and universities in the 1920s. Canadians remained behind on these scores. Two Canadian suffrage pioneers suggested that the relative lack of economic and political involvement by their country's women at that time stemmed from their having not fought as hard, that they "got the vote too easily to appreciate it," that, in the words of one of them, they were "beneficiaries of...greater, earlier crusades in...the United Kingdom and the United States."[59]

Much of the political and economic limits on women's participation have greatly declined on both sides of the border since the 1950s. But a comprehensive analysis completed in the mid-1970s still emphasized that "to the extent that values such as conservatism, greater respect for authority, and ascription in fact characterize Canadian culture," family and gender-related behavior could be expected to "be more traditionalistic...than in the United States."[60] That deduction was borne out by crossnational data reported from the 1960s and early 1970s: the United States had in its labor force a much larger percentage of women in all categories — single, married, and those with children under six years of age.[61] The proportion of women in universities was also much lower in Canada and, consequently, there were fewer in the higher professions.

The situation has improved strikingly in both countries in recent years. Government policy has become more supportive of women's rights, in large measure as an extension of programs developed in reaction to the major minorities in each country, blacks and French Canadians. Thus, most equal rights policies, including affirmative action programs, are applicable to women. Behavioral and opinion poll data from both nations point to the increased acceptance by men, particularly the younger and better educated ones, of women's equality. The increase in gender consciousness has led to a sharp growth in the numbers of women seizing educational, occupational, and, to a lesser degree, elective political opportunities. Canadian women had lagged with respect to labor force participation: 31 percent in the United States and 24 percent in the north at the start of the 1950s. By the mid-1980s, however, the proportions in the labor force were the same on the two sides of the border: 55 percent of the total adult female population. And Canada now leads by 3 percentage points among women who are less than 25 years of age. [62]

These changes did not just happen, of course. The large feminist movements that emerged in both societies from the 1960s on have played a major role in pressing for the removal of barriers based on gender. But in looking at feminist organization and political response, it is noteworthy that the proportionately stronger and more militant American groups have had less success than their Canadian counterparts in achieving political objectives. In the United States during the 1980s, the efforts to pass the ERA (Equal Rights Amendment) to the Constitution failed, while affirmative action quotas and preferences were being undercut by judicial decisions. [63]

Conversely, in Canada, the 1982 constitutional revisions, particularly sections of the Charter of Rights and Freedoms, gave Canadian women extensive guarantees of equal rights and legitimated affirmative action programs. Ontario, Canada's most industrialized, wealthiest, and populous province, has gone much further than any American state in enacting legislation requiring that women receive the same pay as men for jobs of comparable skill. Unlike comparable American state laws, which apply only to public agencies, Ontario's law covers all employers with more than ten workers. Although obviously controversial, this major and costly reform in gender rights was passed *unanimously* in November 1988. [64] In effect, in spite of employer opposition, the province's political elite decided the time had come for the change. All three parties enforced discipline on their legislators, thereby removing the issue from electoral debate. That nothing like this could possibly happen south of the border illustrates again the sharp difference between elitist and populist systems.

Overall, the crossborder differences in the political success of the women's movement result from the dissimilarities in the political systems and the varying emphases on populism, as well as from the diverse religious traditions, which have been more favorable to the position of women and minorities in Canada than in the United States. Thus, the ERA, like all amendments to the American Constitution, had to be ratified by three-quarters of the state legislatures. Although it came very close to the needed 38 states (it passed in 35), it failed in 15, almost all of which were among the more Protestant evangelical and less urbanized ones. In Canada, the constitutional clauses guaranteeing equal rights did not have to be exposed to a popular ratification process. They were incorporated into the Charter by the political elite and accepted without much formal public debate. All three major Canadian churches — Anglican, Roman Catholic, and United — favored the reforms. While the emphasis on individualism and competitive meritocracy increased in the United States during the prosperous postwar decades, the northern country has experienced a growth in redistributive equalitarianism for deprived groups and has not faced a major effort to turn the clock back in the fields of gender and minority rights.

The growth in women's participation in higher education and the labor force in Canada, which now places them in a better position statistically than their peers south of the border, appears to reflect the lesser strength of religious-based traditional values about gender in the north. As we have seen, the United States is one of the most religiously traditional societies in Christendom, and fundamentalist beliefs are linked to attitudes about the role of women in the family and economy. Fewer women in Canada than in the United States are held back by traditional values. The greater liberalism now expressed by Canadians with respect to sexual behavior — for example, their increased disposition to use birth control — and other value changes have brought the Canadian birth rate, particularly in Quebec, well below the American. The current differences in crossborder gender outcomes with respect to education and jobs reflect these shifts.

Although the diverse content of American and Canadian fiction did not affect the position of the sexes in the past, the expansion in the contribution of women to the northern literature in recent decades may reflect and contribute to the greater changes in gender-related attitudes and behavior north of the border. Beyond the variations in the fictional treatment of gender relationships in both countries, a content analysis of all advertisements appearing in the first 20 issues of 1989 in the weekly mass-circulation news magazines *Maclean's* and *Newsweek* finds that women are depicted more fairly in Canada. A larger percentage of subjects in the Canadian advertisements are women (38.3 percent) than in the American ones (31 percent). "Canadian ads appear to portray women and men more equally in employment status and occupation than American ads....More women appear as customers in the U.S. than men, whereas the reverse is true for Canada."[65]

Conclusion

If the two North American countries have reduced some of the differences in the ways they deal with minorities, immigrants, and women, they are more dissimilar than before with respect to the importance of the center and the periphery: the national government versus the regions, states, and provinces. The power of the latter has steadily declined in the United States; it has increased in Canada.[66] The next chapter turns to this subject.

11

Center and Periphery

Samuel Beer, a leading American authority on federalism and comparative government, summarizes the consensus in this field that political and economic modernization inherently lead to a growth in authority at the center and a concomitant decline in state or provincial power at the periphery. As he puts it: "In the United States, as in other modernizing societies, the general historical record has spelled centralization."[1] He emphasizes that

> the main reasons for this change...., the major grounds of centralization and decentralization are to be found not in..."ground rules" [the Constitution and court rulings]...[or] in the personal, partisan or ideological preferences of office-holders, but in the new forces produced by an advanced modernity.[2]

Canada, however, has been different. As Donald Smiley, an expert on federalism, effectively refutes the proposition:

> Modernization had not led to centralization in the Canadian federal system but rather to the power, assertiveness, and competence of the provinces. Furthermore, the provinces where modernization has proceeded most rapidly are the most insistent about preserving and extending their autonomy.[3]

Another Canadian authority, Alan Cairns, refers to this development as the "great mystery for students of Canadian federalism."[4]

Federal-Regional Relationships

Political scientists agree that Canada is already more decentralized than any other industrialized country and that, especially since the early 1960s, decentralization measured by such indices as spending and taxing shares has proceeded apace.[5] Conversely, in the United States, federal power increased steadily from the Great Depression to the election of Ronald Reagan. And although Reagan sought to reverse the tendency, he managed only to slow down the growth.

The differences show up strikingly with respect to revenues. In the United States, federal authorities control most of the funds raised and spent by all the country's governments — federal, state, county, and municipal. In contrast, Canada has fiscally "become the most decentralized federation in the western world....Canada's provinces [and municipalities] have surpassed the Federal Government in total spending and tax revenues." The ratio is the highest among the countries of the Organisation for Economic Co-operation and Development.[6] As of 1985, the federal share of total Canadian tax revenue, *not* including social security funds, was 47.6 percent; the equivalent figure for the United States was 56.3 percent.[7]

Canadian provinces are also much more disposed than American states to challenge the power of the federal government. Movements advocating secession have recurred in this century not only in Quebec but also in some of the Atlantic provinces, the Prairies, and British Columbia. The tensions between Ottawa and the provinces and regions are not simply conflicts among politicians over the distribution of power. Public sentiment in Canada remains much more territorial than in the United States. "Unlike in the United States where voter turnout falls off precipitously in state elections, turnout in [Canadian] provincial elections historically has paralleled that in Dominion elections."[8] In a comparative analysis of voting patterns between 1945 and 1970 in 17 western nations, Canada ranked among the most diversified regionally, while the United States was the most nationalized. "Over the time span of the study, voting in the United States was progressively nationalized whereas Canada experienced no change."[9] Three other studies, two dealing with the elections in English Canada through this century, and the third for all of Canada from 1878 to 1974, each concluded that provincial differences had not declined or had actually increased over time.[10] Moreover, a number of "political socialization studies have discovered that... regional identifications begin early in the learning process and help to produce strong patterns of regional loyalties by the adolescent years."[11] A mid-1970s Canadian research study by Allan Gregg and Michael S. Whittington found "significant regional differences in the basic orientations to politics even among very young children."[12]

Students of crossborder patterns in state-provincial legislative behavior emphasize the different degrees of integration in the two federal polities.[13] During the 1980s, Canadian legislators have been more likely to vary in their views on various issues "depending on their province of representation" than have Americans from different states who are "more like one another in their [party] policy orientations."[14] This crossborder difference probably goes back at least several decades.

The provinces have been steadily growing in political strength, particularly from the 1960s through to the Meech Lake Accord between Ottawa and the provinces in 1987, an agreement (discussed in more detail in the next section) that is designed to give them even more power if it is ever ratified by all of them. (At the time of writing — mid-1989 — there are two holdouts, and the expiration date is June 1990.) The opponents of decentralization have found little support in the national tradition. Even as ardent a federalist and defender of the role of the Canadian central government as Pierre Trudeau argued in 1961, when he was still calling himself a social democrat, that Canadian socialists should be glad of and defend provincial rights, that they must recognize that they live in a highly decentralized country. Hence, "socialists must stand for different things in different parts of Canada."[15]

Similar arguments were made 20 years later by New Democratic Party (NDP) spokespersons Grant Notley, then the leader of the Alberta party, and Allan Blakeney, at the time premier of Saskatchewan. Arguing against socialist centralizers, Notley emphasized that regional variations offer Canadian socialists opportunities for experimentation. He insisted, "[T]he NDP must recognize that many Canadians do not want to be controlled from

Ottawa, that in his home province, the majority of working people, as well as the majority of business men, identify with their provincial government."[16] At conferences dealing with constitutional changes, Blakeney joined Conservative premiers to defend provincial power. Before the adoption of the 1982 constitution, he "expressed his reservations because he did not wish to see his government restricted in its ability to create 'new rights' through social and economic legislation."[17] To mollify such "suspicion of the centralizing effect of the Charter of Rights and Freedoms,"[18] the new constitution includes a clause to protect the provinces from future amendments even after they have been approved by Parliament and two-thirds of the provinces. Subsections 38.2 and 38.3 provide that, in the words of one commentator, a province can "opt out if the amendment affects existing provincial powers."[19]

Contradictory Developments

The sharp discrepancy between developments in Canada and in the United States — in one a weakening of the power of the national government, in the other a strengthening of it — has led social scientists to ask what accounts for these contrary movements. Some, such as John Porter, contend that the difference represents the continued influence in Canada of counterrevolutionary traditions and institutions. Others say basically the same thing but conceptualize the difference as reflecting different sets of values, as "the choice between a preference for the maintenance of group identities or for the diffusion of individualism and universalism."[20] Structuralists point to a variety of macroscopic factors: "*societal* (economic, demographic, and international forces) and *institutional* (the form of constitutional structures of the state)."[21]

The impact of the cultural and institutional variables can be linked to the outcome of the American Revolution, as Porter argues. French Canadians' commitment to survival, discussed earlier, is clearly important, as are the varying effects of the American presidential-congressional system and the British parliamentary model. Certainly some of the variations that have resulted in a much stronger federal government in the United States than in Canada flow directly from the differences between a division-of-powers constitution and a parliamentary one that concentrates authority in the hands of a cabinet supported by a legislative majority.

Ironically, these outcomes were unanticipated by the shapers of each country and, indeed, are contradictory to their intentions. The American founding fathers, suspicious of executive power, consciously devised a constitution designed to weaken and disperse governmental authority. Residual powers were left to the state governments. Almost a century later, Canada's fathers of Confederation, seeing in the American south's attempt at secession what could happen to a weak central government whose powers over subordinate units were ambiguous, deliberately wrote a constitution that gave the federal executive the right to veto provincial legislation. This could be done either directly or through the actions of a federal appointee, the lieutenant-governor (formally the representative to the province of the monarch, which in effect meant the national cabinet). In addition, residual powers were assigned to the federal government.

In practice, things worked out quite differently. In the United States, as a result of the outcome of the Civil War and subsequent sectional, class, and racial struggles, states rights were diminished and the federal government became much more powerful than planned. Conversely, in Canada, the provinces have steadily gained in power at the expense of the central authorities. The latter have rarely used their veto powers — never since the mid-1930s — and they were not included in the 1982 constitution. Although most American states, like Canadian provinces, have sought to maintain or extend their power, the decisive difference between the two polities derives from the fact that Canada's largest minority, French Canadians, control a province, Quebec. The "Québécois...have used the...provincial government as an instrument of cultural survival and, because the stakes are so high, provincial rights have been guarded with a vigor unknown in the United States."[22] Smaller provinces seeking to extend their autonomy have been able to do so because Quebec has always been in the forefront of the struggle.

The effort to persuade Quebec to accept the 1982 constitution, which became law without its ratification, resulted in the 1987 Meech Lake Accord, which, if ratified, will expand provincial powers even further.[23] Its provisions include giving the provinces the right to select immigrants and a share in nominating members of the Supreme Court and the Senate, letting them opt out of federal-provincial shared-cost programs more easily than they can now, and requiring ratification of constitutional amendments by every province, not seven as at present. It will also recognize Quebec as a "distinct society," with special responsibility for the maintenance of Francophone culture.[24] As of the middle of 1989, Manitoba and New Brunswick have not signed the accord, which will be, in effect, a series of constitutional amendments.

Many Canadians fear the proposals will, in the words of Pierre Trudeau, "render the Canadian state totally impotent." Their argument is that, under the accord, the provinces will have "an absolute right of veto over Parliament since the Senate will eventually be composed of persons who owe their appointments to the provinces." The former prime minister contends that the provision to allow provinces to stay out of national shared-cost programs if they undertake one "compatible with national objectives" will "enable the provinces to finish off the balkanization of languages and cultures with the balkanization of social issues."[25]

It is clear that the "[a]ccord is a distinct tilt...to a more provincialist conception" of Canada. Those who defend it argue that it gives only "symbolic recognition of [the country's] basic sociological, legal and political realities." They note that Quebec is in fact a "distinct society" and that Canada is actually "a collection of provincial political communities equally as legitimate as the national community."[26]

The accord points up anew the unique situation of Canadian federalism and the weak hold that the national state has on its citizens and political leaders. Canada is much more statist than the United States, but its statism, as Trudeau noted in 1961, is more provincial than federal.[27]

Conversely, in the United States, the most important and powerful minority is and has been the blacks. And much as their struggle for equal rights has facilitated that of other minorities and women, it has also contributed to political centralization. Unlike the Québécois, American blacks do not control any states. Until the civil rights revolution of the 1960s, they were most oppressed in the deep south, in the states in which they were proportionately most numerous. Hence, they pressed for federal intervention to override state policies in education, social amenities (Jim Crow laws), economics, and politics. Trade unionists, similarly weakest in the less industrialized and least democratic south, also supported enhanced national power.

Thus, the equal rights struggles of the two major minorities within the North American federal unions had diverse and opposing consequences on their center-periphery relationships.

Regional Interests

The Canadian provinces' tendency to engage in recurrent struggles with the federal government may also be related to the fact that regional interests are much less well protected in Parliament than in Congress. As I argued three decades ago:

> Given the tight national party discipline imposed by a parliamentary as compared with a presidential system, Canadians are forced to find a way of expressing their special regional or other group needs....[T]he Canadian solution has been frequently to support different parties on a provincial level than those which they back nationally,

so that provincial governments can carry out the representation tasks that in the United States are fulfilled by congressional interest blocs.[28] Or, as a Canadian political scientist put it more recently, "congressionalism appears to inhibit the direct confrontation of federal and state governments, while the parliamentary forms in their contemporary Canadian variant sharpen the conflict between federal and provincial jurisdictions."[29] Thus, "federal-provincial conferences became the forum where all provinces...seek to negotiate with the federal government as though its interests and those of the provinces are inherently opposed."[30]

In the federal-provincial conference, Canada has, in effect, created an extraparliamentary, unelected legislative body to handle regional representation — a body that is effectively consociational, representative of political units, not the electorate. Policies are adopted through agreement by the heads of the regional and linguistic groupings without the equivalent of a vote in Parliament.

> [T]o create policies in Canada and review how the Canadian federal system works in general a Plenary Conference of the Prime Ministers of the National and Provincial Governments meets at least once a year. The conference has a secretariat; it works out agreements and commissions special studies. In addition, Plenary Conferences of the national and provincial ministers and deputy ministers in specific fields meet several times a year. They too have secretariats, working committees, and special studies by consultants. An office under the Prime Minister of Canada oversees the set of contacts with the provinces in special fields. Within each provincial government an office oversees all the government's contacts with Ottawa.[31]

The many regularly scheduled meetings of deputy ministers in various fields — health, education, labor, and so on — make for an extensive third house. There are many more than one hundred such sessions a year. Although the United States also has many meetings of state government representatives and federal authorities, their range, staff, power, and influence are proportionately very much less than those in Canada. States press their legislative, budgetary, and regulatory concerns through their representatives in the House and Senate, who will act aggressively on their behalf against their president or party leaders if need be.

To oppose and negotiate effectively with the national government, the regional electorates require the opportunity to choose provincial administrations or congressional representatives who can not be controlled by the federal executive. One way to do this is to opt for an opposition party at the provincial level — a route Canadians often take within a year after a national election has changed party control of Parliament. Given tight parliamentary discipline, being able to choose a party not linked to the governing federal party makes the task of regional representation easier.

Electoral Systems

If someone were to give the proverbial political sociologist from Mars a list of Canadian election results, province by province, provincial as well as federal, from 1921 to the present, and ask him with that knowledge alone to guess what kind of country Canada is, I suspect that he would conclude that it is an extremely unstable nation, full of unresolved tensions, with a political system close to collapse. No other country has produced so many electorally effective minor parties in the same period of time. In contrast, the United States has produced very few.

This variation is in some measure a function of the different constitutional structures derivative from the replacement of a monarchy by a presidency in the south and the evolution of a constitutional monarchy-parliamentary government in the north. All efforts to form strong third parties in the United States have proved futile because the effective constituency in presidential elections is the entire country, and in gubernatorial elections the state. The need to elect one person as chief executive has prevented American third parties from developing pluralities among distinct working-class, farmer, religious, or ethnic groups, as has been done in single-member, parliamentary constituency systems such as those in Canada and other Commonwealth countries.[32]

Third Parties

The thesis that constitutional factors have affected the propensity for third parties in the United States is a very old one. In 1893, Friedrich Engels put it at the top of a list of variables preventing the growth of a third, workers' party in the United States, blaming "the Constitution...which causes any vote for any candidate not put up by one of the two governing parties to appear to be lost. And the American...wants to influence his state; he does not throw his vote away."[33]

The electoral factors undermining third parties were spelled out in detail in 1910 by Morris Hillquit, Socialist Party leader. In the first major history of American socialism, he noted that in other parliamentary countries such as Canada or Britain,

> the elections are by district and the ticket of each party is, as a rule, limited to one candidate for each district. Each electoral campaign is thus conducted on the merits of the given district, and is in no way dependent upon conditions in other districts. In an electoral district largely made up of radicals the voters may, therefore, enter the contest with the expectation of victory regardless of the more conservative sentiments in other districts or in the country at large. In the United States...the ticket handed to the voter...contains the names not only of candidates for the state legislature or congress, but also for all local and state officers and even for President of the United States. And since a new party rarely seems to have the chance or prospect of electing its candidate for governor of a state or president of the country, the voter is inclined in advance to consider its entire ticket as hopeless. The fear of "throwing away" the vote is thus a peculiar product of American politics, and it requires a voter of exceptional strength of conviction to overcome it.[34]

Comparing the situation in the United States with that in Canada before the 1930s suggests the importance of the emphasis on electoral systems in explaining the varying success of third parties. The parliamentary system encouraged agrarian and socialist minor-party constituency victories in the early 1920s. Canada's best-known socialist, J.S. Woodsworth, was elected to the House of Commons from Winnipeg as an Independent Labor Party member and remained in the House for the next two decades as the parliamentary leader of Canadian socialism. He initially led a group of two members, who were formally recognized in the House as a fourth party (in addition to the Liberals, the Conservatives, and the agrarian-based Progressives).[35]

South of the border, Robert LaFollette, running for president in 1924 as the candidate of the Progressive and Socialist parties and with the official backing of the American Federation of Labor, secured 17 percent of the national vote. This was the second-largest percentage obtained by a third-party candidate since the Civil War.[36] Yet the considerable support for farmer-labor politics evidenced by the LaFollette candidacy had no consequences for the party system or for third-party representation in Congress.[37]

Conversely, in Canada, the few socialist and United Farmer members of Parliament elected from Manitoba and Alberta had an important

> educational and propagandist function....The...[third-party] group persistently kept the viewpoint of labour before the House and country. In the House they forced discussions and recorded votes. They used Ottawa as "a great broadcasting machine for working class education."[38]

One result was Canada's first effective socialist party on the national level, the Co-operative Commonwealth Federation, which was founded in 1932. As the historian Martin Robin notes:

> The legislative and propagandist activities of Woodsworth and the Ginger Group in parliament support the proposition that the formal structure of the Canadian parliamentary system favored the institutionalization of a third party, and explains in part the relative success and failure of Canadian and American third parties and socialism. The executive and legislative politics in the United States restricted the growth of third parties since they could play no role in executive politics. In Canada, however, a small group of independent MPs, favoured by house rules which recognized their independence and facing disciplined major parties, could effectively claim a separate party existence and use parliament for propaganda and legislative purposes.[39]

In the United States, following more than half a century of electoral defeats, two leaders of the Socialist Party of America, Norman Thomas and Michael Harrington, came to accept this explanation of the general failure of third parties. The former placed particular emphasis on the fact that, unlike the situation in countries with proportional representation or single-member parliamentary districts, third-party supporters in the United States always face the fact that they are casting a "wasted" vote that may help elect the major party candidate they most dislike.[40] Earlier, in 1938, Thomas had noted the weakness of third parties and suggested that they only hurt their cause by running independent candidates for president.[41] By the end of the 1950s, he reluctantly concluded that his party's experience demonstrated the futility of third parties in America, a view that a majority of the Socialist Party, then led by Harrington, soon came to accept.

The American electoral system, with its emphasis on elect-
ing one person from one party to the presidency or governorship,
cannot function with multiparty politics. The various groups
must identify with one or another of the two major electoral alliances on whatever basis of division is most salient to them. Each
major alliance or coalition party contains different interest
groups, which fight it out in the primaries. And within the legislature after the election, issue-based coalitions — such as the
farm bloc, the advocates of equal rights for minorities, and the
economic conservatives — form, cutting across party lines. Legislative majorities shift according to which set of issues is most
salient at the moment.

Canada's multiparty system is the result of the complexity
of its social structure and bases of political division — a pattern
essentially comparable to the American one — while it maintains
a form of government that requires disciplined parliamentary parties, that does not permit cross-party alignments in the House of
Commons or sharp divergences among a party's federal MPs from
province to province, and that does not provide primaries to
resolve internal party cleavages. Consequently, whenever a section, class, ethnic group, or province finds itself in basic conflict
with its traditional party allegiance, it can either go over to the
other major party — with which it may be in even greater disagreement on other issues — or back a third party.[42]

The Canadian and American polities must both face the difficulty of finding means that permit a number of factions based
on distinct interests and values to operate within a country that
spans a continent, while maintaining stable and representative
governments.[43] These two conditions, stability and repre-
sentativeness, are very difficult to meet simultaneously. As we
have seen, the American presidential system seriously discour-
ages third parties. It allows, even encourages, diverse factions to
fight it out in the primaries before elections. The party leaders
who come through the primaries then face the problem of head-
ing what is essentially a coalition — of representing diverse party
segments that are in sharp disagreement with each other. Issue-
oriented or special-interest groups are ultimately forced to find a
place within one of the major parties. But in Canada, as Mildred
Schwartz emphasizes,

> party discipline, along with the dominance of the Cabinet,
> gives relatively little scope for individual legislators to adopt
> a single issue as their own....These properties of government
> mean there is less to fear in Canada from single-issue moral
> campaigns.[44]

Its parliamentary system does not permit the accommodation of factionalism through intraparty contests involving the electorate. As a result, Canada perennially produces new parties.

Canadian political history since World War I "is odd when compared with both the American and Western European experience" in having

> given rise to several [regionally based] social move-
> ments....They have formed provincial governments in British
> Columbia, Alberta, Saskatchewan, Manitoba, [Ontario,] and
> Quebec, but have remained unaligned with the [national] es-
> tablishment parties (Liberal and Progressive Conservative).[45]

Shifts in representation in the federal Parliament have also been much greater than actual variations in public opinion.

Canada's electoral changes have clearly been the result not of great instability or tension, but rather of the electoral system. In effect, the Canadian system encourages the transformation of political protest, of social movements, of discontent with the dominant party in one's region or other aspects of life, into third, fourth, or fifth parties. The American system, on the other hand, favors the emergence of single-issue, extraparliamentary protest movements, almost all of which are absorbed relatively quickly into one of the major parties, which responds by becoming a spokesperson for the grievances or issues. Like the abolitionists who joined the Republicans, the populists who merged with the Democrats, and the radicals who backed the New Deal, they contribute to the policy orientations of the newly formed coalition.

It has been argued that the evidence that the variation in the number of parties in Canada and the United States is in large part a function of the differences in constitutional and electoral frameworks may also account for the varying roles socialist parties play in the two polities. In other words, as Norman Thomas contended in 1963, "had we in the United States had a centralized parliamentary government rather than a federal presidential government, we should have had, under some name or other, a moderately strong socialist party."[46]

There can be little question but that Thomas had a point. But it should also be noted that, as detailed in Chapter 9, Canada has had proportionately greater unionization of its labor force than the United States for five of the seven decades since 1918. That greater union strength points up a greater potential for class-related organizations north of the border.[47] The differential power of labor unions can not be casually linked to the electoral systems, a fact implying that cultural factors affect the propensities for leftist political activity in each country.

Opinion Division and Lobbies

In Canada, the recurrent conflicts between provincial governments and Ottawa, stimulated by the linguistic-cultural concerns of the Québécois and the role of other provinces in representing regional interests, have given the periphery increasing strength and undermined efforts to foster a strong Canadian identity. The country continues to emphasize local communities, both regional and ethnic. The American polity, on the other hand, though marked by ever-weakening party structures as populist reformers make headway, is increasingly nationalized. Its main regional entity, the south, has become incorporated into the national two-party system. The correlates of voter choice and opinion division are increasingly the same in Wyoming as in Arkansas, in California as in New York.

Constitutional structures also serve to give much more encouragement to the activities of lobbies in the United States than in Canada. There are more than 7,000 registered with Congress, plus many others that deal with other levels of government; Ottawa and the provinces have considerably fewer, even in proportion to the smaller Canadian population.[48] The difference lies, in part, in the dissimilarities between the roles of a congressperson and an MP. The former is free to vote as he or she chooses on bills and as the chair or member of a House or Senate committee may have more input on given policies than a cabinet member. Consequently, it pays to lobby Congress. Canada, conversely, "combines the British tradition of a strong executive and centralized leadership [and disciplined parliamentary parties] with a *relative* freedom from mass pressure and popular constraint."[49] Since individual MPs have comparatively little influence on specific policy items, lobbying is best addressed to the cabinet and, more discreetly, to higher-level civil servants. The fact that, as noted in Chapter 2, political appointments reach far lower into the administrative hierarchies in Washington and the state capitals than in Ottawa and the provinces makes for greater lobbying in the United States than in Canada.

Do They Work?

It is impossible to judge whether the American or the Canadian electoral and party system is more representative of voter opinion or interests. It is equally difficult to evaluate which is more efficient. Both countries are complex, continent-spanning federal unions marked by great social heterogeneity and economic diversity. In the United States, the separation of powers, the absence of disciplined congressional parties, and, for most of the period since the 1960s, the division of the federal authority between a president of one party and a congressional majority of the other, make it difficult to reach decisions on major issues. In Canada, in spite of party discipline in Parliament and the ability of the prime minister and the cabinet to have their way on legislation, foreign policy, and the budget, the provinces act as an effective constraint on the power of the central government. In noting that "we have stumbled into a peculiar Canadian version of the American separation of powers," Alan Cairns, one of Canada's most eminent political scientists, also concludes that his country's system "may be more difficult to work than its American counterpart" for it must have the cooperation of governments "jealous of their prerogatives."[50] Both systems require crises to produce the consensus necessary for major changes.

The American system, derived from a founding ideology or creed and operating within a nationalized cleavage system, has greater consensus on central core values. The social distance from the center to the periphery appears much shorter south of the border than in the north. Hence, the United States should be able to reach an agreement on new policies or reforms more easily than its northern neighbor does. But in spite of obvious sharply differentiated regional and provincial politics, Canada has been able to adopt across the continent similar policies on a number of major issues through the separate action of all, or the large majority, of its provincial governments, as in the cases of health care, labor legislation, and higher education.

Regional Cultures

Some Canadian cultural analysts say that their culture, like their politics, is focused much more regionally than nationally. Ethel Goodstein, an architecture critic, contends that Canadians, unlike Americans, have no distinct national style, that their "architecture is distinguished by its inherent regionalism." As she notes, Canada promotes "variety...rather than national identity in the built environment."[51] George Woodcock emphasizes that "Canadian literature, like Canadian painting, has always remained regional in its impulses and origins."[52]

The belief that Canada has no central character, that its identity is defined by its regions, was emphasized in a 1988 television documentary seeking to explain Canada to an American audience.[53] The program used as a takeoff point the 100th anniversary issue of *Saturday Night*, the country's leading cultural magazine, entitled "Our Home and Native Land" — a phrase from the national anthem.[54] As the television writers accurately indicated in translating the essays to the screen, the *Saturday Night* editors emphasized regional variety in their 24 articles. There was no essay that dealt with Canada's distinctiveness, values, or behavior. The editors and the television producers concluded that what makes Canada a country unlike any other is the variety of its communities. Few American intellectuals would say the same about their own nation.

To what extent are these crossborder differences a cause or a consequence of greater political regionalism in one system and centralization in the other? The question is almost impossible to answer, except by saying that the factors are interdependent. As we have seen, political factors press for greater provincial authority in Canada and stronger federal power in the United States. And the emphasis on the province in the north produces a stronger sense of place there. The presence of a national creed — a political religion — in the south fosters a stress on the nation. But Canadian intellectuals' greater commitment to regional and provincial identification must contribute to the resistance, even among Anglophones, to a strong sense of country. Robert Kroetsch emphasizes these crossborder differences in noting:

> Where the impulse in the U.S. is usually to define oneself as American, the Canadian...is always quoting his many sources. Our sense of region resists our national sense. I hear myself saying, I'm from *Western* Canada. Or, even beyond that — because I was born in Alberta and now live in Manitoba — people ask me, seriously, if I think of myself as an Albertan or Manitoban.[55]

The Canadian opinion polls bearing on these issues produce diverse results — in part, perhaps, an outcome of the different wording of questions. The 1974 Canadian National Election Study asked respondents to assign a score from zero to 100 on a "feeling thermometer" to Canada and their own province. The researchers found "that regional consciousness was not declining,....[since] it was highest among the younger and better educated," indicating that they "are more conscious of the regional divisions of the country than their elders."[56] The same study, however, reported that the national and provincial scores were *positively* correlated — that is, those who ranked the country high were also more likely to feel warmly toward their province. As David Elkins notes about this finding, except for Quebec separatists, Canadians' "deep and abiding" sense of place covers *both* nation and province.[57]

Six years later, in 1980, a national cross-section was asked "about the extent of their federal versus provincial attachment." Ontario was the only province in which a majority replied "Canada." Attachment to province was higher in the Atlantic provinces (68 percent), the Prairies (63 percent), Quebec (62 percent), and British Columbia (57 percent). As in the 1974 Election Study, older people were most "attached to Canada as opposed

to their province, or [more disposed] to support the federal government in situations of conflict."[58]

These findings indicating the strength of provincial identities
appear challenged by opinion surveys reporting that when Canadians have been asked to make the choice (which is artificial and
forced) between expressing their "first loyalty with Canada or the
province in which you live" or thinking of themselves "*first* as a
Canadian or as a [named provincial]," 74 percent in 1980 and 73
percent in 1983 replied "Canada" or "Canadian." Provincial loyalties were strongest in Newfoundland, followed by Quebec and the
Maritimes.[59] As in the earlier research, they were weakest in Ontario.

Two statistically sophisticated studies of the effects of province on political attitudes also conclude that regionalism is
important. They sought to evaluate the strength of such influences through analyzing the data of a 1981 survey that included a
number of ideologically relevant questions on social programs,
redistribution, corporate and union power, and other issues.
Michael Ornstein concludes, "[T]he ideological difference between
the Quebec and the English Canadian nations is much greater
than the differences between the provinces of English Canada."[60]
Overall, he reports that there are "distinct provincial political cultures,....that the people of different regions exhibit regional
loyalties, in the sense of preferring the quality of life in their
province and/or supporting their province's claims against the
federal government." He also notes "that the provinces lead distinct political lives."[61] A subsequent analysis of the same data
finds that the correlations with ideological opinions "for province
of residence tend to be consistently higher than for status, class
or ethnicity."[62]

Given the much greater importance of their provincial governments in the lives of Canadians, as compared to the role the
states now play for Americans, and the larger significance given
to place in the literature and art of the northern country than in
the southern, more commitment by the former to their subnational geographical unit is to be expected. I have not been able to
locate comparable surveys in the United States, testimony to the
improbability of asking Americans to choose between state and
nation as sources of identity or loyalty. I would hazard that

Americans faced with a similar choice would opt for the nation over the state by a larger majority than their neighbors. However one estimates the relative feeling Canadians hold for country and province, we have here another example of the interplay of beliefs and structures: Canada is more decentralized politically and more regional culturally, the United States more national on both counts, and the peoples and intellectuals of each reflect the differences.

12

Still Whig, Still Tory

Regardless of whether one emphasizes structural factors or cultural values, Canada and the United States continue to differ considerably. America reflects the influence of its classically liberal, Whig, individualistic, antistatist, populist, ideological origins. Canada, at least from a comparative North American perspective, can still be seen as Tory-mercantilist, group-oriented, statist, deferential to authority — a "socialist monarchy," to use Robertson Davies' phrase. There can be no real argument. As Margaret Atwood concludes, "Americans and Canadians are not the same, they are the products of two very different histories, two very different situations."[1]

At the same time, the two resemble each other more than either resembles any other nation. Both are products of North American settler societies. They have many structures and classically liberal values in common, and they vary in comparable ways from postfeudal, mercantilist Britain and Europe. Their differences, as we have seen from many public opinion polls, are often in the range of 5 to 10 percent.

The interesting fact is that, despite the development of both countries into industrialized, wealthy, urbanized, and ethnically heterogeneous societies, the dissimilarities, particularly the cultural differences, of the past continue. To reiterate an analogy, the two are like trains that have moved thousands of miles along parallel railway tracks. They are far from where they started, but they are still separated.

The End of Ideology

Comparable structural changes in tandem with the continuation of cultural differences have occurred throughout the developed world. Almost all of its countries have experienced close to half a century of prosperity and economic growth since World War II. They have also become better educated, more socially and geographically mobile, more egalitarian in social relations, and more responsive to demands from strata and minorities previously excluded from political influence. These trends have brought about comparable adjustments in culture and policies. On the political level, all, including the United States and Canada, have moved toward greater acceptance of the welfare-planning state. The emphasis in the late 1950s and early 1960s on the "end of ideology" testified to seeming agreement by the democratic left and right on this objective.[2] It reflected the impact of the Great Depression and the war in fostering collectivist policies.

The 1970s, and more especially the 1980s, however, witnessed a crisis of the welfare state both in the west and in the Communist world, as the burden of taxation and growing evidence of the dysfunctional effects of bureaucratic controls and planning on the economy led to a shift in the political cycle. Conservative, more free-enterprise-oriented parties have been elected in many western countries. More significantly, both socialist and Communist leaders are acknowledging the superiority of free-market incentives for spurring productivity and are endorsing increased privatization in the economy. Moves toward competition are occurring within the major Communist systems, China and the Soviet Union, as well as in lesser ones, such as Hungary and Poland. Socialist-led governments, including those of Australia, France, New Zealand, Spain, and Sweden, openly espouse market economics. Felipe Gonzales, prime minister of Spain, says that he knows of no system that works better than the free market, in spite of its immoral aspects. Kjell-Olof Feldt, finance minister of Sweden, proposes to reduce sharply the progressivity of his country's tax system, and discusses the need for "accepting private ownership, the profit motive and differences of income and wealth." Writing in the Social Democratic Party's magazine, this socialist leader states,

The market economy's facility for change and development and therefore economic growth has done more to eliminate poverty and "the exploitation of the working class" than any political intervention in the market's system of distribution.[3]

The leader of the most important opposition social democratic movement, Neil Kinnock of the British Labour Party, contends that to advocate widespread nationalization of industry today is "not socialism: that is dreaming." He argues that his party's efforts should be addressed to making capitalism "work more efficiently, more fairly and more successfully in the world marketplace."[4] More important, perhaps, is the growing British movement, Charter 88. This group, inaugurated by the leftist magazine *The New Statesman and Society* and supported by many associated with the Labour Party, advocates a charter for Britain modeled on the Canadian Charter of Rights and Freedoms and the American Bill of Rights. It seeks to constitutionalize due process and civil liberties guarantees and to limit the power of the Cabinet and Parliament.

This is all happening in the United States and Canada too. The American liberal Democrats are increasingly neo-liberals, who emphasize environmental, cultural, and racial- and gender-equality issues but who agreed with the tax reductions of the early 1980s, accept the need for deregulation (Senator Edward Kennedy has been a leader on this issue), and emphasize the use of market incentives as stimuli to growth. In Canada, Ed Broadbent, the leader of the federal New Democratic Party (NDP), noted early in 1989:

> The serious debate about the future is not about the desirability of a market economy. For most thoughtful people that debate is now closed....We New Democrats believe in the marketplace, including private investment decisions, reduced tariffs, private property, the free disposal of assets, the right to make a profit, decentralized decision making....As the world evolves so must our policies.[5]

If in the 1950s we were all socialists, as we approach the last decade of the 20th century we are all free marketers and libertarians.

Structure and Culture

Some critics of the cultural approach to accounting for Canadian-U.S. differences, such as Arthur K. Davis and Irving Louis Horowitz, contend that they are largely a function of cultural lag — that Canada, traditionally somewhat less developed economically than America, has been slower to give up the values and lifestyles characteristic of a less industrialized, more agrarian society.[6] On this view, Canada should become more like the United States as the structural gap declines.

Proponents of world-system or convergence theories enunciate a similar thesis on a broader scale. They see national differences diminishing, if not vanishing, as the industrial systems of the developed countries come to approximate each other. On that view, Canada and the United States should become even more similar since, say the proponents, the "American connection" has resulted in U.S. companies' having increasing domination over broad sections of Canadian economic life, while Canada has also become more culturally dependent on its large neighbor through the spread of the American mass media, particularly television and various forms of print journalism. Ironically, the argument that Canada inevitably must become American in its values and institutions finds greatest support among Canadian leftist intellectuals, who also most disparage the society to the south of them.

The economic-lag and convergence theories are seductive because parts of them — but only parts — are true. Since World War II, substantial changes in occupational structure, in economic productivity, in degree of urbanization, in education (quantitatively and qualitatively), and in rates of upward social mobility have greatly reduced the economically based structural gaps between the two countries. Canada, as of 1989, is almost as wealthy as the United States on a per capita basis, has been growing more quickly, is more urbanized, and has a more modern (service-oriented) occupational structure. But the economically dependent relationship marked by heavy U.S. investment has been changing rapidly with the steady increase in Canadian business involvement in the south. The latter development has outweighed the reverse relationship for many years in per capita terms, and it is now true *absolutely*. By the end of the 1980s, the outflow of Canadian capital south exceeded the inflow of American capital north.[7]

The two countries continue to vary on other structural dimensions. Canada retains a governmental structure quite different from that of the United States, is dissimilar demo\-graphically in terms of population size and racial, ethnic, and religious composition, and has a harsher climate. All these factors contribute to "overdetermining" the cultural and value variations since they operate largely in the same direction — that is, they reinforce Canada's Tory-socialist values.

More often than not, the structuralists are concerned primarily with economy-linked variables, which they see as the most important determinants of values. Here, the decline of Canadian-U.S. differences has been great, yet there has been no consistent falloff in the patterns of differences in behavior and values. Indeed, some have grown. As elaborated in the preceding pages, significant crossborder dissimilarities remain for a broad range of societal behavior and beliefs.

Both Canadian linguistic cultures continue to differ systematically from the American. As noted, the attitudinal evidence indicates that, on most issues, Francophones are at one end of the spectrum, Anglophones in the middle, and Americans at the other. Quebec, once the most conservative part of Canada, has become the most liberal on social and welfare issues. English Canada is also consistently more progressive than the United States.

Politically, the United States has grown more centralized, while Canada has become more decentralized. Changes in the same directions have occurred with respect to nationalization of politics; south of the border, similar lines of cleavage increasingly cut across all sections, while in the north, regional diversity has grown. The variations in the political systems have increased as well. Canadians retain party discipline in Parliament, while the American organizations have less influence over nominations and the behavior of legislators than at any time since Andrew Jackson. In Canada, the NDP has gained parliamentary strength, while American socialists and proponents of third-party activity are weaker than ever.

Although the productivity gap between the two countries has almost disappeared, behavioral indicators of Canadian and American economic cultures — for example, rates of savings and insurance and the use of credit — point to continued contrasts. Market researchers report consistent differences in consumption patterns. According to Goldfarb Consultants, Americans are much more inclined to use purchases to express their personalities or status; for example, they buy more flamboyant sport cars and prefer elegantly furnished hotel rooms, while Canadians choose more staid transportation and practical hotel accommodations. The dissimilarity in class organizational behavior in the two countries, as reflected in rates of trade union membership, has increased. The two also differ significantly in the degree of intraclass relations at the corporate level; networks are much denser in Canada, as is concentration of ownership of capital.

In other respects, the crossnational differences have narrowed. Canada's legal system is paying closer attention than it did formerly to the interpretations of American courts. The northern liberal tradition, historically much more supportive of group rights than the American, now seeks to encompass its neighbor's emphasis on the protection of individual political rights. Due-process guarantees for the accused have been strengthened in Canada as a result of constitutional changes. Such rights are also under greater juridical protection in the United States as well, as a consequence of many Supreme Court decisions and legislation on civil rights and freedom of information. American courts remain the most powerful in the world. The general distinction between Canadian adherence to a crime-control and group-rights model and American use of a due-process and individual-protection model still holds, but it has lessened. The large variations in rates of violent crimes, however, have not declined. And the gap in the ratio of police to population has widened.

Canada's increased concern with extending equality of opportunity has also helped to make the two societies more comparable with respect to the scope of their educational systems and to opportunities to enter the upper strata. The northern country, particularly at the level of higher education, is moving away from an elitist emphasis on the liberal arts, the humanities, and the classics, to a greater stress on professionalization in both the content of education and the activities of the professorate. Nevertheless, the two still differ somewhat in the proportions attending universities and in the social origins of those in elite occupations.

Both countries have witnessed an ethnic revival. Particularistic demands by minorities have led to increased institutionalization of multiculturalism on both sides of the border. Since the 1960s, each country has liberalized its immigration policies; two-fifths of those who enter both are Asian.

Canada is clearly handling the strains of a multicultural society better than the United States, although the results of the 1989 *Maclean's*-Decima survey raise some doubts about prospects for the future. In spite of a dramatic change in the ethnic composition of its major cities, there has been relatively little overt friction. And as we have seen, Canadian women now enter the labor force and the universities in larger proportions than their peers south of the border. There has simply been less pressure for and less resistance to the changes in ethnic and gender relationships. A handful of Québécois militants excepted, Canadians are less prone than Americans to express themselves violently. Moreover, the problems, particularly those created by ethnic incursions, may be less divisive in Canada, because of the lesser importance of race differences there and the absence of a culturally defined underclass in the proportions found in the United States.

Crossnational variations in religious behavior and attitudes continue, although their content has changed. The United States continues to be the most devout and orthodox of the world's highly industrialized countries. Canada is second, but clearly well behind its neighbor. The parishioners of the ecclesiastical churches, Roman Catholic and Anglican, as well as of the ecumenical, desectarianized United Church, who predominate in Canada, have become more permissive in their social attitudes and have lowered their level of religious participation; the adherents of the evangelical and fundamentalist Protestant sects, much more numerous in the United States, remain highly moralistic and have become more activist.

These differences are reflected in the contrasting emphases toward legalized abortion. The anti-abortion elements in both countries are based on the more orthodox religious forces. Hence, they are stronger and more militant in America, where conservative politicians and judges are more responsive to their fervor for the *rights* of the fetus than those north of the border.

In line with developments elsewhere, both countries have become more permissive with respect to forms of behavior once defined as illegal or deviant, particularly sexual behavior (extramarital relations, homosexuality, bearing children outside marriage, abortion) and personal lifestyles. Concomitant with and — perhaps derived from — the changes in the religious arena, Canadians, once more conservative, are now more libertarian than Americans, Quebecers more so than the rest of the country.

Survey data and impressionistic observations alike continue to sustain the thesis that Canada is a more elitist or deferential society than the United States, although less so than three decades ago. At the same time, the evidence clearly indicates that Canadians are more supportive than Americans of redistributive equalitarianism. Canada's political parties, including the governing Conservatives, remain committed to an activist welfare state, though not as much as in the 1960s and 1970s. American politicians, particularly the Republicans, have returned to advocacy of a weaker government, one less involved in welfare programs and more supportive of the free market.

Culture and Policy

In an effort to account for the severe urban crisis in the United States in contrast to the higher quality of urban life in certain European nations, the American sociologist David Popenoe looks at comparative conditions that exist in Canada as well — fewer slums, less poverty, and the relative absence of urban sprawl. After arguing that the differences cannot be explained by reference to an American underclass or to greater social heterogeneity, he points to dissimilarities in "political culture." Compared to much of Europe and Canada, the United States reflects a much weaker "sense of collective responsibility, and... an exaggerated sense of personal liberty," making it "one of the most *anti-government* of the advanced societies." Popenoe contends that these cultural attitudes affect the quality of urban life, underlying

> the lack of community planning at all levels, the political jus-
> tification of welfare payments not on humanitarian but on
> economic grounds, the aversion toward public housing and
> the inadequate system of public transportation.[8]

The "libertarian impulse" leads Americans to forget that

> those societies which have the most successful cities...are at
> the same time, compared to the United States, socially coer-
> cive societies. They do not provide their citizens the range of
> personal liberties and private property rights found in
> America.[9]

Consequently, the United States simply may not have the ideological resources, found even in such a highly free-
enterprise-oriented society as Switzerland, to deal with its urban
crisis or underclass.

The cultural and political differences between the two North
American nations help to explain their occasional difficulty in understanding each other in the international arena. There are the
obvious effects of the variations in size, power, and awareness of
the other. Canadians object to being taken for granted and to
being ignored by their neighbor. As citizens of a much less
populous power, they sympathize with other small or weak
countries in conflict with the United States. But beyond these dissimilarities of national power and interests, Canadians and
Americans have a somewhat disparate *Weltanschauung* (world
view) ideology. As noted in Chapter 2, Americans, more than other
western peoples, tend to view international politics in nonnegoti-
able moralistic and ideological terms. Canadians, like Europeans,
are more disposed to perceive international conflicts as reflections
of interest differences and, therefore, subject to negotiation and
compromise. The difference can be

> generalized by observing that major thrusts (and some quite
> minor ones) in American foreign policy are called "doctrines"
> while in Canada the term most often employed to describe
> the country's conduct of external relations is "functionalism"

....The Canadian term "functionalism" expresses an essentially European rejection of ideological criteria in foreign relations.[10]

The Tenacity of Culture

Many English-Canadian intellectuals, justly proud of their national culture, mobilized to fight the Canada-U.S. Free Trade Agreement because they saw in it a real threat to the continuity of distinct Canadian values. Without anticipating the results of further declines in tariff barriers, it is important to note how these values have survived what is already an American-dominated *mass* cultural market. As the Canadian playwright Rick Salutin pointed out before the treaty was ratified:

> Only three to five percent of all theatrical screen time in Canada goes to Canadian films; two to four percent of video cassettes are Canadian titles....[T]otal prime-time broadcasting in drama and sitcoms is only two to three percent Canadian; 95 percent of English-language TV drama is non-Canadian; Canadian-owned publishers have only 20 percent of the book market; 77 per cent of magazines sold here are foreign; 85 percent of record and tape sales are non-Canadian; in theatre, Canadian plays are the alternative theatre — they are the equivalent of off-Broadway, or off-off Broadway.[11]

In spite of the foreign (largely American) domination of popular culture in Canada, the vitality of the creative arts north of the border is striking. The country is producing world-class novelists, playwrights, dancers, painters, and other artists in numbers never before witnessed. Canadian complaints about being ignored by American reviewers no longer hold; they now pay considerable attention to the Canadian cultural scene. Robertson Davies properly calls attention to "the acceptance Canadian literature now enjoys all over the world...[since] during the past quarter of a century that literature has grown to an extraordinary maturity."[12] Novelist and historian Harold Horwood notes, "[T]he current period will, in years to come, be regarded as the Canadian renaissance in which Canada's seminal literary texts were being written."[13]

The continued survival of a distinct Anglophone Canadian culture is not surprising when viewed from a worldwide perspective. Minority cultures in many areas have been able to endure even when, like Canada, they have been exposed to powerful influences from larger neighbors who speak the same language. The Irish and the Scots are peoples separate from the English. Norway remains different from Sweden. The French- and Dutch-speaking areas of Belgium retain distinctiveness from both France and the Netherlands. The same is true of the different linguistic parts of Switzerland and their neighbors. The Ukraine has not been absorbed into the culture of Great Russia. As Mikhail Gorbachev is learning, national identities are not easily undermined.[14] Given modern means of communication, the diffusion of mass media, and easy travel, the tenacity of cultures — their ability to hold on within merged economies and polities — is amazing.

Changing Ideological Images

The ideological images of the two countries have fluctuated considerably, particularly since World War II. Canada is now seen by many, both at home and abroad, as being to the left of the United States. This shift is a consequence of the change in the international perception of America, which was seen for much of its history as the center of egalitarian, populist, leftist support for democratic movements of social change. That image was first challenged by the Bolshevik takeover of Russia, which, among other things, ended the Marxist assumption that the United States would be the first socialist country, that socialism as a movement would first come to power in the most advanced industrial country.[15]

Following the Russian Revolution, the United States shifted not only from being regarded as first in line for socialism to last but also from being viewed as a leader of the left to being seen as a defender and exemplar of reaction and a leader of the right.

Although criticism of the United States by people outside of it has changed ideological direction, the substance of the attacks is similar. In Canada and Latin America, the principal supporters of the United States before 1917 and for some time afterwards were the more liberal leftist groups. The Canadian social democratic party, the Co-operative Commonwealth Federation (CCF), was somewhat pro-American and anti-British in the 1930s, holding to the classic leftist position, similar to that of the Canadian rebels a century earlier. The Canadian Conservatives of the day were the pro-British, anti-American party, the defenders of the great refusal. In Latin America as well, the conservatives, the *pensadores*, those identified with Catholic traditional thought, were very anti-North American; the democrats, the liberals, the socialists were more sympathetic. Western hemisphere conservatives, north and south of the American borders, criticized the United States as a mobocracy, as a crude, vulgar, materialist, individualist, technologically oriented society, one unconcerned with high culture, community, the spiritual aspects of life, the decent things.

Today, the content of much of the anti-American criticism is the same, but the arguments that once were advanced by conservatives are now voiced by leftists. Rather than blaming populist democracy and vulgar popular taste, they hold capitalism responsible. Conversely, rightists increasingly defend the country and culture their forebears used to attack. Many Americans are either unaware of or reject this change in image. They still see themselves as citizens of a nation that defends liberty and equality against reaction and dictatorship. When the authoritarian enemy was on the monarchical or fascist right, that position was easy to hold; now that the opposition is the Third World or Communist left, that stance has become more difficult. Since all leftists are seen as progressive, particularly by intellectuals, the United States' international role is perceived as that of the major reactionary defender of the status quo.

The new situation has fostered an ambivalence in the American psyche. The United States is having an identity crisis. Many Americans have become confused about what the United States is and what it stands for abroad. They are not used to thinking in these terms. Unlike Canadians, they rarely have asked: what is our identity? are we a leftist nation? a rightist nation? a reformist nation? a defender of the status quo?

Canada, of course, has also changed. It was once a country many of whose intellectual leaders proudly identified as conser-

vative and elitist, a society on the model of Tory Britain. Now they
think of their country as less elitist, less reactionary, less
stratified, more egalitarian, though also less populist, than the
United States. They believe this is as it should be. And, as noted,
an increasing number of Canadians are critical of the United
States from the left, a view that affects their beliefs as to what
Canada is and should be. They seek to defend the integrity of
Canada against the United States by defining their own country
as more humane, more democratic, more anti-imperialist, and
more social democratic.

This shift in the definition of the character of Canada's main
reference group, the United States, is clearly affecting Canadian
values. Ironically, the change in self-image from that of a nation
to the right of the United States to one on its left may, in the long
run, contribute to eliminating the differences between the values
of the two countries. As Leon Samson argued more than half a
century ago, a democratic socialist ideology is to a considerable
extent synonymous with the social content of Americanism.
Frank Underhill, the author of the Regina Manifesto, the founding document of the CCF, once emphasized to his fellow citizens:
"If we are eventually to satisfy ourselves that we have at last
achieved a Canadian identity, it will be only when we are satisfied that we have arrived at a better American way of life than the
Americans have."[16]

Many Canadian literary critics, such as Ronald Sutherland,
A.J.M. Smith, and T.D. Maclulich, find that Canadian literature
has been coming to resemble American fiction, in line with the
presumed shift in national political identifications and the "modernization" of Canadian society. Sutherland notes,

> [A] new hero, as it were, suddenly exploded from the pages of
> Canadian fiction. In many respects he is an exponent of tradi-
> tional American rather the Canadian values — self-reliance,
> individualism, independence, self-confidence....Clear ex-
> amples of the new hero are found in novels from both French
> and English Canada, indicating that Canadians of each major
> language group are simultaneously and at long last creating
> a new image of themselves.[17]

And if there is a new image, a new hero, the expression of
new national attitudes and behavior cannot be far behind.

Conclusion

Some may argue that I have overemphasized the cultural differences between the two North American democracies, particularly between Anglophone Canada and the United States. They may properly point out that the two are quite similar to each other when compared to European or other nations. I do not question such a judgment. This study is an effort at a detailed comparison of two closely linked neighbors, not of crosscultural variations on a broad international scale. As Marcus Cunliffe notes, "*narrow comparison brings out dissimilarities, and broad comparison brings out similarities.*"[18]

The United States and Canada remain two nations formed around sharply different organizing principles. Their basic myths vary considerably, and national ethoses and structures are determined in large part by such images. One nation's institutions reflect the effort to apply universalistic principles emphasizing competitive individualism and egalitarianism, while the other's are an outgrowth of a particularistic compact to preserve linguistic and provincial cultures and rights and elitism. Ironically, as I have stressed, the conservative effort has stimulated an emphasis on group rights and benefits for the less privileged; the liberal one continues to stress more concern for the individual but exhibits less interest in those who are poor and outcast. The responses to the March 1989 *Maclean's*-Decima question on giving the government the power to suspend civil liberties reaffirm that Americans are much more suspicious of the state than are Canadians, particularly Anglophone Canadians. Those in the north continue to have a more deferential attitude toward government.

Perhaps the most important step that Canada has taken to Americanize itself — far greater in its implications than the signing of the free trade treaty — has been the incorporation into its constitution of a bill of rights, the Charter of Rights and Freedoms, placing the power of the state under judicial restraint. Although the principles of parliamentary supremacy and consideration for group rights are retained, the Charter makes Canada a more individualistic and litigious culture, one that will place more stress on the enforcement of personal rights through adversary procedures rather than governmental adjudication.

The greater institutional emphasis on individualism ultimately should be reflected in the country's values. By enacting the Charter, Canada has gone far toward joining the United States culturally. Yet Pierre Trudeau, the man most responsible for the Charter, is a combination of an American classical liberal and a European social democrat in his social outlook. Like him, Canada retains its Tory-socialist concern for group rights. Whether it can continue to be a "socialist monarchy," a deferential welfare state, will be its basic issue for the 21st century.

The United States moves toward the third millennium with its population as satisfied about their personal life situations as they have been since opinion polling started in the 1930s. Yet most Americans are disturbed by indicators of relative national decline, the trade and budget deficits, the spread of hard drugs and the seeming relationship to increased urban crime and violence, the inability to reduce poverty, and confusion about the country's world role. The enduring sense of moral superiority, of the strong conviction of America as utopia, of passion for a country in covenant with God, which has underlain its foreign policy, has steadily declined. America has returned to its antistatist philosophy in stronger terms that at any time since 1933. But the defense budget for resisting communism, which enhances the role of the state, is far greater than that spent by other developed countries. Gorbachev and the fiscal deficit are helping to bring it down.

Since the changes in western Europe and the Communist world involve moves toward more market-oriented and weaker state systems, the United States may come out of its identity crisis more certain of the correctness of competitive individualism than it has been for a long time. Certainly most of the presidents from Dwight D. Eisenhower to George Bush have pointed in this direction. On a political level, the dramatic events in the Communist countries and in the Third World — the visible influence of American practices and values, the placement of a model of the Statue of Liberty in Tiananmen Square, the spread of democracy in Latin America and Asia — suggest that American values are still in harmony with popular aspirations everywhere.

To end as I began, two countries came out of the American Revolution. Ironically, if that revolution had not succeeded, the continuing British North American polity would now be more left-ist than the revolution's children, more statist, much more social democratic, more disposed to perceive equality in redis-tributionist rather than meritocratic terms. It would operate under a parliamentary system, more conducive to third parties. It would be less individualistic and more deferential to authority. That hypothetical polity would also be less protective of civil liber-ties, free speech, and a free press than the actual populist republic, less inclined to place restrictions on the police, less generally inhibitive of the power of government.

Whose ancestors made the right decision? There is no "right" answer. But there can be an increase in understanding between their descendants. Canadians and Americans will never be alike, but Americans can learn more about Canada, and Canadians can learn more about why Americans are as they are. And by so doing they will come to understand their own countries better.

Notes

Acknowledgments

1. My initial treatment was presented in my book *The First New Nation: The United States in Historical and Comparative Perspective* (New York: Basic Books, 1963; exp. paper ed., New York: W.W. Norton, 1979), see esp. ch. 7.

Preface

1. Much of this is taken from an earlier essay on "History and Sociology: Some Methodological Considerations," in Seymour Martin Lipset, *Revolution and Counterrevolution: Change and Persistence in Social Structures*, 3d ed. (New Brunswick, N.J.: Transaction Books, 1988), pp. 3–34.

2. T.H. Marshall, *Class, Citizenship and Social Development* (Garden City, N.Y.: Doubleday, 1964), p. 38.

3. This survey, which I draw on in various parts of this book, is reported in "Portrait of Two Nations," *Maclean's*, July 3, 1989, pp. 23–56.

4. Ibid.

5. Stuart H. Surlin, Walter I. Romanow, and Walter C. Sonderlund, "TV Network News: A Canadian-American Comparison," *The American Review of Canadian Studies* 18 (Winter 1988): 468.

6. Seymour Martin Lipset, *Agrarian Socialism: The Cooperative Commonwealth Federation in Saskatchewan*, rev. ed. (Berkeley: University of California Press, 1971; first published in 1950).

7. See Seymour Martin Lipset, "American Exceptionalism Reaffirmed," in Byron Shafer, ed., *Is America Different?: A New Look at American Exceptionalism* (Oxford: Oxford University Press, forthcoming).

8. Robin W. Winks, *The Relevance of Canadian History* (Lanham, Md.: Universities Press of America, 1988), pp. xiii–xiv.

1 Revolution and Counterrevolution: The Introduction

1. Alexis de Tocqueville, *Democracy in America*, vol. 2 (New York: Alfred A. Knopf, 1948; first published in French, 1839), pp. 36–37. Friedrich Engels also was impressed by American exceptionalism, point-

ing to "special American conditions" that made Americans more likely than Europeans to idealize "bourgeois conditions" ("Engels to Weydemeyer," August 7, 1851, in Karl Marx and Friedrich Engels, *Letters to Americans* [New York: International Publishers, 1953], pp. 25–26).

2. J. Madison Davis, ed., *Conversations with Robertson Davies* (Jackson: University Press of Mississippi, 1989), p. 7.

3. Ibid., p. 125.

4. As the sociologist Mildred Schwartz notes: "The locus of anti-Americanism is primarily in the intellectual community in universities, in publishing houses, and among those concerned with the dissemination of ideas and popular culture" (*The Environment for Policy-Making in Canada and the United States*, Canada-U.S. Prospects 9 [Montreal: C.D. Howe Research Institute; Washington, D.C.: National Planning Association, 1981], p. 123).

For earlier comments to similar effect, see S.D. Clark, *The Developing Canadian Community* (Toronto: University of Toronto Press, 1962), pp. 232–242.

5. Northrop Frye, *Divisions on a Ground: Essays on Canadian Culture* (Toronto: Anansi, 1982), p. 13.

6. Robertson Davies, "Signing Away Canada's Soul," *Harpers* 278 (January 1989): 44.

7. Patricia Smart, "Our Two Cultures," *Canadian Forum* 64 (December 1984): 15.

8. Peter Brimelow, *The Patriot Game: National Dreams and Political Realities* (Toronto: Key Porter, 1986), pp. 1, 6–7.

9. "Engels to Sorge," September 10, 1888, in Marx and Engels, *Letters to Americans*, p. 204; and James Bryce, *Modern Democracies*, vol. 1 (New York: Macmillan, 1921), p. 471. See also "How Far American Experience Is Available for Europe," in James Bryce, *The American Commonwealth*, vol. 3 (London: Macmillan, 1887), p. 363.

10. Kaspar D. Naegele, "Canadian Society: Some Reflections," in Bernard Blishin et al., eds., *Canadian Society: Sociological Perspectives*, 3d ed. (Toronto: Macmillan of Canada, 1971), pp. 26–29. See also John Porter, *The Measure of Canadian Society: Education, Equality, and Opportunity* (Agincourt, Ont.: Gage, 1979; reprint, Ottawa: Carleton University Press, 1987), p. 180; Kenneth McNaught, "Approaches to the Study of Canadian History," *The* [Japanese] *Annual Review of Canadian Studies* 5 (1984): 94–97; Bernard Blishen, "Continuity and Change in Canadian Values," in Alan Cairns and Cynthia Williams, eds., *The Politics of Gender, Ethnicity and Language in Canada* (Toronto: University of Toronto Press, 1986), pp. 7–9, 22–24.

11. Wallace E. Lambert, Josiane F. Hamers James, and Nancy Frasure-Smith, *Child-Rearing Values. A Cross-National Study* (New York: Praeger, 1979), pp. 144, 346, 348–349. For a comprehensive comparison of aggregate statistics bearing on the ways in which values in the United States and Canada affect the socialization of children — a study that reaches conclusions similar to those of Lambert, James, and Frasure-Smith — see Lyle E. Larson, *The Canadian Family in Comparative Perspective* (Scarborough, Ont.: Prentice-Hall Canada, 1976), esp. pp. 24–25, 28–37.

12. Clifford Geertz, *The Interpretation of Cultures* (New York: Basic Books, 1973), p. 89.

13. "Engels to Sorge," February 8, 1890, in Karl Marx and Friedrich Engels, *Selected Correspondence* (New York: International Publishers, 1942), p. 467.

14. Northrop Frye notes that Canada should be

thought of...as a country that grew out of a Tory opposition to the Whig victory in the American revolution....[Quebec reacted against] the French Revolution with its strongly anti-clerical bias. The clergy remained the ideologically dominant group in Quebec down to a generation ago and the clergy wanted no part of the French Revolution or anything it stood for (*Divisions on a Ground*, p. 66).

15. Louis Hartz, *The Founding of New Societies* (New York: Harcourt, Brace and World, 1964), pp. 1–48; and Kenneth D. McRae, "The Structure of Canadian History," an essay in ibid., pp. 219–274. See also D.V. Bell, "The Loyalist Tradition in Canada," *Journal of Canadian Studies* 5 (May 1970): 22–23; and K.D. McRae, "Louis Hartz' Concept of the Fragment Society and Its Application to Canada," *Études Canadiennes* 5 (1978): 17–30.

16. Hartz, *The Founding*, p. 34.

17. Clark, *The Developing Canadian Community*, pp. 190–191.

18. R.R. Palmer, *The Age of the Democratic Revolution: The Challenge* (Princeton, N.J.: Princeton University Press, 1959), pp. 188–189. "The size of the loyalist migration in proportion to America's population was twenty times greater than in revolutionary France" (Patrice Higonnet, *Sister Republics: The Origins of French and American Republicanism* [Cambridge, Mass.: Harvard University Press, 1988], p. 193).

19. Forrest McDonald, "The Relation of the French Peasant Veterans of the American Revolution to the Fall of Feudalism in France, 1789–1792," *Agricultural History* 25 (October 1951): 151–161.

20. See Seymour Martin Lipset, *The First New Nation: The United States in Historical and Comparative Perspective* (New York: Basic Books,

1963; exp. ed., New York: W.W. Norton, 1979), esp. pp. 74–98; and Gunnar Myrdal, *An American Dilemma*, 2d ed. (New York: Harper and Row, 1962).

21. On the complexity of Jefferson's views, see Edmund S. Morgan, "Slavery and Freedom: The American Paradox," *The Journal of American History* 59 (June 1972): 5–29.

George Washington, who, like Jefferson, owned a plantation, also grew increasingly horrified about the institution and eventually freed all his slaves. Although a rural southerner, his backing of Alexander Hamilton's emphasis on industry against Jefferson's agrarianism was largely linked to the fact that the "Hamilton system had no need for slavery." Presciently, Washington understood that the union could only survive by "rooting out...slavery." And anticipating the possibility that the country might break up because it could not resolve the problem, he said privately to Edmund Randolph, his Attorney General, that should this occur "he had made up his mind to move and be of the northern" (James Thomas Flexner, *Washington: The Indispensable Man* [New York: New American Library, 1984], pp. 389–390).

22. Higonnet, *Sister Republics*, pp. 274, 278–279.

23. Manning Dauer, *The Adams Federalists* (Baltimore: Johns Hopkins University Press, 1953).

24. Reg Whitaker, "Democracy and the Canadian Constitution," in Keith Banting and Richard Simeon, eds., *And No One Cheered* (Toronto: Methuen, 1983), p. 245.

25. Timothy L. Smith, *Revivalism and Social Reform in Mid-Nineteenth Century America* (New York: Abingdon Press, 1957), pp. 24–25.

26. Ibid., pp. 88–89.

27. J. Franklin Jameson, *The American Revolution Considered as a Social Movement* (Princeton, N.J.: Princeton University Press, 1926), p. 157.

28. See McNaught, "Approaches to the Study," pp. 89–102, for a modern socialist's exposition of the Canadian view in these terms.

29. John Conway, "An 'Adapted Organic Tradition,'" *Daedalus* 117 (Fall 1988): 12.

30. W.L. Morton, *The Canadian Identity* (Madison: University of Wisconsin Press, 1961), pp. 105–106.

31. Bryce, *Modern Democracies*, vol. 1, pp. 559–560.

32. S.D. Clark, "The Frontier and Democratic Theory," *Transactions of the Royal Society of Canada* 48 (1954): 72; see also Morton, *The Canadian Identity*, pp. 105–106.

33. Kenneth McNaught, "Canada's European Ambiance" (paper read at the annual meeting of the Italian Association for Canadian Studies, Sicily, May 1988), p. 6.

34. A.R.M. Lower, "Religion and Religious Institutions," in George Brown, ed., *Canada* (Berkeley: University of California Press, 1954), p. 465.

35. Max Weber, *The Methodology of the Social Sciences* (Glencoe, Ill.: The Free Press, 1949; essays first published separately in German in various years, early 20th century), pp. 182–185.

36. Frank Underhill, *In Search of Canadian Liberalism* (Toronto: Macmillan of Canada, 1960), p. 222.

37. J.M.S. Careless, *Canada: A Story of Challenge* (Cambridge: Cambridge University Press, 1963), p. 113.

38. Bryce, *Modern Democracies*, vol. 1, p. 471. For an analysis by a Canadian economist of the implications of the differences in population sizes, see Richard G. Lipsey, "Canada and the United States: The Economic Dimension," in John F. Sigler and Charles H. Doran, eds., *Canada and the United States: Enduring Friendship, Persistent Stress* (Englewood Cliffs, N.J.: Prentice-Hall, 1985), pp. 70–72, 77–82.

39. Some economic historians advance a theory called the Laurentian thesis, which includes the assumption that Canada could not have survived as a separate country without state intervention and economic links to Europe.

40. "Engels to Sorge," September 10, 1888, in Marx and Engels, *Letters to Americans*, p. 204.

41. Harold A. Innis, *Essays in Canadian Economic History* (Toronto: University of Toronto Press, 1956), p. 406.

2 The American Ideology

1. Quoted in Michael Kazin, "The Right's Unsung Prophet," *The Nation* 248 (February 20, 1989): 242.

2. Kenneth McNaught, "Approaches to the Study of Canadian History," *The* [Japanese] *Annual Review of Canadian Studies* 5 (1984): 89.

3. For an excellent comparative discussion of American values, see Steven Kelman, *Regulating America, Regulating Sweden: A Comparative Study of Occupational Safety and Health Policy* (Cambridge, Mass.: MIT Press, 1981), pp. 123–127, 236–237.

4. This meaning of "antistatist" was to win wide acceptance a half-century later when presented in more detail by Louis Hartz (see *The Liberal Tradition in America* [New York: Harcourt Brace, 1955]).

5. H.G. Wells, *The Future in America* (New York: Harper and Brothers, 1906), pp. 72–76. The same thesis was presented by Gunnar Myrdal, *An American Dilemma* (New York: Harper's, 1944), pp. 7–9.

6. Leo Strauss, *Thoughts on Machiavelli* (Glencoe, Il.: The Free Press, 1958), p. 13.

7. For references to earlier opinion surveys, see Seymour Martin Lipset and William Schneider, *The Confidence Gap: Business, Labor and Government in the Public Mind*, rev. ed. (Baltimore, Md.: Johns Hopkins University Press, exp., 1987), pp. 379–380.

8. Quoted in Michael T. Kaufman, "Canada: An American Discovers Its Difference," *New York Times Magazine*, May 15, 1983, pp. 60–61, 80–85, 88.

9. J.P. Nettl, "The State as a Conceptual Variable," *World Politics* 20 (4:1968): 561, 574, 585.

10. L.H. Butterfield et al., eds., *The Book of Abigail and John: Selected Letters of the Adams Family 1762–1784* (Cambridge, Mass.: Harvard University Press, 1975), p. 121.

11. Ibid., pp. 122–123.

12. Edward Pessen, *Most Uncommon Jacksonians* (Albany: State University of New York Press, 1967), pp. 183–189; and Walter Hugins, *Jacksonian Democracy and the Working Class, A Study of the New York Workingmen's Movement 1829–1837* (Stanford, Cal.: Stanford University Press, 1960), pp. 13, 18–20, 132–134.

Although the Workingmen's Party received between 15 and 20 percent of the vote in some cities, it merged with the Democrats within a few years. It was thus the first of many leftist third parties that wound up walking down the road to the Democratic Party; from 1830 to 1990 that pattern seems to have been repeated almost like an invariant necessity.

13. That is, Marx developed his beliefs about working-class consciousness and the possibilities of socialism by reading about the Jacksonian United States. See Lewis S. Feuer, *Marx and the Intellectuals* (Garden City, N.Y.: Doubleday-Anchor Books, 1969), pp. 198–209; Maximilien Rubel, "Notes on Marx's Conception of Democracy," *New Politics* 1 (1961): 84–85; and Karl Marx and Friedrich Engels, *The German Ideology* (New York: International Publishers, 1960; first published in its entirety, International, 1939), p. 123.

14. See S.D. Clark, *Movements of Political Protest in Canada* (Toronto: University of Toronto Press, 1959); idem, *Canadian Society in Historical Perspective* (Toronto: McGraw-Hill Ryerson, 1976); Frank Underhill, *In Search of Canadian Liberalism* (Toronto: Macmillan of Canada, 1960); idem, *The Image of Confederation* (Toronto: Canadian Broadcasting Corporation, 1964); A.R.M. Lower, *Colony to Nation* (Toronto: Longman's, 1964); and John Porter, *The Vertical Mosaic: An Analysis of Social Class and Power in Canada* (Toronto: University of Toronto Press, 1965).

15. Alexis de Tocqueville, *Democracy in America*, vol. 1 (New York: Alfred A. Knopf, 1963; first published in French, 1835), p. 51.

16. Philip Schaff, *America: A Sketch of the Political, Social, and Religious Character of the United States of North America* (New York: C. Scribner, 1855), p. 259.

17. "Engels to Sorge," February 8, 1890, in Karl Marx and Friedrich Engels, *Selected Correspondence* (New York: International Publishers, 1942), p. 467.

18. Max Weber, *The Protestant Ethic and the Spirit of Capitalism* (New York: Scribner, 1935; first published in German, 1905), pp. 55–56.

19. Antonio Gramsci, *Selections from the Prison Notebooks* (New York: International Publishers, 1971; first published in Italian, 1955), pp. 21–22, 272, 318.

20. Weber, *The Protestant Ethic*, pp. 155–183; and idem, "The Protestant Sects and the Spirit of Capitalism," in Max Weber, *Essays in Sociology*, trans. and ed. by Hans Gerth and C.W. Mills (New York: Oxford University Press, 1946; first published in German, various dates, early 20th century), pp. 309, 313.

21. Hermann Keyserling, *America Set Free* (New York: Harper and Brothers, 1929), pp. 237–240, 244–252; Leon Samson, *Toward a United Front* (New York: Farrar and Rinehart, 1935), pp. 16–17. For my earlier discussions of Samson, see Seymour Martin Lipset, "Why No Socialism in the United States?" in S. Bialer and S. Sluzar, eds., *Sources of Contemporary Radicalism*, vol. 1 (Boulder, Col.: Westview Press, 1977), pp. 75–77; and idem, *The First New Nation: The United States in Historical and Comparative Perspective*, rev. ed. (New York: W.W. Norton, 1979), pp. 393–394.

22. Samson, *Toward a United Front*, pp. 16–17.

23. Michael Harrington, *Socialism* (New York: Saturday Review Press, 1972), p. 118.

24. "MacNeil/Lehrer News Hour," Public Broadcasting System, Washington, D.C.

25. Kelman, *Regulating America, Regulating Sweden*, pp. 122–123.

26. Robert N. Bellah, *The Broken Covenant: American Civil Religion in Time of Trial* (New York: Seabury Press, 1975), p. 124.

27. William M. Dick, *Labor and Socialism in America: The Gompers Era* (Port Washington, N.Y.: Kennikat Press, 1972), p. 184. See also Melvyn Dubofsky, *We Shall Be All: A History of the Industrial Workers of the World* (Chicago: Quadrangle Books, 1955), pp. 483–484.

28. William Appleman Williams, *The Great Evasion* (Chicago: Quadrangle Books, 1964), p. 155.

29. James Weinstein and David W. Eakins, eds., *For a New America* (New York: Random House, 1970), p. 162.

30. C. Wright Mills, *White Collar* (New York: Oxford University Press, 1951), p. 10.

31. David Deitch, "Libertarians Unite in Drive to Reduce Tax Burden," Boston *Globe*, April 10, 1971, p. 7. See also "What's This?" *Dissent* 18 (August 1971): 395.

32. Deitch, "Libertarians Unite," p. 7.

33. Agar Adamson, "We Were Here Before: The Referendum in Canadian Experience," in Ronald G. Landes, ed., *Canadian Politics, A Comparative Reader* (Scarborough, Ont.: Prentice-Hall Canada, 1985), pp. 333–345.

34. Henry H. Bull, "The Career Prosecutor of Canada," *The Journal of Criminal Law, Criminology, and Police Science* 53 (1962): 89–96.

35. Richard Morin, "A Half a Million Choices for American Votes," *Washington Post*, national weekly ed., February 6–12, 1989, p. 38.

36. Andrew Sancton, "Conclusion: Canadian City Politics in Comparative Perspective," in Warren Magnusson and Andrew Sancton, eds., *City Politics in Canada* (Toronto: University of Toronto Press, 1983), p. 300.

37. Albert Shanker, "European vs. U.S. Students: Why Are We So Behind?" *New York Times*, News of the Week section, April 23, 1989, p. E7.

38. Morin, "A Half a Million Choices," p. 38.

39. Austin Ranney, "Referendums," *Public Opinion* 11 (January/February 1989): 15.

40. This figure is based on the total populations of voting ages. The percentage would be one to two points higher if residents who are not citizens (and thus not eligible to vote) were excluded from the base. See Walter Dean Burnham, "The 1980 Earthquake: Realignment, Reaction, or What?" in Thomas Ferguson and Joel Rogers, eds., *The Hidden Election* (New York: Pantheon,1981), p. 101.

41. Walter Dean Burnham, "The Appearance and Disappearance of the American Voter," in Richard Rose, ed., *Electoral Participation: A Comparative Analysis* (Beverly Hills, Cal.: Sage Publications, 1980), pp. 35–73.

42. Raymond E. Wolfinger and Steven Rosenstone, *Who Votes?* (New Haven, Conn.: Yale University Press, 1980); and Frances Fox Piven and Richard A. Cloward, *Why Americans Don't Vote* (New York: Pantheon, 1988).

43. Alexander Brady, "Canada and the Model of Westminster," in William B. Hamilton, ed., *The Transfer of Institutions* (Durham, N.C.: Duke University Press, 1964), p. 77.

44. Edward C. Banfield and James Q. Wilson, *City Politics* (Cambridge, Mass.: Harvard University Press and MIT Press, 1963), p. 1.

45. Max Beloff, "Of Lords, Senators, & Plain Misters," *Encounter* 68 (April 1987): 69–71; and "An Exchange between Max Beloff and Irving Kristol," *Encounter* 69 (June 1987): 69–71.

46. George Grant, *Lament for a Nation* (Princeton, N.J.: Van Nostrand, 1965), pp. 64–65.

47. Ibid.

48. Richard Rose, "How Exceptional Is American Government?" *Studies in Public Policy* (Centre for the Study of Public Policy, University of Strathclyde, Glasgow) 150 (1985).

49. Nathan Glazer, "Welfare and 'Welfare' in America," in Richard Rose and Rei Shiratori, eds., *The Welfare State East and West* (New York: Oxford University Press, 1986), p. 62; Harold Wilensky, *The Welfare State and Equality* (Berkeley: University of California Press, 1975), pp. 28–39; and Arnold Heidenheimer et al., *Comparative Public Policy: The Politics of Social Choice in Europe and America* (New York: St. Martin's Press, 1983).

50. For a sophisticated analysis of the changes, see Hugh Heclo, "The Emerging Regime," in Richard A. Harris and Sidney M. Milkis, eds., *Remaking American Politics* (Boulder, Col.: Westview Press, 1989), pp. 290–320.

51. For a comprehensive analysis of the meanings of equality in America and ambivalence about opportunities and results, see Sidney Verba and Gary R. Orren, *Equality in America: The View from the Top* (Cambridge, Mass.: Harvard University Press, 1985), pp. 1–3, 5–9, 18–20.

52. For a detailed discussion, see Lipset, *The First New Nation*, pp. xxxiv–xxxv.

53. Brigitte Buhmann et al., "Equivalence Scales, Well-Being, Inequality, and Poverty: Sensitivity Estimates across Ten Countries Using the Luxembourg Income Study (LIS) Database," *Review of Income and Wealth* 34 (June 1988): 126–133; and Timothy M. Smeeding and Barbara Boyld Torrey, "Poor Children in Rich Countries," *Science* 242 (November 11, 1988): 873–877.

54. It should be noted, however, that complex composite measures of inequality, which include items such as social security programs, physicians per capita, infant mortality, caloric and protein consumption per capita, educational attainments, social mobility into elite categories, in addition to income distribution, place the United States close to the top, most equal (only Switzerland is possibly higher) among 120 polities (Michael Don Ward, *The Political Economy of Distribution: Equality versus Inequality* [New York: Elsevier, 1978], pp. 43, 65).

55. Martin Dooley, "Demography of Child Poverty in Canada: 1873–1986" (paper presented to the Population Association of America, Baltimore, Md., March 28–April 1, 1989), tables 18 and 19.

56. Quoted in Sacvan Bercovitch, "The Rites of Assent: Rhetoric, Ritual, and the Ideology of American Consensus," in Sam B. Girgus, ed., *The American Self: Myth, Ideology and Popular Culture* (Albuquerque: University of New Mexico Press, 1981), p. 21.; see also idem, *The American Jeremiad* (Madison: University of Wisconsin Press, 1978), pp. 140–152, 176.

57. Bercovitch, "Rites of Assent," pp. 5–6.

58. Ibid. (italics in original).

59. Gramsci, *Selections*, pp. 21–22, 272, 318.

60. See Seymour Martin Lipset, *Consensus and Conflict: Essays in Political Sociology* (New Brunswick, N.J.: Transaction Books, 1985), pp. 187–217; and idem, "American Exceptionalism Reaffirmed," in Byron Shafer, ed., *Is America Different?: A New Look at American Exceptionalism* (Oxford: Oxford University Press, forthcoming).

3 The Canadian Identity

1. Ramsay Cook, *The Maple Leaf Forever: Essays on Nationalism and Politics in Canada* (Toronto: Macmillan of Canada, 1977), pp. 188–189.

2. Margaret Atwood, *The Journals of Suzanna Moodie: Poems* (Toronto: Oxford University Press, 1970), p. 62.

3. See Seymour Martin Lipset, "Why No Socialism in the United States?" in S. Bialer and S. Sluzar, eds., *Sources of Contemporary Radicalism*, vol. 1 (Boulder, Col.: Westview Press, 1977), pp. 74–79, 81–83, for other references.

4. See Harold Innis, *The Fur Trade in Canada* (Toronto: University of Toronto Press, 1973), p. 396.

5. Peter J. Smith, "The Ideological Origins of Canadian Confederation," *Canadian Journal of Political Science* 20 (March 1987): 25, 27.

6. William A. Stahl, "'May He Have Dominion...': Civil Religion and the Legitimation of Canadian Confederation" (Luther College, University of Regina, 1986), p. 4 (italics in original).

7. Quoted in ibid.

8. Ibid., p. 14.

9. Pierre Berton, *Why We Act Like Canadians* (Toronto: McClelland and Stewart, 1982), pp. 16–17.

10. Ibid., p. 16.

11. Alan F.J. Artibise, "Exploring the North American West: A Comparative Urban Perspective," *The American Review of Canadian Studies* 14 (Spring 1984): 32.

12. "O Canada Eh!" prepared by McLuhan Productions, Toronto, 1986.

13. Charles Gordon, "No One Called In the Helicopters," *Maclean's*, May 1, 1989, p. 35.

14. There were, of course, opponents of these actions, especially among French Canadians. Not enamored with the British tie (although they preferred an Anglican monarchy to absorption into a Protestant sectarian republic), Francophones argued that Canada had become a North American nation and that the decision on whether or not to go to war should depend on its interests as an independent state. Pointing to the fact that the United States did not enter either world war at its beginning, they contended that if Canada were truly independent, it too would stay out of wars unless and until it was felt necessary to enter for Canadian reasons. At times, this opposition became vehement. The imposition of conscription evoked riots and public disobedience in Quebec during both world wars.

15. "Bleeding-Heart Conservatives," Canada survey, *The Economist*, October 8, 1988, p. 4.

16. Philip Resnick, *Parliament vs. People: An Essay on Democracy and Canadian Political Culture* (Vancouver: New Star Books, 1984), p. 13.

17. Frank Underhill, *In Search of Canadian Liberalism* (Toronto: Macmillan of Canada, 1960) p. 222.

18. Mason Wade, "Quebec and the French Revolution of 1789," in J.M. Bumsted, ed., *Canadian History before Confederation: Essays and Interpretations* (Georgetown, Ont.: Irwin-Dorsey, 1972), p. 252.

19. "Engels to Sorge," February 8, 1890, in Karl Marx and Friedrich Engels, *Selected Correspondence* (New York: International Publishers, 1942), p. 467; and "Engels to Sorge," September 10, 1888, in idem, *Letters to Americans* (New York: International Publishers, 1953), p. 204.

20. Arthur K. Davis, "Canadian Society and History as Hinterland versus Metropolis," in Richard J. Ossenberg, ed., *Canadian Society: Pluralism, Change and Conflict* (Scarborough, Ont.: Prentice-Hall Canada, 1971), pp. 22–29.

21. Reg Whitaker, "Images of the State in Canada," in Leo Panitch, ed., *The Canadian State: Political Economy and Political Power* (Toronto: University of Toronto Press, 1977), pp. 34, 39 (italics in original). See also Gordon T. Stewart, *The Origins of Canadian Politics: A Comparative Approach* (Vancouver: University of British Columbia Press, 1986), pp. 92–93, 96–99.

22. See, for example, Louis Hartz, *The Liberal Tradition in America* (New York: Harcourt, Brace, 1955); and Gad Horowitz, "Notes on 'Con-

servatism, Liberalism and Socialism in Canada,"" *Canadian Journal of Political Science* 11 (June 1978): 390.

23. Gad Horowitz, "Red Tory," in William Kilbourn, ed., *Canada: A Guide to the Peaceable Kingdom* (New York: St. Martin's Press, 1970), p. 255 (emphasis in original). See also idem, *Canadian Labour in Politics* (Toronto: University of Toronto Press, 1968), pp. 1–52.

24. Northrop Frye, "Letters in Canada: 1952, Part I: Publications in English," *University of Toronto Quarterly* 22 (April 1953): 273.

25. See S.D. Clark, *Church and Sect in Canada* (Toronto: University of Toronto Press, 1948).

26. Rodney Stark and William Sims Bainbridge, *The Future of Religion* (Berkeley: University of California Press, 1985), p. 461.

27. William Christian and Colin Campbell, *Political Parties and Ideologies in Canada* (Toronto: McGraw-Hill Ryerson, 1983), p. 29, 31.

28. S.D. Clark, *The Developing Canadian Community* (Toronto: University of Toronto Press, 1962), p. 232. See also Harold A. Innis, *Essays in Canadian Economic History* (Toronto: University of Toronto Press, 1956), pp. 62–77, 78–96, 97–107, 156–175, 200–210; idem, *The Fur Trade in Canada*; and Donald G. Creighton, *The Empire of the St. Lawrence* (Toronto: Houghton Mifflin, 1958). For an evaluation of the literature, see J.T. McLeod, "The Free Enterprise Dodo Is No Phoenix," *The Canadian Forum* 56 (August 1976): 6–13.

29. Richard Gwyn, *The 49th Paradox: Canada in North America* (Toronto: McClelland and Stewart, 1985), p. 11. For a critique of the geographic argument about Canadian character, see Carl Berger, "The True North Strong and Free," in Peter Russell, ed., *Nationalism in Canada* (Toronto: McGraw-Hill, 1966), pp. 3–26.

30. Gwyn, *The 49th Paradox*, pp. 185–187. See also Alan F.J. Artibise, "Canada as an Urban Nation," *Daedalus* 117 (Fall 1988): 237–239.

31. Michael A. Goldberg and John Mercer, *The Myth of the North American City: Continentalism Challenged* (Vancouver: University of British Columbia Press, 1986), p. 116.

32. Edgar W. McInnis, *The Unguarded Frontier* (Garden City, N.Y.: Doubleday, 1942), pp. 306–307. See also Douglas Fetherling, *The Gold Crusades: A Social History of Gold Rushes 1849–1969* (Toronto: Macmillan of Canada, 1989).

33. Sacvan Bercovitch, "The Rites of Assent: Rhetoric, Ritual, and the Ideology of American Consensus," in Sam B. Girgus, ed., *The American Self: Myth, Ideology and Popular Culture* (Albuquerque: University of New Mexico Press, 1981), pp. 5–6.

34. Alan C. Cairns, "Political Science in Canada and the Americanization Issue," *Canadian Journal of Political Science* 8 (June 1975): 217.

35. A.J.M. Smith, "Evolution and Revolution as Aspects of English-Canadian and American Literature," in R.A. Preston, ed., *Perspectives on Revolution and Evolution* (Durham, N.C.: Duke University Press, 1979), p. 234.

36. Margaret Atwood, *Survival: A Thematic Guide to Canadian Literature* (Boston: Beacon Press, 1972), pp. 31–32.

37. Stanley Fogel, *A Tale of Two Countries: Contemporary Fiction in English Canada and the United States* (Toronto: ECW Press, 1984), p. 19. For a discussion of the impact of the American myth on writers, see pp. 14–18.

38. W.L. Morton, *The Canadian Identity* (Madison: University of Wisconsin Press, 1961), p. 86.

39. Bercovitch, "The Rites of Assent," p. 24.

40. Underhill, *In Search of Canadian Liberalism*, p. 222.

41. Blair Fraser, *The Search for Identity: Canada, 1945–67* (Garden City, N.Y.: Doubleday, 1967), p. 301. See also S.D. Clark, in H.F. Angus, ed., *Canada and Her Great Neighbor: Sociological Surveys of Opinions and Attitudes in Canada Concerning the United States* (Toronto: Ryerson Press, 1938), pp. 243, 245.

42. Robin Winks, "'Whodunit?': Canadian Society as Reflected in Its Detective Fiction," *The American Review of Canadian Studies* 17 (Winter 1987–88): 377.

43. David M. Potter, "Canadian Views of the United States as a Reflex of Canadian Values: A Commentary," in S.F. Wise and R.C. Brown, *Canada Views the United States: Nineteenth-Century Political Attitudes* (Toronto: Macmillan of Canada, 1976), pp. 127–129.

44. John Charles Weaver, "Imperiled Dreams: Canadian Opposition to the American Empire, 1918–1930" (Ph.D. diss., Department of History, Duke University, 1973), pp. 78–79.

45. James Bryce, *Modern Democracies*, vol. 1 (New York: Macmillan, 1921), pp. 495–496.

46. Ibid., pp. 467, 501–502.

47. Weaver, "Imperiled Dreams," pp. 159–160.

48. H. Blair Neatby, *The Politics of Chaos: Canada in the Thirties* (Toronto: Macmillan of Canada, 1972), pp. 10–14. He summarizes research reported in Angus, ed., *Canada and Her Great Neighbor*, especially the section by S.D. Clark, pp. 392–438.

49. For a statement by Canada's foremost contemporary conservative philosopher on the differences between American and Canadian conservatism, see George Grant, *Lament for a Nation* (Princeton, N.J.: Van Nostrand, 1965), pp. 64–65, 70–71. See also Charles Taylor, *Radical Tories: The Conservative Tradition in Canada* (Toronto: Anansi, 1982).

50. Gwyn, *The 49th Paradox*, p. 11.

51. From a speech to the House of Commons, Ottawa, June 18, 1936.

52. Resnick, *Parliament vs. People*, pp. 16–17.

4 Literature and Myths: Canadian Perspectives

1. Ronald Sutherland, "A Literary Perspective: The Development of a National Consciousness," in William Metcalfe, ed., *Understanding Canada* (New York: New York University Press, 1982), p. 402.

2. Robertson Davies, *The Lyre of Orpheus* (Toronto: Macmillan of Canada, 1988), pp. 131–132.

3. John Irving, *A Prayer for Owen Meany* (New York: William Morrow, 1989), pp. 203–204 (italics in original).

4. See Robert L. McDougall, "The Dodo and the Cruising Auk," *Canadian Literature* 18 (Autumn 1973): 10–11; and Gaile McGregor, *The Wacousta Syndrome: Explorations in the Canadian Langscape* (Toronto: University of Toronto Press, 1985), pp. 59–60, 113–115, 256–257.

5. See McDougall, "The Dodo and the Cruising Auk," pp. 8–9; Russell M. Brown, "Telemachus and Oedipus: Images and Authority in Canadian and American Fiction" (Department of English, University of Toronto, 1979), p. 1; and R. Bruce Elder, *Image and Identity: Reflections on Canadian Film and Culture* (Waterloo, Ont.: Wilfrid Laurier University Press, 1989), p. 313.

6. Brown, "Telemachus and Oedipus," p. 1.

7. For references to "the fact that many of Canada's leading writers are women," see Geoff Hancock, *Canadian Writers at Work* (Toronto: Oxford University Press, 1987), p. 15; to "a literature dominated by women writers," see David Stouck, *Major Canadian Authors*, 2d ed. (Lincoln: University of Nebraska Press, 1988), pp. 28, 256; and Michelle Gadpaille, *The Canadian Short Story* (Toronto: Oxford University Press, 1988), p. vii.

8. I do not seek to evaluate the validity of these observations, some of which, like American creedal statements, are inherently self-serving from a nationalist perspective.

9. Ronald Sutherland, *The New Hero: Essays in Comparative Quebec/Canadian Literature* (Toronto: Macmillan of Canada, 1977), p. 2. For an analysis of regional literature making similar points, see Dick Harrison, *Unnamed Country: The Struggle for a Canadian Prairie Fiction* (Edmonton: University of Alberta Press, 1977), esp. pp. 73–79, 87–90. Dealing with the writing of the 1920s, Harrison notes "the general anti-revolutionary tendency of the society this literature expresses" (p. 89). Dennis Duffy traces the continuing impact of the Loyalist tradi-

tion on the literature of Ontario in *Gardens, Covenants, Exiles: Loyalism in the Literature of Upper Canada/Ontario* (Toronto: University of Toronto Press, 1982).

10. Northrop Frye, *Divisions on a Ground: Essays on Canadian Culture* (Toronto: Anansi, 1982), p. 46. See also Douglas Le Pan, "The Outlook for the Relationship: A Canadian View," in John S. Dickey, ed., *The United States and Canada* (Englewood Cliffs, N.J.: Prentice-Hall, 1964), pp. 158–159.

11. Northrop Frye, *The Bush Garden: Essays on the Canadian Imagination* (Toronto: Anansi, 1971), p. 248.

12. Claude A. Bissell, "A Common Ancestry: Literature in Australia and Canada," *University of Toronto Quarterly* 25 (January 1956): 133–134.

13. Claude A. Bissell, "The Place of Learning and the Arts in Canadian Life," in Richard A. Preston, ed., *Perspectives on Revolution and Evolution* (Durham, N.C.: Duke University Press, 1979), p. 208.

14. T.D. Maclulich, *Between Europe and America: The Canadian Tradition in Fiction* (Oakville, Ont.: ECW Press, 1988), pp. 13–14, 204–217.

15. Margaret Atwood, *Survival: A Thematic Guide to Canadian Literature* (Boston: Beacon Press, 1972), p. 33. On the same point, see Robert Kroetsch, *The Lovely Treachery of Words: Essays Selected and New* (Toronto: Oxford University Press, 1989), p. 55.

16. Atwood, *Survival*, p. 171.

17. Ibid., p. 131.

18. J. Madison Davis, ed., *Conversations with Robertson Davies* (Jackson: University Press of Mississippi, 1989), p. 78.

19. Dick Harrison, "The Search for an Authentic Voice in Canadian Literature," in Friedel H. Bastein, ed., *Kanada Heute* (Frankfurt am Main: Verlag Peter Lang, 1987), p. 156.

20. In Davis, ed., *Conversations with Robertson Davies*, p. 78.

21. Brown, "Telemachus and Oedipus," pp. 1, 2.

22. Ibid., p. 2.

23. Brown cites D.H. Lawrence as having said, "The American motto was really 'Henceforth be masterless' — an articulation of a deep-seated rebellion against the parenthood of Europe"; and Earl Rovid as writing that beneath the surface of the American novel of adolescence lies "the bloody ritual of parricide" a feature so pervasive that, he feels, in the American mythos, "Isaac has reversed positions with Abraham" (Ibid., pp. 5–6).

24. Ibid., p. 7.

25. Ibid., p. 8.

26. The critic George Woodcock particularly emphasizes Mac-Lennan's books as examples of the consciously didactic character of much Canadian fiction, which in his case involved using "archetypal" myths, notably those of Oedipus and Odysseus, to express concern for the country. And Woodcock asks, "what more potent image can a [Canadian] writer find...— an image that at the same time disguises and justifies his didacticism — than the relationship of orphans and surrogate fathers that recurs so often in the novels?" (George Woodcock, *Northern Spring: The Flowering of Canadian Literature* [Vancouver: Douglas and McIntyre, 1987], pp. 83, 93).

27. Brown, "Telemachus and Oedipus," pp. 16–17.

28. Ibid., p. 18. Written after Brown's essay was another Canadian retelling of the story of Noah: Timothy Findlay, *Not Wanted on the Voyage* (Toronto: Viking Press, 1984).

On the American emphasis on the present and the Canadian on history, see also Elder, *Image and Identity*, p. 313.

29. Mary Jean Green, "Writing in a Motherland" (French Department, Dartmouth College, Hanover, N.H., 1984).

30. Hugh MacLennan, "The Psychology of Canadian Nationalism," *Foreign Affairs* 27 (April 1949): 414–415. Robert Kroetsch points to the greater importance of heroines, who are much stronger than the men, in his country's fiction. The female figures tend to be strong and powerful. They seemingly have little need of men or have weak companions of the opposite sex (*The Lovely Treachery of Words*, pp. 66–67, 70).

31. McGregor, *The Wacousta Syndrome*, pp. 137, 143–147 (italics in original). See also Elder, *Image and Identity*, p. 33.

32. Robert Fothergill, "Coward, Bully, or Clown: The Dream-Life of a Younger Brother," in Seth Feldman and Joyce Nelson, eds., *Canadian Film Reader* (Toronto: Peter Martin Associates, 1977), pp. 235–236, 239–241.

33. Green, "Writing in a Motherland."

34. Frye, *The Bush Garden*, pp. 136–137.

35. Norman Newton, "Classical Canadian Poetry and the Public Muse," *Canadian Literature* 51 (Winter 1972): 40.

36. Northrop Frye, "Preface to an Uncollected Anthology," in Eli Mandel, ed., *Contexts of Canadian Criticism* (Chicago: University of Chicago Press, 1971), p. 184.

37. Bissell, "A Common Ancestry," pp. 133–134.

38. Bissell, "The Place of Learning," pp. 206–207.

39. Ross Skoggard, "Old Master," *Saturday Night* 103 (May 1988): 68–69.

40. Elder, *Image and Identity*, pp. 104–110.

41. See ibid., pp. 34–35, 109–111, for discussion of painting and film.

42. George Bowering, "Modernism Could Not Last Forever," *Canadian Fiction Magazine*, nos. 32–33 (1979–80): 4.

43. Stanley Fogel, *A Tale of Two Countries: Contemporary Fiction in English Canada and the United States* (Toronto: ECW Press, 1984), p. 23.

44. Linda Hutcheon, *The Canadian Postmodern: A Study of Contemporary English-Canadian Fiction* (Toronto: Oxford University Press, 1988), esp. pp. 193–208.

45. Edgar Z. Friedenberg, *Deference to Authority* (White Plains, N.Y.: M.E. Sharpe, 1980), p. 20.

46. Hugh MacLennan, "A Society in Revolt," in Judith Webster, ed., *Voices of Canada: An Introduction to Canadian Culture* (Burlington, Vt.: Association for Canadian Studies in the United States, 1977), p. 30; and idem, "The Psychology of Canadian Nationalism," pp. 417–419.

47. Quoted in Andrew H. Malcolm, *The Canadians* (New York: Times Books, 1985), pp. 58–59; see also idem, "Canada's Deeper Identity Not Made in the U.S.A.," *New York Times*, November 20, 1988, p. 1.

48. Robertson Davies, "Signing Away Canada's Soul," *Harper's* 278 (January 1989): 45.

49. Stouck, *Major Canadian Authors*, p. 27.

50. Scott Symons, "The Canadian Bestiary: Ongoing Literary Depravity," *West Coast Review* 11 (January 1977): 14.

51. Frances W. Kaye, "The 49th Parallel and the 98th Meridian: Some Lines for Thought," *Mosaic: A Journal for the Interdisciplinary Study of Literature* 14 (Spring 1981): 170.

52. McGregor, *The Wacousta Syndrome*, p. 256.

53. Atwood, *Survival*, p. 32.

54. "Beautiful Losers," *Saturday Night* 101 (January 1986): 25.

55. R.E. Walters, "A Special Tang: Stephen Leacock's Canadian Humour," *Canadian Literature* 5 (Summer 1960): 25, 27, 32. For more recent comments, see Tom Marshall, "Re-Visioning: Comedy and History in the Canadian Novel," *Queen's Quarterly* 93 (Spring 1986): 52–65.

56. Hutcheon, *The Canadian Postmodern*, pp. 198–199.

57. Kroetsch, *The Lovely Treachery of Words*, pp. 68–69.

58. Hancock, *Canadian Writers*, pp. 140–141.

59. Eleanor Cook, "'A Seeing and Unseeing in the Eye': Canadian Literature and the Sense of Place," *Daedalus* 117 (Fall 1988): 233. See also Richard Gwyn, *The 49th Paradox: Canada in North America* (Toronto: McClelland and Stewart, 1985), p. 183.

246 Notes to pp. 69–73

60. McGregor, *The Wacousta Syndrome*, p. 415. For a similar analysis, see William Kilbourn, "The Peaceable Kingdom Still," *Daedalus* 117 (Fall 1988): 25.

61. Walters, "A Special Tang," p. 32.

62. Beverly Kasporich, "Canadian Humour and Culture: Regional and National Expressions" (Faculty of General Studies, University of Calgary, 1986), pp. 13–15. See also Edmund Wilson, *O Canada: An American's Notes on Canadian Culture* (New York: Farrar, Strauss and Giroux, 1965), p. 92.

63. Fothergill, "Coward, Bully, or Clown," pp. 242–243.

64. Geoff Pevere, "Images of Men," *The Canadian Forum* 64 (February 1985): 24, 28.

65. Geoff Pevere, "Projections," *The Canadian Forum* 65 (March 1986): 42.

66. Quoted in Philip Marchand, *Marshall McLuhan, The Medium and the Messenger* (New York: Ticknor and Fields, 1989), pp. 210–211.

67. Russell M. Brown, "A Search for America: Some Canadian Literary Responses," *Journal of American Culture* 2 (1980): 676.

68. Quoted in ibid., pp. 675–676 from Beth Harvor, *Women and Children.*

69. Susan Swan, *The Biggest Modern Woman of the World* (Toronto: Lester and Orpen Dennys, 1983), pp. 273–274.

70. Brown, "A Search for America," p. 679.

71. Doug Fetherling, ed., *A George Woodcock Reader* (Ottawa: Deneau and Greenberg, 1980), pp. 56–60.

72. Richard Hofstadter, *Anti-Intellectualism in American Life* (New York: Alfred A. Knopf, 1963), p. 39; Seymour Martin Lipset, "Academia and Politics in America," in T.J. Nossiter et al. eds., *Imagination and Precision in the Social Sciences* (London: Faber and Faber, 1972), pp. 211–269; and Seymour Martin Lipset and Richard Dobson, "The Intellectual as Critic and Rebel: With Special Reference to the United States and the Soviet Union," *Daedalus* 101 (Summer 1972): 137–198.

73. Sutherland, *The New Hero*, p. 413; A.J.M. Smith, "Evolution and Revolution as Aspects of English Canadian and American Literature," in R.A. Preston, ed., *Perspectives on Revolution and Evolution* (Durham, N.C.: Duke University Press, 1978), p. 213.

74. Maclulich, *Between Europe and America*, p. 217.

75. William Christian and Colin Campbell, *Political Parties and Ideologies in Canada* (Toronto: McGraw-Hill Ryerson, 1983), p. 209.

76. Rodney Stark and William Sims Bainbridge, *The Future of Religion* (Berkeley: University of California Press, 1985), pp. 457–458.

5 The Impact of Religion

1. Edmund Burke, *Selected Works* (Oxford: Clarendon Press, 1904), pp. 180–181.

2. John Conway, "An 'Adapted Organic Tradition,'" *Daedalus* 117 (Fall 1988): 382. Ronald Sutherland sums up the differences from a more organizational perspective: "American puritanism, developing as it did from the peculiar notions of a small and persecuted sect, underlined self-reliance and the responsibility of the individual....Canada, by contrast, had relatively sophisticated church systems among both Catholics and Protestants....Canadians...had the security of reliance upon a church establishment, detailed codes of behaviour, a controlling system" (Ronald Sutherland, *The New Hero: Essays in Comparative Quebec/Canadian Literature* [Toronto: Macmillan of Canada, 1977], pp. 2–3).

3. Max Weber, "The Protestant Sects and the Spirit of Capitalism," in idem, *Essays in Sociology*, trans. and ed. by Hans Gerth and C.W. Mills (New York: Oxford University Press, 1946; first published in German, various years, early 20th century).

4. Max Weber, *The Protestant Ethic and the Spirit of Capitalism* (New York: Scribner, 1935; first published in German, 1905), pp. 55–56.

5. Ibid., pp. 48–50.

6. For a discussion of relevant data, see Chapter 8.

7. Alexis de Tocqueville, *Democracy in America*, vol. 1 (New York: Alfred A. Knopf, 1963; first published in French, 1835), p. 314. For quantitative documentation, see Walter Dean Burnham, "The 1980 Earthquake: Realignment, Reaction or What?" appendix A on religion, in Thomas Ferguson and Joel Rogers, eds., *The Hidden Election* (New York: Pantheon Books, 1981), pp. 132–136.

8. Samuel Huntington, *American Politics: The Promise of Disharmony* (Cambridge, Mass.: Harvard University Press, Belknap Press, 1981), p. 154.

9. Robert N. Bellah, *The Broken Covenant: American Civil Religion in Time of Trial* (New York: Seabury Press, 1975), p. 48.

10. Seymour Martin Lipset, *The First New Nation: The United States in Historical and Comparative Perspective*, exp. ed. (New York: W.W. Norton, 1979), pp. 166–169.

11. This is, of course, part of what some people see as problematic about foreign policy. See George Kennan, *Realities of American Foreign Policy* (New York: W.W Norton, 1966), pp. 3–50; and Robert Bellah, *Beyond Belief* (New York: Harper and Row, 1970), pp. 182–183.

12. Huntington, *American Politics*, pp. 158–159.

13. Bellah, *Beyond Belief,* p. 175. See also Kenneth D. Wald, *Religion and Politics in the United States* (New York: St. Martin's Press, 1987), pp. 48–55.

14. Bellah, *The Broken Covenant,* p. 60.

15. Sol Tax, "War and the Draft," in Morton Fried, Marvin Harris, and Robert Murphy, eds., *War* (Garden City, N.Y.: Doubleday, The Natural History Press, 1968), pp. 199–203. Actually, Tax concludes that seven wars out of 12 fought by the United States were less popular than the Vietnam War. The 12, however, include various Indian wars.

16. See Samuel Eliot Morison, "Dissent in the War of 1812," in Samuel Eliot Morison, Frederick Merk, and Frank Freidel, *Dissent in Three American Wars* (Cambridge, Mass.: Harvard University Press, 1970), pp. 3–31.

17. See Frederick Merk, "Dissent in the Mexican War," in ibid., pp. 33–63; and Edward S. Wallace, "Notes and Comment — Deserters in the Mexican War," *The Hispanic American Historical Review* 15 (1935): 374.

18. See David Donald, "Died of Democracy," in David Donald, ed., *Why the North Won the Civil War* (Baton Rouge: Louisiana State University Press, 1960), pp. 85–89; James McCague, *The Second Rebellion: The New York City Riots of 1863* (New York: Dial, 1968); and Basil L. Lee, *Discontent in New York City, 1861–65* (Washington, D.C.: Catholic University of America Press, 1943).

19. See H.C. Peterson and Gilbert C. Fite, *Opponents of War, 1917–1918* (Seattle: University of Washington Press, 1957), pp. 39, 123–135, 234; and Daniel Bell, "The Background and Development of Marxian Socialism in the United States," in Donald Drew Egbert and Stow Persons, eds., *Socialism and American Life,* vol. 1 (Princeton, N.J.: Princeton University Press, 1952), pp. 314–315.

20. Hazel Erskine, "The Polls: Is War a Mistake?" *Public Opinion Quarterly* 34 (1970): 138-141; and Edward Suchman, Rose K. Goldsen, and Robin Williams, Jr., "Attitudes Toward the Korean War," *Public Opinion Quarterly* 17 (1953): 173, 182.

21. Kennan, *Realities of American Foreign Policy.*

22. Reginald Bibby, *Fragmented Gods: The Poverty and Potential of Religion in Canada* (Toronto: Irvine, 1987), pp. 217–218.

23. Conway, "An 'Adapted Organic Tradition,'" p. 388.

24. Kenneth McNaught, "Canada's European Ambiance" (paper read at the annual meeting of the Italian Association for Canadian Studies, Sicily, May 1988), p. 16.

25. Tocqueville, *Democracy in America,* vol. 1, p. 312.

26. Harold Innis, *Essays in Canadian Economic History* (Toronto: University of Toronto Press, 1956), p. 385.

27. John Webster Grant, "'At Least You Knew Where You Stood with Them': Reflections on Religious Pluralism in Canada and the United States," *Studies in Religion* 2 (Spring 1973): 341.

28. William Kilbourn, *Canada: A Guide to the Peaceable Kingdom* (New York: St. Martin's Press, 1970), p. xvi.

29. S.D. Clark, "The Canadian Community," in George W. Brown, ed., *Canada* (Berkeley: University of California Press, 1954), p. 388.

30. Kenneth McNaught, *The Pelican History of Canada* (Harmondsworth, England: Penguin Books, 1976), pp. 46–50.

31. Roger O'Toole, "Some Good Purpose: Notes on Religion and Political Culture in Canada," *Annual Review of the Social Sciences of Religion* (The Hague) 6 (1982): 184.

32. Ibid., pp. 184–185.

33. Rodney Stark and William Sims Bainbridge, *The Future of Religion* (Berkeley: University of California Press, 1985), p. 461. See also O'Toole, "Some Good Purpose," p. 184.

34. Kenneth Westhues, "Stars and Stripes, The Maple Leaf, and the Papal Coat of Arms," *Canadian Journal of Sociology* 3 (Spring 1978): 251.

35. See R.L. Bruckberger, "The American Catholics as a Minority," in Thomas T. McAvoy, ed., *Roman Catholicism and the American Way of Life* (Notre Dame, Ind.: University of Notre Dame Press, 1960), pp. 45–47.

36. Westhues, "Stars and Stripes," pp. 256–257.

37. Ibid., pp. 254–255, 257.

38. See Bellah, *The Broken Covenant*; and idem, *Beyond Belief*, p. 175.

39. Harold Fallding, "Mainline Protestantism in Canada and the United States of America: An Overview," *Canadian Journal of Sociology* 3 (Spring 1978): 143.

40. Ibid.

41. Reginald W. Bibby, "Religious Encasement in Canada: An Argument for Protestant and Catholic Entrenchment," *Social Compass* 32 (1985): 287–303. See also Reginald Bibby and Harold R. Weaver, "Cult Consumption in Canada: A Further Critique of Stark and Bainbridge," *Sociological Analysis* 46 (1985): 445–460; and Merlin A. Brinkerhoff and Reginald W. Bibby, "Circulation of the Saints in South America: A Comparative Study," *Journal for the Scientific Study of Religion* 24 (March 1985): 39–40.

42. Harry H. Hiller, "Continentalism and the Third Force in Religion," *Canadian Journal of Sociology* 3 (Spring 1978): 191.

43. Bibby, *Fragmented Gods*, pp. 218–219.

44. Douglas F. Campbell, "The Canadian and Australian Church Unions: A Comparison," *International Journal of Comparative Sociology* 26 (3–4:1985): 184–185. See also C.E. Silcox, *Church Union in Canada* (New York: Institute of Social and Religious Research, 1933).

45. Gallup International Research Institute, *Human Needs and Satisfaction: A Global Survey* (Princeton, N.J., 1977); and Center for Applied Research in the Apostolate, *Values Study of Canada* (Washington, D.C.: May 1983). In the CARA study, the percentages for the United States are based on 1,729 respondents and those for Canada on 1,251 respondents — 338 French-speaking and 913 English-speaking.

46. Alex C. Michalos, *North American Social Report: A Comparative Study of the Quality of Life in Canada and the USA from 1964 to 1974*, vol. 5 (Dordrecht, The Netherlands: D. Reidel, 1980–82), p. 145.

47. H. Wesley Perkins, "Research Note: Religious Content in American, British and Canadian Popular Publications from 1937 to 1979," *Sociological Analysis* 45 (1984): 163.

48. Michalos, *North American Social Report*, vol. 5, p. 167.

49. Ibid., p. 179.

50. Canadian Conference of Catholic Bishops, "A Statement on Social Policy," *Dissent* 34 (Summer 1988): 314–321. See also Gregory Baum and Duncan Cameron, *Ethics and Economics: Canada's Catholic Bishops on the Economic Crisis* (Toronto: James Lorimer, 1984).

51. John F. Burns, "Canadian Church Approves Homosexual Ministers," *New York Times*, August 28, 1988, p. 19.

52. Brinkerhoff and Bibby, "Circulation of the Saints," pp. 39–40; and Bibby, "Religious Encasement," pp. 287–289. John Burbidge contends that "Bibby's percentage figures for the number of conservative Protestants in Canada may well be high," since he includes all the Baptists, "even though there is evidence that there is now little difference between many of their units and those of the United Church" ("Religion in Canada," *Journal of Canadian Studies* 22 [Winter 1987–88]: 163–164).

53. "Religion in America," *The Gallup Report*, no. 236 (May 1985), pp. 29, 38, 47–48.

54. Nathan R. Kollar, "Controversial Issues in North American Fundamentalism" (St. John Fisher College, Rochester N.Y., 1989), pp. 14–16.

6 Law and Deviance

1. Margaret Atwood, *Survival: A Thematic Guide to Canadian Literature* (Boston: Beacon Press, 1972), p. 171. See also Robertson Davies, "Signing Away Canada's Soul," *Harper's* 278 (January 1989): 43.

2. Gaile McGregor, *The Wacousta Syndrome: Explorations in the Canadian Langscape* (Toronto: University of Toronto Press, 1985), p. 61.

3. Ibid. For similar comments, see also Robert Kroetsch, *The Lovely Treachery of Words: Essays Selected and New* (Don Mills, Ont.: Oxford University Press, 1989), p. 28; and David Stouck, *Major Canadian Authors*, 2d ed. (Lincoln: University of Nebraska Press, 1988), pp. 44–47.

4. Frances Kaye, "The 49th Parallel and the 98th Meridian: Some Lines for Thought," *Mosaic: A Journal for the Interdisciplinary Study of Literature* 14 (Spring 1981): 167.

5. Wallace Stegner, *Wolf Willow* (New York: Viking Press, 1962), pp. 97-123.

6. Kenneth McNaught, *The Pelican History of Canada* (Harmondsworth, England: Penguin Books, 1982), p. 146.

7. For an excellent analysis of American western novels, see John G. Cawelti, *The Six-Gun Mystique* (Bowling Green, Ohio: Bowling Green University Popular Press, 1975).

8. Robert Thacker, "Canada's Mounted: The Evolution of a Legend," *Journal of Popular Culture* 14 (Fall 1980): 299, 303–311; and Dick Harrison, "The Insignificance of the Frontier in Western Canadian Fiction," in Wolfgang Klooss and Hartmut Lutz, eds., *Kanada Geschichte: Politik Kultur*, German-English Yearbook Band 19 (Berlin: Argument-Verlag, 1987), pp. 49–57.

9. Dick Harrison, "Popular Fiction of the Canadian Prairies: Autopsy on a Small Corpse," *Journal of Popular Culture* 14 (Fall 1980): 329.

10. Thacker, "Canada's Mounted," pp. 307–308.

11. Douglas Fetherling, *The Gold Crusades: A Social History of Gold Rushes 1849–1969* (Toronto: Macmillan of Canada, 1989), pp. 80–81, 150–151, 188–190; J. Bartlett Brebner, *Canada* (Ann Arbor: University of Michigan Press, 1960), p. 255; James Bryce, *Modern Democracies*, vol. 2 (New York: Macmillan, 1921), pp. 486–487; and Paul F. Sharp, "Three Frontiers: Some Comparative Studies of Canadian, American and Australian Settlement," *Pacific Historical Review* 24 (1955): 373–374.

12. Lawrence Jackson, "Fever," *Books in Canada* 18 (April 1989): 28.

13. Edgar W. McInnis, *The Unguarded Frontier* (Garden City, N.Y.: Doubleday, 1942), p. 307.

14. Richard G. Lipsey, *The Great Free Trade Debate and the Canadian Identity: A Convocation Address* (Ottawa: Carleton University, 1987), p. 9.

15. Guy Rocher, "Comments on Seymour Martin Lipset's 'Canada and the United States: The Cultural Dimension'" (Faculty of Law, University of Quebec at Montreal, 1988), p. 2. See also idem, "Canadian Law

from a Sociological Perspective," in Ivan Bernier and André Lajoie, eds., *Law, Society and the Economy* (Toronto: University of Toronto Press, 1986), esp. pp. 160–176.

16. Rocher, "Comments," pp. 4, 7, 8–9.

17. These models are taken from the work of Herbert Packer, "Two Models of the Criminal Process," *University of Pennsylvania Law Review* 113 (1964): 1–68.

18. John Hagan and Jeffrey Leon, "Philosophy and Sociology of Crime Control," in Harry M. Johnson, ed., *Social System and Legal Process* (San Francisco: Jossey-Bass, 1978), p. 182. See also Curt Griffiths, John Fiklein, and Simon N. Verdon-Jones, *Criminal Justice in Canada* (Toronto: Butterworths, 1980); Lorne Tepperman, *Crime Control: The Urge toward Authority* (Toronto: McGraw-Hill Ryerson, 1977); and John Hagan, "Crime, Deviance, and Legal Order," in James Curtis and Lorne Tepperman, eds., *Understanding Canadian Society* (Toronto: McGraw-Hill Ryerson, 1988), pp. 426–427, 435–439.

19. See June Callwood, *Portrait of Canada* (Garden City, N.Y.: Doubleday, 1981), pp. 333–334, 341–342; David Bell and Lorne Tepperman, *The Roots of Disunity* (Toronto: McClelland and Stewart, 1979), pp. 83–84; and Denis Smith, *Bleeding Hearts...Bleeding Country: Canada and the Quebec Crisis* (Edmonton: Hurtig, 1971).

20. Alan F. Westin, "The United States Bill of Rights and the Canadian Charter: A Socio-Political Analysis," in William R. McKercher, ed., *The U.S. Bill of Rights and the Canadian Charter of Rights and Freedoms* (Toronto: Ontario Economic Council, 1983), p. 41.

21. Robert K. Merton, *Social Theory and Social Structure* (Glencoe, Il.: The Free Press, 1957), p. 169.

22. John Hagan, "Comparing Crime and Criminalization in Canada and the U.S.A.," *Canadian Journal of Sociology* 14 (Fall 1989).

23. For data on the two countries, see ibid., table 1; idem, "Crime, Deviance, and Legal Order," pp. 433–438; and Dane Archer and Rosemary Gartner, *Violence and Crime in Cross-National Perspective* (New Haven: Yale University Press, 1984), "Comparative Crime Data File: Nations," unnumbered appendix.

24. Hagan, "Comparing Crime"; and idem, "Toward A Structural Theory of Crime, Race and Gender," in Robert A. Silverman and James V. Teevan, Jr., eds., *Crime in Canadian Society*, 3d ed. (Toronto: Butterworths, 1986), p. 199. These conclusions have been challenged by Rhonda Lenton, "Homicide in Canada and the U.S.A.: A Critique of the Hagan Thesis," *Canadian Journal of Sociology* 14 (Spring 1989): 163–178. Lenton is responded to as statistically naive by Hagan in "Comparing Crime."

25. For detailed comparative statistics from the mid-1960s to the mid-1980s, see Alex C. Michalos, *North American Social Report: A Com-*

parative Study of the Quality of Life in Canada and the USA from 1964 to 1974, vol. 2 (Dordrecht, The Netherlands: D. Reidel, 1980–1982), pp. 74–150; John Hagan, *The Disreputable Pleasures*, 2d ed. (Toronto: McGraw-Hill Ryerson, 1984), pp. 48–54; and Louise I. Shelley, "American Crime: An International Anomaly?" *Comparative Social Research* 8 (1985): 81–95. The most recent data are reported in "Profiles in Numbers," *Maclean's*, July 3, 1989, p. 51.

26. James F. Kirkham, Sheldon G. Levy, and William J. Crotty, *Assassination and Political Violence* (New York: Praeger, 1970), pp. 156–159, 170, 190, 204; William Mishler, *Political Participation in Canada: Prospects for Democratic Citizenship* (Toronto: Macmillan of Canada, 1979), pp. 52–53; and Hagan, *The Disreputable Pleasures*, p. 48.

27. For comparable data from 1965 to 1974, see Michalos, *North American Social Report*, vol. 2, p. 81.

28. More recently, Hagan also notes that the data "on self-reported delinquency [are] consistent with the impression that serious offences are more frequent in the United States than in Canada....[The] data indicate that as the value of property reported stolen increases, so too do the national differences." (*The Disreputable Pleasures*, p. 48).

29. It is hard to believe that the shift over four years — from 45 percent of Americans fearful in the Gallup poll to 31 in the Decima — represents a "real" change. The difference could be a result of sample variation, of the content of the two questionnaires, or of the many other sources of potential error in polling.

30. Hagan, *The Disreputable Pleasures*, pp. 52–53. In 1987, drug arrests were 169 per 100,000 population in Canada and 385 in the United States, according to "Profiles in Numbers," p. 51.

31. William A. Westley, *Violence and the Police: A Sociological Study of Law, Custom and Morality* (Cambridge: MIT Press, 1970), pp. 92-94; and Jerome Skolnick, *Justice without Trial: Law Enforcement in a Democratic Society* (New York: John Wiley, 1966).

32. Callwood, *Portrait of Canada*, p. xii.

33. James C. Hackler and Christian T.L. Janssen, "Police Killings in Perspective," in Robert A. Silverman and James V. Teevan, Jr., eds., *Crime in Canadian Society*, 3d ed. (Toronto: Butterworths, 1986), p. 241. See also John F. Klein, Jim R. Webb, and J.R. DeSanto, "Experience with Police and Attitudes towards the Police," *Canadian Journal of Sociology* 3 (1978): 441–456.

34. Daniel J. Koenig, "Police Perceptions of Public Respect and Extra-Legal Use of Force: A Reconsideration of Folk Wisdom and Pluralistic Ignorance," *Canadian Journal of Sociology* 1 (Summer, 1975): 316; and Griffiths, Fiklein, and Verdon-Jones, *Criminal Justice in Canada*, 1980), p. 66.

35. Ted E. Thomas, "The Gun Control Issue: A Sociological Analysis of United States and Canadian Attitudes and Policies" (Department of Sociology, Mills College, Oakland, Cal., 1983), p. 40. For a comprehensive report, see Elisabeth Scarff, *Evaluation of the Canadian Gun Control Legislation* (Ottawa: Supply and Services Canada, 1983).

36. Thomas, "The Gun Control Issue," p. 6.

37. Michalos, *North American Social Report*, vol. 2, p. 147; see also pp. 58–59.

38. My analysis of the 1975 Canadian data at the Roper Center reveals no difference in the attitudes of the two Canadian linguistic groups on this issue.

39. David R. Francis, "Why Canada Is Safer Than US," *Christian Science Monitor*, January 2, 1987, pp. 9–10.

40. Ibid.

41. "A North-South Dialogue," *Maclean's*, July 3, 1989, p. 48.

42. Michalos, *North American Social Report*, vol. 2, p. 65.

43. Ibid., p. 141.

44. These data have been made available for secondary analysis. Besides my work on them, they are reported in Doug Baer, Edward Grabb, and William A. Johnston, "Canadian and American Values: Reassessing the Differences," in James Curtis and Lorne Tepperman, eds., *Images of Canada: The Sociological Tradition* (Scarborough, Ont.: Prentice-Hall Canada, 1989).

It is worth remembering that responses to a single question, which in any case was worded differently than in the earlier surveys, are not definitive; clearly, the area needs to be explored.

45. "The United States is the most litigious society known to the world" (Westin, "The United States Bill of Rights," p. 33).

46. "Bleeding-Heart Conservatives," Canada survey, *The Economist* 309 (October 8, 1988): 5.

47. Richard L. Abel, "United States: The Contradictions of Professionalization," in Richard Abel and Philip S.C. Lewis, eds., *Lawyers in Society*, vol. 1 (Berkeley: University of California Press, 1988), pp. 240–242; and Harry W. Arthurs, Richard Weisman, and Frederick H. Zemans, "Canadian Lawyers: A Peculiar Professionalism," in ibid., pp. 126, 169. The Canadian figure includes Quebec notaries, who are lawyers under the French system of civil law used in that province.

48. John Hagan and Jeffrey Leon, "The Rehabilitation of Law: A Social and Historical Comparison of Probation in Canada and the United States," *Canadian Journal of Sociology* 5 (Summer 1980): 237–238, as summarized in Hagan, *The Disreputable Pleasures*, p. 232.

49. Hagan, *The Disreputable Pleasures*, p. 233.

50. F.L. Morton and Leslie A. Pal, "The Impact of the Charter on Public Administration," *Canadian Public Administration* 28 (Summer 1985): 241.

51. Kenneth McNaught, "Political Trials and the Canadian Political Tradition," in Martin L. Friedland, ed., *Courts and Trials: A Multidisciplinary Approach* (Toronto: University of Toronto Press, 1975), p. 138. See also John D. Whyte, "Civil Liberties and the Courts," *Queen's Quarterly* 83 (Winter 1976): 656–657; and Katherine Swinton, "Judicial Policy Making: American and Canadian Perspectives," *The Canadian Review of American Studies* 10 (Spring 1979): 91–93.

52. Edgar Friedenberg, "Culture in Canadian Context," in M. Michael Rosenberg et al., eds., *An Introduction to Sociology* (Toronto: Methuen, 1983), p. 128.

53. Robert A. Sedler, "Constitutional Protection of Individual Rights in Canada: The Impact of the New Canadian Charter of Rights and Freedoms," *Notre Dame Law Review* 59 (June 1984): 1215–1217.

54. Morris C. Shumiatcher, "Property and the Canadian Charter of Rights and Freedoms," *The Canadian Journal of Law and Jurisprudence* 1 (July 1988): 190.

55. Mark B. Lapping, "Peoples of Plenty: A Note on Agriculture as a Planning Metaphor and National Character in North America," *Journal of Canadian Studies* 22 (Spring 1987): 123–124.

56. Kenneth McNaught, "Canada's European Ambience" (paper read at the annual meeting of the Italian Association for Canadian Studies, Sicily, May 1988).

57. Paul Weiler, "The Evolution of the Charter: A View from the Outside," in Joseph Weiler and Robin Elliot, eds., *Litigating the Values of a Nation: The Canadian Charter of Rights and Freedoms* (Toronto: Carswell, 1986), pp. 53, 57. See also Dale Gibson, "Reasonable Limits under the Canadian Charter of Rights and Freedoms," *Manitoba Law Review* 15 (1:1985): 27–52.

58. Anne F. Bayefsky, "The Judicial Function under the Canadian Charter of Rights and Freedoms," *McGill Law Journal* 32 (September 1987): 817–818. See also A. Kenneth Pye, "The Rights of Persons Accused of Crime under the Canadian Constitution: A Comparative Perspective," *Law and Contemporary Problems* 45 (Autumn 1982): 221–248; and Edward McWhinney, *Canada and the Constitution, 1979–1982* (Toronto: University of Toronto Press, 1982), pp. 55–67, 61. See also Westin, "The United States Bill of Rights," pp. 27–44; and the other articles in William R. McKercher, ed., *The U.S. Bill of Rights and the Canadian Charter of Rights and Freedoms* (Toronto: Ontario Economic Council, 1983).

59. F.L. Morton, "The Political Impact of the Canadian Charter of Rights and Freedoms," *Canadian Journal of Political Science* 20 (March 1987): 54–55.

60. José Woehrling, "Minority Cultural and Linguistic Rights and Equality Rights in the Canadian Charter of Rights and Freedoms," *McGill Law Journal* 31 (1985): 88–89.

61. Ibid., p. 90.

62. For a review of various cases, see A. Alan Borovoy, *When Freedoms Collide: The Case for Our Civil Liberties* (Toronto: Lester and Orpen Dennys, 1988), pp. 34–53.

63. David Bercuson and Douglas Wertheimer, *A Trust Betrayed* (Toronto: Doubleday Canada, 1985).

64. B.P. Elman, "The Promotion of Hatred and the Canadian Charter of Rights and Freedoms: A Review of Keegstra v. The Queen," *Canadian Public Policy* 15 (March 1989): 74–75.

65. Jeffrey Miller, "Speak No Evil," *Saturday Night* 104 (May 1989): 31.

66. Ibid., pp. 29–30.

67. Ibid., p. 30.

68. Elman, "The Promotion of Hatred," p. 80.

69. Miller, "Speak No Evil," pp. 30–31.

70. Paul M. Sniderman et al., "Liberty, Authority, and Community: Civil Liberties and the Canadian Political Culture" (Centre of Criminology, University of Toronto, and Survey Research Center, University of California, Berkeley, 1988), figures 9A–9D.

71. Michael A. Goldberg and John Mercer, *The Myth of the North American City: Continentalism Challenged* (Vancouver: University of British Columbia Press, 1986), p. 31.

72. "A North-South Dialogue," p. 49.

73. Goldberg and Mercer, *The Myth of the North American City*, pp. 24, 140.

74. Alan F.J. Artibise, "Canada as an Urban Nation," *Daedalus* 117 (Fall 1988): 244. A comparably positive evaluation of Toronto is given by Yasmin Alibhai, "Canadian Club," *The New Statesman and Society*, September 2, 1988, pp. 26–27.

75. Elise F. Jones et al., *Teenage Pregnancy in Industrialized Countries* (New Haven, Conn.: Yale University Press, 1986).

76. Ibid., pp. 8–11, 25, 36.

77. Ibid., pp. 72, 86.

78. Ibid., pp. 26, 76, 78.

79. Ibid., p. 78.

80. Ibid., pp. 72, 86.

81. Ibid., p. 223.

82. Ibid., pp. 89, 92.

7 Economic Behavior and Culture

1. "The Italian Economy," *The Economist*, February 27, 1988, survey, p. 9. The data are from the OECD and are expressed in terms of purchasing power parities.

2. Samuel P. Huntington, "The U.S. — Decline or Renewal," *Foreign Affairs* 67 (Winter 1988/89): 82–83.

3. Ibid.

4. Maurice Ernst, "How Not To Create Jobs: Lessons from the West European Experience," *Journal of Labor Research* 10 (Winter 1989): 39.

5. Robert J. Brym with Bonnie J. Fox, *From Culture to Power* (Toronto: Oxford University Press, 1989), p. 37.

6. Max Weber, *The Protestant Ethic and the Spirit of Capitalism* (New York: Scribner, 1935; first published in German, 1905); and idem, "The Protestant Sects and the Spirit of Capitalism," in Max Weber, *Essays in Sociology*, trans. and ed. by Hans Gerth and C.W. Mills (New York: Oxford University Press, 1946; first published in German, various years, early 20th century), pp. 302–322.

7. For a discussion of past variations between English and French Canada, see Seymour Martin Lipset, "Values, Education and Entrepreneurship," in S.M. Lipset and Aldo Solari, eds., *Elites in Latin America* (New York: Oxford University Press, 1967), pp. 11–12.

8. "Engels to Sorge," September 10, 1888, in Karl Marx and Friedrich Engels, *Letters to Americans* (New York: International Publishers, 1953), p. 204 (italics added).

9. For a further discussion and references to the relevant writings of Marx and Engels, see Seymour Martin Lipset, "Racial and Ethnic Tensions in the Third World," in W. Scott Thompson, ed., *The Third World: Premises of U.S. Policy* (San Francisco: Institute for Contemporary Studies, 1978), pp. 123–148.

10. Herschel Hardin, *A Nation Unaware: The Canadian Economic Culture* (Vancouver: J.J. Douglas, 1974), p. 62 (italics in original).

11. Peter Karl Kresl, "An Economics Perspective: Canada in the International Economy," in William Metcalfe, ed., *Understanding Canada* (New York: New York University Press, 1982), p. 240; and Alistair Horne, *Canada and the Canadians* (London: Macmillan, 1961), p. 245.

12. "O Canada Eh!" prepared by McLuhan Productions, Toronto, 1986.

13. Quoted in Andy Stark, "Canadian Conundrums: Nationalism, Socialism, and Free Trade," *The American Spectator*, April 1989, p. 21.

14. Hardin, *A Nation Unaware*, pp. 102–105. See also J.J. Brown, *Ideas in Exile: A History of Canadian Invention* (Toronto: McClelland and Stewart, 1967); and Pierre L. Bourgault, *Innovation and the Structure of Canadian Industry*, Science Council of Canada Background Paper 23 (Ottawa: Information Canada, 1972).

15. Science Council of Canada, "Innovation in a Cold Climate: 'Impediments to Innovation,'" in Abraham Rothstein and Gary Lax, eds., *Independence: The Canadian Challenge* (Toronto: Committee for an Independent Canada, 1972), pp. 123—24. For a description of similar conclusions in a 1988 government report, see David Spurgeon, "A Psychiatrist Crusades to Bring Risk Taking to Canadian Science," *The Scientist*, July 11, 1988, p. 2.

16. Charles J. McMillan, "The Changing Competitive Environment of Canadian Business," *Journal of Canadian Studies* 13 (Spring 1978): 45. Canadian novelist Mordecai Richler comments "on the curious reluctance of Canadians to seize economic opportunity with vigour needed to develop and operate their own economy" ("Letter from Ottawa: The Sorry State of Canadian Nationalism," *Harper's* 250 [June 1975]: 32). See also Edgar Z. Friedenberg, *Deference to Authority* (White Plains, N.Y.: M.E. Sharpe, 1980), p. 142.

17. Geraldine A. Kenney-Wallace and J. Fraser Mustard, "From Paradox to Paradigm: The Evolution of Science and Technology in Canada," *Daedalus* 117 (Fall 1988): 199, 201–202, 208–209.

18. Canadian Institute for Advanced Research, *Innovation and Prosperity: The Transforming Power of Science, Engineering and Technology* (Toronto, 1988), pp. 53–54.

19. David Crane, "Study of Trade Data Highlights Canada's High-Tech Problem," *Toronto Star*, August 12, 1989, p. D2.

20. Quoted in Harry H. Hiller, *Canadian Society: A Sociological Analysis* (Scarborough, Ont.: Prentice-Hall Canada, 1976), p. 144.

21. From Keizzi Koho Center, *Japan 1983: An International Comparison* (Tokyo, 1983), p. 8. The data are from United Nations, *Monthly Bulletin of Statistics*, July 1983.

22. Robert Sexty, "Canadian Business: Who Owns It? Who Controls It? Who Cares?" (Memorial University of Newfoundland, St. John's, 1988); and New York Stock Exchange, *New York Stock Exchange Fact Book* (New York, 1987), p. 58.

23. Science Council of Canada, "Innovation," pp. 123–124.

24. Hiller, *Canadian Society*, p. 144. John Crispo also notes the "propensity among Canadians to invest more abroad" (*Mandate for*

Canada [Don Mills, Ont.: General Publishing, 1979], p. 28). See also Kresl, "An Economics Perspective," pp. 240–241.

25. Kenneth M. Glazier, "Canadian Investment in the United States: 'Putting Your Money Where Your Mouth Is,'" *Journal of Contemporary Business* 1 (Autumn 1972): 61.

26. R.T. Naylor, *The History of Canadian Business, 1867–1914*, vol. 2, *Industrial Development* (Toronto: Lorimer, 1973), p. 241.

27. Ibid., pp. 246, 252. For a similar point about Victorian Canada, see James Eayrs, "Sharing a Continent: The Hard Issues," in John S. Dickey, ed., *The United States and Canada* (Englewood Cliffs, N.J.: Prentice-Hall, 1964), p. 78.

28. Jorge Niosi, "Continental Nationalism: The Strategy of the Canadian Bourgeoisie," in Robert J. Brym, ed., *The Structure of the Canadian Capitalist Class* (Toronto: Garamond Press, 1985), pp. 61–63.

29. Martin Tolchin and Susan Tolchin, *Buying into America* (New York: Times Books, 1988), table 4, pp. 295–302.

30. "Britain, Netherlands Still Lead Japan in Total Direct Investment in U.S.," *Wall Street Journal*, February 24, 1989 (italics added).

31. Ibid. (italics added).

32. Alan M. Rugman, *Outward Bound: Canadian Direct Investment in the United States* (Toronto; Washington, D.C.: Canadian-American Committee, 1987), pp. 3–6.

33. Lukin Robinson, "Fortunes of Trade," *The Canadian Forum* 68 (March 1989): 7.

34. Prospectus Investment and Trade Partners, *1989 Canada Facts: An International Business Comparison* (Ottawa, 1989), p. 40. The data are from Statistics Canada.

35. Glazier, "Canadian Investment," p. 65.

36. Robert J. Brym, "Canada," in Tom Bottomore and Robert J. Brym, eds., *The Capitalist Class: An International Study* (New York: Harvester Wheatsheaf, 1989), p. 186.

37. Geert Hofstede, *Culture's Consequences: International Differences in Work-Related Values* (Beverly Hills, Cal.: Sage Publications, 1984), pp. 121–122.

38. Science Council of Canada, "Innovation," p. 123.

39. American Council of Life Insurance, *Life Insurance Fact Book 1983* (Washington, D.C., 1983), pp. 14, 102–103.

40. Michael Goldberg and John Mercer, *The Myth of the North American City: Continentalism Challenged* (Vancouver: University of British Columbia Press, 1986), pp. 83 84.

41. American Council of Life Insurance, *Life Insurance Fact Book 1985* (Washington, D.C., 1985), pp. 4, 47.

42. Prospectus Investment and Trade Partners, *1989 Canada Facts*, p. 70. See also Janet Jarrett, "Why Canadians Save More Than Americans," *Canadian Business Review* 7 (Autumn 1980): 37; and Charles A. Barrett, "Why Are Canadians Saving So Much?" *Canadian Business Review* 5 (Summer 1978): 5–8.

43. Andrew H. Malcolm, "Canada's Deeper Identity Not Made in the U.S.A.," *New York Times*, November 20, 1988, pp. 1, 18.

44. See Stephen J. Arnold and Douglas J. Tigert, "Canadians and Americans: A Comparative Analysis," *International Journal of Comparative Sociology* 15 (March–June 1974): 68–83; and Stephen J. Arnold and James G. Barnes, "Canadians and Americans: Implications for Marketing," in Donald M. Thompson, ed., *Problems in Canadian Marketing* (Chicago: American Marketing Association, 1977), pp. 13–14.

45. Arnold and Tigert, "Canadians and Americans: A Comparative Analysis," pp. 75–76.

46. Arnold and Barnes, "Canadians and Americans: Implications," pp. 13–14.

47. I have reported only items for which there was a consistent difference of 5 percent or more. Items for which there were no large differences included good manners and politeness, honesty, patience, tolerance of others, self-control, and obedience.

48. Tom Atkinson and Michael Murray, *Values, Domains and the Perceived Quality of Life: Canada and the United States* (Toronto: Institute for Behavioural Research, 1982), pp. 17, 28.

49. Brym with Fox, *From Culture to Power*, pp. 33, 38.

50. William K. Carroll, John Fox, and Michael D. Ornstein, "The Network of Directorate Links among the Largest Canadian Firms," *Canadian Review of Sociology and Anthropology* 19 (February:1982): 62. They refer to the writings of Tom Naylor and Wallace Clement.

51. Ibid.; and William K. Carroll, *Corporate Power and Canadian Capitalism* (Vancouver: University of British Columbia Press, 1986).

52. Robert J. Brym, "The Canadian Capitalist Class, 1965–1985," in idem, ed., *The Structure of the Canadian Capitalist Class* (Toronto: Garamond Press, 1985), pp. 9–10.

53. Patricia Marchak, *Ideological Perspectives on Canada* (Toronto: McGraw-Hill Ryerson, 1988), pp. 70–72.

54. Peter C. Newman, "The Dark Side of Merger Mania," *Maclean's*, February 6, 1989, p. 37.

55. Diane Francis, *Controlling Interest: Who Owns Canada?* (Toronto: McClelland-Bantam, 1987), pp. 1–2. See also Jorge Niosi, *The Economy of Canada: Who Controls It?* (Montreal: Black Rose Books,

1978), pp. 90–119; and idem, *Canadian Capitalism* (Toronto: Lorimer, 1981).

56. Francis, *Controlling Interest*, p. 5.

57. Ibid., p. 365–367. See also Kristine Chase, "National Banking: A Comparison of Policy towards Nationwide Banking and Concentration of Power in Banking Markets in Canada and the U.S.," *Policy Studies Journal* 14 (June 1986): 641, 647.

58. Francis, *Controlling Interest*, p. 2.

59. Anthony J. Obadal, "Tax Law Makes It Harder to Keep Firms in Family," *Wall Street Journal*, May 2, 1989, p. A18.

60. Michael Ornstein, "The Social Organization of the Canadian Capitalist Class in Comparative Perspective," *Canadian Review of Sociology and Anthropology* 26 (1:1989): 151–177.

61. Francis, *Controlling Interest*, pp. 12–15.

62. Scott Bennett, "Issues in Pharmaceutical Policy: A Comparison of Canada and the United States," in Martin Lubin, ed., *Canadian and U.S. Public Policy and Process: The Interplay between Institutions, Values and Interdependence* (forthcoming).

63. Sylvia Ostry, "Government Intervention: Canada and the United States Compared," in Ronald G. Landes, ed., *Canadian Politics: A Comparative Reader* (Scarborough, Ont.: Prentice-Hall Canada, 1985, p. 261.

64. Ibid., pp. 261–262.

65. Urban planning, however, is much stricter in Canada than in the United States.

66. Peter N. Nemetz, W.T. Stanbury, and Fred Thompson, "Social Regulation in Canada: An Overview and Comparison with the American Model," *Policy Studies Journal* 14 (June 1986): 594.

67. Ibid., p. 595.

68. See the essays in Joseph P. Jiang, ed., *Confucianism and Modernization: A Symposium* (Taipei, Taiwan: The Freedom Council—Wu Nan Publishing, 1987), esp. Benjamin A. Elman, "Confucianism and Modernization: A Reevaluation," pp. 1–19; and Fu Pei-jung, "Confucianism and an Ethic for Modernization — In Response to Weber's Critique," pp. 149–159.

69. See Francis, *Controlling Interest*.

70. See Seymour Martin Lipset, "A Unique People in an Exceptional Country," in idem, ed., *American Pluralism and the Jewish Community* (New Brunswick, N.J.: Transaction Books, 1989).

71. Mira Wilkins, *The History of Foreign Investment in the United States to 1914* (Cambridge, Mass.: Harvard University Press, 1989).

8 Government, Welfare, and Philanthropy

1. Pierre Lemieux, "Will Canada's Tax Reform Have a Supply-Side Effect?" *Wall Street Journal,* September 2, 1988, p. 13. See also Michael Goldberg and John Mercer, *The Myth of the North American City: Continentalism Challenged* (Vancouver: University of British Columbia Press, 1986), table 4-6, pp. 85, 100.

2. See United States, Arms Control and Disarmament Agency, *World Military Expenditures and Arms Transfers, 1971–1980* (Washington, D.C., 1982), pp. 42, 71.

3. "Canada Fails Litmus Test," *Wall Street Journal,* May 1, 1989, p. A14.

4. J.T. McLeod, "The Free Enterprise Dodo Is No Phoenix," *The Canadian Forum* 56 (August 1976): 6, 9. See also H.G.J. Aitkin, "Defensive Expansionism: The State and Economic Growth in Canada," in idem, ed., *The State and Economic Growth* (New York: Social Science Research Council, 1959), pp. 79–114; H.V. Nelles, "Defensive Expansionism Revisited: Federalism, the State and Economic Nationalism in Canada, 1959–1979," *The* [Japanese] *Annual Review of Canadian Studies* 2 (1980): 127–129; and J. Robert S. Pritchard, *Crown Corporations in Canada* (Toronto: Butterworths, 1983).

5. John Mercer and Michael Goldberg, "Value Differences and Their Meaning: Urban Development in the United States" (Faculty of Commerce Working Paper no. 12, UBC Research in Land Economics, University of British Columbia, Vancouver, 1982), p. 27. See also Sylvia Ostry, "Government Intervention: Canada and the United States Compared," in K.J. Rea and Nelson Wiseman, eds., *Government and Enterprise in Canada* (Toronto: Methuen, 1985), p. 23.

6. Keith G. Banting, "Images of the Modern State," in idem, ed., *State and Society: Canada in Comparative Perspective* (Toronto: University of Toronto Press, 1986), pp. 3–4. As of 1980, 18.8 percent of jobs in Canada were in government, compared to 16.7 percent in the United States ("The Role of Government in Employment, Investment and Income," *OECD Observer,* no. 121 [March 1983], pp. 6–10).

7. Robert G. Evans, "'We'll Take Care of It for You': Health Care in the Canadian Community," *Daedalus* 117 (Fall 1988): 169.

8. Robert J. Blendon, "Three Systems: A Comparative Survey," *Health Management Quarterly* 11 (first quarter 1989): 8–9.

9. Ibid.

10. William Glaser, "Health Politics: Lessons from Abroad," in Theodore J. Litman, ed., *Health Politics and Policy* (New York: John Wiley, 1984), pp. 319–322.

11. Part of the comparability results from standards established by the *Canada Health Act* as a condition for federal funding.

12. Robert T. Kudrle and Theodore R. Marmor, "The Development of Welfare States in North America," in Peter Flora and Arnold J. Heidenheimer, eds., *The Development of Welfare States in Europe and America* (New Brunswick, N.J.: Transaction Books, 1981), pp. 110–111.

13. Ostry, "Government Intervention," p. 27.

14. Robert Presthus, *Elites in the Policy Process* (London: Cambridge University Press, 1974), p. 463.

15. Robert Presthus, "Aspects of Political Culture and Legislative Behavior: United States and Canada," in idem, ed., *Cross-National Perspectives: United States and Canada* (Leiden: E.J. Brill, 1977), p. 15. For an analysis of the ideology of Canadian Conservatives, which differs greatly from that of Ronald Reagan and Margaret Thatcher, see William Christian and Colin Campbell, *Political Parties and Ideologies in Canada* (Toronto: McGraw-Hill Ryerson, 1983), pp. 83–136.

16. Colin Campbell, "The Interplay of Institutionization and the Assignment of Tasks in Parliamentary and Congressional Systems," in Presthus, ed., *Cross-National Perspectives*, pp. 142–143, 149.

17. Vicki L. Templin, "Predicting the Policy Choices of Individual Legislators: A Comparative Study of Canada and the United States," *Population Research and Policy Review* 6 (1987): 254–256.

18. "Bleeding-Heart Conservatives," Canada survey, *The Economist*, October 8, 1988, p. 4.

19. John Hutcheson, "A Political Re-alignment," *The Canadian Forum* 68 (March 1989): 6.

20. Maurice Lamontagne, "The Role of Government," in G.P. Gilmour, ed., *Canada's Tomorrow* (Toronto: Macmillan, 1954), p. 125. For a discussion by James Bryce of Canada's opposition to laissez faire written in the 1920s, see *Modern Democracies*, vol. 1 (New York: Macmillan, 1921), p. 471.

21. Stephen J. Arnold and Douglas J. Tigert, "Canadians and Americans: A Comparative Analysis," *International Journal of Comparative Sociology* 15 (March–June 1974): 68–83.

22. Stephen J. Arnold and James G. Barnes, "Canadian and American National Characteristics as a Basis for Market Segmentation," in J. Sheth, ed., *Research in Marketing*, vol. 2 (Greenwich, Conn.: JAI Press, 1979), p. 32.

23. James Curtis and Ronald Lambert, "Culture and Social Organization," in Robert Hagedorn, ed., *Sociology* (Toronto: Holt, Rinehart and Winston of Canada, 1980), p. 117.

24. Task Force on Funding Higher Education, *From Patrons to Partners, Corporate Support for Universities* (Montreal: Corporate Higher Education Forum, 1987), p. 84. See also Allan Arlett, "Unchartered Chari-Tory," *Foundation News* 30 (March–April 1989): 18–23. A more

recent report indicates that "American corporations give four times as much as Canadian companies" (Eve Drobut, "Social and Personal," *Saturday Night* 104 [August 1989]: 15).

25. Task Force on Funding Higher Education, *From Patrons to Partners*, p. 84.

26. See Drobut, "Social and Personal," p. 15, for further elaboration.

27. Merle Curti, *American Philanthropy Abroad: A History* (New Brunswick, N.J.: Rutgers University Press, 1963), p. 625.

28. Aileen Ross, "Philanthropy," in David L. Sills, ed., *International Encyclopedia of the Social Sciences*, vol. 12 (New York: Macmillan and The Free Press, 1968), p. 76. See also the essays in Teresa Odendahl, ed., *America's Wealthy and the Future of Foundations* (Washington, D.C.: The Foundation Center, 1987).

29. Robert H. Bremner, *American Philanthropy* (Chicago: University of Chicago Press, 1988), p. 138.

30. Philip Hart, *Orpheus in the New World: The Symphony Orchestra as an American Cultural Institution* (New York: W.W. Norton, 1973), pp. 349, 354.

31. David Deitch, "Libertarians Unite in Drive to Reduce Tax Burdens," *Boston Globe*, April 10, 1971, p. 7. See also "What's This?" *Dissent* 18 (August 1971): 395.

32. Quoted in Martin Green, *The Problem of Boston* (New York: W.W. Norton, 1966), p. 4.

33. Ibid., p. 56.

34. Quoted in Ben Whitaker, *The Foundations: An Anatomy of Philanthropy and Society* (London: Eyre Methuen, 1974), p. 53.

35. Joseph C. Goulden, *The Money Givers* (New York: Random House, 1971), p. 47.

36. Ibid., p. 28; Whitaker, *The Foundations*, pp. 64–66; and Bremner, *American Philanthropy*, p. 106.

37. Bremner, *American Philanthropy*, p. 210. See also Ann Lowrey Bailey and Vince Stehle, "Link to Religion Called Significant for Fund Raisers," *The Chronicle of Philanthropy* 1 (March 21, 1989): 1, 8; Edward C. Jenkins, *Philanthropy in America* (New York: Association Press, 1950), p. 91; William S. Vickrey, "One Economist's View of Philanthropy," in Frank Dickinson, ed., *Philanthropy and Public Policy* (New York; National Bureau of Economic Research, 1962), p. 33; and George G. Kirstein, *Better Giving* (Boston: Houghton Mifflin, 1975), pp. 59–71. For detailed statistics, see American Association of Fund-Raising Counsel Trust for Philanthropy, New York, *Giving USA*, a report that has been published annually since 1954.

38. Vickrey, "One Economist's View," p. 45.

39. Ross, "Philanthropy," p. 78.

40. Merrimon Cuninggim, *Private Money and Public Service* (New York: McGraw-Hill, 1972), pp. 169–170.

41. Bremner, *American Philanthropy*, p. 178.

42. American Association of Fund-Raising Counsel Trust for Philanthropy, *Giving USA 88*, p. 11.

43. Drobut, "Social and Personal," p. 15.

44. American Association of Fund-Raising Counsel Trust for Philanthropy, *Giving USA 88*, pp. 28–29.

45. Nathan Glazer, "Welfare and 'Welfare' in America," in Richard Rose and Rei Shiratori, eds., *The Welfare State East and West* (New York: Oxford University Press, 1986), p. 62.

46. Seymour Martin Lipset, "Canada and the United States: The Cultural Dimension," in Charles F. Doran and John H. Sigler, eds., *Canada and the United States: Enduring Friendship, Persistent Stress* (Englewood Cliffs, N.J.: Prentice-Hall, 1985), pp. 141–142. See also idem, "Historical Traditions and National Characteristics: A Comparative Analysis of Canada and the United States," *Canadian Journal of Sociology* 11 (Summer 1986): 135.

47. James E. Curtis, Ronald D. Lambert, Steven D. Brown, and Barry J. Kay, "Affiliation with Voluntary Associations: Canadian-American Comparisons," *Canadian Journal of Sociology* 14 (Spring 1989): 143–161.

48. See Seymour Martin Lipset, "Voluntary Activities: More Canadian-American Comparisons — A Reply," *Canadian Journal of Sociology* 14 (Fall 1989).

49. An example in a somewhat similar vein is the evidence indicating a shift in the proportion of Americans who favored more, rather than less, spending for defense. It was very high under President Carter, while he was cutting the military budget (a position that softened, it should be noted, after the Soviet invasion of Afghanistan). The percentage of survey respondents who favored more defense spending began to decline greatly within a year of Ronald Reagan's taking office and sharply increasing such expenditures.

50. Robert Y. Shapiro and John T. Young, "Public Opinion and the Welfare State: The United States in Comparative Perspective," *Political Science Quarterly* 104 (Spring 1989): 69–70.

51. Louis Hartz, *The Liberal Tradition in America* (New York: Harcourt, Brace and World, 1955); idem, *The Founding of New Societies* (New York: Harcourt, Brace, 1964), pp. 1–48; Gad Horowitz, *Canadian Labour in Politics* (Toronto: University of Toronto Press, 1968), pp. 3–57;

Seymour Martin Lipset, "Why No Socialism in the United States?" in S. Bialer and S. Sluzar, eds., *Sources of Contemporary Radicalism*, vol. 1 (Boulder, Col.: Westview Press, 1977), pp. 79–83; and idem, "Socialism in America," in P. Kurtz, ed., *Sidney Hook: Philosopher of Democracy and Humanism* (Buffalo: Prometheus Books, 1983), pp. 52–53.

52. See Robert J. Brym, "Social Movements and Third Parties," in S.D. Berkowitz, ed., *Models and Myths in Canadian Sociology* (Toronto: Butterworths, 1984), pp. 34–35.

53. Christian and Campbell, *Political Parties and Ideologies*, p. 36.

9 Social Stratification, Trade Unions, and Politics

1. Kenneth McNaught, "Approaches to the Study of Canadian History," *The* [Japanese] *Annual Review of Canadian Studies* 5 (1984): 95, 96.

2. Kenneth McNaught, "American Progressives and the Great Society," *Journal of American History* 53 (December 1966): 508, 511–512.

3. Michael A. Goldberg and John Mercer, *The Myth of the North American City: Continentalism Challenged* (Vancouver: University of British Columbia Press, 1986), p. 247.

4. Craig Crawford and James Curtis, "English Canadian–American Differences in Value Orientations," *Studies in Comparative International Development* 14 (1979); Peter C. Pineo and John Porter, "Occupational Prestige in Canada," in James E. Curtis and William G. Scott, eds., *Social Stratification in Canada* (Scarborough, Ont.: Prentice-Hall Canada, 1973); L. Neil Guppy, "Dissensus or Consensus: A Cross-National Comparison of Occupational Prestige Scales," *Canadian Journal of Sociology* 9 (Winter 1983–84); and Wallace E. Lambert, Josiane F. Hamers, and Nancy Frasure-Smith, *Child Rearing Values: A Cross-National Study* (New York: Praeger, 1979).

5. Crawford and Curtis, "English Canadian–American Differences," pp. 32–33.

6. Pineo and Porter, "Occupational Prestige," p. 60.

7. Guppy, "Dissensus or Consensus," pp. 79–80.

8. Lambert, Hamers, and Frasure-Smith, *Child Rearing Values*, p. 152.

9. The same finding is reported from other surveys in Allan Kornberg, *Politics and Culture in Canada* (Ann Arbor, Mich.: Center for Political Studies, Institute for Social Research, University of Michigan, 1988), pp. 18–19.

10. See John Goyder and Peter C. Pineo, "Social Class Self-Identification," in James G. Curtis and William G. Scott, eds., *Social Strat-*

ification in Canada, 2d ed. (Scarborough, Ont.: Prentice-Hall Canada, 1979), p. 437.

11. The lowest estimates were by the National Opinion Research Center of the University of Chicago; the highest by the Survey Research Center of the University of Michigan.

12. Goyder and Pineo, "Social Class Self-Identification," pp. 441–442.

13. See Goldberg and Mercer, *The Myth*, p. 51.

14. Seymour Martin Lipset, *The First New Nation: The United States in Historical and Comparative Perspective*, exp. ed. (New York: W.W. Norton, 1979), p. 211.

15. Milton Rokeach, "Some Reflections about the Place of Values in Canadian Social Science," in T.N. Guinsberg and G.L. Reuber, eds., *Perspectives on the Social Sciences in Canada* (Toronto: University of Toronto Press, 1974), p. 164.

16. Elizabeth H. Hastings and Philip K. Hastings, eds., *Index to International Public Opinion, 1980–1981* (Westport, Conn.: Greenwood Press, 1982), p. 519.

17. Ibid., pp. 520, 525. Further evidence that Americans emphasize achievement more than Canadians may be found in Geert Hofstede's multinational comparison of work-related employee attitudes, *Culture's Consequences: International Differences in Work-Related Values* (Beverly Hills, Cal.: Sage Publications, 1984), pp. 155–158, 186–189.

18. Ralph H. Turner, "Sponsored and Contest Mobility and the School System," *American Sociological Review* 25 (1960): 855–867.

19. Frank J. Mifflen and Sydney C. Mifflen, *The Sociology of Education: Canada and Beyond* (Calgary: Detselig Enterprises, 1982), p. 22.

20. Richard A. Wanner, "Educational Inequality: Trends in Twentieth-Century Canada and the United States," *Comparative Social Research* 9 (1986): 53–55.

21. Dennis Wrong, *American and Canadian Viewpoints* (Washington, D.C.: American Council on Education, 1955), p. 19.

22. Lawrence W. Donney, "A Canadian Image of Education," in Bernard Blishen et al., eds., *Canadian Society* (Toronto: Macmillan of Canada, 1971), pp. 148–149.

23. Mark M. Orkin, *Speaking Canadian English: An Informal Account of the English Language in Canada* (Toronto: General Publishing, 1970), p. 42.

24. T.D. Maclulich, *Between Europe and America: The Canadian Tradition in Fiction* (Oakville, Ont.: ECW Press, 1988), p. 201.

25. World Bank, *World Development Report 1987* (New York: Oxford University Press, 1987), p. 263.

26. United States, Department of Education, Center for Education Studies, *Digest of Education Statistics 1987* (Washington D.C., 1987), p. 132; United States, Department of Commerce, *Statistical Abstract of the U.S. 1988*, 108th ed. (Washington D.C., 1988), pp. 13, 140; and Canada, Statistics Canada, *Canada Year Book 1988*, cat. no. 11-402E (Ottawa, 1988), sec. 4, p. 17.

27. For summaries of the literature, see S.M. Lipset and Reinhard Bendix, *Social Mobility in Industrial Society* (Berkeley: University of California Press, 1959), pp. 11–75; S.M. Lipset, "Equality and Inequality," in Robert K. Merton and Robert Nisbet, eds., *Contemporary Social Problems* (New York: Macmillan, 1976), pp. 305–353; and idem, "Social Mobility in Industrial Societies," *Public Opinion* 5 (June/July, 1982): 107–115.

28. Robert J. Brym with Bonnie J. Fox, *From Culture to Power* (Toronto: Oxford University Press, 1989), pp. 93–95.

29. Sid Gilbert, "The Selection of Educational Aspirations," in R.A. Carlton, L.A. Colley, and N.J. MacKinnon, eds., *Education, Change, and Society* (Toronto: Gage, 1977), pp. 281–285, 287–289, 294. See also idem, "Educational and Occupational Aspirations of Ontario High School Students: A Multivariate Analysis" (Ph.D. diss., Department of Sociology, Carleton University, Ottawa, 1973).

30. Wanner, "Educational Inequality," p. 62.

31. Claude A. Bissell, "The Place of Learning and the Arts in Canadian Life," in Richard A. Preston, ed., *Perspectives on Revolution and Evolution* (Durham, N.C.: Duke University Press, 1979), p. 198.

32. Ibid., pp. 198–199. See also Maclulich, *Between Europe and America*, p. 202.

33. Geraldine A. Kenney-Wallace and J. Fraser Mustard, "From Paradox to Paradigm: The Evolution of Science and Technology in Canada," *Daedalus* 117 (Fall 1988): 204.

34. Charles J. McMillan, "The Changing Competitive Environment of Canadian Business," *Journal of Canadian Studies* 13 (Spring 1978): 45. He suggests that the gap still exists in spite of the growth in numbers of business students.

35. Wallace Clement, *Continental Corporate Power* (Toronto: McClelland and Stewart, 1977), pp. 183, 209.

36. Robert M. Pike, "Education and the Schools," in James Curtis and Lorne Tepperman, eds., *Understanding Canadian Society* (Toronto: McGraw-Hill Ryerson, 1988), pp. 276–277.

37. Canadian Institute for Advanced Research, *Innovation and Prosperity: The Transforming Power of Science, Engineering and Technology* (Toronto, 1988), p. 54.

38. Clement, *Continental Corporate Power*, pp. 144, 215–250, esp. p. 216. See also A.E. Safarian, *The Performance of Foreign-Owned Firms in Canada* (Washington, D.C.; Montreal: Canadian-American Committee, 1969), p. 13.

39. Robert Presthus and William V. Monopoli, "Bureaucracy in the United States and Canada: Social, Attitudinal and Behavioral Variables," in Robert Presthus, ed., *Cross-National Perspectives: United States and Canada* (London: E.J. Brill, 1977), pp. 178-199; and Colin Campbell, *Governments under Stress* (Toronto: University of Toronto Press, 1983).

40. Robert Presthus, *Elite Accommodation in Canadian Politics* (Cambridge: Cambridge University Press, 1973), pp. 34, 98.

41. Campbell, *Governments under Stress*, pp. 311–314.

42. Colin Campbell and George J. Szablowski, *The Superbureaucrats: Structure and Behavior in Central Agencies* (Toronto: Macmillan of Canada, 1979), pp. 105, 121.

43. R. Manzer, *Canada: A Socio-Political Report* (Toronto: McGraw-Hill Ryerson, 1974), pp. 188–206.

44. Christopher Huxley, David Kettler, and James Struthers, "Is Canada's Experience 'Especially Instructive?'" in Seymour Martin Lipset, ed., *Unions in Transition: Entering the Second Century* (San Francisco: Institute for Contemporary Studies, 1986), pp. 116–120.

45. Seymour Martin Lipset, "Roosevelt and the Protest of the 1930s," *University of Minnesota Law Review* 68 (December 1983): 273–298.

46. Richard Hofstadter, *The Age of Reform* (New York: Vintage Books, 1967), p. 308.

47. Samuel Lubell, "Post-Mortem: Who Elected Roosevelt?" *Saturday Evening Post*, January 25, 1941, p. 9; see also idem, *The Future of American Politics* (New York: Doubleday–Anchor Books, 1965), pp. 55–68.

48. See Louis Uchitelle, "Election Placing Focus on the Issue of Jobs vs. Wages," *New York Times*, September 4, 1988, pp. 1, 14; and Joyanna Moy, "Recent Trends in Unemployment and the Labor Force, 10 Countries," *Monthly Labor Review* 108 (August 1985): 11.

49. Peter T. Kilborn, "A Fight to Win the Middle Class," *New York Times*, business section, September 4, 1988, p. 5.

50. Paul Blustein, "The Great Jobs Debate," *Washington Post*, national weekly edition, September 5 11, 1988, p. 20.

51. Seymour Martin Lipset and William Schneider, *The Confidence Gap: Business, Labor and Government in the Public Mind*, rev. ed. (Baltimore: Johns Hopkins University Press, 1987), pp. 265–266.

52. Ibid., pp. 285–287.

53. For an earlier effort to account for a socialist party in Canada and the absence of one in the United States, see Seymour Martin Lipset, "Radicalism in North America: A Comparative View of the Party Systems in Canada and the United States," *Transactions of the Royal Society of Canada*, 4th series, 16 (1976): 19–55. In that paper, I emphasize the role of diverse electoral and constitutional structures in facilitating a multiparty system in Canada and a two-party one in the United States. Analyzing the reasons for greater union density in Canada has convinced me that the emphasis in the 1976 paper was wrong — that political cultural values are more important.

54. Henry Phelps Brown, *The Origins of Union Power* (Oxford: Clarendon Press, 1983), p. 240.

55. Gad Horowitz, "Red Tory," in William Kilbourn, ed., *Canada: A Guide to the Peaceable Kingdom* (New York: St. Martin's Press, 1970), p. 256 (italics in original).

56. For a general historical analysis of the tensions between the two since the formation of the AFL, see Robert H. Babcock, *Gompers in Canada: A Study in American Continentalism before the First World War* (Toronto: University of Toronto Press, 1974).

57. Gad Horowitz, *Canadian Labour in Politics* (Toronto: University of Toronto Press, 1968), p. 59 (italics in original). See also Charles Lipton, *The Trade Union Movement of Canada* (Toronto: University of Toronto Press, 1973), pp. 75–76, 118–121, 233–236; Harold A. Logan, *The History of Trade-Union Organization in Canada* (Chicago: University of Chicago Press, 1928), pp. 245–248, 274–286; and Babcock, *Gompers in Canada*, pp. 60–66, 160–162, 179–182.

58. Horowitz, *Canadian Labour*, p. 184.

59. Mark A. Thompson and Albert A. Blum, "International Unionism in Canada: The Move to Local Control," *Industrial Relations* 22 (Winter 1983): 83.

60. During the provincial election campaign in Manitoba in March 1986, Gary Filmon, the leader of the Conservative opposition to the incumbent NDP, told an American reporter that he had decided not to campaign against socialism because "the talk of socialism doesn't seem to have a sting" in Canada. In fact, he accused "the socialist government of 'neglecting' and 'starving' Manitoba's elaborate health and social welfare system," and he promised to restore services cut by the NDP (Herbert N. Denton, "Socialists Seek Reelection in Manitoba," *Washington Post*, March 18, 1986, p. A21). As premier, he has kept his promise to some extent.

61. Leo Panitch and Donald Swartz, *The Assault on Trade Union Freedoms: From Consent to Coercion Revisited* (Toronto: Garamond Press, 1988).

62. For an analysis of the variations, see Seymour Martin Lipset, "North American Labor Movements: A Comparative Perspective," in idem, ed., *Unions in Transition,* pp. 421–477.

63. Noah M. Meltz, "Labor Movements in Canada and the United States," in Thomas A. Kochan, ed., *Challenges and Choices Facing American Labor* (Cambridge, Mass.: MIT Press, 1985), p. 322.

64. Roy J. Adams, "North American Industrial Relations: Divergent Trends in Canada and the United States" (Working Paper no. 307, Faculty of Business, McMaster University, Hamilton, Ont., 1988), pp. 12–24.

65. Harvey Krahn and Graham S. Lowe, "Public Attitudes Towards Unions: Some Canadian Evidence," *Journal of Labor Research* 5 (Spring 1984): 160–161.

66. Robertson Davies, "Dark Hamlet with the Features of Horatio: Canada's Myths and Realities," in Judith Webster, ed., *Voices of Canada: An Introduction to Canadian Culture* (Burlington, Vt.: Association for Canadian Studies in the United States, 1977), p. 43.

10 Mosaic and Melting Pot

1. Morton Weinfeld, "Canadian Jews and Canadian Pluralism," in S.M. Lipset, ed., *American Pluralism and the Jewish Community* (New Brunswick, N.J.: Transaction Books, 1989 forthcoming).

2. Nathan Glazer and Daniel P. Moynihan, *Beyond the Melting Pot* (Cambridge, Mass.: Harvard University Press, 1965), pp. 6–7.

3. For an earlier discussion, see Seymour Martin Lipset, "Racial and Ethnic Tensions in the Third World," in W. Scott Thompson, ed., *The Third World: Premises of U.S. Policy* (San Francisco: Institute for Contemporary Studies, 1978), pp. 146–148.

4. Marie Haug, "Social and Cultural Pluralism as a Concept in Social System Analysis," *American Journal of Sociology* 73 (November 1967): 296–297, 299, 302.

5. Arthur K. Davis, "Canadian Society and History as Hinterland versus Metropolis," in Richard J. Ossenberg, ed., *Canadian Society: Pluralism, Change and Conflict* (Scarborough, Ont.: Prentice-Hall Canada, 1971), p. 27.

6. John Hagan, "Toward a Structural Theory of Crime, Race and Gender," in Robert A. Silverman and James V. Teevan, Jr., eds., *Crime in Canadian Society,* 3d ed. (Toronto: Butterworths, 1986), p. 200.

7. Wallace Stegner, *Wolf Willow* (New York: Viking Press, 1962), p. 101. "The redcoat associated first with British dragoons and later with the Mounties meant, to Indian minds, a force that was non- and sometimes anti-American...[while] the blue of the American calvary had become an abomination to the Plains Indians" (ibid.).

8. Frances W. Kaye, "The 49th Parallel and the 98th Meridian: Some Lines for Thought," *Mosaic: A Journal for the Interdisciplinary Study of Literature* 14 (Spring 1981): 170. See also Stegner, *Wolf Willow*, pp. 114–118.

9. Kenneth McNaught, *The Pelican History of Canada* (Harmondsworth, England: Penguin Books, 1982), p. 176.

10. Hagan, "Toward a Structural Theory," p. 200.

11. Robin W. Winks, *The Relevance of Canadian History* (Lanham, Md.: Universities Press of America, 1988), p. 23.

12. Gaile McGregor, *The Wacousta Syndrome: Explorations in the Canadian Langscape* (Toronto: University of Toronto Press, 1985), pp. 217–218. See also Kaye, "The 49th Parallel," p. 170.

13. Linda Hutcheon, *The Canadian Postmodern: A Study of Contemporary English-Canadian Fiction* (Toronto: Oxford University Press, 1988), pp. 194–195.

14. Anthony H. Richmond, *Immigration and Ethnic Conflict* (New York: St. Martin's Press, 1988), p. 129.

15. Gillian Porter Ladousse, "The Unicorn and the Booby Hatch: An Interview with Margaret Atwood," *Études Canadiennes* 5 (1978): 98.

16. Leslie Laczko, "Ethnic Diversity in Canada: A Macrosociological Look at Some Recent Trends" (Department of Sociology, University of Ottawa, 1984); Victor Valentine, "Native Peoples and Canadian Society: A Profile of Issues and Trends," in Raymond Breton et al., eds., *Cultural Boundaries and the Cohesion of Canada* (Montreal: Institute for Research on Public Policy, 1980); and James S. Frideres, "Institutional Structures and Economic Deprivation: Native People in Canada," in B. Singh Bolaria and Peter S. Li, eds., *Racial Oppression in Canada* (Toronto: Garamond Press, 1988).

17. Laczko, "Ethnic Diversity," p. 7.

18. Valentine, "Native Peoples," p. 81; and Frideres, "Institutional Structures," p. 73. Canadians, unlike Americans, differentiate between status Indians — people legally defined under the *Indian Act* — and nonstatus Indians — people of Indian ancestry who have lost their legal status by abandoning their rights or, in the case of women, by marrying non-Indians. Status Indians are divided into treaty Indians and registered (nontreaty) Indians; except for the details of treaty specifications, the two groups have the same rights and benefits. Nonstatus Indians have none of this legal protection, although many retain their Indian identity and are "indistinguishable from status Indians in appearance, language, culture and lifestyle" (Laczko, "Ethnic Diversity," p. 7).

For a detailed discussion of the legal and socioeconomic situation of the different categories, see Roger Gibbins and J. Rick Ponting, "An

Assessment of the Probable Impact of Aboriginal Self-Government in Canada," in Alan Cairns and Cynthia Williams, eds., *The Politics of Gender, Ethnicity and Language in Canada* (Toronto: University of Toronto Press, 1986), pp. 171–245. See also Richmond, *Immigration and Ethnic Conflict*, p. 130.

19. Donald Purich, *Our Land: Native Rights in Canada* (Toronto: Lorimer, 1986), pp. 47–60.

20. Dale Gibson, "Protection of Minority Rights under the Canadian Charter of Rights and Freedoms: Can Politicians and Judges Sing Harmony?" in Neil Nevitte and Allan Kornberg, eds., *Minorities and the Canadian State* (Oakville, Ont.: Mosaic Press, 1985), p. 46.

21. See Alan Cairns, "The Embedded State: State-Society Relations in Canada," in Keith G. Banting, ed., *State and Society: Canada in Comparative Perspective* (Toronto: University of Toronto Press, 1986), p. 66. For the full story, see Bryan Schwartz, *First Principles, Second Thoughts: Aboriginal Peoples, Constitutional Reform and Canadian Statecraft* (Montreal: Institute for Research on Public Policy, 1986).

22. Purich, *Our Land*, pp. 213–231.

23. C.E.S. Franks, "Indian Self-Government: Canada and the United States Compared," in Martin Lubin, ed., *Canadian and U.S. Public Policy and Process: The Interplay between Institution, Values and Interdependence* (forthcoming). On the Arctic grant, see Paul Lewis, "Canada About to Sign Major Land Agreement with Eskimos," *New York Times*, national ed., August 21, 1989, p. A3.

24. Rodney J. Sawatsky, "Domesticated Sectarianism: Mennonites in the U.S. and Canada in Comparative Perspective," *Canadian Journal of Sociology* 3 (Spring 1978): 239.

25. Ruth Wisse, in a discussion among Ruth Wisse, Mervin Butovsky, Howard Roiter, and Morton Weinfeld, "Jewish Culture and Canadian Culture," in M. Weinfeld, W. Shaffir, and I. Cotler, eds., *The Canadian Jewish Mosaic* (Toronto: John Wiley, 1981), p. 321.

26. Jonathan D. Sarna, "The Value of Canadian Jewish History to the American Jewish Historian and Vice Versa," *Canadian Jewish Historical Society Journal* 5 (Spring 1981): 18–19.

27. Ibid., p. 20.

28. Stuart Schoenfeld, "The Jewish Religion in North America: Canadian and American Comparisons," *Canadian Journal of Sociology* 3 (Spring 1978): 209–231. For an update and elaboration, see Weinfeld, "Canadian Jews and Canadian Pluralism." It also should be noted that private Jewish schools in Montreal, one of the two Canadian cities with a sizable Jewish population, can be eligible for tax support.

29. McGregor, *The Wacousta Syndrome*, p. 66.

30. In Wisse et al., "Jewish Culture," p. 321.

31. Sarna, "The Value of Canadian Jewish History," p. 20.

32. Richard Simeon and David J. Elkins, "Conclusion: Province, Nation, Country and Confederation," in David J. Elkins and Richard Simeon, eds., *Small Worlds: Provinces and Parties in Canadian Political Life* (Toronto: Methuen, 1980), p. 287.

33. Morton Weinfeld, "Myth and Reality in the Canadian Mosaic: 'Affective Ethnicity,'" *Canadian Ethnic Studies* 13 (1981): 94.

34. Canada, Royal Commission on Bilingualism and Biculturalism, *Report*, vol. 4, *The Cultural Contribution of the Other Ethnic Groups* (Ottawa: Queen's Printer, 1969).

35. Canada, Parliament, House of Commons, *Debates* [Hansard], October 8, 1971.

36. Peter Woolfson, "An Anthropological Perspective: The Ingredients of a Multicultural Society," in William Metcalfe, ed., *Understanding Canada* (New York: New York University Press, 1982), pp. 303–305.

37. Raymond Breton, "Multiculturalism and Canadian Nation-Building," in Cairns and Williams, eds., *The Politics of Gender, Ethnicity and Language in Canada*, pp. 50–51.

38. Quoted in Alan Anderson and James Frideres, *Ethnicity in Canada: Theoretical Perspectives* (Toronto: Butterworths, 1981), p. 100.

39. Thomas Flanigan, "The Manufacture of Minorities," in Nevitte and Kornberg, eds., *Minorities and the Canadian State*, pp. 107–123.

40. Italics S.M.L. See Gibson, "Protection of Minority Rights," p. 40.

41. Cairns, "The Embedded State," pp. 66–67.

42. Thomas Jefferson, *Notes on the State of Virginia* (New York: Harper and Row, Torchbooks, 1964; first published 1784–85), p. 156.

43. Gunnar Myrdal, *An American Dilemma*, 2d ed. (New York: Harper and Row, 1962), pp. 460–462.

44. Freda Hawkins, *Canada and Immigration: Public Policy and Public Concern* (Kingston, Ont.; Montreal: McGill-Queen's University Press, 1988), p. 34.

45. Seymour Martin Lipset and Earl Raab, *The Politics of Unreason: Right-Wing Extremism in the United States 1790–1977*, 2d ed. (Chicago: University of Chicago Press, 1978), pp. 110–147.

46. For these and other immigration data, see Hawkins, *Canada and Immigration*, pp. 53–64; and idem, *Critical Years in Immigration: Canada and Australia Compared* (Kingston, Ont.; Montreal: McGill-Queen's University Press, 1989), pp. 258–263; and Barry R. Chiswick, "Immigration Policy, Source Countries and Immigrant Skills: Australia,

Canada and the United States," in Lyle Baker and Paul Miller, eds., *The Economics of Immigration* (Canberra: Australian Government Publishing Service, 1988), pp. 165–171.

47. Chiswick, "Immigration Policy," pp. 166–171.

48. Ibid.

49. Peter Kopvillem, "An Angry Racial Backlash," *Maclean's*, July 10, 1989, pp. 14–15.

50. "A North-South Dialogue," *Maclean's*, July 3, 1989.

51. Kopvillem, "An Angry Racial Backlash," p. 15.

52. Ibid.

53. J. Paul Grayson, "Male Hegemony and the English-Canadian Novel," *Canadian Review of Sociology and Anthropology* 20 (February 1983): 1–21.

54. Catherine Lyle Cleverdon, *The Woman Suffrage Movement in Canada* (Toronto: University of Toronto Press, 1950), pp. 274–275.

55. Chaviva Hosek, "Women and the Constitutional Process," in Keith Banting and Richard Simeon, eds., *And No One Cheered* (Toronto: Methuen, 1983), p. 281.

56. Cleverdon, *The Woman Suffrage Movement in Canada*, pp. 112–113.

57. See Alison Prentice et al., *Canadian Women: A History* (Toronto: Harcourt Brace Jovanovich, 1988), pp. 194–209.

58. See S.J. Wilson, "Gender Inequality," in James Curtis and Lorne Tepperman, eds., *Understanding Canadian Society* (Toronto: McGraw-Hill Ryerson, 1988), p. 248; and Sandra Burt, "Women's Issues and the Women's Movement of Canada since 1970," in Cairns and Williams, eds., *The Politics of Gender, Ethnicity and Language in Canada*, p. 121.

59. Cleverdon, *The Woman Suffrage Movement in Canada*, p. 273.

60. Lyle E. Larson, *The Canadian Family in Comparative Perspective* (Scarborough, Ont.: Prentice-Hall Canada, 1976), pp. 24–25.

61. Ibid., pp. 28–35.

62. Prospectus Investment and Trade Partners, *1989 Canada Facts: An International Business Comparison* (Ottawa, 1989), pp. 23-24; and reports by Statistics Canada and the U.S. Department of Commerce, Bureau of the Census.

63. See Jane Mansbridge, *Why We Lost the E.R.A.* (Chicago: University of Chicago Press, 1986).

64. Milt Fredenheim, "A New Ontario Law Matches Women's Wages with Men's," *New York Times*, July 7, 1989, pp. A1, A18.

65. Nancy J. Church and Lise Héroux, "A Comparison of Sex Roles in American and Canadian News Magazines: A Pictorial Content An-

alysis" (School of Business Administration, State University of New York, Plattsburgh, N.Y., 1989), pp. 7, 12.

66. See Mildred A. Schwartz, *Politics and Territory: The Sociology of Regional Persistence in Canada* (Montreal: McGill-Queen's University Press, 1974), which is the most comprehensive sociological work on the subject. See also Robin Matthews, "Regional Differences in Canada: Social versus Economic Interpretations," in Dennis Forcese and Stephen Richter, eds., *Social Issues: Sociological Views of Canada* (Scarborough, Ont.: Prentice-Hall Canada, 1982), pp. 82–123.

11 Center and Periphery

1. Samuel Beer, "The Modernization of American Federalism," *Publius: The Journal of Federalism* 3 (February 1973): 52. See also Sidney Tarrow, "Introduction," in S. Tarrow, P.J. Katzenstein, and L. Graziano, eds., *Territorial Politics in Industrial Nations* (New York: Praeger, 1978), pp. 6–14. For an argument that a decentralized federal system, such as the Canadian, runs against the current of modernization, see John Porter, *The Measure of Canadian Society: Education, Equality and Opportunity* (Ottawa: Carleton University Press, 1979; reprint, 1987), pp. 172–173.

2. Beer, "The Modernization of American Federalism," p. 95.

3. Donald V. Smiley, "Public Sector Politics, Modernization and Federalism: The Canadian and American Experience," *Publius: The Journal of Federalism* 14 (Winter 1984): 59. For a comprehensive discussion of the factors making for centralization and decentralization, see Richard Simeon, "Considerations on Centralization and Decentralization," *Canadian Public Administration* 29 (Autumn 1986): 445–461.

4. Alan C. Cairns, *Constitution, Government, and Society in Canada* (Toronto: McClelland and Stewart, 1988), p. 144.

5. Richard Simeon, "Some Questions of Governance in Contemporary Canada" (School of Public Administration, Queen's University, Kingston, Ont., 1987), p. 17.

6. Thomas S. Axworthy, "Colliding Visions: The Debate over the Charter of Rights and Freedoms, 1980–81" (paper presented to the Conference on the Canadian Charter of Human Rights and Freedoms, Pacific Institute of Law and Public Policy, University of British Columbia, Vancouver, March 28–29, 1985), p. 7; Alan Cairns, "The Embedded State: State-Society Relations in Canada," in Keith G. Banting, ed., *State and Society: Canada in Comparative Perspective* (Toronto: University of Toronto Press, 1986), pp. 59–60; and Richard Bird, "Federal Finance in Comparative Perspective," in Thomas J. Courchene, David W. Conklin, and Gail C.A. Cook, eds., *Ottawa and the Provinces: The Distribution of Money and Power*, vol. 1 (Toronto: Ontario Economic Council, 1985), pp. 137–177..

7. Organisation for Economic Co-Operation and Development, *Revenue Statistics of OECD Member Countries, 1965–1986* (Paris, 1987), pp. 213, 232.

8. William Mishler, *Political Participation in Canada: Prospects for Democratic Citizenship* (Toronto: Macmillan of Canada, 1979), p. 31.

9. Roger Gibbins, *Regionalism: Territorial Politics in Canada and the United States* (Toronto: Butterworths, 1982), p. 158. This book is an excellent detailed analysis of the greater emphasis on territorial regional politics in Canada than in the United States. See also Richard Johnston, "Federal and Provincial Voting," in David J. Elkins and Richard Simeon, eds., *Small Worlds: Provinces and Parties in Canadian Political Life* (Toronto: Methuen, 1980), pp. 131–178, for a documentation that "Canadian politics are becoming less national and more provincial" (p. 172). See also Dennis Forcese, "Canada's Politics: Class, Region and Continentalism," in S.D. Berkowitz, ed., *Models and Myths in Canadian Sociology* (Toronto: Butterworths, 1984), pp. 115–120.

10. These studies are described in Gibbins, *Regionalism*, p. 158.

11. Ronald G. Landes, "The Political Socialization of Political Support," in Allan Kornberg and Harold P. Clarke, eds., *Political Support in Canada: The Crisis Years* (Durham, N.C.: Duke University Press, 1983), p. 111.

12. Quoted in ibid.

13. Robert Presthus, *Elites in the Policy Process* (London: Cambridge University Press, 1974), p. 25.

14. Vicki L. Templin, "Predicting the Policy Choices of Individual Legislators: A Comparative Study of Canada and the United States," *Population Research and Policy Review* 6 (1987): 267.

15. Pierre Elliott Trudeau, "The Practice and Theory of Federalism," *Federalism and the French Canadians* (New York: St. Martin's Press, 1968), p. 128; The article is an extended argument to Canadian socialists to oppose centralization. It was first published in a volume of socialist essays, Michael Oliver, ed., *Social Purpose for Canada* (Toronto: University of Toronto Press, 1961).

16. Grant Notley, "Comments," in John Richards and Don Kerr, eds., *Canada, What's Left?* (Edmonton: NeWest Press, 1986), pp. 154–155.

17. David Close, "Politics and Constitutional Reform in Canada: A Study in Political Opposition," *Publius: The Journal of Federalism* 15 (Winter 1985): 169. For an expression of Blakeney's support for provincial experimentation, see Allan Blakeney, "Decentralization: A Qualified Defence," in Richards and Kerr, eds., *Canada*, pp. 147–152.

18. Roger Gibbins, Rainer Knopff, and F.L. Morton, "Canadian Federalism, the Charter of Rights and the 1984 Election," *Publius: The Journal of Federalism* 15 (Summer 1985): 167.

19. Ivo D. Duchacek, "Consociational Cradle of Federalism," *Publius: The Journal of Federalism* 15 (Spring 1985): 41.

20. Summarized in Thomas O. Huegelin, "The End of Institutional Tidiness? Trends of Late Federalism in the United States and Canada" (Department of Political Science, Queen's University, Kingston, Ont. 1984), p. 22 (this is not his position).

21. Milton J. Esman, "Federalism and Modernization: Canada and the United States," *Publius: The Journal of Federalism* 14 (Winter 1984): 23 (italics in original). See also Smiley, "Public Sector Politics," pp. 52–59.

22. Gibbins, *Regionalism*, p. 192. See also Ronald L. Watts, "The American Constitution in Comparative Perspective: A Comparison of Federalism in the United States and Canada," *Journal of American History* 74 (3:1987): 778–779.

23. For a comprehensive discussion, see the articles in the special supplement entitled "The Meech Lake Accord," *Canadian Public Policy* 14 (September 1988).

24. R. Simeon, "Meech Lake and Shifting Conceptions of Canadian Federalism," *Canadian Public Policy* 14 (September 1988): pp. S7–S24. See also Kenneth McRoberts, "The Case for Meech Lake," *The Canadian Forum* 67 (December 1987): 12–13; and Andrew Cohen, "Power to the Provinces," *Saturday Night* 103 (August 1988): 12–14.

25. Quoted in Mary Janigan, "Trudeau's Power Punch," *Maclean's*, June 8, 1987, p. 10.

26. Simeon, "Meech Lake," pp. S19–S22.

27. Trudeau, "The Practice and Theory of Federalism."

28. I first elaborated this analysis in Seymour Martin Lipset, "Democracy in Alberta," *The Canadian Forum* 34 (November/December 1954): 175–177, 196–198. The above summary is taken from an extension of the argument in idem, "Radicalism in North America: A Comparative View of the Party System in Canada and the United States," *Transactions of the Royal Society of Canada*, 4th series, 16 (1976): 37–41.

29. Smiley, "Public Sector Politics," p. 55. See also Watts, "The American Constitution," pp. 782–784.

30. Harry H. Hiller, *Canadian Society: A Macro Analysis* (Scarborough, Ont.: Prentice-Hall Canada, 1986), p. 110.

31. William Glaser, "Improving Federalism in American Health Services: Some Ideas from Abroad," in Christa Altenstetter, ed., *Changing National-Subnational Relations in Health: Opportunities and Constraints* (Washington, D.C.: Public Health Services, National Institutes of Health, Department of Health, Education and Welfare, 1978), p. 391.

32. For the argument and evidence, see E.E. Schattschneider, *Party Government* (New York: Rinehart, 1942), pp. 65–98.

33. "Engels to Sorge," December 2, 1893, in Karl Marx and Friedrich Engels, *Letters to Americans* (New York: International Publishers, 1953), p. 258 (italics in original).

34. Morris Hillquit, *History of Socialism in the United States* (New York: Funk and Wagnalls, 1910), pp. 359–360.

35. Kenneth McNaught, *A Prophet in Politics: A Biography of J.S. Woodsworth* (Toronto: University of Toronto Press, 1959), pp. 165–192.

36. The largest was the vote secured by Theodore Roosevelt running as the candidate of the Progressive wing of the divided Republicans in 1912.

37. Daniel Bell, *Marxian Socialism in the United States* (Princeton N.J.: Princeton University Press, 1967), pp. 120–121; and Michael Harrington, *Socialism* (New York: Saturday Review Press, 1972), p. 252.

38. Martin Robin, *Radical Politics and Canadian Labour 1880–1930* (Kingston, Ont.: Queen's University Press, 1968), p. 254.

39. Ibid., p. 273.

40. Norman Thomas, *Socialism Re-Examined* (New York: W.W. Norton, 1963), pp. 117–120; and idem, *A Socialist's Faith* (New York: W.W. Norton, 1951), pp. 90–95.

41. Harrington, *Socialism*, p. 262.

42. For an excellent analysis of the Canadian system, see Cairns, *Constitution, Government, and Society in Canada*, pp. 111–140.

43. See Leon D. Epstein, "A Comparative Study of Canadian Parties," *American Political Science Review* 58 (March 1964): 46–59.

44. Mildred Schwartz, "Politics and Moral Causes in Canada and the United States," *Comparative Social Research* 4 (1981): 84.

45. Robert Brym, "Social Movements," in Lorne Tepperman and R. Jack Richardson, eds., *The Social World* (Toronto: McGraw-Hill Ryerson, 1986), p. 294.

46. Thomas, *Socialism Re-Examined*, pp. 117–120.

47. See Christopher Huxley, David Kettler, and James Struthers, "Is Canada's Experience 'Especially Instructive?'" in Seymour Martin Lipset, ed., *Unions in Transition: Entering the Second Century* (San Francisco: Institute for Contemporary Studies, 1986), pp. 116–120.

48. Val Scars, "High-Tech Lobbying: It's Just a Byte Away," in Robert J. Jackson, Doreen Jackson, and Nicolas Baxter-Moore, eds., *Contemporary Canadian Politics: Readings and Notes* (Scarborough, Ont.: Prentice-Hall Canada, 1987), p. 293.

49. Richard Simeon, "The 'Overload Thesis' and Canadian Government," *Canadian Public Policy* 2 (June 1976): 550 (italics in original).

50. Cairns, *Constitution, Government, and Society in Canada,* p. 169.

51. Ethel S. Goodstein, "Contemporary Architecture and Canadian National Identity," *The American Review of Canadian Studies* 18 (Summer 1988): 156.

52. George Woodcock, *Northern Spring: The Flowering of Canadian Literature* (Vancouver: Douglas and McIntyre, 1987), p. 32. See also Eleanor Cook, "'A Seeing and Unseeing in the Eye': Canadian Literature and the Sense of Place," *Daedalus* 117 (Fall 1988): 215–235.

53. "Where Is Here?" Public Broadcasting System, September 19, 1988.

54. *Saturday Night* 102 (January 1987).

55. Robert Kroetsch, *The Lovely Treachery of Words: Essays Selected and New* (Don Mills, Ont.: Oxford University Press, 1989), p. 27 (italics in original).

56. Harold D. Clarke et al., *Political Choice in Canada* (Toronto: McGraw-Hill Ryerson, 1979), pp. 37–38.

57. David J. Elkins, "The Sense of Place," in Elkins and Simeon, eds., *Small Worlds,* pp. 16–17, 21. For a report on a 1965 study of Canadian opinion also indicating the strength of provincial loyalties, see Porter, *The Measure of Canadian Society,* pp. 175–183.

58. Ralph Matthews and J. Campbell Davis, "The Comparative Influence of Region, Status, Class and Ethnicity on Canadian Attitudes and Values," in Robert J. Brym, ed. *Regionalism in Canada* (Toronto: Irwin, 1986), p. 100. Unfortunately, this publication does not give the wording of the question. The sample size was 2,046.

59. Roger Gibbins, *Conflict and Unity: An Introduction to Canadian Political Life* (Scarborough, Ont.: Nelson Canada, 1988), pp. 114–117. See also Allan Kornberg and Marianne C. Stewart, "National Identification and Political Support," in Kornberg and Clarke, eds., *Political Support in Canada,* pp. 85–94.

60. Michael D. Ornstein, "Regionalism and Canadian Political Ideology," in Brym, ed. *Regionalism,* p. 61. The sample included "nearly 3,000 cases."

61. Ibid., p. 80.

62. Matthews and Davis, "The Comparative Influence," pp. 118–120.

12 Still Whig, Still Tory

1. Margaret Atwood, *Second Words: Selected Critical Prose* (Boston: Beacon Press, 1984), p. 392.

2. For a detailed history and review of the application of the concept of the "end of ideology," see Seymour Martin Lipset, *Consensus and Conflict: Essays in Political Sociology* (New Brunswick, N.J.: Transaction Books, 1985), pp. 81–109.

3. "Sweden Mensheviksson," *The Economist,* April 1, 1989, pp. 42–44.

4. Quoted in Jeff Greenfield, "Challenging the Liturgy," *The West Side Spirit,* May 28, 1989, p. 13. For a discussion of the Labour Party's swing to the right, toward acceptance of a market economy, in the spring of 1989, see David Marquand, "Keep Right On," *The New Statesman and Society,* June 2, 1989, pp. 20–21.

5. Quoted in Charlotte Gray, "Designer Socialism," *Saturday Night* 104 (August 1989): 8.

6. Arthur K. Davis, "Canadian Society and History as Hinterland versus Metropolis," in Richard J. Ossenberg, ed., *Canadian Society: Pluralism, Change and Conflict* (Scarborough, Ont.: Prentice-Hall Canada, 1971), pp. 6–32; and Irving Louis Horowitz, "The Hemispheric Connection: A Critique and Corrective to the Entrepreneurial Thesis of Development with Special Emphasis on the Canadian Case," *Queen's Quarterly* 80 (Autumn 1973): 327–359.

7. Lukin Robinson, "Fortunes of Trade," *The Canadian Forum* 68 (March 1989): 7.

8. David Popenoe, "The Political Culture of Metropolitan Communities in the United States: A Cross-National Perspective," in Dan A. Chekki, ed., *Contemporary Community: Change and Challenge* (forthcoming) (italics in original).

9. Ibid.

10. Kenneth McNaught, "Canada's European Ambiance" (paper read at the Annual Meeting of the Italian Association for Canadian Studies, Sicily, May 1988), p. 16.

11. Quoted in Robert E. Babe, "Copyright and Culture," *The Canadian Forum* 67 (February/March 1988): 28–29.

12. Robertson Davies, "Signing Away Canada's Soul," *Harpers* 278 (January 1989): 47. See also Matt Cohen, "Literary Nationalism in English Canada: Bogus or Magus?" *American Book Review* 10 (May–June 1988): 4; and "Bleeding-Heart Conservatives," Canada survey, *The Economist,* October 8, 1988, pp. 15–16.

13. In Stanley Fogel, *A Tale of Two Countries: Contemporary Fiction in English Canada and the United States* (Toronto: ECW Press, 1984), p. 4. The statement is a paraphrase by Fogel from an interview with Horwood.

14. For a comparable argument made more than a quarter of a century ago by a distinguished Canadian economist, which I read after

writing these words, see Harry Johnson, "Unlovely Canadianism," in William Kilbourn, ed., *Canada: A Guide to the Peaceable Kingdom* (New York: St. Martin's Press, 1970), p. 208.

15. For a review of the extensive Marxist literature arguing that socialism would emerge first in the United States, see Seymour Martin Lipset, "Why No Socialism in the United States?" in S. Bialer and S. Sluzar, eds., *Sources of Contemporary Radicalism*, vol. 1 (Boulder, Col.: Westview Press, 1977), pp. 32–33, 48–49.

16. Quoted in Frank Underhill, *The Image of Confederation* (Toronto: Canadian Broadcasting Corporation, 1964), p. 69.

17. Ronald Sutherland, "A Literary Perspective: The Development of a National Consciousness," in William Metcalfe, ed., *Understanding Canada* (New York: New York University Press, 1982) p. 413.

18. Marcus Cunliffe, "New World, Old World: The Historical Antithesis," in Richard Rose, ed., *Lessons from America* (London: Macmillan 1974), p. 45 (italics in original).

Bibliography

Abel, Richard L. "United States: The Contradictions of Professionalization. In *Lawyers in Society*, edited by Richard Abel and Philip S.C. Lewis, vol. 1. Berkeley: University of California Press, 1988.

Adams, Roy J. "North American Industrial Relations: Divergent Trends in Canada and the United States." Working Paper no. 307, Faculty of Business, McMaster University, Hamilton, Ont., 1988.

Adamson, Agar. "We Were Here Before: The Referendum in Canadian Experience." In *Canadian Politics, A Comparative Reader*, edited by Ronald G. Landes. Scarborough, Ont.: Prentice-Hall Canada, 1985.

Aitkin, H.G.J. "Defensive Expansionism: The State and Economic Growth in Canada." In *The State and Economic Growth*, edited by H.G.J. Aitkin. New York: Social Science Research Council, 1959.

Alibhai, Yasmin. "Canadian Club." *The New Statesman and Society*, September 2, 1988.

American Association of Fund-Raising Counsel Trust for Philanthropy, New York. *Giving USA*. Annual.

American Council of Life Insurance. *Life Insurance Fact Book*. Washington, D.C. Annual.

Anderson, Alan, and James Frideres. *Ethnicity in Canada: Theoretical Perspectives*. Toronto: Butterworths, 1981.

Archer, Dane, and Rosemary Gartner. *Violence and Crime in Cross-National Perspective*. New Haven: Yale University Press, 1984.

Arlett, Allan. "Unchartered Chari-Tory." *Foundation News* 30 (March–April 1989).

Arnold, Stephen J., and James G. Barnes. "Canadian and American National Characteristics as a Basis for Market Segmentation." In *Research in Marketing*, edited by J. Sheth, vol. 2. Greenwich, Conn.: JAI Press, 1979.

———, and James G. Barnes. "Canadians and Americans: Implications for Marketing." In *Problems in Canadian Marketing*, edited by Donald M. Thompson. Chicago: American Marketing Association, 1977.

———, and Douglas J. Tigert. "Canadians and Americans: A Comparative Analysis." *International Journal of Comparative Sociology* 15 (March–June 1974).

Arthurs, Harry W., Richard Weisman, and Frederick H. Zemans. "Canadian Lawyers: A Peculiar Professionalism." In *Lawyers in Society*, edited by Richard Abel and Philip S.C. Lewis, vol. 1. Berkeley: University of California Press, 1988.

Artibise, Alan F.J. "Canada as an Urban Nation." *Daedalus* 117 (Fall 1988).

———. "Exploring the North American West: A Comparative Urban Perspective." *The American Review of Canadian Studies* 14 (Spring 1984).

Atkinson, Tom, and Michael Murray. *Values, Domains and the Perceived Quality of Life: Canada and the United States*. Toronto: Institute for Behavioural Research, 1982.

Atwood, Margaret. *The Journals of Suzanna Moodie: Poems*. Toronto: Oxford University Press, 1970.

———. *Second Words: Selected Critical Prose*. Boston: Beacon Press, 1984.

———. *Survival: A Thematic Guide to Canadian Literature*. Boston: Beacon Press, 1972.

Axworthy, Thomas S. "Colliding Visions: The Debate over the Charter of Rights and Freedoms, 1980–81." Paper presented to the Conference on the Canadian Charter of Human Rights and Freedoms, Pacific Institute of Law and Public Policy, University of British Columbia, Vancouver, March 28-29, 1985.

Babcock, Robert H. *Gompers in Canada: A Study in American Continentalism before the First World War*. Toronto: University of Toronto Press, 1974.

Babe, Robert E. "Copyright and Culture." *The Canadian Forum* 67 (February/March 1988).

Baer, Doug, Edward Grabb, and William A. Johnston. "Canadian and American Values: Reassessing the Differences." In *Images of Canada: The Sociological Tradition*, edited by James Curtis and Lorne Tepperman. Scarborough, Ont.: Prentice-Hall Canada, 1989.

Bailey, Ann Lowrey, and Vince Stehle. "Link to Religion Called Significant for Fund Raisers." *The Chronicle of Philanthropy* 1 (March 21, 1989).

Banfield, Edward C., and James Q. Wilson. *City Politics*. Cambridge, Mass.: Harvard University Press and MIT Press, 1963.

Banting, Keith G. "Images of the Modern State." In *State and Society: Canada in Comparative Perspective*, edited by Keith G. Banting. Toronto: University of Toronto Press, 1986.

Barrett, Charles A. "Why Are Canadians Saving So Much?" *Canadian Business Review* 5 (Summer 1978).

Baum, Gregory, and Duncan Cameron. *Ethics and Economics: Canada's Catholic Bishops on the Economic Crisis.* Toronto: James Lorimer, 1984.

Bayefsky, Anne F. "The Judicial Function under the Canadian Charter of Rights and Freedoms." *McGill Law Journal* 32 (September 1987).

"Beautiful Losers." *Saturday Night* 101 (January 1986).

Beer, Samuel. "The Modernization of American Federalism." *Publius: The Journal of Federalism* 3 (February 1973).

Bell, D.V. "The Loyalist Tradition in Canada." *Journal of Canadian Studies* 5 (May 1970).

Bell, Daniel. "The Background and Development of Marxian Socialism in the United States." In *Socialism and American Life*, edited by Donald Drew Egbert and Stow Persons, vol. 1. Princeton, N.J.: Princeton University Press, 1952.

———. *Marxian Socialism in the United States.* Princeton N.J.: Princeton University Press, 1967.

Bell, David, and Lorne Tepperman. *The Roots of Disunity.* Toronto: McClelland and Stewart, 1979.

Bellah, Robert N. *Beyond Belief.* New York: Harper and Row, 1970.

———. *The Broken Covenant: American Civil Religion in Time of Trial.* New York: Seabury Press, 1975.

Beloff, Max. "Of Lords, Senators, & Plain Misters." *Encounter* 68 (April 1987).

Bennett, Scott. "Issues in Pharmaceutical Policy: A Comparison of Canada and the United States." In *Canadian and U.S. Public Policy and Process: The Interplay between Institutions, Values and Interdependence*, edited by Martin Lubin. Forthcoming.

Bercovitch, Sacvan. *The American Jeremiad.* Madison: University of Wisconsin Press, 1978.

———. "The Rites of Assent: Rhetoric, Ritual, and the Ideology of American Consensus." In *The American Self: Myth, Ideology and Popular Culture*, edited by Sam B. Girgus. Albuquerque: University of New Mexico Press, 1981.

Bercuson, David, and Douglas Wertheimer. *A Trust Betrayed.* Toronto: Doubleday Canada, 1985.

Berger, Carl. "The True North Strong and Free." In *Nationalism in Canada*, edited by Peter Russell. Toronto: McGraw-Hill, 1966.

Berton, Pierre. *Why We Act Like Canadians.* Toronto: McClelland and Stewart, 1982.

Bibby, Reginald. *Fragmented Gods: The Poverty and Potential of Religion in Canada.* Toronto: Irvine, 1987.

———. "Religious Encasement in Canada: An Argument for Protestant and Catholic Entrenchment." *Social Compass* 32 (1985).

———, and Harold R. Weaver. "Cult Consumption in Canada: A Further Critique of Stark and Bainbridge." *Sociological Analysis* 46 (1985).

Bird, Richard. "Federal Finance in Comparative Perspective." In *Ottawa and the Provinces: The Distribution of Money and Power,* edited by Thomas J. Courchene, David W. Conklin, and Gail C.A. Cook, vol. 1. Toronto: Ontario Economic Council, 1985.

Bissell, Claude A. "A Common Ancestry: Literature in Australia and Canada." *University of Toronto Quarterly* 25 (January 1956).

———. "The Place of Learning and the Arts in Canadian Life." In *Perspectives on Revolution and Evolution,* edited by Richard A. Preston. Durham, N.C.: Duke University Press, 1979.

Blakeney, Allan. "Decentralization: A Qualified Defence." In *Canada, What's Left?,* edited by John Richards and Don Kerr. Edmonton: NeWest Press, 1986.

"Bleeding-Heart Conservatives," Canada survey. *The Economist,* October 8, 1988.

Blendon, Robert J. "Three Systems: A Comparative Survey." *Health Management Quarterly* 11 (first quarter 1989).

Blishen, Bernard. "Continuity and Change in Canadian Values." In *The Politics of Gender, Ethnicity and Language in Canada,* edited by Alan Cairns and Cynthia Williams. Toronto: University of Toronto Press, 1986.

Blustein, Paul. "The Great Jobs Debate." *Washington Post,* national weekly edition, September 5–11, 1988.

Borovoy, A. Alan. *When Freedoms Collide: The Case for Our Civil Liberties.* Toronto: Lester and Orpen Dennys, 1988.

Bourgault, Pierre L. *Innovation and the Structure of Canadian Industry,* Science Council of Canada Background Paper 23. Ottawa: Information Canada, 1972.

Bowering, George. "Modernism Could Not Last Forever." *Canadian Fiction Magazine,* nos. 32–33 (1979–80).

Brady, Alexander. "Canada and the Model of Westminster." In *The Transfer of Institutions,* edited by William B. Hamilton. Durham, N.C.: Duke University Press, 1964.

Brebner, J. Bartlett. *Canada.* Ann Arbor: University of Michigan Press, 1960.

Bremner, Robert H. *American Philanthropy*. Chicago: University of Chicago Press, 1988.

Breton, Raymond. "Multiculturalism and Canadian Nation-Building." In *The Politics of Gender, Ethnicity and Language in Canada*, edited by Alan Cairns and Cynthia Williams. Toronto: University of Toronto Press, 1986.

Brimelow, Peter. *The Patriot Game: National Dreams and Political Realities*. Toronto: Key Porter, 1986.

Brinkerhoff, Merlin A., and Reginald W. Bibby. "Circulation of the Saints in South America: A Comparative Study." *Journal for the Scientific Study of Religion* 24 (March 1985).

"Britain, Netherlands Still Lead Japan in Total Direct Investment in U.S.." *Wall Street Journal*, February 24, 1989.

Brown, Henry Phelps. *The Origins of Union Power*. Oxford: Clarendon Press, 1983.

Brown, J.J. *Ideas in Exile: A History of Canadian Invention*. Toronto: McClelland and Stewart, 1967.

Brown, Russell M. "A Search for America: Some Canadian Literary Responses." *Journal of American Culture* 2 (1980).

———. "Telemachus and Oedipus: Images and Authority in Canadian and American Fiction." Department of English, University of Toronto, 1979.

Bryce, James. *The American Commonwealth*, 3 vols. London: Macmillan, 1887.

———. *Modern Democracies*, 2 vols. New York: Macmillan, 1921.

Brym, Robert J. "Canada." In *The Capitalist Class: An International Study*, edited by Tom Bottomore and Robert J. Brym. New York: Harvester Wheatsheaf, 1989.

———. "The Canadian Capitalist Class, 1965–1985." In *The Structure of the Canadian Capitalist Class*, edited by Robert J. Brym. Toronto: Garamond Press, 1985.

———. "Social Movements." In *The Social World*, edited by Lorne Tepperman and R. Jack Richardson. Toronto: McGraw-Hill Ryerson, 1986.

———. "Social Movements and Third Parties." In *Models and Myths in Canadian Sociology*, edited by S.D. Berkowitz. Toronto: Butterworths, 1984.

———, with Bonnie J. Fox. *From Culture to Power*. Toronto: Oxford University Press, 1989.

Buhmann, Brigitte, et al. "Equivalence Scales, Well-Being, Inequality, and Poverty: Sensitivity Estimates across Ten Countries Using the Luxembourg Income Study (LIS) Database." *Review of Income and Wealth* 34 (June 1988).

Bull, Henry H. "The Career Prosecutor of Canada." *The Journal of Criminal Law, Criminology, and Police Science* 53 (1962).

Burbidge, John. "Religion in Canada." *Journal of Canadian Studies* 22 (Winter 1987–88).

Burke, Edmund. *Selected Works.* Oxford: Clarendon Press, 1904.

Burnham, Walter Dean. "The Appearance and Disappearance of the American Voter." In *Electoral Participation: A Comparative Analysis,* edited by Richard Rose. Beverly Hills, Cal.: Sage Publications, 1980.

———. "The 1980 Earthquake: Realignment, Reaction, or What?" In *The Hidden Election,* edited by Thomas Ferguson and Joel Rogers. New York: Pantheon, 1981.

Burns, John F. "Canadian Church Approves Homosexual Ministers." *New York Times,* August 28, 1988.

Burt, Sandra. "Women's Issues and the Women's Movement of Canada since 1970." In *The Politics of Gender, Ethnicity and Language in Canada,* edited by Alan Cairns and Cynthia Williams. Toronto: University of Toronto Press, 1986.

Butterfield, L.H., et al., eds. *The Book of Abigail and John: Selected Letters of the Adams Family 1762–1784.* Cambridge, Mass.: Harvard University Press, 1975.

Cairns, Alan C. *Constitution, Government, and Society in Canada.* Toronto: McClelland and Stewart, 1988.

———. "The Embedded State: State-Society Relations in Canada." In *State and Society: Canada in Comparative Perspective,* edited by Keith G. Banting. Toronto: University of Toronto Press, 1986.

———. "Political Science in Canada and the Americanization Issue." *Canadian Journal of Political Science* 8 (June 1975).

Callwood, June. *Portrait of Canada.* Garden City, N.Y.: Doubleday, 1981.

Campbell, Colin. *Governments under Stress.* Toronto: University of Toronto Press, 1983.

———. "The Interplay of Institutionization and the Assignment of Tasks in Parliamentary and Congressional Systems." In *Cross-National Perspectives: United States and Canada,* edited by Robert Presthus. Leiden: E.J. Brill, 1977.

———, and George J. Szablowski. *The Superbureaucrats: Structure and Behavior in Central Agencies.* Toronto: Macmillan of Canada, 1979.

Campbell, Douglas F. "The Canadian and Australian Church Unions: A Comparison." *International Journal of Comparative Sociology* 26 (3–4:1985).

Canada. Royal Commission on Bilingualism and Biculturalism. *Report*, vol. 4, *The Cultural Contribution of the Other Ethnic Groups*. Ottawa: Queen's Printer, 1969.

————. Statistics Canada. *Canada Year Book 1988*. Cat. No. 11-402E. Ottawa, 1988.

"Canada Fails Litmus Test." *Wall Street Journal*, May 1, 1989.

Canadian Conference of Catholic Bishops. "A Statement on Social Policy." *Dissent* 34 (Summer 1988).

Canadian Institute for Advanced Research. *Innovation and Prosperity: The Transforming Power of Science, Engineering and Technology*. Toronto, 1988.

Careless, J.M.S. *Canada: A Story of Challenge*. Cambridge: Cambridge University Press, 1963.

Carroll, William K. *Corporate Power and Canadian Capitalism*. Vancouver: University of British Columbia Press, 1986.

————, John Fox, and Michael D. Ornstein. "The Network of Directorate Links among the Largest Canadian Firms." *Canadian Review of Sociology and Anthropology* 19 (February 1982).

Cawelti, John G. *The Six-Gun Mystique*. Bowling Green, Ohio: Bowling Green University Popular Press, 1975.

Center for Applied Research in the Apostolate. *Values Study of Canada*. Washington, D.C., May 1983.

Chase, Kristine. "National Banking: A Comparison of Policy towards Nationwide Banking and Concentration of Power in Banking Markets in Canada and the U.S." *Policy Studies Journal* 14 (June 1986).

Chiswick, Barry R. "Immigration Policy, Source Countries and Immigrant Skills: Australia, Canada and the United States." In *The Economics of Immigration*, edited by Lyle Baker and Paul Miller. Can-berra: Australian Government Publishing Service, 1988.

Christian, William, and Colin Campbell. *Political Parties and Ideologies in Canada*. Toronto: McGraw-Hill Ryerson, 1983.

Church, Nancy J., and Lise Héroux. "A Comparison of Sex Roles in American and Canadian News Magazines: A Pictorial Content Analysis." School of Business Administration, State University of New York, Plattsburgh, N.Y., 1989.

Clark, S.D. In *Canada and Her Great Neighbor: Sociological Surveys of Opinions and Attitudes in Canada Concerning the United States*, edited by H.F. Angus. Toronto: Ryerson Press, 1938.

————. "The Canadian Community." In *Canada*, edited by George W. Brown. Berkeley: University of California Press, 1954.

————. *Canadian Society in Historical Perspective*. Toronto: McGraw-Hill Ryerson, 1976.

———. *Church and Sect in Canada.* Toronto: University of Toronto Press, 1948.

———. *The Developing Canadian Community.* Toronto: University of Toronto Press, 1962.

———. "The Frontier and Democratic Theory." *Transactions of the Royal Society of Canada* 48 (1954).

———. *Movements of Political Protest in Canada.* Toronto: University of Toronto Press, 1959.

Clarke, Harold D., et al. *Political Choice in Canada.* Toronto: McGraw-Hill Ryerson, 1979.

Clement, Wallace. *Continental Corporate Power.* Toronto: McClelland and Stewart, 1977.

Cleverdon, Catherine Lyle. *The Woman Suffrage Movement in Canada.* Toronto: University of Toronto Press, 1950.

Close, David. "Politics and Constitutional Reform in Canada: A Study in Political Opposition." *Publius: The Journal of Federalism* 15 (Winter 1985).

Cohen, Andrew. "Power to the Provinces." *Saturday Night* 103 (August 1988).

Cohen, Matt. "Literary Nationalism in English Canada: Bogus or Magus?" *American Book Review* 10 (May–June 1988).

Conway, John. "An 'Adapted Organic Tradition.'" *Daedalus* 117 (Fall 1988).

Cook, Eleanor. "'A Seeing and Unseeing in the Eye': Canadian Literature and the Sense of Place." *Daedalus* 117 (Fall 1988).

Cook, Ramsay. *The Maple Leaf Forever: Essays on Nationalism and Politics in Canada.* Toronto: Macmillan of Canada, 1977.

Crane, David. "Study of Trade Data Highlights Canada's High-Tech Problem." *Toronto Star,* August 12, 1989.

Crawford, Craig, and James Curtis. "English Canadian–American Differences in Value Orientations." *Studies in Comparative International Development* 14 (1979).

Creighton, Donald G. *The Empire of the St. Lawrence.* Toronto: Houghton Mifflin, 1958.

Crispo, John. *Mandate for Canada.* Don Mills, Ont.: General Publishing, 1979.

Cuninggim, Merrimon. *Private Money and Public Service.* New York: McGraw-Hill, 1972.

Cunliffe, Marcus. "New World, Old World: The Historical Antithesis." In *Lessons from America,* edited by Richard Rose. London: Macmillan, 1974.

Curti, Merle. *American Philanthropy Abroad: A History.* New Brunswick, N.J.: Rutgers University Press, 1963.

Curtis, James, and Ronald Lambert. "Culture and Social Organization." In *Sociology*, edited by Robert Hagedorn. Toronto: Holt, Rinehart and Winston of Canada, 1980.

———, Ronald D. Lambert, Steven D. Brown, and Barry J. Kay. "Affiliation with Voluntary Associations: Canadian-American Comparisons." *Canadian Journal of Sociology* 14 (Spring 1989).

Dauer, Manning. *The Adams Federalists.* Baltimore: Johns Hopkins University Press, 1953.

Davies, Robertson. "Dark Hamlet with the Features of Horatio: Canada's Myths and Realities." In *Voices of Canada: An Introduction to Canadian Culture*, edited by Judith Webster. Burlington, Vt.: Association for Canadian Studies in the United States, 1977.

———. *The Lyre of Orpheus.* Toronto: Macmillan of Canada, 1988.

———. "Signing Away Canada's Soul." *Harpers* 278 (January 1989).

Davis, Arthur K. "Canadian Society and History as Hinterland versus Metropolis." In *Canadian Society: Pluralism, Change and Conflict*, edited by Richard J. Ossenberg. Scarborough, Ont.: Prentice-Hall Canada, 1971.

Davis, J. Madison, ed. *Conversations with Robertson Davies.* Jackson: University Press of Mississippi, 1989.

Deitch, David. "Libertarians Unite in Drive to Reduce Tax Burden." Boston *Globe*, April 10, 1971.

Denton, Herbert N. "Socialists Seek Reelection in Manitoba." *Washington Post*, March 18, 1986.

Dick, William M. *Labor and Socialism in America: The Gompers Era.* Port Washington, N.Y.: Kennikat Press, 1972.

Donald, David. "Died of Democracy." In *Why the North Won the Civil War*, edited by David Donald. Baton Rouge: Louisiana State University Press, 1960.

Donney, Lawrence W. "A Canadian Image of Education." In *Canadian Society*, edited by Bernard Blishen et al. Toronto: Macmillan of Canada, 1971.

Dooley, Martin. "Demography of Child Poverty in Canada: 1873–1986." Paper presented to the Population Association of America, Baltimore, Md., March 28–April 1, 1989.

Drobut, Eve. "Social and Personal." *Saturday Night* 104 (August 1989).

Dubofsky, Melvyn. *We Shall Be All: A History of the Industrial Workers of the World.* Chicago: Quadrangle Books, 1955.

Duchacek, Ivo D. "Consociational Cradle of Federalism." *Publius: The Journal of Federalism* 15 (Spring 1985).

Duffy, Dennis. *Gardens, Covenants, Exiles: Loyalism in the Literature of Upper Canada/Ontario.* Toronto: University of Toronto Press, 1982.

Eayrs, James. "Sharing a Continent: The Hard Issues." In *The United States and Canada,* edited by John S. Dickey. Englewood Cliffs, N.J.: Prentice-Hall, 1964.

Elder, R. Bruce. *Image and Identity: Reflections on Canadian Film and Culture.* Waterloo, Ont.: Wilfrid Laurier University Press, 1989.

Elkins, David J. "The Sense of Place." In *Small Worlds: Provinces and Parties in Canadian Political Life,* edited by David J. Elkins and Richard Simeon. Toronto: Methuen, 1980.

Elman, B.P. "The Promotion of Hatred and the Canadian Charter of Rights and Freedoms: A Review of Keegstra v. The Queen." *Canadian Public Policy* 15 (March 1989).

Elman, Benjamin A. "Confucianism and Modernization: A Re-evaluation." In *Confucianism and Modernization: A Symposium,* edited by Joseph P. Jiang. Taipei, Taiwan: The Freedom Council—Wu Nan Publishing, 1987.

Epstein, Leon D. "A Comparative Study of Canadian Parties." *American Political Science Review* 58 (March 1964).

Ernst, Maurice. "How Not to Create Jobs: Lessons from the West European Experience." *Journal of Labor Research* 10 (Winter 1989).

Erskine, Hazel. "The Polls: Is War a Mistake?" *Public Opinion Quarterly* 34 (1970).

Esman, Milton J. "Federalism and Modernization: Canada and the United States." *Publius: The Journal of Federalism* 14 (Winter 1984).

Evans, Robert G. "'We'll Take Care of It for You': Health Care in the Canadian Community." *Daedalus* 117 (Fall 1988).

"An Exchange between Max Beloff and Irving Kristol." *Encounter* 69 (June 1987).

Fallding, Harold. "Mainline Protestantism in Canada and the United States of America: An Overview." *Canadian Journal of Sociology* 3 (Spring 1978).

Fetherling, Douglas, ed. *A George Woodcock Reader.* Ottawa: Deneau and Greenberg, 1980.

————. *The Gold Crusades: A Social History of Gold Rushes 1849–1969.* Toronto: Macmillan of Canada, 1989.

Feuer, Lewis S. *Marx and the Intellectuals.* Garden City, N.Y.: Doubleday–Anchor Books, 1969.

Findlay, Timothy. *Not Wanted on the Voyage*. Toronto: Viking Press, 1984.

Flanigan, Thomas. "The Manufacture of Minorities." In *Minorities and the Canadian State*, edited by Neil Nevitte and Allan Kornberg. Oakville, Ont.: Mosaic Press, 1985.

Flexner, James Thomas. *Washington: The Indispensable Man*. New York: New American Library, 1984.

Fogel, Stanley. *A Tale of Two Countries: Contemporary Fiction in English Canada and the United States*. Toronto: ECW Press, 1984.

Forcese, Dennis. "Canada's Politics: Class, Region and Continentalism." In *Models and Myths in Canadian Sociology*, edited by S.D. Berkowitz. Toronto: Butterworths, 1984.

Fothergill, Robert. "Coward, Bully, or Clown: The Dream-Life of a Younger Brother." In *Canadian Film Reader*, edited by Seth Feldman and Joyce Nelson. Toronto: Peter Martin Associates, 1977.

Francis, David R. "Why Canada Is Safer Than US." *Christian Science Monitor*, January 2, 1987.

Francis, Diane. *Controlling Interest: Who Owns Canada?*. Toronto: McClelland-Bantam, 1987.

Franks, C.E.S. "Indian Self-Government: Canada and the United States Compared." In *Canadian and U.S. Public Policy and Process: The Interplay between Institution, Values and Interdependence*, edited by Martin Lubin. Forthcoming.

Fraser, Blair. *The Search for Identity: Canada, 1945–67*. Garden City, N.Y.: Doubleday, 1967.

Fredenheim, Milt. "A New Ontario Law Matches Women's Wages with Men's." *New York Times*, July 7, 1989.

Frideres, James S. "Institutional Structures and Economic Deprivation: Native People in Canada." In *Racial Oppression in Canada*, edited by B. Singh Bolaria and Peter S. Li. Toronto: Garamond Press, 1988.

Friedenberg, Edgar. "Culture in Canadian Context." In *An Introduction to Sociology*, edited by M. Michael Rosenberg et al. Toronto: Methuen, 1983.

———. *Deference to Authority*. White Plains, N.Y.: M.E. Sharpe, 1980.

Frye, Northrop. *The Bush Garden: Essays on the Canadian Imagination*. Toronto: Anansi, 1971.

———. *Divisions on a Ground: Essays on Canadian Culture*. Toronto: Anansi, 1982.

———. "Letters in Canada: 1952, Part I: Publications in English." *University of Toronto Quarterly* 22 (April 1953).

――――. "Preface to an Uncollected Anthology." In *Contexts of Canadian Criticism*, edited by Eli Mandel. Chicago: University of Chicago Press, 1971).

Fu Pei-jung. "Confucianism and an Ethic for Modernization — In Response to Weber's Critique." In *Confucianism and Modernization: A Symposium*, edited by Joseph P. Jiang. Taipei, Taiwan: The Freedom Council—Wu Nan Publishing, 1987.

Gadpaille, Michelle. *The Canadian Short Story*. Toronto: Oxford University Press, 1988.

Gallup International Research Institute. *Human Needs and Satisfaction: A Global Survey*. Princeton, N.J., 1977.

Geertz, Clifford. *The Interpretation of Cultures*. New York: Basic Books, 1973.

Gibbins, Roger. *Conflict and Unity: An Introduction to Canadian Political Life*. Scarborough, Ont.: Nelson Canada, 1988.

――――. *Regionalism: Territorial Politics in Canada and the United States*. Toronto: Butterworths, 1982.

――――, Rainer Knopff, and F.L. Morton. "Canadian Federalism, the Charter of Rights and the 1984 Election." *Publius: The Journal of Federalism* 15 (Summer 1985).

――――, and J. Rick Ponting. "An Assessment of the Probable Impact of Aboriginal Self-Government in Canada." In *The Politics of Gender, Ethnicity and Language in Canada*, edited by Alan Cairns and Cynthia Williams. Toronto: University of Toronto Press, 1986.

Gibson, Dale. "Protection of Minority Rights under the Canadian Charter of Rights and Freedoms: Can Politicians and Judges Sing Harmony?" In *Minorities and the Canadian State*, edited by Neil Nevitte and Allan Kornberg. Oakville, Ont.: Mosaic Press, 1985.

――――. "Reasonable Limits under the Canadian Charter of Rights and Freedoms." *Manitoba Law Review* 15 (1:1985).

Gilbert, Sid. "Educational and Occupational Aspirations of Ontario High School Students: A Multivariate Analysis." Ph.D. diss., Department of Sociology, Carleton University, Ottawa, 1973.

――――. "The Selection of Educational Aspirations." In *Education, Change, and Society*, edited by R.A. Carlton, L.A. Colley, and N.J. MacKinnon. Toronto: Gage, 1977.

Glaser, William. "Health Politics: Lessons from Abroad." In *Health Politics and Policy*, edited by Theodore J. Litman. New York: John Wiley, 1984.

――――. "Improving Federalism in American Health Services: Some Ideas from Abroad." In *Changing National-Subnational Relations in Health: Opportunities and Constraints*, edited by Christa Altenstetter.

Washington, D.C.: Public Health Services, National Institutes of Health, Department of Health, Education and Welfare, 1978.

Glazer, Nathan. "Welfare and 'Welfare' in America." In *The Welfare State East and West*, edited by Richard Rose and Rei Shiratori. New York: Oxford University Press, 1986.

————, and Daniel P. Moynihan. *Beyond the Melting Pot.* Cambridge, Mass.: Harvard University Press, 1965.

Glazier, Kenneth M. "Canadian Investment in the United States: 'Putting Your Money Where Your Mouth Is.'" *Journal of Contemporary Business* 1 (Autumn 1972).

Goldberg, Michael A., and John Mercer. *The Myth of the North American City: Continentalism Challenged.* Vancouver: University of British Columbia Press, 1986.

Goodstein, Ethel S. "Contemporary Architecture and Canadian National Identity." *The American Review of Canadian Studies* 18 (Summer 1988).

Gordon, Charles. "No One Called In the Helicopters." *Maclean's,* May 1, 1989.

Goulden, Joseph C. *The Money Givers.* New York: Random House, 1971.

Goyder, John, and Peter C. Pineo. "Social Class Self-Identification." In *Social Stratification in Canada.* 2d ed., edited by James G. Curtis and William G. Scott. Scarborough, Ont.: Prentice-Hall Canada, 1979.

Gramsci, Antonio. *Selections from the Prison Notebooks.* New York: International Publishers, 1971; first published in Italian, 1955.

Grant, George. *Lament for a Nation.* Princeton, N.J.: Van Nostrand, 1965.

Grant, John Webster. "'At Least You Knew Where You Stood with Them': Reflections on Religious Pluralism in Canada and the United States." *Studies in Religion* 2 (Spring 1973).

Gray, Charlotte. "Designer Socialism." *Saturday Night* 104 (August 1989).

Grayson, J. Paul. "Male Hegemony and the English-Canadian Novel." *Canadian Review of Sociology and Anthropology* 20 (February 1983).

Green, Martin. *The Problem of Boston.* New York: W.W. Norton, 1966.

Green, Mary Jean. "Writing in a Motherland." French Department, Dartmouth College, Hanover, N.H, 1984.

Greenfield, Jeff. "Challenging the Liturgy." *The West Side Spirit,* May 28, 1989.

Griffiths, Curt, John Fiklein, and Simon N. Verdon-Jones. *Criminal Justice in Canada.* Toronto: Butterworths, 1980.

Guppy, L. Neil. "Dissensus or Consensus: A Cross-National Comparison of Occupational Prestige Scales." *Canadian Journal of Sociology* 9 (Winter 1983–84).

Gwyn, Richard. *The 49th Paradox: Canada in North America.* Toronto: McClelland and Stewart, 1985.

Hackler, James C., and Christian T.L. Janssen, "Police Killings in Perspective." In *Crime in Canadian Society.* 3d ed., edited by Robert A. Silverman and James V. Teevan, Jr. Toronto: Butterworths, 1986.

Hagan, John. "Comparing Crime and Criminalization in Canada and the U.S.A.." *Canadian Journal of Sociology* 14 (Fall 1989).

―――. "Crime, Deviance, and Legal Order." In *Understanding Canadian Society,* edited by James Curtis and Lorne Tepperman. Toronto: McGraw-Hill Ryerson, 1988.

―――. *The Disreputable Pleasures.* 2d ed. Toronto: McGraw-Hill Ryerson, 1984.

―――. "Toward A Structural Theory of Crime, Race and Gender." In *Crime in Canadian Society.* 3d ed., edited by Robert A. Silverman and James V. Teevan, Jr. Toronto: Butterworths, 1986.

―――, and Jeffrey Leon. "Philosophy and Sociology of Crime Control." In *Social System and Legal Process,* edited by Harry M. Johnson. San Francisco: Jossey-Bass, 1978.

―――, and Jeffrey Leon. "The Rehabilitation of Law: A Social and Historical Comparison of Probation in Canada and the United States." *Canadian Journal of Sociology* 5 (Summer 1980).

Hancock, Geoff. *Canadian Writers at Work.* Toronto: Oxford University Press, 1987.

Hardin, Herschel. *A Nation Unaware: The Canadian Economic Culture.* Vancouver: J.J. Douglas, 1974.

Harrington, Michael. *Socialism.* New York: Saturday Review Press, 1972.

Harrison, Dick. "The Insignificance of the Frontier in Western Canadian Fiction." In *Kanada Geschichte: Politik Kultur,* German-English Yearbook Band 19, edited by Wolfgang Klooss and Hartmut Lutz. Berlin: Argument-Verlag, 1987.

―――. "Popular Fiction of the Canadian Prairies: Autopsy on a Small Corpse." *Journal of Popular Culture* 14 (Fall 1980).

―――. "The Search for an Authentic Voice in Canadian Literature." In *Kanada Heute,* edited by Friedel H. Bastein. Frankfurt am Main: Verlag Peter Lang, 1987.

————. *Unnamed Country: The Struggle for a Canadian Prairie Fiction.* Edmonton: University of Alberta Press, 1977.

Hart, Philip. *Orpheus in the New World: The Symphony Orchestra as an American Cultural Institution.* New York: W.W. Norton, 1973.

Hartz, Louis. *The Founding of New Societies.* New York: Harcourt, Brace and World, 1964.

————. *The Liberal Tradition in America.* New York: Harcourt Brace, 1955.

Hastings, Elizabeth H., and Philip K. Hastings, eds. *Index to International Public Opinion, 1980–1981.* Westport, Conn.: Greenwood Press, 1982.

Haug, Marie. "Social and Cultural Pluralism as a Concept in Social System Analysis." *American Journal of Sociology* 73 (November 1967).

Hawkins, Freda. *Canada and Immigration: Public Policy and Public Concern.* Kingston, Ont.; Montreal: McGill-Queen's University Press, 1988.

————. *Critical Years in Immigration: Canada and Australia Compared.* Kingston, Ont.; Montreal: McGill-Queen's University Press, 1989.

Heclo, Hugh. "The Emerging Regime." In *Remaking American Politics,* edited by Richard A. Harris and Sidney M. Milkis. Boulder, Col.: Westview Press, 1989.

Heidenheimer, Arnold, et al. *Comparative Public Policy: The Politics of Social Choice in Europe and America.* New York: St. Martin's Press, 1983.

Higonnet, Patrice. *Sister Republics: The Origins of French and American Republicanism.* Cambridge, Mass.: Harvard University Press, 1988.

Hiller, Harry H. *Canadian Society: A Sociological Analysis.* Scarborough, Ont.: Prentice-Hall Canada, 1976.

————. "Continentalism and the Third Force in Religion." *Canadian Journal of Sociology* 3 (Spring 1978).

Hillquit, Morris. *History of Socialism in the United States.* New York: Funk and Wagnalls, 1910.

Hofstadter, Richard. *The Age of Reform.* New York: Vintage Books, 1967.

————. *Anti-Intellectualism in American Life.* New York: Alfred A. Knopf, 1963.

Hofstede, Geert. *Culture's Consequences: International Differences in Work-Related Values.* Beverly Hills, Cal.: Sage Publications, 1984.

Horne, Alistair. *Canada and the Canadians.* London: Macmillan, 1961.

Horowitz, Gad. *Canadian Labour in Politics*. Toronto: University of Toronto Press, 1968.

―――. "Notes on 'Conservatism, Liberalism and Socialism in Canada.'" *Canadian Journal of Political Science* 11 (June 1978).

―――. "Red Tory." In *Canada: A Guide to the Peaceable Kingdom*, edited by William Kilbourn. New York: St. Martin's Press, 1970.

Horowitz, Irving Louis. "The Hemispheric Connection: A Critique and Corrective to the Entrepreneurial Thesis of Development with Special Emphasis on the Canadian Case." *Queen's Quarterly* 80 (Autumn 1973).

Hosek, Chaviva. "Women and the Constitutional Process." In *And No One Cheered*, edited by Keith Banting and Richard Simeon. Toronto: Methuen, 1983.

Huegelin, Thomas O. "The End of Institutional Tidiness? Trends of Late Federalism in the United States and Canada." Department of Political Science, Queen's University, Kingston, Ont. 1984.

Hugins, Walter. *Jacksonian Democracy and the Working Class, A Study of the New York Workingmen's Movement 1829–1837*. Stanford, Cal.: Stanford University Press, 1960.

Huntington, Samuel. *American Politics: The Promise of Disharmony*. Cambridge, Mass.: Harvard University Press, Belknap Press, 1981.

―――. "The U.S. — Decline or Renewal." *Foreign Affairs* 67 (Winter 1988/89).

Hutcheon, Linda. *The Canadian Postmodern: A Study of Contemporary English-Canadian Fiction*. Toronto: Oxford University Press, 1988.

Hutcheson, John. "A Political Re-alignment." *The Canadian Forum* 68 (March 1989).

Huxley, Christopher, David Kettler, and James Struthers. "Is Canada's Experience 'Especially Instructive?'" In *Unions in Transition: Entering the Second Century*, edited by Seymour Martin Lipset. San Francisco: Institute for Contemporary Studies, 1986.

Innis, Harold A. *Essays in Canadian Economic History*. Toronto: University of Toronto Press, 1956.

―――. *The Fur Trade in Canada*. Toronto: University of Toronto Press, 1973.

Irving, John. *A Prayer for Owen Meany*. New York: William Morrow, 1989.

"The Italian Economy." *The Economist*, February 27, 1988.

Jackson, Lawrence. "Fever." *Books in Canada* 18 (April 1989).

Jameson, J. Franklin. *The American Revolution Considered as a Social Movement.* Princeton, N.J.: Princeton University Press, 1926.

Janigan, Mary. "Trudeau's Power Punch." *Maclean's,* June 8, 1987.

Jarrett, Janet. "Why Canadians Save More Than Americans." *Canadian Business Review* 7 (Autumn 1980).

Jefferson, Thomas. *Notes on the State of Virginia.* New York: Harper and Row, Torchbooks, 1964; first published 1784–85.

Jenkins, Edward C. *Philanthropy in America.* New York: Association Press, 1950.

Jiang, Joseph P., ed. *Confucianism and Modernization: A Symposium.* Taipei, Taiwan: The Freedom Council—Wu Nan Publishing, 1987.

Johnson, Harry. "Unlovely Canadianism." In *Canada: A Guide to the Peaceable Kingdom,* edited by William Kilbourn. New York: St. Martin's Press, 1970.

Johnston, Richard. "Federal and Provincial Voting." In *Small Worlds: Provinces and Parties in Canadian Political Life,* edited by David J. Elkins and Richard Simeon. Toronto: Methuen, 1980.

Jones, Elise F., et al. *Teenage Pregnancy in Industrialized Countries.* New Haven, Conn.: Yale University Press, 1986.

Kasporich, Beverly. "Canadian Humour and Culture: Regional and National Expressions." Faculty of General Studies, University of Calgary, 1986.

Kaufman, Michael T. "Canada: An American Discovers Its Difference." *New York Times Magazine,* May 15, 1983.

Kaye, Frances W. "The 49th Parallel and the 98th Meridian: Some Lines for Thought." *Mosaic: A Journal for the Interdisciplinary Study of Literature* 14 (Spring 1981).

Kazin, Michael. "The Right's Unsung Prophet." *The Nation* 248 (February 20, 1989).

Keizzi Koho Center. *Japan 1983: An International Comparison.* Tokyo, 1983.

Kelman, Steven. *Regulating America, Regulating Sweden: A Comparative Study of Occupational Safety and Health Policy.* Cambridge, Mass.: MIT Press, 1981.

Kennan, George. *Realities of American Foreign Policy.* New York: W.W Norton, 1966.

Kenney-Wallace, Geraldine A., and J. Fraser Mustard. "From Paradox to Paradigm: The Evolution of Science and Technology in Canada." *Daedalus* 117 (Fall 1988).

Keyserling, Hermann. *America Set Free*. New York: Harper and Brothers, 1929.

Kilborn, Peter T. "A Fight to Win the Middle Class." *New York Times*, business section, September 4, 1988.

Kilbourn, William. *Canada: A Guide to the Peaceable Kingdom*. New York: St. Martin's Press, 1970.

———. "The Peaceable Kingdom Still." *Daedalus* 117 (Fall 1988).

Kirkham, James F., Sheldon G. Levy, and William J. Crotty. *Assassination and Political Violence*. New York: Praeger, 1970.

Kirstein, George G. *Better Giving*. Boston: Houghton Mifflin, 1975.

Klein, John F., Jim R. Webb, and J.R. DeSanto. "Experience with Police and Attitudes towards the Police." *Canadian Journal of Sociology* 3 (1978).

Koenig, Daniel J. "Police Perceptions of Public Respect and Extra-Legal Use of Force: A Reconsideration of Folk Wisdom and Pluralistic Ignorance." *Canadian Journal of Sociology* 1 (Summer, 1975).

Kollar, Nathan R. "Controversial Issues in North American Fundamentalism." St. John Fisher College, Rochester, N.Y., 1989.

Kopvillem, Peter. "An Angry Racial Backlash." *Maclean's*, July 10, 1989.

Kornberg, Allan. *Politics and Culture in Canada*. Ann Arbor, Mich.: Center for Political Studies, Institute for Social Research, University of Michigan, 1988.

———, and Marianne C. Stewart. "National Identification and Political Support." In *Political Support in Canada: The Crisis Years*, edited by Allan Kornberg and Harold P. Clarke. Durham, N.C.: Duke University Press, 1983.

Krahn, Harvey, and Graham S. Lowe. "Public Attitudes towards Unions: Some Canadian Evidence." *Journal of Labor Research* 5 (Spring 1984).

Kresl, Peter Karl. "An Economics Perspective: Canada in the International Economy." In *Understanding Canada*, edited by William Metcalfe. New York: New York University Press, 1982.

Kroetsch, Robert. *The Lovely Treachery of Words: Essays Selected and New*. Toronto: Oxford University Press, 1989.

Kudrle, Robert T., and Theodore R. Marmor. "The Development of Welfare States in North America." In *The Development of Welfare States in Europe and America*, edited by Peter Flora and Arnold J. Heidenheimer. New Brunswick, N.J.: Transaction Books, 1981.

Laczko, Leslie. "Ethnic Diversity in Canada: A Macrosociological Look at Some Recent Trends." Department of Sociology, University of Ottawa, 1984.

Ladousse, Gillian Porter. "The Unicorn and the Booby Hatch: An Interview with Margaret Atwood." *Études Canadiennes* 5 (1978).

Lambert, Wallace E., Josiane F. Hamers James, and Nancy Frasure-Smith. *Child-Rearing Values: A Cross-National Study*. New York: Praeger, 1979.

Lamontagne, Maurice. "The Role of Government." In *Canada's Tomorrow*, edited by G.P. Gilmour. Toronto: Macmillan, 1954.

Landes, Ronald G. "The Political Socialization of Political Support." In *Political Support in Canada: The Crisis Years*, edited by Allan Kornberg and Harold P. Clarke. Durham, N.C.: Duke University Press, 1983.

Lapping, Mark B. "Peoples of Plenty: A Note on Agriculture as a Planning Metaphor and National Character in North America." *Journal of Canadian Studies* 22 (Spring 1987).

Larson, Lyle E. *The Canadian Family in Comparative Perspective*. Scarborough, Ont.: Prentice-Hall Canada, 1976.

Le Pan, Douglas. "The Outlook for the Relationship: A Canadian View." In *The United States and Canada*, edited by John S. Dickey. Englewood Cliffs, N.J.: Prentice-Hall, 1964.

Lee, Basil L. *Discontent in New York City, 1861–65*. Washington, D.C.: Catholic University of America Press, 1943.

Lemieux, Pierre. "Will Canada's Tax Reform Have a Supply-Side Effect?" *Wall Street Journal*, September 2, 1988.

Lenton, Rhonda. "Homicide in Canada and the U.S.A.: A Critique of the Hagan Thesis." *Canadian Journal of Sociology* 14 (Spring 1989).

Lewis, Paul. "Canada About to Sign Major Land Agreement with Eskimos." *New York Times*, national ed., August 21, 1989.

Lipset, Seymour Martin. "Academia and Politics in America." In *Imagination and Precision in the Social Sciences*, edited by T.J. Nossiter et al. London: Faber and Faber, 1972.

———. *Agrarian Socialism: The Cooperative Commonwealth Federation in Saskatchewan*. rev. ed. Berkeley: University of California Press, 1971; first published in 1950.

———. "American Exceptionalism Reaffirmed." In *Is America Different?: A New Look at American Exceptionalism*, edited by Byron Shafer. Oxford: Oxford University Press, forthcoming.

———. "Canada and the United States: The Cultural Dimension." In *Canada and the United States: Enduring Friendship, Persistent Stress*, edited by Charles F. Doran and John H. Sigler. Englewood Cliffs, N.J.: Prentice-Hall, 1985.

———. *Consensus and Conflict: Essays in Political Sociology*. New Brunswick, N.J.: Transaction Books, 1985.

————. "Democracy in Alberta." *The Canadian Forum* 34 (November/December 1954).

————. "Equality and Inequality." In *Contemporary Social Problems*, edited by Robert K. Merton and Robert Nisbet. New York: Macmillan, 1976.

————. *The First New Nation: The United States in Historical and Comparative Perspective*. New York: Basic Books, 1963; exp. paper ed., New York: W.W. Norton, 1979.

————. "Historical Traditions and National Characteristics: A Comparative Analysis of Canada and the United States." *Canadian Journal of Sociology* 11 (Summer 1986).

————. "North American Labor Movements: A Comparative Perspective." In *Unions in Transition: Entering the Second Century*, edited by Seymour Martin Lipset. San Francisco: Institute for Contemporary Studies, 1986.

————. "Racial and Ethnic Tensions in the Third World." In *The Third World: Premises of U.S. Policy*, edited by W. Scott Thompson. San Francisco: Institute for Contemporary Studies, 1978.

————. "Radicalism in North America: A Comparative View of the Party Systems in Canada and the United States." *Transactions of the Royal Society of Canada*, 4th series, 16 (1976).

————. *Revolution and Counterrevolution: Change and Persistence in Social Structures*. 3d ed. New Brunswick, N.J.: Transaction Books, 1988.

————. "Roosevelt and the Protest of the 1930s." *University of Minnesota Law Review* 68 (December 1983).

————. "Social Mobility in Industrial Societies." *Public Opinion* 5 (June/July, 1982).

————. "Socialism in America." In *Sidney Hook: Philosopher of Democracy and Humanism*, edited by P. Kurtz. Buffalo: Prometheus Books, 1983.

————. "A Unique People in an Exceptional Country." In *American Pluralism and the Jewish Community*, edited by Seymour Martin Lipset. New Brunswick, N.J.: Transaction Books, 1989.

————. "Values, Education and Entrepreneurship." In *Elites in Latin America*, edited by S.M. Lipset and Aldo Solari. New York: Oxford University Press, 1967.

————. "Voluntary Activities: More Canadian-American Comparisons — A Reply." *Canadian Journal of Sociology* 14 (Fall 1989).

————. "Why No Socialism in the United States?" In *Sources of Contemporary Radicalism*. vol. 1, edited by S. Bialer and S. Sluzar. Boulder, Col.: Westview Press, 1977.

————, and Reinhard Bendix. *Social Mobility in Industrial Society*. Berkeley: University of California Press, 1959.

————, and Richard Dobson. "The Intellectual as Critic and Rebel: With Special Reference to the United States and the Soviet Union." *Daedalus* 101 (Summer 1972).

————, and Earl Raab. *The Politics of Unreason: Right-Wing Extremism in the United States 1790–1977*. 2d ed. Chicago: University of Chicago Press, 1978.

————, and William Schneider. *The Confidence Gap: Business, Labor and Government in the Public Mind*. rev. ed. Baltimore, Md.: Johns Hopkins University Press, 1987.

Lipsey, Richard G. "Canada and the United States: The Economic Dimension." In *Canada and the United States: Enduring Friendship, Persistent Stress*, edited by John F. Sigler and Charles H. Doran. Englewood Cliffs, N.J.: Prentice-Hall, 1985.

————. *The Great Free Trade Debate and the Canadian Identity: A Convocation Address*. Ottawa: Carleton University, 1987.

Lipton, Charles. *The Trade Union Movement of Canada*. Toronto: University of Toronto Press, 1973.

Logan, Harold A. *The History of Trade-Union Organization in Canada*. Chicago: University of Chicago Press, 1928.

Lower, A.R.M. *Colony to Nation*. Toronto: Longman's, 1964.

————. "Religion and Religious Institutions." In *Canada*, edited by George Brown. Berkeley: University of California Press, 1954.

Lubell, Samuel. *The Future of American Politics*. New York: Doubleday–Anchor Books, 1965.

————. "Post-Mortem: Who Elected Roosevelt?" *Saturday Evening Post*, January 25, 1941.

McCague, James. *The Second Rebellion: The New York City Riots of 1863*. New York: Dial, 1968.

McDonald, Forrest. "The Relation of the French Peasant Veterans of the American Revolution to the Fall of Feudalism in France, 1789–1792." *Agricultural History* 25 (October 1951).

McDougall, Robert L. "The Dodo and the Cruising Auk." *Canadian Literature* 18 (Autumn 1973).

McGregor, Gaile. *The Wacousta Syndrome: Explorations in the Canadian Langscape*. Toronto: University of Toronto Press, 1985.

McInnis, Edgar W. *The Unguarded Frontier*. Garden City, N.Y.: Doubleday, 1942.

McKercher, William R., ed. *The U.S. Bill of Rights and the Canadian Charter of Rights and Freedoms*. Toronto: Ontario Economic Council, 1983.

MacLennan, Hugh. "The Psychology of Canadian Nationalism." *Foreign Affairs* 27 (April 1949).

———. "A Society in Revolt." In *Voices of Canada: An Introduction to Canadian Culture*, edited by Judith Webster. Burlington, Vt.: Association for Canadian Studies in the United States, 1977.

McLeod, J.T. "The Free Enterprise Dodo Is No Phoenix." *The Canadian Forum* 56 (August 1976).

Maclulich, T.D. *Between Europe and America: The Canadian Tradition in Fiction.* Oakville, Ont.: ECW Press, 1988.

McMillan, Charles J. "The Changing Competitive Environment of Canadian Business." *Journal of Canadian Studies* 13 (Spring 1978).

McNaught, Kenneth. "American Progressives and the Great Society." *Journal of American History* 53 (December 1966).

———. "Approaches to the Study of Canadian History." *The* [Japanese] *Annual Review of Canadian Studies* 5 (1984).

———. "Canada's European Ambiance." Paper read at the annual meeting of the Italian Association for Canadian Studies, Sicily, May 1988.

———. *The Pelican History of Canada.* Harmondsworth, England: Penguin Books, 1976.

———. "Political Trials and the Canadian Political Tradition." In *Courts and Trials: A Multidisciplinary Approach.* edited by Martin L. Friedland. Toronto: University of Toronto Press, 1975.

———. *A Prophet in Politics: A Biography of J.S. Woodsworth.* Toronto: University of Toronto Press, 1959.

"MacNeil/Lehrer NewsHour." Public Broadcasting System, Washington, D.C.

McRae, Kenneth D. "Louis Hartz' Concept of the Fragment Society and Its Application to Canada." *Études Canadiennes* 5 (1978).

———. "The Structure of Canadian History." In Louis Hartz, *The Founding of New Societies.* New York: Harcourt, Brace and World, 1964.

McRoberts, Kenneth. "The Case for Meech Lake." *The Canadian Forum* 67 (December 1987).

McWhinney, Edward. *Canada and the Constitution, 1979–1982.* Toronto: University of Toronto Press, 1982.

Malcolm, Andrew H. "Canada's Deeper Identity Not Made in the U.S.A." *New York Times*, November 20, 1988.

———. *The Canadians.* New York: Times Books, 1985.

Mansbridge, Jane. *Why We Lost the E.R.A.* Chicago: University of Chicago Press, 1986.

Manzer, R. *Canada: A Socio-Political Report.* Toronto: McGraw-Hill Ryerson, 1974.

Marchak, Patricia. *Ideological Perspectives on Canada.* Toronto: McGraw-Hill Ryerson, 1988.

Marchand, Philip. *Marshall McLuhan, The Medium and the Messenger.* New York: Ticknor and Fields, 1989.

Marquand, David. "Keep Right On." *The New Statesman and Society,* June 2, 1989.

Marshall, T.H. *Class, Citizenship and Social Development.* Garden City, N.Y.: Doubleday, 1964.

Marshall, Tom. "Re-Visioning: Comedy and History in the Canadian Novel." *Queen's Quarterly* 93 (Spring 1986).

Marx, Karl, and Friedrich Engels. *The German Ideology.* New York: International Publishers, 1960; first published in its entirety, International, 1939.

———. *Letters to Americans.* New York: International Publishers, 1953.

———. *Selected Correspondence.* New York: International Publishers, 1942.

Matthews, Ralph, and J. Campbell Davis. "The Comparative Influence of Region, Status, Class and Ethnicity on Canadian Attitudes and Values." In *Regionalism in Canada,* edited by Robert J. Brym. Toronto: Irwin, 1986.

Matthews, Robin. "Regional Differences in Canada: Social versus Economic Interpretations." In *Social Issues: Sociological Views of Canada,* edited by Dennis Forcese and Stephen Richter. Scarborough, Ont.: Prentice-Hall Canada, 1982.

"The Meech Lake Accord." *Canadian Public Policy* 14 (September 1988).

Mercer, John, and Michael Goldberg. "Value Differences and Their Meaning: Urban Development in the United States." Faculty of Commerce Working Paper no. 12, UBC Research in Land Economics, University of British Columbia, Vancouver, 1982.

Meltz, Noah M. "Labor Movements in Canada and the United States." In *Challenges and Choices Facing American Labor,* edited by Thomas A. Kochan. Cambridge, Mass.: MIT Press, 1985.

Merk, Frederick. "Dissent in the Mexican War." In Samuel Eliot Morison, Frederick Merk, and Frank Freidel, *Dissent in Three American Wars.* Cambridge, Mass.: Harvard University Press, 1970).

Merton, Robert K. *Social Theory and Social Structure.* Glencoe, Il.: The Free Press, 1957.

Michalos, Alex C. *North American Social Report: A Comparative Study of the Quality of Life in Canada and the USA from 1964 to 1974.* Dordrecht, The Netherlands: D. Reidel, 1980-82.

Mifflin, Frank J., and Sydney C. Mifflen. *The Sociology of Education: Canada and Beyond.* Calgary: Detselig Enterprises, 1982.

Miller, Jeffrey. "Speak No Evil." *Saturday Night* 104 (May 1989).

Mills, C. Wright. *White Collar.* New York: Oxford University Press, 1951.

Mishler, William. *Political Participation in Canada: Prospects for Democratic Citizenship.* Toronto: Macmillan of Canada, 1979.

Morgan, Edmund S. "Slavery and Freedom: The American Paradox." *The Journal of American History* 59 (June 1972).

Morin, Richard. "A Half a Million Choices for American Votes." *Washington Post*, national weekly ed., February 6–12, 1989.

Morison, Samuel Eliot. "Dissent in the War of 1812." In Samuel Eliot Morison, Frederick Merk, and Frank Freidel, *Dissent in Three American Wars.* Cambridge, Mass.: Harvard University Press, 1970.

Morton, F.L. "The Political Impact of the Canadian Charter of Rights and Freedoms." *Canadian Journal of Political Science* 20 (March 1987).

————, and Leslie A. Pal. "The Impact of the Charter on Public Administration." *Canadian Public Administration* 28 (Summer 1985).

Morton, W.L. *The Canadian Identity.* Madison: University of Wisconsin Press, 1961.

Moy, Joyanna. "Recent Trends in Unemployment and the Labor Force, 10 Countries." *Monthly Labor Review* 108 (August 1985).

Myrdal, Gunnar. *An American Dilemma.* 2nd ed. New York: Harper and Row, 1962.

Naegele, Kaspar D. "Canadian Society: Some Reflections." In *Canadian Society: Sociological Perspectives.* 3d ed., edited by Bernard Blishin et al. Toronto: Macmillan of Canada, 1971.

Naylor, R.T. *The History of Canadian Business, 1867–1914.* Toronto: Lorimer, 1973.

Neatby, H. Blair. *The Politics of Chaos: Canada in the Thirties.* Toronto: Macmillan of Canada, 1972.

Nelles, H.V. "Defensive Expansionism Revisited: Federalism, the State and Economic Nationalism in Canada, 1959–1979." *The* [Japanese] *Annual Review of Canadian Studies* 2 (1980).

Nemetz, Peter N., W.T. Stanbury, and Fred Thompson. "Social Regulation in Canada: An Overview and Comparison with the American Model." *Policy Studies Journal* 14 (June 1986).

Nettl, J.P. "The State as a Conceptual Variable." *World Politics* 20 (4:1968).

New York Stock Exchange. *New York Stock Exchange Fact Book* (New York, 1987).

Newman, Peter C. "The Dark Side of Merger Mania." *Maclean's*, February 6, 1989.

Newton, Norman. "Classical Canadian Poetry and the Public Muse." *Canadian Literature* 51 (Winter 1972).

Niosi, Jorge. *Canadian Capitalism.* Toronto: Lorimer, 1981.

————. "Continental Nationalism: The Strategy of the Canadian Bourgeoisie." In *The Structure of the Canadian Capitalist Class*, edited by Robert J. Brym. Toronto: Garamond Press, 1985.

————. *The Economy of Canada: Who Controls It?*. Montreal: Black Rose Books, 1978.

Notley, Grant. "Comments." In *Canada, What's Left?*, edited by John Richards and Don Kerr. Edmonton: NeWest Press, 1986.

"A North-South Dialogue." *Maclean's*, July 3, 1989.

"O Canada Eh!" Prepared by McLuhan Productions, Toronto, 1986.

Obadal, Anthony J. "Tax Law Makes It Harder to Keep Firms in Family." *Wall Street Journal*, May 2, 1989.

Odendahl, Teresa, ed. *America's Wealthy and the Future of Foundations.* Washington, D.C.: The Foundation Center, 1987.

Oliver, Michael, ed. *Social Purpose for Canada.* Toronto: University of Toronto Press, 1961.

Organisation for Economic Co-Operation and Development. *Revenue Statistics of OECD Member Countries, 1965–1986.* Paris, 1987.

Orkin, Mark M. *Speaking Canadian English: An Informal Account of the English Language in Canada.* Toronto: General Publishing, 1970.

Ornstein, Michael D. "Regionalism and Canadian Political Ideology." In *Regionalism in Canada*, edited by Robert J. Brym. Toronto: Irwin, 1986.

————. "The Social Organization of the Canadian Capitalist Class in Comparative Perspective." *Canadian Review of Sociology and Anthropology* 26 (1:1989).

Ostry, Silvia. "Government Intervention: Canada and the United States Compared." In *Canadian Politics: A Comparative Reader*, edited by Ronald G. Landes. Scarborough, Ont.: Prentice-Hall Canada, 1985.

O'Toole, Roger. "Some Good Purpose: Notes on Religion and Political Culture in Canada." *Annual Review of the Social Sciences of Religion.* (The Hague) 6 (1982).

Packer, Herbert. "Two Models of the Criminal Process." *University of Pennsylvania Law Review* 113 (1964).

Palmer, R.R. *The Age of the Democratic Revolution: The Challenge.* Princeton, N.J.: Princeton University Press, 1959.

Panitch, Leo, and Donald Swartz. *The Assault on Trade Union Freedoms: From Consent to Coercion Revisited.* Toronto: Garamond Press, 1988.

Perkins, H. Wesley. "Research Note: Religious Content in American, British and Canadian Popular Publications from 1937 to 1979." *Sociological Analysis* 45 (1984).

Pessen, Edward. *Most Uncommon Jacksonians.* Albany: State University of New York Press, 1967.

Peterson, H.C., and Gilbert C. Fite. *Opponents of War, 1917–1918.* Seattle: University of Washington Press, 1957.

Pevere, Geoff. "Images of Men." *The Canadian Forum* 64 (February 1985).

———. "Projections." *The Canadian Forum* 65 (March 1986).

Pike, Robert M. "Education and the Schools." In *Understanding Canadian Society,* edited by James Curtis and Lorne Tepperman. Toronto: McGraw-Hill Ryerson, 1988.

Pineo, Peter C., and John Porter. "Occupational Prestige in Canada." In *Social Stratification in Canada,* edited by James E. Curtis and William G. Scott. Scarborough, Ont.: Prentice-Hall Canada, 1973.

Piven, Frances Fox, and Richard A. Cloward. *Why Americans Don't Vote.* New York: Pantheon, 1988.

Popenoe, David. "The Political Culture of Metropolitan Communities in the United States: A Cross-National Perspective." In *Contemporary Community: Change and Challenge,* edited by Dan A. Chekki. Forthcoming.

Porter, John. *The Measure of Canadian Society: Education, Equality, and Opportunity.* Agincourt, Ont.: Gage, 1979; reprint, Ottawa: Carleton University Press, 1987.

———. *The Vertical Mosaic: An Analysis of Social Class and Power in Canada.* Toronto: University of Toronto Press, 1965.

"Portrait of Two Nations." *Maclean's,* July 3, 1989.

Potter, David M. "Canadian Views of the United States as a Reflex of Canadian Values: A Commentary." In *Canada Views the United States: Nineteenth-Century Political Attitudes,* by S.F. Wise and R.C. Brown. Toronto: Macmillan of Canada, 1976.

Prentice, Alison, et al. *Canadian Women: A History.* Toronto: Harcourt Brace Jovanovich, 1988.

Presthus, Robert. "Aspects of Political Culture and Legislative Behavior: United States and Canada." In *Cross-National Perspectives: United States and Canada,* edited by Robert Presthus. Leiden: E.J. Brill, 1977.

———. *Elite Accommodation in Canadian Politics.* Cambridge: Cambridge University Press, 1973.

———. *Elites in the Policy Process.* London: Cambridge University Press, 1974.

———, and William V. Monopoli. "Bureaucracy in the United States and Canada: Social, Attitudinal and Behavioral Variables." In *Cross-National Perspectives: United States and Canada,* edited by Robert Presthus. London: E.J. Brill, 1977.

Pritchard, J. Robert S. *Crown Corporations in Canada.* Toronto: Butterworths, 1983.

"Profiles in Numbers." *Maclean's,* July 3, 1989.

Prospectus Investment and Trade Partners. *1989 Canada Facts: An International Business Comparison.* Ottawa, 1989.

Purich, Donald. *Our Land: Native Rights in Canada.* Toronto: Lorimer, 1986.

Pye, A. Kenneth. "The Rights of Persons Accused of Crime under the Canadian Constitution: A Comparative Perspective." *Law and Contemporary Problems* 45 (Autumn 1982).

Ranney, Austin. "Referendums." *Public Opinion* 11 (January/February 1989).

"Religion in America." *The Gallup Report,* no. 236 (May 1985).

Resnick, Philip. *Parliament vs. People: An Essay on Democracy and Canadian Political Culture.* Vancouver: New Star Books, 1984.

Richler, Mordecai. "Letter from Ottawa: The Sorry State of Canadian Nationalism." *Harper's* 250 (June 1975).

Richmond, Anthony H. *Immigration and Ethnic Conflict.* New York: St. Martin's Press, 1988.

Robin, Martin. *Radical Politics and Canadian Labour 1880–1930.* Kingston, Ont.: Queen's University Press, 1968.

Robinson, Lukin. "Fortunes of Trade." *The Canadian Forum* 68 (March 1989).

Rocher, Guy. "Canadian Law from a Sociological Perspective." In *Law, Society and the Economy,* edited by Ivan Bernier and Andre Lajoie. Toronto: University of Toronto Press, 1986.

———. "Comments on Seymour Martin Lipset's 'Canada and the United States: The Cultural Dimension.'" Faculty of Law, University of Quebec at Montreal, 1988.

Rokeach, Milton. "Some Reflections about the Place of Values in Canadian Social Science." In *Perspectives on the Social Sciences in Canada,* edited by T.N. Guinsberg and G.L. Reuber. Toronto: University of Toronto Press, 1974.

"The Role of Government in Employment, Investment and Income." *OECD Observer*, no. 121 (March 1983).

Rose, Richard. "How Exceptional Is American Government?" *Studies in Public Policy* (Centre for the Study of Public Policy, University of Strathclyde, Glasgow) 150 (1985).

Ross, Aileen. "Philanthropy." In *International Encyclopedia of the Social Sciences*. vol. 12, edited by David L. Sills. New York: Macmillan and The Free Press, 1968.

Rubel, Maximilien. "Notes on Marx's Conception of Democracy." *New Politics* 1 (1961).

Rugman, Alan M. *Outward Bound: Canadian Direct Investment in the United States*. Toronto; Washington, D.C.: Canadian-American Committee, 1987.

Safarian, A.E. *The Performance of Foreign-Owned Firms in Canada.* Washington, D.C.; Montreal: Canadian-American Committee, 1969.

Samson, Leon. *Toward a United Front.* New York: Farrar and Rinehart, 1935.

Sancton, Andrew. "Conclusion: Canadian City Politics in Comparative Perspective." In *City Politics in Canada*, edited by Warren Magnusson and Andrew Sancton. Toronto: University of Toronto Press, 1983.

Sarna, Jonathan D. "The Value of Canadian Jewish History to the American Jewish Historian and Vice Versa." *Canadian Jewish Historical Society Journal* 5 (Spring 1981).

Sawatsky, Rodney J. "Domesticated Sectarianism: Mennonites in the U.S. and Canada in Comparative Perspective." *Canadian Journal of Sociology* 3 (Spring 1978).

Scarff, Elisabeth. *Evaluation of the Canadian Gun Control Legislation.* Ottawa: Supply and Services Canada, 1983.

Schaff, Philip. *America: A Sketch of the Political, Social, and Religious Character of the United States of North America.* New York: C. Scribner, 1855.

Schattschneider, E.E. *Party Government.* New York: Rinehart, 1942.

Schoenfeld, Stuart. "The Jewish Religion in North America: Canadian and American Comparisons." *Canadian Journal of Sociology* 3 (Spring 1978).

Schwartz, Bryan. *First Principles, Second Thoughts: Aboriginal Peoples, Constitutional Reform and Canadian Statecraft.* Montreal: Institute for Research on Public Policy, 1986.

Schwartz, Mildred A. *The Environment for Policy-Making in Canada and the United States.* Canada-U.S. Prospects 9. Montreal: C.D. Howe Research Institute; Washington, D.C.: National Planning Association, 1981.

————. "Politics and Moral Causes in Canada and the United States." *Comparative Social Research* 4 (1981).

————. *Politics and Territory: The Sociology of Regional Persistence in Canada.* Montreal: McGill-Queen's University Press, 1974.

Science Council of Canada. "Innovation in a Cold Climate: 'Impediments to Innovation.'" In *Independence: The Canadian Challenge,* edited by Abraham Rothstein and Gary Lax. Toronto: Committee for an Independent Canada, 1972.

Sears, Val. "High-Tech Lobbying: It's Just a Byte Away." In *Contemporary Canadian Politics: Readings and Notes,* edited by Robert J. Jackson, Doreen Jackson, and Nicolas Baxter-Moore. Scarborough, Ont.: Prentice-Hall Canada, 1987.

Sedler, Robert A. "Constitutional Protection of Individual Rights in Canada: The Impact of the New Canadian Charter of Rights and Freedoms." *Notre Dame Law Review* 59 (June 1984).

Sexty, Robert. "Canadian Business: Who Owns It? Who Controls It? Who Cares?" Memorial University of Newfoundland, St. John's, 1988.

Shanker, Albert. "European vs. U.S. Students: Why Are We So Behind?" *New York Times,* News of the Week section, April 23, 1989.

Shapiro, Robert Y., and John T. Young. "Public Opinion and the Welfare State: The United States in Comparative Perspective." *Political Science Quarterly* 104 (Spring 1989).

Sharp, Paul F. "Three Frontiers: Some Comparative Studies of Canadian, American and Australian Settlement." *Pacific Historical Review* 24 (1955).

Shelley, Louise I. "American Crime: An International Anomaly?" *Comparative Social Research* 8 (1985).

Shumiatcher, Morris C. "Property and the Canadian Charter of Rights and Freedoms." *The Canadian Journal of Law and Jurisprudence* 1 (July 1988).

Silcox, C.E. *Church Union in Canada.* New York: Institute of Social and Religious Research, 1933.

Simeon, Richard. "Considerations on Centralization and Decentralization." *Canadian Public Administration* 29 (Autumn 1986.

————. "Meech Lake and Shifting Conceptions of Canadian Federalism." *Canadian Public Policy* 14 (September 1988).

————. "The 'Overload Thesis' and Canadian Government." *Canadian Public Policy* 2 (June 1976).

————. "Some Questions of Governance in Contemporary Canada." School of Public Administration, Queen's University, Kingston, Ont., 1987.

————, and David J. Elkins. "Conclusion: Province, Nation, Country and Confederation." In *Small Worlds: Provinces and Parties in*

Canadian Political Life, edited by David J. Elkins and Richard Simeon. Toronto: Methuen, 1980.

Skoggard, Ross. "Old Master." *Saturday Night* 103 (May 1988).

Skolnick, Jerome. *Justice without Trial: Law Enforcement in a Democratic Society*. New York: John Wiley, 1966.

Smart, Patricia Smart. "Our Two Cultures." *The Canadian Forum* 64 (December 1984).

Smeeding, Timothy M., and Barbara Boyld Torrey. "Poor Children in Rich Countries." *Science* 242 (November 11, 1988).

Smiley, Donald V. "Public Sector Politics, Modernization and Federalism: The Canadian and American Experience." *Publius: The Journal of Federalism* 14 (Winter 1984).

Smith, A.J.M. "Evolution and Revolution as Aspects of English-Canadian and American Literature." In *Perspectives on Revolution and Evolution*, edited by R.A. Preston. Durham, N.C.: Duke University Press, 1979.

Smith, Denis. *Bleeding Hearts...Bleeding Country: Canada and the Quebec Crisis*. Edmonton: Hurtig, 1971.

Smith, Peter J. "The Ideological Origins of Canadian Confederation." *Canadian Journal of Political Science* 20 (March 1987).

Smith, Timothy L. *Revivalism and Social Reform in Mid-Nineteenth Century America*. New York: Abingdon Press, 1957.

Sniderman, Paul M., et al. "Liberty, Authority, and Community: Civil Liberties and the Canadian Political Culture." Centre of Criminology, University of Toronto, and Survey Research Center, University of California, Berkeley, 1988.

Spurgeon, David. "A Psychiatrist Crusades to Bring Risk Taking to Canadian Science." *The Scientist*, July 11, 1988.

Stahl, William A. "'May He Have Dominion...': Civil Religion and the Legitimation of Canadian Confederation." Luther College, University of Regina, 1986.

Stark, Andy. "Canadian Conundrums: Nationalism, Socialism, and Free Trade." *The American Spectator*, April 1989.

Stark, Rodney, and William Sims Bainbridge. *The Future of Religion*. Berkeley: University of California Press, 1985.

Stegner, Wallace. *Wolf Willow*. New York: Viking Press, 1962.

Stewart, Gordon T. *The Origins of Canadian Politics: A Comparative Approach*. Vancouver: University of British Columbia Press, 1986.

Stouck, David. *Major Canadian Authors*. 2d ed. Lincoln: University of Nebraska Press, 1988.

Strauss, Leo. *Thoughts on Machiavelli*. Glencoe, Ill.: The Free Press, 1958.

Suchman, Edward, Rose K. Goldsen, and Robin Williams, Jr. "Attitudes Toward the Korean War." *Public Opinion Quarterly* 17 (1953).

Surlin, Stuart H., Walter I. Romanow, and Walter C. Sonderland. "TV Network News: A Canadian-American Comparison." *The American Review of Canadian Studies* 18 (Winter 1988).

Sutherland, Ronald. "A Literary Perspective: The Development of a National Consciousness." In *Understanding Canada*, edited by William Metcalfe. New York: New York University Press, 1982.

————. *The New Hero: Essays in Comparative Quebec/Canadian Literature*. Toronto: Macmillan of Canada, 1977.

Swan, Susan. *The Biggest Modern Woman of the World*. Toronto: Lester and Orpen Dennys, 1983.

"Sweden Mensheviksson." *The Economist*, April 1, 1989.

Swinton, Katherine. "Judicial Policy Making: American and Canadian Perspectives." *The Canadian Review of American Studies* 10 (Spring 1979).

Symons, Scott. "The Canadian Bestiary: Ongoing Literary Depravity." *West Coast Review* 11 (January 1977).

Tarrow, Sidney. "Introduction." In *Territorial Politics in Industrial Nations*, edited by S. Tarrow, P.J. Katzenstein, and L. Graziano. New York: Praeger, 1978.

Task Force on Funding Higher Education. *From Patrons to Partners, Corporate Support for Universities*. Montreal: Corporate Higher Education Forum, 1987.

Tax, Sol. "War and the Draft." In *War*, edited by Morton Fried, Marvin Harris, and Robert Murphy. Garden City, N.Y.: Doubleday, The Natural History Press, 1968.

Taylor, Charles. *Radical Tories: The Conservative Tradition in Canada*. Toronto: Anansi, 1982.

Taylor, Charles L., and David A. Jodice. *World Handbook of Political and Social Indicators*. 3d ed. New Haven: Yale University Press, 1983.

Templin, Vicki L. "Predicting the Policy Choices of Individual Legislators: A Comparative Study of Canada and the United States." *Population Research and Policy Review* 6 (1987).

Tepperman, Lorne. *Crime Control: The Urge toward Authority*. Toronto: McGraw-Hill Ryerson, 1977.

Thacker, Robert. "Canada's Mounted: The Evolution of a Legend." *Journal of Popular Culture* 14 (Fall 1980).

Thomas, Norman. *Socialism Re-Examined*. New York: W.W. Norton, 1963.

————. *A Socialist's Faith.* New York: W.W. Norton, 1951.

Thomas, Ted E. "The Gun Control Issue: A Sociological Analysis of United States and Canadian Attitudes and Policies." Department of Sociology, Mills College, Oakland, Cal., 1983.

Thompson, Mark A., and Albert A. Blum. "International Unionism in Canada: The Move to Local Control." *Industrial Relations* 22 (Winter 1983).

Tocqueville, Alexis de. *Democracy in America.* 2 vols. New York: Alfred A. Knopf, 1948; first published in French, 1839.

Tolchin, Martin, and Susan Tolchin. *Buying into America.* New York: Times Books, 1988.

Trudeau, Pierre Elliott. *Federalism and the French Canadians.* New York: St. Martin's Press, 1968.

Turner, Ralph H. "Sponsored and Contest Mobility and the School System." *American Sociological Review* 25 (1960).

Uchitelle, Louis. "Election Placing Focus on the Issue of Jobs vs. Wages." *New York Times,* September 4, 1988.

Underhill, Frank. *The Image of Confederation.* Toronto: Canadian Broadcasting Corporation, 1964.

————. *In Search of Canadian Liberalism.* Toronto: Macmillan of Canada, 1960.

United Nations. *Monthly Bulletin of Statistics,* July 1983.

United States. Arms Control and Disarmament Agency. *World Military Expenditures and Arms Transfers, 1971–1980.* Washington, D.C., 1982.

————. Department of Commerce. *Statistical Abstract of the U.S. 1988.* 108th ed. Washington D.C., 1988.

————. Department of Education. Center for Education Studies. *Digest of Education Statistics 1987.* Washington D.C., 1987.

Valentine, Victor. "Native Peoples and Canadian Society: A Profile of Issues and Trends." In *Cultural Boundaries and the Cohesion of Canada,* edited by Raymond Breton et al. Montreal: Institute for Research on Public Policy, 1980.

Verba, Sidney, and Gary R. Orren. *Equality in America: The View from the Top.* Cambridge, Mass.: Harvard University Press, 1985.

Vickrey, William S. "One Economist's View of Philanthropy." In *Philanthropy and Public Policy,* edited by Frank Dickinson. New York: National Bureau of Economic Research, 1962.

Wade, Mason. "Quebec and the French Revolution of 1789." In *Canadian History before Confederation: Essays and Interpretations,* edited by J.M. Bumsted. Georgetown, Ont.: Irwin-Dorsey, 1972.

Wald, Kenneth D. *Religion and Politics in the United States.* New York: St. Martin's Press, 1987.

Wallace, Edward S. "Notes and Comment — Deserters in the Mexican War." *The Hispanic American Historical Review* 15 (1935).

Walters, R.E. "A Special Tang: Stephen Leacock's Canadian Humour." *Canadian Literature* 5 (Summer 1960).

Wanner, Richard A. "Educational Inequality: Trends in Twentieth-Century Canada and the United States." *Comparative Social Research* 9 (1986).

Ward, Michael Don. *The Political Economy of Distribution, Equality versus Inequality.* New York: Elsevier, 1978.

Watts, Ronald L. "The American Constitution in Comparative Perspective: A Comparison of Federalism in the United States and Canada." *Journal of American History* 74 (3:1987).

Weaver, John Charles. "Imperiled Dreams: Canadian Opposition to the American Empire, 1918–1930." Ph.D. diss., Department of History, Duke University, 1973.

Weber, Max. *The Methodology of the Social Sciences.* Glencoe, Ill.: The Free Press, 1949; essays first published separately in German in various years, early 20th century.

————. *The Protestant Ethic and the Spirit of Capitalism.* New York: Scribner, 1935; first published in German, 1905.

————. "The Protestant Sects and the Spirit of Capitalism." In Max Weber, *Essays in Sociology.* trans. and ed. by Hans Gerth and C.W. Mills. New York: Oxford University Press, 1946; first published in German, various dates, early 20th century.

Weiler, Paul. "The Evolution of the Charter: A View from the Outside." In *Litigating the Values of a Nation: The Canadian Charter of Rights and Freedoms,* edited by Joseph Weiler and Robin Elliot. Toronto: Carswell, 1986.

Weinfeld, Morton. "Canadian Jews and Canadian Pluralism." In *American Pluralism and the Jewish Community,* edited by S.M. Lipset. New Brunswick, N.J.: Transaction Books, 1989.

————. "Myth and Reality in the Canadian Mosaic: 'Affective Ethnicity.'" *Canadian Ethnic Studies* 13 (1981).

Weinstein, James, and David W. Eakins, eds. *For a New America.* New York: Random House, 1970.

Wells, H.G. *The Future in America.* New York: Harper and Brothers, 1906.

Westhues, Kenneth. "Stars and Stripes, The Maple Leaf, and the Papal Coat of Arms." *Canadian Journal of Sociology* 3 (Spring 1978).

Westin, Alan F. "The United States Bill of Rights and the Canadian Charter: A Socio-Political Analysis." In *The U.S. Bill of Rights and the Canadian Charter of Rights and Freedoms*, edited by William R. Mc-Kercher. Toronto: Ontario Economic Council, 1983.

Westley, William A. *Violence and the Police: A Sociological Study of Law, Custom and Morality.* Cambridge: MIT Press, 1970.

"What's This?" *Dissent* 18 (August 1971).

Whitaker, Ben. *The Foundations: An Anatomy of Philanthropy and Society.* London: Eyre Methuen, 1974.

Whitaker, Reg. "Democracy and the Canadian Constitution." In *And No One Cheered*, edited by Keith Banting and Richard Simeon. Toronto: Methuen, 1983.

————. "Images of the State in Canada." In *The Canadian State: Political Economy and Political Power*, edited by Leo Panitch. Toronto: University of Toronto Press, 1977.

Whyte, John D. "Civil Liberties and the Courts." *Queen's Quarterly* 83 (Winter 1976).

Wilensky, Harold. *The Welfare State and Equality.* Berkeley: University of California Press, 1975.

Wilkins, Mira. *The History of Foreign Investment in the United States to 1914.* Cambridge, Mass.: Harvard University Press, 1989.

Williams, William Appleman. *The Great Evasion.* Chicago: Quadrangle Books, 1964.

Wilson, Edmund. *O Canada: An American's Notes on Canadian Culture.* New York: Farrar, Strauss and Giroux, 1965.

Wilson, S.J. "Gender Inequality." In *Understanding Canadian Society*, edited by James Curtis and Lorne Tepperman. Toronto: McGraw-Hill Ryerson, 1988.

Winks, Robin W. *The Relevance of Canadian History.* Lanham, Md.: Universities Press of America, 1988.

————. "'Whodunit?': Canadian Society as Reflected in Its Detective Fiction." *The American Review of Canadian Studies* 17 (Winter 1987–88).

Wisse, Ruth, Mervin Butovsky, Howard Roiter, and Morton Weinfeld. "Jewish Culture and Canadian Culture." In *The Canadian Jewish Mosaic*, edited by M. Weinfeld, W. Shaffir, and I. Cotler. Toronto: John Wiley, 1981.

Woehrling, José. "Minority Cultural and Linguistic Rights and Equality Rights in the Canadian Charter of Rights and Freedoms." *McGill Law Journal* 31 (1985).

Wolfinger, Raymond E., and Steven Rosenstone. *Who Votes?.* New Haven, Conn.: Yale University Press, 1980.

Woodcock, George. *Northern Spring: The Flowering of Canadian Literature.* Vancouver: Douglas and McIntyre, 1987.

Woolfson, Peter. "An Anthropological Perspective: The Ingredients of a Multicultural Society." In *Understanding Canada,* edited by William Metcalfe. New York: New York University Press, 1982.

World Bank. *World Development Report 1987.* New York: Oxford University Press, 1987.

Wrong, Dennis. *American and Canadian Viewpoints.* Washington, D.C.: American Council on Education, 1955.

Index